Wayward Servants

Wayward Servants

The Two Worlds of the African Pygmies

Colin M. Turnbull

PUBLISHED FOR THE AMERICAN MUSEUM OF NATURAL HISTORY

THE NATURAL HISTORY PRESS / GARDEN CITY, NEW YORK

The Natural History Press, publisher for The American Museum of Natural History, is a division of Doubleday & Company, Inc. Directed by a joint editorial board made up of members of the staff of both the Museum and Doubleday, the Natural History Press publishes books and periodicals in all branches of the life and earth sciences, including anthropology and astronomy. The Natural History Press has its editorial offices at The American Museum of Natural History, Central Park West at 79th Street, New York 24, New York, and its business offices at 501 Franklin Avenue, Garden City, New York.

The photographs for this book were taken by the author; the line illustrations were prepared by Nicholas Amarosi of The American Museum of Natural History.

TO MY PARENTS,
WITH GRATITUDE AND LOVE

Acknowledgments

The present study is based on field work conducted during the years 1957 and 1958, under the support of a grant from the Emslie Horniman Anthropological Trust. To the trustees I owe thanks not only for their financial aid, but also for their personal interest and encouragement.

My academic debt lies above all to the Institute of Social Anthropology at Oxford and to its members under whom I studied. To them all I am sincerely grateful, and I hope that this work will to some extent justify their constantly cheerful, if at times somewhat skeptical, encouragement and optimism.

But for the patience and endurance of Professor E. E. Evans-Pritchard, I might never have enjoyed the privilege of being an anthropologist. Dr. John Peristiany was my first teacher, and his personal interest and understanding helped me to find my way during the first erratic years. But to Dr. Rodney Needham I owe more than I can say, for he undertook to supervise this study and has nursed it along over a period of several years and across many thousands of miles of land and water. Despite all too infrequent opportunities for meeting, he persisted in his attempts to make the work more sound and perceptive. I am most conscious of many shortcomings; some due to the ever-restricting factor of time, but others due to the sheer difficulty of dealing with a theoretical and geographical area for which there is so little published material of real use. Largely because of this factor, the study is isolated and does not attempt to draw upon the comparative material that is available. Such comparisons can most fruitfully be made after further intensive field studies of the Mbuti have been made. The inherent problems of the field work have created many serious gaps that remain to be filled on the next field study, and this, together with the necessity for presenting a lengthy ethnographic description, has made the task of analysis infinitely more difficult. Dr. Needham's perceptiveness as well as his own field experience have been invaluable, but shortcomings still persist and are in no way his fault.

I would also like to thank the staff of the Anthropology Department of The American Museum of Natural History for their constant interest, agreement and disagreement, the Museum for allowing time for the work to be completed, and its library for their most friendly and helpful co-operation.

To the late Dr. Franz Olbrechts I also owe much for encouragement and very practical help, and to him and the staff of the then Musée Royal du Congo Belge my thanks for assistance both before and during the field trip, including free access to all their facilities, and for help in the less academic chore of clearing away much administrative red tape.

To Father Paul Schebesta I also owe thanks, for he first pioneered the field, and although we have had and still have sources of disagreement he has been as generous with his help as he has been with his criticism. In conversation and through correspondence he has at all times been willing to offer whatever help he could.

It is impossible to mention all those in Africa who helped make the study possible, most of all those among whom I worked. Of the others my thanks are particularly due to Mr. and Mrs. Patrick Putnam, Father Longo of the Mission Catholique at Nduye, Father Brisson of Teturi, the Reverend Mr. and Mrs. George Bell of Biasiku, Pastor Chaptal of Bangui, and the Mission Evangélique de l'Oubangi, all of whom gave freely of their rich experience of many years spent among the peoples of the Congo.

Finally my thanks to those often neglected helpers who are invariably left to do the real donkeywork: Eleanor Skinner and Joseph Towles for typing and retyping, for checking and cross-checking, and for generally keeping track of where the various parts of the manuscript were; Nicholas Amorosi for his painstaking labors with the charts, plans and maps; and Merilee Oakes for checking on all references, quotations and translations.

However incomplete this work may be, it would have been far more incomplete without such help. It is hoped that at least it is another step forward, and a sound one, offering a springboard for the further research that is so urgently needed.

Contents

LIST OF MAPS, TABLES AND PLANS

INTRODUCTION

CHAPTER 1

Objectives

The general purpose here is to add as much as possible to our knowledge of the Mbuti pygmies and of their much misunderstood relationship with the neighboring tribes of forest cultivators. The account is drawn from first-hand field experience, and is primarily intended to be of use to anthropologists.

In the belief, however, that anthropologists are human beings, and that other human beings might equally well find much of interest in works of this kind, the currently fashionable academic jargon has been discarded. Such jargon in most cases only obscures what are often essentially simple basic truths, and so another objective is to present an academic study in plain language. I cannot claim to have been thoroughly consistent, for to have striven too hard would have led only to an equally artificial form.

Even so there may be those who will object, for the mystery, formerly obscured by an abuse of the English language, in this way becomes unveiled and accessible to all. I hope that what I say is plain, so that others may more easily and more usefully take issue with it. Before embarking on the account itself, however, a certain amount of ground-clearing for purely academic purposes is necessary.

LIMITATIONS

It is important at the outset to define very clearly the objectives of the present study, so that its limitations may be plainly understood. Both the objectives and the limitations were a carefully preconsidered part of the field project, and form an integral part of the subsequent analysis. The reasons for accepting such limitations were, I believe, insuperable in the given circumstances.

The title perhaps indicates a wider scope than is covered by the work, but it is believed that there are good grounds for using this study as a comparative base from which the study of the Mbuti as a whole may be more speedily and accurately advanced. It is also believed that although the bulk of the study involves a single hunting band, much of the basic structure uncovered applies to other Mbuti bands. The major limitation, however, is that we are here concerned primarily with one band rather than with the Mbuti as a whole, yet this was an inevitable necessity.

Other limitations arise from the lack of monographs on comparable groups of forest nomads, from my consequent reluctance to generalize too far from so narrow a base, and from the difficulty of presenting the principles of organization of a society that does not possess the formal institutions found in larger and more sedentary societies. Nonetheless, such principles plainly must exist, and while our general objective is to outline the form and structure of the Mbuti hunters and gatherers of the Ituri Forest in the northeast Congo (Leopoldville), we also have the more particular objective of searching for the elusive principles that integrate each apparently autonomous Mbuti band, giving it an identity of its own by which it recognizes itself and its integral but diffuse relationship with other bands. For it is in light of these principles that we must try to understand the effective but problematical relationship that pertains between any Mbuti band and the village cultivators who are its neighbors.

Another limitation derives from the lack of reference material on the Mbuti, which necessitated the gathering of ethnographic minutiae in the field and their presentation here, adding considerably to the bulk despite vigorous sifting. However, without a firm ethnographic base no analysis would be possible, so the provision of such a base is considered a prime prerequisite.

I have elsewhere (Turnbull, 1956) given reasons for rejecting existing sources for both purposes of general comparison and particular analysis, though this is not to deny their possible value in other fields. My own subsequent account of the Mbuti (Turnbull, 1961) was in no way intended as an academic study, nor is it suited for use as such, though it served a useful purpose in helping the field worker detach himself from the subject of his study, enabling him to examine it more critically.

In my examination of other sources (1956) it was suggested that subsequent field work might discover a more meaningful division of the Ituri Mbuti than the linguistic division made by Schebesta, as the languages referred to, although spoken by the Mbuti, were evidently of non-Mbuti origin. Consequently another objective of the present study, based on further field work, is to begin to look for valid structural differences that do exist, following up the contention (*ibid.*) that one would expect to find such differences between the Mbuti who hunt by net and those who hunt with bow and arrow. The boundaries of the net-hunters and archers incidentally correspond, very roughly, to the linguistic boundaries drawn by Schebesta between the Sua- and Efe-speaking Mbuti: the Aka, to the north, although somewhat divided amongst themselves, offer a third category, some of them using the spear as their prime weapon.

To all these ends it was decided to make a further field trip in which one hunting band would be studied intensively throughout a calendar year, and in which as much comparative material as time and field conditions permitted would be gathered from other hunting bands. It was decided in advance, in the light of previous personal experience, that the sacrifice of a whole year to the study of one small band was essential, even though it would mean that any final conclusions about the general nature of Mbuti society would have to be delayed until a number of other such studies had been made. A band of either archers or net-hunters is a highly mobile, volatile entity, demanding of the field worker the utmost persistence in both physical and intellectual pursuit. It was quite obvious, also from previous experience, that the band not only constantly changes location, but it also constantly changes in composition. The significance of these fluctuations would only be discovered, it was felt, by following them right through their course in one given hunting territory before attempting any comparative studies among other bands. Above all it was essential in one band to find out what the significant social groupings were, and what principles enabled them to maintain any kind of consistency and continuity in the face of perpetual change. How was the band divided, along exactly what lines did the characteristic splits occur, what forces operated to hold the band together and to divide it? The scope of the one-band study was aimed at answering such questions and others that concern band relationships with local villages of cultivators. It was hoped to arrive at an understanding of the true nature of the over-all Mbuti/Villager relationship in this area, following up on the suggestion made earlier (Turnbull, 1956, 363–64) that this relationship was not one of master/servant, still less of slavery, and probably not even of symbiosis.

In paying special attention to this relationship it was felt that the otherwise intangible value-system of the Mbuti would be more clearly revealed, leading to an understanding of the ritual relationship that appeared to exist between the Mbuti and the forest, as implied in the accounts of other observers and in my own prior experience, but nowhere made explicit.

EXECUTION

Field work was undertaken between the summer of 1957 and the late winter of 1958, entering the then Belgian Congo by driving through from the West Coast, collecting as many local accounts of pygmy or pygmoid hunters and gatherers along the way as possible, for future reference. Such accounts were gathered in Dahomey, Nigeria (particularly towards the east), the Cameroons, Gabon, and throughout the Congo, but few hunting bands were encountered until well towards the Ubangi River (see Map 1). It was decided not to spend time trying to make contact, except on the far side of the Ubangi, where contact was relatively easy, and where there were also some Binga pygmies from the west bank of the river.

From the Ubangi over to the Ituri it was quite obvious that, as elsewhere, true hunting bands only existed where there was substantial primary forest, and that elsewhere not only was the hunting and gathering economy defunct, but there had been so much intermarriage that one could not truly speak of a pygmy physical type any more than one could speak of a pygmy culture.

Leaving aside the forested area south of the Congo River, which I did not cover but for which pygmoid groups are reported, I found relatively isolated bands of pygmy and pygmoid hunters and gatherers to exist in the forests of the Gabon and the Cameroons, and in the Congo Republic (Brazzaville) as well as in the forested regions around the Ubangi River. But by far the heaviest concentration is in the Ituri Forest, where all the pygmies recognize their unity in the name Mbuti, and where both the physical and the cultural integrity of the hunters and gatherers seems to have been best preserved.

There was no question that this was the right area for the major bulk of the field work, but there was some question as to which band to select for the intensive study. I eventually decided on the Epulu

net-hunters for a variety of reasons, their central location (see Map
2) being only one.

There were several more immediate reasons, which I give now, as
the choice may be a point of some criticism:

1) I had already been among this band on two prior occasions,
and had established with them a most friendly relationship that I
knew would guarantee me immediate access to their forest hunting
camps. Although I was known among other bands, there did not
exist the same degree of intimacy and trust, and the Mbuti are by
nature reserved and suspicious when faced with the prospect of having a stranger in their forest camps.

2) I was also well known to the Epulu villagers, and could antici-
pate the need for understanding and tolerance from this direction.

3) Father Schebesta (1957) had previously attacked my discussion of the significance of the music and ceremonial (Turnbull, 1955,
1957[1]) by saying that this same band was particularly acculturated
and therefore not representative.[1] As the whole point of my argument was the superficiality of the acculturation, and granting that
this band had all the appearances of gross acculturation, this seemed
like an excellent opportunity for testing a hypothesis that I felt to be
valid, and that I also suspected to have far deeper significance in the
total Mbuti social structure than I at present recognized.

4) In selecting a net-hunting band I would at least be adding to
Schebesta's general ethnographic description, which was mostly concerned with the archers, rather than be duplicating it.

5) Because of its central location I would be able to move relatively rapidly to other areas in the forest if the occasion demanded,
and when in other areas I would still be able to stay within a few
days' reach of the Epulu band, in case I needed to return. Also because of its central location, there seemed to be some possibility of
establishing contact not only with other net-hunting bands, but also
possibly with archer bands, in the normal course of the year's migrations.

6) The continued existence of Camp Putnam, on the Epulu River,
offered me a base where I could keep essential supplies in safety, and
where I would not alienate myself from the villagers with whom
I would eventually have to work by having to stay at a government

---

[1] For a further clarification of Schebesta's attitude, see my article on the *nkumbi* initiation (Turnbull, 1957), his rejoinder and subsequent recantation (Schebesta, 1958,
1963).

rest-house or with other Europeans. Mr. and Mrs. Putnam had long established their own *bona fides,* and indeed fitted perfectly into the traditional village structure in this area, where a number of different village tribes converge. Their friendship for me placed me on a particularly favorable footing with both the villagers and the Mbuti, and I knew that I could count on protection from any interference from other Europeans, administrators included, who might wish to visit me. (Naturally I established perfect accord with the central and local administration, who offered every co-operation, but I was particularly concerned that I should not receive "friendly visits," as it was the policy of both villagers and Mbuti, for different reasons, to keep Europeans out of the forest.)

Having established my headquarters, building a somewhat larger but otherwise typical mud house on the fringe of the village where the Mbuti had their semi-permanent village camp (see Plan 1A, 1B), I paid my respects to the divers local village chiefs and head men, mostly of the Bira, Ndaka, and Ngwana tribes. At this time the local Mbuti band was in the village, but a sudden epidemic of stomach disorders, resulting in a number of unexpected deaths, caused them to leave for a prolonged hunting spell in the forest, taking me with them.

While the deaths, which included men, women and children, were most untimely and unhappy from a personal point of view, they achieved everything else that I could have wished for as an anthropologist. Prior to precipitating the flight back to the forest, they gave me an opportunity to study in the greatest detail the reaction to the death of an Mbuti in the village, both from the village point of view and from that of the Mbuti themselves. I at once witnessed what I had seen on my previous visit when observing the *nkumbi* initiation; namely, the almost desperate attempt of the villagers to assert authority over the Mbuti. In this case the attempt was made by controlling the mourning and burial proceedings, claiming that the Mbuti had no ritual authority in this respect and were dependent on their *kpara* ("masters"). The villagers attempted to subject the Mbuti to the supernatural sanctions of village lore, and then they attempted to assert more direct political control by calling on their own ritual specialists to determine the cause of the deaths, and to search for the witch responsible. This will be described later (pp. 74 *seq.*); it is mentioned here to show how closely I was thrown into contact, at the outset, with the Mbuti/Villager relationship.

Upon establishing what was, for me, the first hunting camp of the year, there commenced what I might here call the real mourning festivities, as opposed to the festivities imposed upon the Mbuti when in the village. One of the persons to die had been an old and much respected and beloved Mbuti lady, Balekimito. Her death was made the occasion for a great *molimo* festival, which within the first three months of my field trip brought me right to the heart of the Mbuti magico-religious system. Subsequent investigation elsewhere, even among archer bands, revealed a degree of similarity that makes it possible to generalize widely from the base of this single band study, in this realm at least.

I followed the same band throughout its entire series of migrations, living in every camp it established during the course of some fourteen months. During this time the band was sometimes entirely in residence in the Epulu village, in which case I was there with it; on occasion it was entirely in the forest, and sometimes it was divided between the two. When it divided I simply had to distribute my attentions as the occasion seemed to demand. Sometimes I was able to make use of an informant in the other division, and I trained three Mbuti youths for this purpose.

On two occasions I was able to take quick side trips to other parts of the forest, but I left the bulk of my search for comparative material among other bands until I felt that one complete annual cycle had been completed. It so happened that the process of fission and fusion was more systemized than I had anticipated, and my records of consecutive changes in the composition of the hunting band clearly showed the pattern in time for me to be able to spend a few months in different parts of the forest, with both net-hunters and archers, and even allowed me to make a brief excursion to the Kivu district and to Ruanda and Burundi, though the material gathered there was not immediately comparable.

FIELD TECHNIQUE

Before myself assessing the results, and in order to enable others to assess and evaluate the material here presented, it is important that field method should be discussed. The particular technique I employed was born of the particular situation. I do not claim that any other technique was impossible, but I do claim that for the re-

sults I wanted I had no alternative. Other methods would have produced different, though not necessarily contrary, results.

However, there were inherent limitations in the technique followed, which involved close identification and integration between
myself and the Epulu net-hunters. For one, by identifying myself
with the Mbuti, my relationships with the villagers were automatically worsened; the mere fact that I preferred to study the Mbuti
rather than the villagers was ground enough for hostility. But being
accepted by the Mbuti in their forest hunting camps was a privilege
denied to most villagers (though few would have wanted it), and
learning to speak the village language with a strong Mbuti accent
that made it almost unintelligible except to other Mbuti added further fuel to the fire. This all made it extremely difficult for me to see
the Mbuti/Villager relationship from any but the Mbuti point of
view, though I tried, at the end of 1958, to establish a better rapport
with villages both in and beyond the Epulu area.

However, it was impossible for me not to take sides. Had I wished
to work as an outside observer I am not even sure that it could have
been done, as I do not think such an observer would have been
tolerated for long in the forest camps. And as an outsider I would
certainly have been denied familiarity with many aspects of Mbuti
life, particularly the all-important *molimo* festival. In fact, as an "in-
sider" I was able to observe the process of exclusion of the few out-
siders temporarily admitted to a forest camp. But in any case I was
quickly forced by purely practical considerations to take sides.

During the burial proceedings in the village, for instance, in the
first month of my stay, I was invited by both Mbuti and villagers to
take part. But whereas the villagers wanted me to stand by and watch
the digging of the grave under villager supervision, the Mbuti wanted
me to help out with the digging. By acceding to the latter wish I
automatically lost my status among the supervisors, and in fact became unclean and had to ritually wash myself with the other grave-
diggers. And during the post-burial meeting of the men, when the
villagers all argued among themselves as to which Mbuti witch had
caused the death, I had the choice of listening on one side of the
grave with the villagers or of standing on the other side with the
Mbuti and being associated in this way with their mirth and their
ridicule of what was, to them, an utterly nonsensical procedure. And
when on one occasion a burial took place on the morning of the day
that a wedding was to be held in a neighboring village, I had the

choice of staying to listen to the villagers ceremonially wail on behalf of the dead Mbuti, or of going off with the rest of the burial party, as soon as the grave was filled, to the wedding. I found it more sensible as well as more congenial to prefer the wedding to the wailing.

These are only a few of the many instances where a choice had to be made, where no middle road was possible even had it been desirable. The result is then necessarily to some extent one-sided, for no matter how I tried to effect a balance by subsequent investigation, I still feel an urgent need to conduct further field work, taking the village standpoint.

Once started on the road, the process of identification was swift, but never complete enough to render it impossible to observe intelligently and with deliberate detachment. Such temporary blindness to other points of view as occurred took some time to wear off, and this was perhaps the major drawback of the technique, and one that should be borne in mind in the more interpretive parts of this work, for it resulted in a number of unasked and therefore unanswered questions.

Integration demanded a number of things, one of which was that I should at all times be as fully mobile as any Mbuti. This cut down the belongings that I could carry with me; a blanket, a single change of clothes, a typewriter, paper and pencils. With a bundle of this size on my back I was able to travel as fast as was necessary whenever the band moved from one camp to another. It meant that I was economically dependent upon the band, however, so some kind of equilibrium had to be reached. I was not successful as a hunter, being too large and clumsy, and I did not carry a gun nor did I wish to acquire food in this way. When within easy reach of the village, then, I would acquire supplies of village foods, such as plantains, beans, rice and peanuts, at the same time that the Mbuti got their supplies. Instead of barter or theft I used currency, but bought only comparable quantities of exactly the same kind of food as the Mbuti. It was then cooked, usually by a youth who acted as general assistant, informant, guide, mentor and censor, but sometimes by myself or by another bachelor, and shared, as was the custom, among any bachelors who were around at the time. As was also the custom, I was adopted by a woman whose husband was away, but who still had his hunting net and sent it out each day with her stepson. She also sometimes cooked for me, and always built my hut, as she did for the rest of her family.

Being a bachelor made my integration into family life somewhat easier than it might have been otherwise, and my reciprocal duties were not heavy, mainly involving my working with other bachelors in collecting the saplings and leaves used for making the huts. But being unable to make any great contribution to the food economy, although I participated in the hunt, I found myself pushed into another category that I subsequently discovered to be a perfectly traditional one for incompetent hunters and some others—that of buffoon. This was very convenient, as it meant that I was the recipient of threats, ridicule, jokes and gossip, all of significance, and being made a general scapegoat I was also the center of a number of disputes. I have observed similar buffoons in almost every other hunting band, fulfilling the same function, harmlessly dispelling the many little jealousies and hostilities that arise in everyday camp life.

Later on I acquired a hunting net of my own, by virtue of my proven adult status, and was so able to contribute to the food economy. At this time I was able to watch another bachelor take my place as buffoon.

The advantages of this kind of participation are obvious enough, and particularly desirable when a six-foot field worker is living among four-foot pygmies is the way it helps him blend into the social landscape, at least. Among the Mbuti, however, there was an additional advantage. The amount of information I could get from them, even the extent to which I would be allowed to participate, depended upon my attitude to the forest. Fortunately this was something of which I was well aware. But the fact that I was prepared to eat the same food, and that often entirely excluded village plantation foods, and the fact that I was prepared to carry my few belongings myself, to sleep on leaves or branches, and take part in the forest songs that were sung almost nightly around a central fire, conveyed enough of my respect for the forest for the Mbuti to admit me still further.

The process was an interesting one, because it again demonstrated the close relationship between the Mbuti and the forest world around them. But it was also an exhausting and arduous one, and because of the very nature of forest life it was impossible for me to observe all that went on. As will be seen, in the normal course of events a number of different things are going on in different places at different times, and even in the course of the year I cannot be sure that I saw everything of significance. During the *molimo*, for instance, men were expected to stay awake and sing throughout the night until about an hour before dawn, then be up at dawn in preparation for the hunt. This much I could manage, but whereas during the day individual men could stretch out and snatch an hour or two of sleep whenever they felt like it, I never had the chance to feel the same freedom. Acts associated with the *molimo*, such as the ritual gathering of food from every hut, continued throughout the day and I did not wish to miss anything new that might happen.

However, with all its drawbacks (and perhaps the physical and mental strain are not the least) the technique seems in this instance to have been justified by the results.

RESULTS

Both the general and the particular objectives were answered to some extent during the course of the field work. The general form and structure of the Mbuti hunting band became evident, as did certain differentiations between the structure of the archers and that of the net-hunters. Further, certain principles were found that accounted for the cohesion of the band within itself, while at the same time enabling the band to present to the villagers a structure so fluid that any formal relationship of the kind envisaged by the villagers was impossible. Perhaps it is as well to point out here that the kinship system (or lack of it) that characterizes the Mbuti band today is not necessarily representative of what it was yesterday; indeed it may well be that the current ambivalence is in itself a response to the attempts of the patrilineal village society to enforce control through the myth of hereditary unilineal relationships. The origin does not concern us here, only the system as it exists in the present context.

The structural differences between archers and net-hunters are not perhaps as wide as might have been supposed, but before any final conclusions can be drawn there is great need for a detailed study to be made among the archers. Certain differences in behavior are shown, however, to achieve the same structural ends—for instance the process of fission and fusion, where the net-hunters and the archers behave in diametrically opposed cyclic patterns but to the same structural end.

The detailed study of the Epulu net-hunters was backed by sufficient field work among other net-hunting bands to enable us to generalize with reasonable safety. Where generalization is not possible, I cite the specific, and where it is possible but not with absolute cer-

tainty, then I cite supporting evidence; otherwise it may be taken
that generalization for all net-hunters is considered valid. In point of
fact there seem to be few differences of structural interest.

Enough work was done among archer bands to get some idea of
the extent and nature of the structural differences to be expected
between them and the net-hunters, but again I must emphasize
the considered need for further studies, one of which should include
a detailed study of an archer band over a similar period and with
similar intensity, and another of which should tackle the Mbuti/
Villager relationship from the village point of view. Finally, there is
need for detailed studies of the various local village tribes, at which
point those who are interested may begin to sort out which elements
of the present Mbuti culture may be considered as original, and
which as borrowed.

The over-all picture is one of a society where the lack of formal
structure is so evident that one wonders why there is not complete
disintegration. There are not only no chiefs or councils of elders, but
no ritual specialists, and no lineage system that in any way contributes directly to order and cohesion. There is no legal system, and no
body of belief in supernatural sanctions. The secret begins to reveal
itself when you look at the band one day, to see what it really *is*, and
look at it the next day and find it is something else.

As suggested above, the constant state of flux that characterizes
the Mbuti band may be in response to the attempts of the villager
cultivators to assert a formal relationship with it. The lack of chiefs
and the lack of priests and the lack of unilineal descent system certainly prevent the formation of political, ritual or domestic ties, and
as stated elsewhere (Turnbull, 1956) the economic relationship is
one of mutual convenience rather than of dependency. What emerges
that seems to be of particular significance is the central theme of the
forest, a theme that not only orders the hunting and gathering world
of the Mbuti, but also divides them from the world of the villagers
as if dividing the sacred from the profane.

If social flux is what prevents the formation of a relationship that
would necessarily involve the subordination of the Mbuti to the villagers, the central value of the forest is what maintains internal stability and cohesion, at the same time determining the relationship
of opposition with the outside world. This opposition in fact creates
a kind of voluntary indigenous system of apartheid, where two peoples live side by side, exploiting the same environment in totally dif-

ferent ways, with totally different values, with only the minimum of contact, and that based on nothing more than territorial propinquity and mutual convenience. In this way each is able to extract some benefit from the presence of the other without sacrificing its integrity, while maintaining a sense of absolute superiority that, however illusory in terms of economics or politics, is thoroughly justified by the opposition of the value systems.

The fact that this opposition does not erupt into open hostility is due largely to the size of the forest, which can easily support the two populations and the two economies. But the moment some element upsets the precarious balance, rendering one economy or the other ineffective, then collision will be inevitable; and insofar as it is the hunting and gathering way of life that is most likely to be affected, the onus of change will be upon the Mbuti, and they are the ones who, because of the intimate relationship they have with their forest environment, are the least fitted for change. The present study will indicate in some measure the extent to which the Mbuti society is capable of assimilation or adaptation, and the extent to which change can come to it only through subordination or extermination.

Considerable space is devoted to setting out a fairly straightforward ethnography of the Mbuti. This is considered essential because of the present paucity of information that can be used for the kind of analysis here envisaged. The details may seem unnecessarily minute at times, and there are certain total blanks, but the picture is given as fully as possible so that the closeness of the reliance of the Mbuti on their environment may be recognized. And insofar as the environment or territory is going to take precedence over political systems, instability over stability, music over sex and death, and mere age over kinship, it is felt that all the available evidence, however slight it may at first seem, is going to be needed.

CHAPTER 2

Orientation

THE PEOPLE AND THE ENVIRONMENT

The Mbuti pygmies form the largest single group of pygmy hunters and gatherers in Africa, and are probably also the purest in both the biological and cultural senses. Throughout the equatorial rain forest other similar groups exist, but while some of them (notably in the Gabon and in the Ubangi area) appear to be comparable with the Mbuti, the majority, like the Twa and the Tswa of the Kivu and central Congo districts (see Map 3), have at one time or another intermarried with Negro tribes of cultivators, losing many of the true pygmy physical characteristics and at the same time losing a great deal of their original hunting and gathering culture.

Far more important, from the structural point of view, is the altered relationship between all these pygmoids and the world they live in, for as we shall see, the structure of Mbuti society pivots around a powerful forest-oriented system of values. This value system to a large extent overrides economic considerations in determining the relationship between the Mbuti and their village neighbors, whereas among the pygmoids the economic factor appears to be dominant, and the consequent dependency of the pygmoids upon the villagers in other respects is also greater.

This is in no way to say that the structure to be found among the Mbuti is representative of an original pygmy hunting and gathering structure; in fact probably far from it, for the repercussions of the invasion of the forest by the village cultivators have been enormous. But the response of the Mbuti, for whatever reason, has been different from that of the Twa and the Tswa and it is of much greater structural interest and significance, incidentally throwing light on the whole process of acculturation. At the same time, however, the peculiar structural development of the Mbuti does enable us to observe a pure hunting and gathering economy at work not only side by side with, but in opposition to, a cultivation economy. With the pygmoid Twa and Tswa, and possibly only excepting a few small groups in the Gabon and among the Ubangi Binga pygmies, the rest of the population of pygmy hunters and gatherers has become largely dependent for food upon cultivation, either by adopting it themselves or by entering into symbiosis with neighboring village farmers. The Mbuti solution to the contact situation is very different, and so it is in its contemporary context that we study it; any light the study may throw on an earlier form of pygmy society is incidental.

The habitat of the Mbuti is the Ituri Forest. This is a primary rain forest that runs across the equator from the fringes of the Saharan desert, in the north, into the Kivu mountains, in the south. To the east it is bounded clearly by a succession of lakes (Lake Albert, Lake Edward and Lake Kivu) but to the west the boundary is less definable, the forest thinning out as it approaches the Congo River's commercial centers. Effectively, the Mbuti occupy only the dense forest where the migration of game and the nature of vegetation have alike been virtually unaffected by outside influences. Their forest home, some 50,000 square miles in extent, is traversed by a number of roads built, for the most part, since the 1930's, but the purpose of the roads has been merely for transport and has not led to any significant exploitation of the forest, which in most places comes right to the very edge of the roadway (see Map 4).

There are a number of significant features concerning the forest that have to be taken into account. In general it is considered as generous and friendly from the point of view of the Mbuti hunters and gatherers, and as niggardly and hostile from the point of view of the villager cultivators.

For example, the forest is, in most places, gently undulating, though even the mountainous sections in the east and in the south are as thickly wooded at their highest points as at the lowest. In all the territory to the north of the Kivu mountains the average height above sea level is somewhere around a thousand meters. This height, together with the over-all denseness of the forest, and an almost daily rainfall that averages from 70 to 80 inches per year, makes the temperatures within the forest remain remarkably constant and agreeable, seldom departing far from either side of 80° F., never below 70° or above 90°. The relative humidity is fairly constant at 95 per cent.

Where in the villages, and in the plantations that surround them, the midday temperatures soar well into the nineties, and the ground is covered with a dry, choking dust that quickly turns to mud, in the shade of the forest the world is cool and fresh, with only rare places, such as along river banks or at salt licks, where sunlight reaches the ground without first being filtered through a leafy roof. Also from the point of view of comfort, and of health, where village conditions lead to gatherings of flies and mosquitoes, these disease bearers are seldom if ever seen in the depths of the forest, except at such sites as are easily avoided. The Mbuti frequently compare their lot, in these respects, with that of the villagers, who in turn grudgingly admit to some advantages of forest life.

Another important contrast between forest and village life is in the water supply. The forest is interlaced with innumerable streams, any of which can be drunk from with impunity. A hunting camp is always located near a stream, but never stays in the one vicinity long enough to foul the water. A village remains in the same location, however, for three years or so, and the local water supply invariably becomes polluted. The villagers have some resistance to infection, but the Mbuti often have none and quickly become sick if they stay too long in a village.

But it is with regard to food even more than shelter or water that the forest seems to favor the Mbuti. Throughout the year, without fail, there is an abundant supply of game and of vegetable foods. There are half a dozen different kinds of antelope that are particularly abundant, apart from supplementary sources of meat such as birds, monkeys, chimpanzees, and divers grubs and insects. The forest also supplies a number of edible roots, notably the sweet *itaba*, and many different varieties of mushrooms, nuts, berries and fruits. All the latter may vary in abundance the one from the other, according to the time of year, but throughout the year at any one time there will be an ample supply, in both quantity and variety.

The only truly seasonal food in the forest economy of the Mbuti is honey, and it is of major importance in the diet. It is also of major importance as a focal point in the constant process of fission and fusion that characterizes Mbuti society.

The apparent benevolence of the forest towards the Mbuti extends still further. The materials for the making of shelter, clothing, and all other necessary items of material culture are all to hand at a moment's notice. Firewood, equally, is everywhere in abundance. It is not surprising, then, that the Mbuti recognize their dependence upon the forest and refer to it as "Father" or "Mother" (I have heard both used, it seems without discrimination) because, as they say, it gives them food, warmth, shelter and clothing, just like their parents. What is, perhaps, surprising is that the Mbuti add that the forest also, like their parents, gives them affection.

If it has been thought that this stress on the environmental factor is overweighted, the last observation should make it clear why. The forest is more than mere environment to the Mbuti. It is a living, conscious thing, both natural and supernatural, something that has to be depended upon, respected, trusted, obeyed and loved. The love demanded of the Mbuti is no romanticism, and perhaps it might be better included under "respect," but I make the distinction here because the Mbuti make the distinction, and because it is all part of the structural relationship of opposition between the Mbuti and the villagers.

More of the intimacy of the relationship between the Mbuti and the forest will emerge as we proceed; indeed there is not a single aspect of their lives where it is not evident. Here let us take a quick look at the relationship of the neighboring villagers to the same forest.

In the Ituri the tribal composition is thoroughly confused, a succession of invasions from different directions having taken place over the past four hundred years. From the north came the Mangbetu, pursued later and driven westward by the Zande. At the present day these two large tribes stretch right across the northern edges of the forest, a large proportion of each remaining in relatively open savannah. Also in the north and in the east are the populous Budo and the Mamvu-Lesé. From the southeast came the Bira, a Bantu-speaking plains people who split on reaching the forest, some pressing up by Lake Albert and retaining something of their cattle culture[1], the others turning westward through the middle of the forest, segmenting into a number of isolated villages loosely held together by the principle of patrilineal descent and recognition of a common ancestor manifest in the chiefs and sub-chiefs. In recent years, apparently since the imposition of Belgian authority, the Forest Bira (the Plains Bira do not concern us here, directly) divided into two main chieftainships, with territorial headquarters at Koki and Bahaha. (Map 5 illustrates

[1] There is some uncertainty as to whether the Bira were originally cultivators or pastoralists. Among the present Plains Bira, however, cattle plays an important role and the people themselves claim to have always had cattle. They now practice a mixed economy.

the territorial division of the Bira, with the location of chiefs and sub-
chiefs, and also of the Lesé.) The Bira stretch as far as the junction of
the Nduye and Epulu rivers, west of which are the Ndaka and the
related Mbo, also Bantu speakers. Further to the west are the Bali, who
are at the westward extremity of Mbuti territory.

All these tribes, whose total forest population numbers some forty
thousand, have taken to a specialized form of forest cultivation, growing both plantains and manioc as staples, some dry rice, beans and
groundnuts. Palm-oil trees are more common in the north and west
of the forest, but palm oil is used and traded throughout. Elsewhere,
however, groundnut oil is widely used. The leaf of the manioc plant is
cooked with the oil, and sometimes with groundnuts, to make a sauce,
and other leaves are also sometimes used this way. Various wines are
extracted or made from the palm trees and their fruits, and liquor is
commonly distilled from both manioc and plantains. Hemp is grown
in illicit plantations.

There is a fair amount of fishing practiced throughout the area, but
fish is never more than a supplementary food. Pits and spear-falls are
placed around plantations, partly to protect the plantations and
partly in the hope of acquiring meat, but their yield is negligible. For
reasons that will emerge, the villagers dislike going far into the forest,
away from their plantations, and do little hunting. For their meat they
are dependent either upon trade supplies, available only very recently
(and even then only to the few who can afford them), or upon the
Mbuti.

The major difficulty in the life of the villager is the forest itself.
Owing to the size of its enormous trees (many 12 feet in diameter
and 150 in height) and the speed with which secondary vegetation
grows up once the trees are cut down, the work of cutting a new plantation for a village may take months to finish; and once cleared, the
ground has to be constantly worked on to prevent it from being overgrown. When the cutting and burning are completed there is little
danger of the newly planted crop not coming up, but in each succeeding season the yield becomes less, and after three years may cease altogether. Thus whole villages and plantations have to move every few
years. Yet once a site is abandoned the apparently barren land suddenly bursts forth with a luxuriant forest vegetation that soon destroys the buildings and makes access to the old plantation all but
impossible.

The villagers, like the Mbuti, find themselves in a very personal relationship with the forest, but a very different one. The forest surrounds them on all sides, but they do not live in it or by it, only despite it. Their initial act is one of destruction, the cutting down of the forest to make way for village and plantation which in turn are destroyed in the final act. The hostility is mutual, as the villagers see it. They have to fight not only the forest itself, but also the creatures that live in it. Elephants, leopards, baboons and Mbuti, all are a menace to life and livelihood. A whole plantation can be destroyed in a few hours by even a modest sprinkling of elephants. The excessive and sometimes erratic rainfall can cause hunger for a whole season. Baboons and Mbuti come in the night and steal the ripening fruit. Leopards prey on the few scrawny goats and chickens the villagers manage to raise.

As for the Mbuti, so for the villagers is the forest an entity to be reckoned with, upon which life and death depend; it is also an entity that is natural and supernatural. But instead of acceding to the natural, the villagers with their superior technology combat it; and instead of respecting the supernatural in the sense that the Mbuti respect it, the villagers oppose it with fear, mistrust and occasional hate. They people the forest with evil spirits, and they fill their lives with magic, witchcraft and a belief in sorcery.

The forest achieves the establishment of two virtually irreconcilable systems of values. It further determines, for both Mbuti and villagers, a certain degree of nomadism, and it tends to fragment large populations into small, relatively isolated bands or villages. For the Mbuti the forest merely indicates natural boundaries, such as valleys, ridges, rivers, caves and so forth, within which a band can conveniently roam at will throughout the years, economically self-sufficient. Within that nomadic framework there is an enormous sense of permanence and of territory. But for the villagers the forest announces, at the end of every three years or so, that the village must pack up and move, it does not much matter where. The move will inevitably bring the village into renewed conflict with the forest, and may well bring it into conflict with a neighboring village which has also been forced to move. In spite of the vast size of the forest and its small population, the villagers are unwilling to go off entirely on their own. At the present time they move up and down the long road that connects Stanleyville with Irumu, or Wamba with Nia-Nia and Mambasa. Formerly it seems that villages were similarly stretched out along recognized trails, and seldom moved away from them. On any given trail, or road, the number of suitable sites for a semi-permanent village is limited, but friction between villages is due only in part to rivalry for territory. It is also due to suspicion of witchcraft and sorcery, a suspicion that seems to increase as the distance of separation decreases. This, of course, can also be interpreted as an expression of territorial friction, but it is conceived in personal rather than territorial terms, and is accompanied by a general dislike and mistrust of strangers.

Nor must we lose sight of the fact that whereas the Mbuti, even with their nomadism, in which hunting camps are shifted every month, have a strong sense of basic territorial permanence, the villagers have none, and this gives rise to further instability. To mention only one example, it is believed among the Bira that the dead should be buried according to a prescribed ritual, and that the grave should be cared for in a prescribed manner. The burial is always carried out but it is a constant source of conflict having to care for a grave that may be some miles away. Every time a village moves the villagers have to face the fact that they are abandoning their dead, to some extent, and they are unpleasantly reminded of the uncertainty of their own future. We do not know what the original burial practice was before the Bira moved into the forest; undoubtedly changes have been made, but they have not adequately met the new situation.

It is only in light of the relationship between each of these peoples and the environment in which they live that we can understand the relationship between the people themselves. It is in part ignorance of this factor that has led to the gross misunderstanding of Mbuti/ Villager relationship, and indeed of Mbuti society itself. Before considering either the Mbuti or their relationship with the villagers, however, a certain amount of further ground-clearing is necessary.

MBUTI, BΛMBUTI, BAMBUTI

A certain amount of confusion concerning the Mbuti arises out of conflicting terminology, some of it totally inapplicable or lacking in significance. First we have to be clear why we group together, under any one name, all the pygmy hunters of the Ituri Forest, even though they speak different languages and use different hunting techniques.

Racially, they are clearly one people, quite distinct from any of the surrounding Negro tribes. They form a strongly, visibly distinct unit. Culturally, they are equally distinguished from their neighbors as a unit, being hunters and gatherers, and not cultivators, with a consequently totally distinct social structure. Differences in hunting techniques do not affect the basic structural unity. The fact that the Mbuti fall into different linguistic groups is no more than accidental, and is of recent historic origin. The linguistic division is that propounded by Schebesta (1938, pp. 24–26). In effect he uses the terms Aka, Efe and Sua to refer to those pygmies who were in territories invaded and settled by the Ngbetu/Zande, the Lesé, and the Forest Bira respectively; these pygmies apparently adopted the languages of the newcomers to their respective areas and they have maintained some kind of relationship with their Negro neighbors ever since.

The question of language is by no means settled yet, and it may be that either KiLesé or KiBira may in fact prove to be a language of pygmy origin adopted by the Negro invaders. At the moment there is no significant evidence available to this effect, and given a situation where small isolated hunting bands (of an absolute maximum of thirty nuclear families and a possible minimum of three) are brought sharply into contact with larger, more permanent, technologically more advanced peoples with a tribal system, we can only assume the likelihood that the pygmies adopted the languages of the newcomers, losing most of their own.

In this case the linguistic division suggested by Schebesta most certainly only refers to a post-contact situation and does not necessarily point to any indigenous difference between these three groups of Ituri hunters and gatherers. The fact that, very approximately, the linguistic boundaries also correspond to the boundaries between pygmy hunters who emphasize the spear, the bow and arrow, and the net may be no more than a mark of acculturation with the three distinct Negro groups; on the other hand it may point to some earlier distinction, but in any case is of much more significance in any contemporary study of social structure.

In dismissing the linguistic differences as any indication of internal differentiation it is worth pointing out that any pygmy from any area in the Ituri can recognize though not comprehend any other pygmy speaking a totally different language because, throughout, the intonation is remarkably similar, absolutely distinctive, and different by far from the intonation used by the Negroes whose language is being spoken. This is one small pointer toward an earlier linguistic unity among all Ituri pygmies, as is the fact that they all seem to recognize themselves by the term Mbuti. One hears this term far more frequently than any other when pygmies are distinguishing themselves from villagers, in all parts of the forest. Even in distinguishing themselves from neighboring pygmies, place names are more likely to be used than the terms Aka, Efe or Sua. Although I have formerly used both BaMbuti and Bambuti, I here use the form Mbuti, as this eliminates difficulty in accurately representing singular and plural forms, and is in keeping with the current practice of the International African Institute.

In previous writings and occasionally in this work, the term "Negro" is used to differentiate the pygmy hunters from the immigrant farmers, but it now seems far better to use the term "villager," for the significant difference, as seen by the people concerned as well as seen by the anthropologist, is one between a forest people and a village people; the racial factor is structurally negligible. Precise tribal names cannot always be used, as in some villages the tribal composition is mixed, and as any one band of Mbuti may have contact with two or even three different village tribal groups.

I have made other modifications to my earlier terminology, necessary simply because of increased understanding. I now use the term "band" where previously I used the term "group" to refer to a unit of Mbuti hunters, who, regardless of their kin relationships, recognize and share a common hunting territory. As will be seen, the term refers more to territorial boundaries than to the boundaries of kinship. The term "group" I now employ to refer generally to one villager group as opposed to another; i.e., Sudanic and Bantu, say, or to distinguish between all net-hunters and all archers. But wherever used, it is used only in its general sense, the context making its meaning plain. It does not have any specific academic significance, not being a translation, for instance, of Schebesta's (1948, p. 291) "Lokalgruppe."

By "family" is meant a nuclear family of a man, his wife and their sociologically recognized children, who are cared for and brought up in all respects in the same way whether or not they are biological offspring. The terms "clan" and "lineage" do not enter much into our analysis of actual Mbuti kinship, but are used as theoretical concepts by comparison with which we can more satisfactorily understand the Mbuti system. A discussion of their meaning is, then, an integral part of the test.

In the course of discussion of the magico-religious system, certain usages specific to the situation will be defined; here I would just mention my own understanding of the terms "ceremony" and "festival." "Ceremony" has, when I use it, the connotation of formal ritual, of an established pattern of behavior that must be followed according to rule if the ceremony is to be effective, whatever its purpose. By "festival" I mean something rather different. It in no way necessarily implies an annual or regularly recurrent event; its objectives may be precisely the same as those of a ceremony, but the means employed are different. There is no precisely regulated pattern of behavior. On the contrary, there is an important element of spontaneity that gives the occasion a vital immediacy, keeping it in the current context rather than connecting it with the past. I confess that the term "festival" has, for me, other less easily definable connotations that make it more suitable for use in the Mbuti situation, the most important of these being that it implies wider, freer participation, less pomposity and more enjoyment, an abandonment that is almost subversive with respect to the commonly accepted norms of behavior.

Most important, I have to revoke my earlier usage of the term "Essumba" or "Lusumba" (Turnbull, 1955, 1957[1], 1957[2]). The context in earlier writing, I hope, makes it plain when I am referring to a magico-religious festival of the Mbuti as distinct from a ceremony practiced under the same name by the villagers. The misleading terminology employed before my last field trip was due in part to the difficulties of the linguistic situation and the fact that I was then using the lingua franca, KiNgwana, as my major means of communication. The importance and significance of the confusion will appear later in the text, but as I now wish to use a terminology that will clarify the situation as much as the actual linguistic confusion permits, I have to state that wherever in the past I have referred to the magico-religious festival of the net-hunting Mbuti, in which the men play a predominant part, and where I have used either "Essumba" or "Lusumba," it would have been more correct to have used the term *molimo*. Even this term, however, has its counterpart in the Bira *molimo* ceremony, but at least we can now distinguish more easily between both of these and the other local ceremonies known variously as *essumba*, *lusumba* and *ishumba*, which ceremonies are connected primarily with the Ngwana villagers and their earlier slave-trading and ivory-collecting practices.

One last small correction of past usage; whereas before I once or twice (Turnbull, 1955, 1957[1]) used the spelling *Alima* for the festival associated with the puberty of Mbuti girls, I now use the form and spelling *elima*.

ETHNOGRAPHIC BACKGROUND

There are two major difficulties facing any discussion of the Mbuti. One is the fact that while they are true hunters and gatherers, they are nonetheless associated in some way, and apparently closely so, with the surrounding forest cultivators. The inseparability of the two peoples makes it especially difficult to know where to begin, as the Mbuti are one thing in one context and a quite different thing in another context.

The other difficulty lies in the fact that previous sources have not given us a clear idea of the structure of either group, Mbuti or villagers, and have completely misled us as to the nature of the relationship between the two. I have dealt somewhat with the latter difficulty elsewhere (Turnbull, 1956) and propose to deal with the former difficulty by giving a brief sketch of the nature of Mbuti society that will adequately provide a basis for a preliminary investigation of the actual nature of the relationship between the Mbuti and the villagers. Only then can we safely attempt to understand the nature of Mbuti social structure, even in their forest society, as divorced as it may seem to be from the village context.

It is impossible to give an accurate estimate of the population of the Mbuti of the Ituri Forest, as there has been nothing approaching an efficient census. Owing to the mobility of the individual hunting bands, and the lack of co-operation offered by villagers whenever queries are made about the number of Mbuti they "own," we must regard with suspicion any figures based on a count of bands attached to villages and an average band population. From my own experience, and from discussion with missionaries and administrators who have attempted counts, one way or another, I would hazard a guess at somewhere around 40,000, with no evidence to show that the population is increasing, but certainly none to show that it is decreasing.

The total population may be divided, as we have seen, into groups that emphasize one hunting technology or another, the two main groups being the archers and the net-hunters. The spear-hunters also use bows and arrows for defense as well as for occasional individual hunting. None of these groups can be said to have any political identity, however, any more than can the Mbuti totality, except in opposition to the villagers.

The only effective political unit is the band, which we have defined as a unit of Mbuti hunters sharing and recognizing a common hunting territory.[2] No matter what group the band falls under, the definition holds. The territory is clearly defined by natural boundaries, though the law of trespass depends somewhat on the location of the home band within its territory at the moment of trespass. The boundaries, though fixed, are under certain circumstances capable of penetration without causing offense.

The composition of the band is fluid, to say the least, and does not follow any clear unilineal or cognatic descent system. Throughout the forest, the bands are in a constant state of fragmentation as well as in a constant process of fission and fusion. Members of any band are quite likely at any moment to leave and join another band, temporarily or permanently, for any one of a number of reasons. In-law visiting is common, and permanent attachments to the band are sometimes accomplished this way. But at the same time, with each successive, monthly change of site, the hunting camp also shows another stage in the over-all process of fission and fusion along recognizable lines of structural cleavage. At certain times of the year, different for net-hunters and archers, the band splits up into a number of smaller sub-bands, all still hunting within the same over-all territory, but as independent units.

It has generally been stated, sometimes citing the apparent lack of an Mbuti language as an example, that the Mbuti are a people without a culture of their own, adopting the culture of their villager neighbors just as they adopt their language. A superficial look at a hunting society, with its lack of easily recognizable social institutions, might seem to confirm that opinion. There is no chieftainship, no council of elders, but sometimes an individual who assumes the villager title of *sultani* or *capita*. There is no legal system supported by effective or formal supernatural sanctions. There is an evident lack of any kinship system except an apparently slavish imitation of the villager clan and lineage system, whereby certain individuals related through the principle of patrilineal descent recognize a common ancestor and symbolize their unity by the respect of a common totem. Any attempt to integrate this system with other institutions, indigenous or adopted,

---

[2] Throughout, except where otherwise specified, I use the term "band" in this sense of a unit that is primarily territorial. It is essentially composed of peoples bound together by bonds other than lineage. Insofar as affines are an important part of any band, and affinal relationships as important in most respects as lineal relationships, the band cannot even be defined as cognatic or bilateral without qualification stressing its ad-hoc nature.

falls unhappily apart however, and it looks indeed as if the Mbuti are
in the process of adopting villager institutions wholesale, without
adopting the system that would relate them.

Further evidence in favor of this interesting half-truth of Mbuti
dependence is plainly discernible in the adoption by the Mbuti of village ceremonials connected with *rites de passage*, in which they subject themselves completely to villager ritual authority. But again these
adopted institutions seem to have little structural relationship to the
Mbuti hunting life, divorced as it is from the village context. Once
one grants that divorce, then one is left with an apparent vacuum, a
lack of internal system that is almost anarchical. Yet there is no an-
archy; law and order exist without the villager context as within, and
without as in their villager institutions. In default of any clear exposi-
tion of internal system, however, it has been assumed by many that
the actual situation is one of total Mbuti dependence upon the villagers.

The economy of the Mbuti is hunting and gathering, and they are
perfectly capable of independent subsistence. Hunger, in absence of
village food supplies, is due only to laziness. The alleged economic
dependence of the Mbuti will be discussed in the next chapter. Here
it is only necessary to stress the possibility of their actual independence of the village, and point to a dependence upon each other, best
seen in the fact that all the hunting techniques involve some measure of co-operation between men, women and children. The net-hunt
demands the greatest measure of co-operation; the little I was able
to discover about spear-hunts indicates a preference for hunting parties of five or six men; and while archers can hunt successfully in threes,
there are among the archers annual beat-hunts (*begbe*) which demand
the same high degree of co-operation demanded by the net-hunt, involving the entire band. Some elementary principles of unity can be
discerned, then, in these various hunting techniques, but they are not
sufficient to fill the gap left by the absence of developed kinship or
political systems.

In the hunting band, as we have seen, the population is somewhat
mercurial and composite. Only when the band fragments into smaller
units do we occasionally get a fragment that has some appearance of
being a kin group. System still eludes us. Nor do the *sultani* and *capita*
offer any effective replacement for the missing political system. No
one individual is effectively a leader; issues are settled by common

discussion. The discussion is not entirely haphazard, but once again the structural factor is elusive.

When first we look at the religious life of the Mbuti we feel the pulse beating clearly. The *elima* and the *molimo* are outstandingly evident as institutions connected with crisis, but the moment we try to analyze their function the beat becomes less distinct. Here the picture is again confused by the fact that the villagers have similar names for ceremonies of their own that are alike enough to lead to the assumption that the Mbuti adopted these institutions into their own disorganized framework. Then the pulse stops altogether.

I suggested earlier (Turnbull, 1956) that part of the answer lay in a vital opposition between the two worlds of the Mbuti, the forest and the village. Recognizing that opposition is no less a relationship than any other form of relationship, we can at least theoretically separate the two worlds temporarily, if they are truly in opposition, and study them apart. Using this device we are free to look at the Mbuti in the village context almost as though this were their sole existence, and discern there what system we can. We are also free to examine the same people in the forest context, living in small nomadic hunting bands, virtually independent of the village world. But by looking at the village world first, when we turn to the forest world we shall be able to follow the Mbuti not only as they move from one hunting camp to another, but also when they abandon the forest for a brief spell in the village, seized by a whim, by the desire for relaxation, or by their taste for village foods, wine and tobacco. In this way we shall arrive at a better understanding of both worlds of the Mbuti, and of the actual relationship between them. We shall also, in the process, test our hypothesis of opposition, and, if it be proven, discover the elusive principle that binds together the otherwise apparently lawless, leaderless, un-kin-conscious forest society.

PART TWO

THE VILLAGE WORLD

CHAPTER 3

The Mbuti/Villager Relationship

THE QUESTION OF DEPENDENCE

Although we are primarily concerned with the structure of Mbuti society, there are a number of valid reasons why we should first concern ourselves with the relationship between the Mbuti and the villagers.

For one, this has been the area of greatest misunderstanding and this misunderstanding has consequently affected attitudes toward an understanding of the forest hunting and gathering life of the Mbuti even when apart from the villagers. It is widely believed that the Mbuti are subject to village authority, that they are a subordinate people. This belief rests on the assumption that the Mbuti are dependent upon the villagers, and the theory of dependence has been extended to political and ritual fields as well as economic. The exact degree of dependence is something that we have to examine carefully throughout our study, though we can only take it up specifically after we have considered the Mbuti in both the village and the forest worlds.

The notion of dependence has led to the theory that Mbuti culture, such as it is, is in itself derived from the superordinate village culture, and we shall see that this is far from the truth. Even when we look at the Mbuti in the village world it is not hard to see the superficiality of his alleged acculturation, for the very willingness with which he adopts village institutions and falls in with village ways leads him inevitably into one contradiction after another, which contradictions are possible only because the institutions do not have the same structural significance for the Mbuti as for the villager.

The cause of the misunderstanding is largely that previous accounts and investigations have been derived from experience of the Mbuti in the village context, in almost complete ignorance of even

the most general nature of the forest context and in absolute ignorance of the structure of the forest world. But this in turn leads to
another reason for considering the village world first, for the universal-
ity of the misconception and its common cause are in themselves
highly significant. The misconception, that is to say the notion of the
Mbuti as a subordinate and dependent people is, although a myth in
actuality, nonetheless a structural factor of the greatest importance,
and it is the relationship of the Mbuti to the village world that leads
to some of the most interesting elements in the over-all social framework of Mbuti society as it is today. It is not our intent to say what
elements of Mbuti society are caused by their relationship with the
villagers, but it is certain that many elements, such as the constant
process of fragmentation, fission and fusion, take on special significance in light of that relationship. Even the most central religious
institutions, sacred to the forest, appear to be in the process of adaptation, allowing for and encouraging a widening of the Mbuti social
horizon, bringing about a wider sense of unity (both religious and
political) than apparently existed before.

Ostensibly the relationship is based upon the economic dependence
of the Mbuti on the villagers for food and metal. Both manioc and
bananas (sweet as well as plantain) are grown throughout the Ituri
region and jointly form the staple. Both foods are eagerly sought and
consumed by all Mbuti, who in the forest have nothing akin to the
banana or to the large manioc root. The small, sweet forest *itaba* root
has to be grubbed for, and, as the Mbuti say, it is much easier to get
manioc from the villagers. Other village foods consumed by the Mbuti
are groundnuts, corn, rice and beans but, as for the villagers, they are
supplementary. Any of these foods may be carried off to the forest
camps and consumed there. Indeed in any village on almost any day
one is likely to see a pygmy woman or two filling her carrying basket to
capacity with such foods and returning to the forest camp. If the
hunting camp is nearby, a regular supply line is maintained, and even
forest food becomes supplementary in Mbuti diet.

When in the village the Mbuti also have access to luxuries such as
palm wine, and to certain trade goods; tobacco and second-hand
clothes are the most important such items.

Having no knowledge of metalworking,[1] the Mbuti are without a

---

[1] A few Mbuti prisoners were taught by the Belgian administrator at Mambasa how
to hammer arrow tips as part of his campaign to "liberate" the Mbuti from their dependence upon the villagers.

doubt wholly dependent upon the villagers for all metal goods. So also with pottery, there being absolutely no knowledge of pottery manufacture among the Mbuti.

But it is significant that none of the authorities who cite the lack of these foodstuffs and metallurgical and ceramic skills among the Mbuti as an example of their economic dependence also cite the absence, among the Mbuti, of all knowledge of fire-making.[2] By the same reasoning this should make them dependent on the villagers for matches. The point is that mere lack does not constitute a necessary structural dependence, unless the lack is vital. We have to ask ourselves how *necessary* is this apparent economic dependence of the Mbuti upon the villagers.

It will be shown in the section on "The Forest World" that there is no question of any absolute dependence of the Mbuti upon the villagers for food, in that context, except insofar as luxuries ultimately tend to become necessities. It will be seen that in the forest their technology is sufficient to keep them supplied with all their basic needs. It will also be seen that metal is not a necessary part of their technology, any more than is pottery, or knowledge of fire-making.

In the village world, however, the Mbuti are completely dependent upon the villagers. Hunting and gathering in the neighborhood of any village are likely to be equally poor, and it would be difficult if not impossible for an Mbuti band to keep itself supplied with forest foodstuffs from a village headquarters. It would involve a half day's march, at least, to reach a suitable hunting area, and the physical effort alone would be enough to discourage even the most ardent hunter. But even more important is the fact that by living in the village the Mbuti would be out of touch with the forest, and would have no way of knowing the exact whereabouts of the game at any given time. Living in a hunting camp with the forest all around them, the Mbuti know only what is going on in their immediate vicinity. As the game moves

---

[2] Some Mbuti have learned to use matches, when available, and a few know of the fire drill from contact with their village neighbors. There is absolutely no indigenous method of making fire, however, and it is a point of no small importance to their social life that each household maintains its own hearth. Embers from this hearth are carried, usually by the woman, wrapped in fire-resistant leaves, during the hunt or while on the trail. At each new camp site, the family hearths are kindled from embers of the old family hearths, preserving a distinct sense of continuity. Whenever a communal hearth is required, as for the *molimo*, communal participation is accentuated by the compulsory contribution of embers from each family hearth. Whereas matches are rarely used, becoming quickly damp and useless, even if available, they are *never* used for kindling family or communal hearths, but only for such relatively mundane purposes as lighting a pipe or cigarette.

out of that vicinity, however, they keep track of it, and they send out scouts to help them decide the best location for their next hunting camp.

Insofar as the Mbuti are dependent upon the villagers for village foods, thus far are they dependent also for certain items of material culture, in metal, pottery and wood. Even so, of the village foods only rice and beans (neither of which can be considered as staples even among the villagers) demand pottery or metal cooking vessels. Trade vessels of aluminum are rapidly replacing all pottery vessels. Manioc, plantains, corn and peanuts can be roasted, the sweet banana and peanut can be eaten raw, and manioc can also be eaten without cooking if it is first soaked in cold water for several days.

However, in every Mbuti village camp each household will boast at least one metal vessel, and there will be one or two wooden mortars and pestles for common usage. In addition, there is only the metal knife blade which might be said to be necessary to the Mbuti in their village life, for peeling, scraping and cutting the manioc root, and the metal ax blade needed for cutting the saplings used in the construction of either village-type houses or forest-style huts. The technological dependence of the Mbuti upon the villagers, in the village, is then not great, and is directly contingent upon Mbuti dependence upon village foods in the same context.

We shall see that in the forest context, as with food, there is no essential dependence either on materials such as metal, or on skill in working them. It has been argued that the Mbuti hunt is dependent upon metal arrow-points, spear blades, and knife blades. It is not. We shall see that the Mbuti frequently prefer to use the poisoned arrows that have only a fire-hardened tip, for sound practical reasons; that they use the spear primarily for defense rather than offense, and in any case still retain knowledge of the fire-hardened point and the belief that it is as effective as metal except, possibly, against buffalo and elephant. Old Mbuti assert that fire-hardened spears are effective even against the largest game. Slit bamboo and slit reeds offer adequate cutting surfaces, though they dull quickly and are seldom used today; they could, however, successfully replace the metal knife as far as the forest life of the Mbuti is concerned. There are certain types of vine that have a highly abrasive surface and can be used for scraping *itaba* roots. Of all the village utensils, the two that the Mbuti would miss the most would be the machete and the ax blade. The machete is used for cutting the light *fito* saplings that form the framework for the huts and the shafts for spears; the ax is used for enlarging the boles in which bees make their hives, so that the honey can be extracted more easily. Younger Mbuti do not know what they would do without the machete for cutting saplings. Both they and the older men realize that the ax is not absolutely essential, and I have seen ax-shaped clubs used for breaking away the wood from around a hive, where the wood is rotten, as it frequently is. The older men say that if they did not have machetes for cutting saplings they would use stone tools, but they have no knowledge at all of how to make such tools, and are probably prompted to make this remark by the presence in the forest of early stone axheads.

Accepting, for the moment, that the Mbuti in their forest world are not in any position of necessary dependence upon the villagers for food or material, or technological skill, and admitting that in the village context they are dependent, the question arises as to why they choose to place themselves in that position of dependence. It is certainly not out of economic necessity. The truth of the matter is simply that the village offers, for a brief while, an agreeable change of pace, an opportunity for a relaxation that is not always possible in the forest, and, one might say, better hunting, on occasion. An Mbuti band or an Mbuti family or an Mbuti individual may descend upon a village either because of sheer whim, or because of laziness if the forest hunting gets too strenuous, or because of dissension, or indeed for almost any reason except necessity. Whatever the reason, and most commonly it at least involves an expressed desire for relaxation and freedom from care, the reason is on the side of the Mbuti, the choice is theirs, and the dependence that follows is as voluntary as it is temporary.

ECONOMIC RECIPROCITY

We then have to ask what the Mbuti offer in return for the food and metal products that they receive, and to determine at least the economic structure of the relationship. In so doing we are inevitably led to consider the domestic, political and religious aspects and their interrelationship with the economic system, and it is in these interrelationships that inconsistency and conflict emerge.

Even in terms of sheer economic reciprocity the relationship is inherently unstable. Continuing to grant, for the moment, the fact that no economic necessity is involved on the part of the Mbuti, and that their dependence is voluntary and temporary, the forest world remain-

ing an ever-present, ever-accessible sanctuary of independence, then
we are left with a situation which, if anything, is rather the reverse
of what it is normally stated to be; for we find that the villagers have
far more need of the Mbuti than the Mbuti have of the villagers.

Here we have to look briefly at the historical genesis of the relationship, which began with the invasion of the first non-Mbuti tribes
three or four hundred years ago, and continued until the invasion
reached its climax in the nineteenth century. The Mbuti found themselves caught between a number of warring tribes, and according to
legend (also according to what one might reasonably expect) each
isolated hunting band found it convenient to attach itself to one or
another group of villagers. The villagers, on their part, needed the
Mbuti as guides, scouts and spies, and, as related today by both sides,
employed them as such, feeding them in return. When the situation
became more stable, and notably when the last vestiges of open hostility were suppressed by the Belgian administration, this original
relationship came to an end, neither side having any absolute need
of the other. The Mbuti, however, had developed a strong taste for
plantation foods and maintained their demands on the villagers. To
this day, if a villager does not accede to such demands his plantation is
simply raided and he has no recourse. Recognizing the difficulty of
making an effective claim for theft, the villagers continued to supply
food at request, but attempted to secure certain services in return.

We have already mentioned the attitude of the villagers toward
the forest as a hostile place, and a place that they people with evil
spirits. One of the services that they have tried to elicit from the
Mbuti, then, is the supply of forest necessities such as saplings and
leaves for housebuilding, bark for clothmaking (now almost obsolete
among all the villagers), and meat and honey. The longer a village is
in existence, the more scarce these supplies become in the immediate
vicinity, and the villagers are mostly loath to venture far into the forest. However, plainly, as with the Mbuti, it is a question of convenience rather than necessity, though the Mbuti say that the villagers
could never be successful as hunters, being far too clumsy and slow.

This is all largely a matter of historical conjecture, but it helps in
providing a sense of direction, and in indicating that the onus for
maintaining a reasonable degree of reciprocity is all the time upon
the villagers, not upon the Mbuti. For today the villagers are still unwilling to go into the forest, and the Mbuti are still their major source
of meat, honey and building materials. But there is, today, an addi-

tional factor that increases the degree of necessity and dependence on the part of the villagers. By "today" I refer to the period of Belgian administration, for which we have historic record. During this period additional demands were made by the administration upon the villagers; notably, able-bodied men were recruited into the road gangs for building and maintaining the thousand-odd miles of road that cross the forest, linking the widely separated administrative posts; and it was also demanded of the villagers that they produce certain specific crops in excess, and cultivate other new crops, particularly cotton, in addition. The food surplus was used to feed immigrant laborers, the cotton to produce some revenue in an otherwise highly unprofitable region.

These demands thus increased the amount of plantation work that had to be undertaken by each village, and at the same time reduced the labor force available. Penalties for failure were severe, and the villagers naturally turned to the Mbuti for help. Equally naturally, the Mbuti declined to help, except when the nature of the work suited their convenience and the rewards were adequate, and a long struggle began that continued right up to the time that independence somewhat altered the situation.

From the villagers' point of view, their relationship with the Mbuti, which had begun to prove rather tiresome and unprofitable, quickly became a matter of acute anxiety. Instead of regarding the Mbuti merely as parasites, which is effectively what they were, the villagers began to regard them as indispensable to the new village economy. From the Mbuti point of view, however, the situation had not changed. The forest was still there as a sanctuary to which they could retire with impunity at, literally, a moment's notice, and the village was still a place where they could relax, enjoy luxury foods, wine and tobacco, in return for a minimum amount of service. Being a practical people, however, they responded, to a token extent, to the new demands for service, in the form of plantation labor. But it was not to their taste, and it proved highly detrimental to their health. The villagers in many cases realized this and compromised by using the Mbuti mainly to maintain guard over the plantations, so they would not be affected by the unaccustomed sunlight or exercise, and only in emergencies asked them to actually work in the fields.

Such emergencies, however, became more and more frequent as administrative demands upon the villagers were increased. The cotton crop became the major issue, and the time of the cotton harvest was the one time when, above all others, the villagers needed the help of the Mbuti. And that was precisely the time when the Mbuti were least available, for this work was least to their taste, and beyond a certain point even the Mbuti cannot be bribed.

THE NEED FOR CONTROL

In 1957, and again in 1958, Chief Kachui of the Ndaka tribe found himself in difficulty over his cotton harvest. Of all the tribal chiefs in the Ituri, Kachui was one of the most powerful and one of the most influential. He had the advantage of a government-supported police force at his disposal, but on both occasions when I was at Bafwakoa at the time of cotton harvest he was without his usual retinue of Mbuti parasites. He had his sons deployed nearly to the Epulu to the east, and halfway to Wamba to the north, in an effort to learn the whereabouts of "his" Mbuti, but to no avail. He even used me in the hope that I would be able to discover at least one hunting camp, and I was led to where a few Mbuti maintained a plantation camp, living in the shade of the forest but acting as guards against raids on the plantation by monkeys, baboon and elephant, on the strict under-standing that they were not used for work in the cotton fields. Al-though I was known there, and would normally have been taken straight to the hunting camp, all knowledge of the whereabouts of their fellows was denied. It may indeed have been that the band had broken up and gone in different directions to join neighboring bands that were less pressed, or it may simply have gone far off into the depths of the forest where it could never be found. None of Chief Kachui's threats or exhortations was of the least avail.

At the same time, Chief Kayumba of the Mbo, just across the Ituri River, was having the same trouble, and I saw some seven re-cently deserted village camps with not a single Mbuti to be found. Kayumba did not conceal the fact that he had constant difficulty of this kind, never being able to rely on the Mbuti to be on hand when he wanted them, and at other times being surrounded and consumed by them. Hamadi, one of the two major Bira chiefs, and probably the most unscrupulous, generally maintained a retinue of Mbuti in village camps, but as far as I could assess it was a floating population that seldom worked on the plantations. Chief Lupao of the Lesé at Nduye complained of being without Mbuti when he needed them, and this was true on the one occasion when I was at Nduye at the time of the cotton harvest. On the other hand, Chief Nakubai, another Lesé Chief to the north, always seemed to have Mbuti at his beck and call, though he maintained them in rather distant plantations, not close to his village, and as far as I know used them only to provide supplies of forest products, and to help guard the plantations.

The lesser chiefs and village headmen, with no police force at their disposal and with less wealth to use in bribes, were rather more successful because the relationship was more intimate and personal. It is not infrequent for a strong attachment to grow between the villagers and Mbuti, and in such cases the economic exchange is much more balanced. In all other cases there can be no doubt that the Mbuti, with less necessity on their side, have all the advantages while the villagers are the losers. It is significant that on the one hand the Mbuti delight in deliberately shortchanging their exchange partners, thus in their eyes proving their own superiority, while on the other hand the villagers are forced by lack of political control to accept such short change with relative passivity, and indeed find ways of rationalizing it. They do this either by referring to the Mbuti as *nyama*, or animals, thus excluding them from the realm of normal, moral human behavior, or else they openly admit the Mbuti are right to help themselves to plantation products.

This latter admission is one of respect for the anteriority of the Mbuti in the forest and is common throughout the Ituri, and beyond, though by no means always open. It is manifest in certain rituals, such as when villagers offer firstfruits from a new plantation to "their" Mbuti (effectively, any Mbuti that happen to be on hand at the time), or when Mbuti are offered places of honor during funerary ceremonies for important villagers. An exceptional example of this respect occurs among the Tembo/Rega populations of the Kivu district (Map 4), one instance of which occurred in September of 1958 at Mayolo village, where a new chief, Butahiri, was inaugurated. I did not witness the occasion, but he told me that on the day that he was crowned with the traditional bead hat, he had to sleep with his sister ("same stomach"). The next night he had to sleep with an Mbuti girl presented to him by the Mbuti "Chief." Butahiri insisted that there was such a Chief, and said that traditionally the girl was meant to be his daughter, but this was not always possible and in that case it was "some other" unmarried female relative. He said he only had to sleep with her once, after which she was sent back to the forest and was never again to be allowed to see him or any of his family, but would be well cared for.

On attempting to find this Mbuti Chief, I discovered that he was in fact just an elderly hunter, and that the girl was his granddaughter. The local Mbuti denied any system of chieftainship, but said that they always appointed one person to deal with the villagers, as in this instance. Both they and the villagers claimed that the legitimate heirs to the chieftainship had to be born of either one of these two formal unions, and that in fact the Chief would sleep again with one or the other girl until she bore him at least two boys. They also said that obviously he would not sleep again with his sister (he himself seemed somewhat disgusted at the recollection of his first night as Chief), and so it would be his Mbuti wife who would provide the tribe with its heir.

There are also firstfruit offerings to the Mbuti in this area, and the same elements of respect and of economic unbalance extend right out of the forest into Ruanda and Burundi, even to the Twa in their relationship with the Tussi. For our present purposes, however, the two situations are not strictly comparable.

But however the villagers might rationalize the economic advantages that accrue to the Mbuti, they do not accept the situation entirely passively. They attempt to create some mechanism by which they can exert authority over the Mbuti and compel them to their service. It is quite evident that if the powerful tribal chiefs backed by armed police are unable to pursue the Mbuti in the forest (even the Belgian administration did not attempt to extend their authority this far), the lesser chiefs are going to be that much more incapable of asserting direct political control. Chiefs such as Kachui, Hamadi, Lupao and Nakubai did not even enter disputes concerning Mbuti in their tribunal records, preferring to deal with such cases "directly." I have witnessed a number of such cases, most of them involving alleged theft, or failure to reciprocate in the exchange of food. The Mbuti claim is invariably that the land is his (even when the charge is for theft of property, not of food), and the villager claim is, equally invariably, that the Mbuti are servants of the villagers, bound to them by indissoluble bonds of heredity and by the fact that the villagers "rescued" the Mbuti from the forest. To this the Mbuti may reply that they "dug" the villagers from a hole in the ground and taught them "how to see and smell and hear and talk." If the case involves food, each side claims original ownership of the plantain tree and the Mbuti alleges that the villager stole the stem by trickery, leaving him only the leaves, so that the villager was able to replant the trees and grow more, but when the Mbuti planted the leaves they just withered and died.[3] It is seldom that the Mbuti deny possession of the stolen goods; what they deny is the act of stealing. But whatever the fact, and however judgment is given, the essential point is that there is no mechanism for enforcing that judgment. Judgment being given by a villager is in my experience without exception against the Mbuti, and orders restitution of the property, or service in lieu. If the Mbuti complies, however, it is merely because in his own estimation it is expedient to do so. If he feels that he has exhausted the goodwill of the injured villager he will simply leave, and thenceforth deal with another villager. If any attempt is made to inflict physical punishment on an Mbuti, or to imprison him, then the whole band will initiate reprisal raids on the plantations of the individual who brought the complaint. This seldom happens, because villagers seek other means for achieving some measure of control over the Mbuti, and it is with those that we shall now concern ourselves.

[3] See Appendix I: "The Legend of the Mbuti Plantation."

CHAPTER 4

The Notion of Hereditary Ownership

A superficial glimpse of the Mbuti/Villager relationship in any village might well tend to confirm the belief that the Mbuti are dependent upon the villagers for the very principles of their social organization. This is the claim of the villagers, the more sophisticated of which use a popular description of the Mbuti as *"les gens sans culture."* The Mbuti themselves will readily admit it, and investigation will, up to a point, confirm it. But we have already witnessed one contradiction; namely, that if the situation is one of superordination, and one of total cultural dependence of the Mbuti upon the villagers, then the villagers would have and be able to exercise some form of political control, and they do not. Indeed there are only the most tenuous political mechanisms for relating the two groups, such as the supposition that each hunting band has a headman or chief (entitled *capita* or *sultani*) who is answerable to the village headman. The villagers accord the Mbuti headman due respect, not far different from the respect they would accord a junior headman of another village, and hold him responsible for the behavior of his band. But even supposing that the Mbuti headman had any actual authority over his band, we have seen that the villagers are incapable of enforcing their will by taking either retributive or restitutive action against the band or the *capita* for fear of reprisal, and because of their very real need for the continued, if minimal, service of the Mbuti and their fear of losing even that.

The Mbuti *capita*, in any case, is merely a village creation and carries no authority whatsoever and little influence among members of the hunting band. The other Mbuti accord him his title when in the village, or even when in the forest, if discussing a village problem. They use him as a convenient link who can also serve as a scapegoat. Through their "chief" the other Mbuti are freed of many of the cares and considerations involved in their relationship with the village, but the position is by no means always popular, and there are instances of dispute as to who should fill a vacant position as *capita*. Usually it is an Mbuti who has a highly developed taste for village foods, tobacco, wine and hemp. Most frequently he fills a dual role, also being the hunting band's clown, an important figure in the settling of internal disputes, again essentially a scapegoat. He will convey to the hunting band the wishes of the villagers, and discuss with the band the questions of food exchange or supply of labor. Among the net-hunters this is about as far as he will go, any decisions after that being taken by group discussion. Among the archers, however, the *capita* may go further, translating the villagers' demands into more practical terms, and suggesting how the band can best effect a compromise. He may even allocate specific tasks to specific individuals or families, but if he is heeded it is with notably bad grace, and again only because those concerned deem it expedient. The Mbuti headman has absolutely no authority in the band, even in its village context.

The greater importance of the *capita* among the archers is related to the fact that, unlike the net-hunters, the archer bands are for the most part of the year fragmented into smaller sections, each virtually independent of the other. There is, then, a greater need to co-ordinate their response to village demands, as the villagers take advantage of the fragmentation by attempting to exploit each section simultaneously. Among the net-hunters, whose bands are much more closely knit, and hunt throughout most of the year as large co-operative units, the only function the *capita* serves, from the point of view of the band, is as an intermediary, little more than a message bearer. Certain *capita*, however, among both archers and net-hunters, acquire great renown among their fellow Mbuti by the success with which they cheat the villagers. This indeed is the only way in which the *capita*, as such, can acquire any prestige at all among his own people.

The major inconsistency of the system lies in the fact that it conflicts directly with a much more subtle means by which the villagers seek to gain control over the Mbuti. Being familiar only with tribal systems of a formal nature, whose organization rests upon the principle of patrilineal descent, the villagers can only conceive of Mbuti society in the same way. Not finding a chief or headman, they impose one, likening a hunting band to a village. They use him in much the same way they would use their own headmen. But the imposition of this institution implies also the imposition of the principle of the patrilineal, patrilocal unit. Perhaps at one time it was; it now certainly is not.[1]

Finding political relations difficult to maintain and enforce, and although they still continue to attempt to deal with bands as one village would deal with another, through the *capita*, the villagers then look to interpersonal relationships as a means of acquiring their ends. They impose the village kinship system upon the Mbuti, keeping as accurate an account of the growth of an Mbuti family as they do of their own, and they ally the resultant Mbuti "clans" to village clans. It is easy enough to visualize the origins of the system, when hunting bands found they had to side with villages, the villagers mistaking (or perhaps correctly taking) the bands for unilineal-descent groups. In this way the relationship between the two groups would be hereditary and self-perpetuating. But the band today is not a unilineal-descent group, and may be comprised of a score or more lineages. Thus a village that is a kinship unit, recognizing the senior male-lineage representative as its headman, finds itself in relationship with a band under a *capita* who may only be remotely related to other male members of the band, by affinal or consanguineal ties. The band itself, consisting of different clans, evidently owes its allegiance, under the village system, to different villages.

On the one hand, the village claims to "own" the band, recognizing the *capita* as its representative. On the other hand, as a lineal unit the village claims a hereditary relationship with another lineal unit, and de facto dissociates itself, perhaps with the major portion of the band, and involves itself in politico-economic difficulties with the neighboring villages who may claim the other portions of that band.

The villagers claim to be saviors of the Mbuti, to have freed them from the necessity of living in the forest like animals, and they justify their claim to ownership in this way. If the Mbuti band were indeed a stable, localized patrilineal unit, then some effective basis for a relationship between the two groups along these lines might persist; but given the cognatic and fluid nature of the contemporary band, the notion of hereditary ownership seldom tallies with effective economic relationships. Consequently there are continuous disputes be-

---

[1] This is not to say that one could not find a band that, at one time of the year or another, is not in effect a patrilineage. It is, rather, to say that lineality would in such a case not be the essence of band structure, but incidental.

tween villagers arising out of the migratory tendencies of "their" Mbuti.

The effective system is that each band maintains an exchange relationship with the village or villages closest to its hunting territory, and effectively the relationship is an exchange not between band and village, except as territorial units only, but between nuclear families or mere individuals. If the exchange relationship follows descent lines, it is no more than incidental. From the Mbuti point of view, in any case, it makes not the slightest difference. All villagers are animals to be "eaten" without discrimination. It only makes a difference from the villager point of view, the question of compensation of the rightful "owner" continually arising.

Leaving the theoretical system for the moment, and looking at the effective system of exchange, we find that the tendency to think of the relationship as hereditary, on the part of the villagers, is irrepressible. As far as the Mbuti are concerned, they pick and choose. As a child an Mbuti may grow accustomed to a number of "owners," as his parents move from band to band, or village to village. When he is old enough to hunt he will choose whichever "owner" happens to be convenient at the time, but if he does not get the treatment he expects, he will without hesitation get himself "adopted" by another villager, even in the same village. The only consideration countenanced by the Mbuti is their own convenience.

A wise villager will treat his Mbuti well, and in return will be able to get the minimum service from them without too much difficulty, and there are instances where such relationship has apparently persisted over several generations (see Table 1). But the contemporary situation militates against persistence. For instance, among the Epulu net-hunters one of the larger "clan" units that made up the total composition of the band was the Puemi clan. In its entirety it was claimed by a prominent Bira named Ngoma. But Ngoma had to spend most of his time in Mambasa, the administrative post some fifty miles from his village, so in his absence his Mbuti were divided, according to the Bira system of inheritance, between his two brothers, Isa and Takalili. But the system did not specify where the dividing line should be drawn, and in any case the Puemi had moved a number of miles in the opposite direction and were on the other side of the Epulu River, in the territory of Chief Kachui of the Ndaka tribe. There they formed allegiances to local villagers, ignored the demands of Isa and Takalili to return to hunt for them, saying that they were

still Ngoma's Mbuti. Ngoma himself said he had no objections to the
Puemi, or any other of his Mbuti, hunting for other villagers while
he was away, so long as they still acknowledged him as their *kpara*,
or owner. He was wealthy enough to have no economic need of the
Mbuti, but he was greatly concerned with his status, which was, he
said, determined largely by the number of Mbuti who called him
kpara. Certainly status was an important consideration for the villagers, and ownership, effective or otherwise, of a large number of
Mbuti would add to it, but there were few who could afford to ignore
the economic aspect of the relationship as could Ngoma.

The situation then becomes seriously complicated for the field
worker who is trying to disentangle the system of ownership. Any
villager will claim hereditary rights over even the most recent newcomer. But he will also claim rights over the Mbuti who have left
him, and in some instances over those that he would have inherited
from his father had they not left his father. As hereditary ownership
can be transferred by adoption with compensation (a sum in cash
or goats, and a promise of a share of any meat that falls into the net
of the Mbuti transferred, or of that of his senior male descendants)
and as the "clan" names also sometimes become adopted in this way,
any attempt to discover a system of hereditary ownership becomes
doubly hazardous, if indeed such a system exists except in theory.

The Epulu situation is perhaps more complicated than others because most of the Mbuti in that band are claimed by Bira villagers,
whereas the band itself is in Ndaka territory and has formed effective
links with both Ndaka and Bira villagers, offering forest foodstuffs
to the local villagers, who are mostly Ndaka, and performing some
service for their more remote Bira owners. In this way, of course,
they maintain two sources of supply of village goods. But the actual
distribution of the clans that contributed to the composition of the
Epulu band, as shown in Table 2, indicates how ineffective the principle of hereditary ownership is, in fact. The same kind of picture can
be drawn for most net-hunting bands, and when we come to consider
the forest world, among both net-hunters and archers we shall find a
situation that militates against any effective stable and durable exchange relationships between Mbuti and villagers, particularly if
based on the principle of unilineal descent.

The myth of hereditary ownership, then, does not seem to provide
a much more effective means of control for the villagers than does
the creation of mythical but comparable political systems. But it is

not totally ineffective. Mbuti genealogical perspective is limited, to say the least, and from their point of view any allegiances formed by a deceased grandfather are of minimal significance, if indeed they are even remembered. In terms of kinship, neither man nor woman will be able to name their great-grandparents, nor may they even be able to name any brothers or sisters of their grandparents unless they have a vivid personal recollection of them. The only occasion on which it would be of any significance for them to know such details would be marriage, and there the parents of the youths concerned will have the necessary access to the (for them) parental, genealogical level by which the permissibility or otherwise of marriage is determined.

Thus the Mbuti can accept with perfect ease, and even with conviction, the villager notion of hereditary ownership. That is not to say that they acknowledge the obligations claimed by the villagers, but only that they recognize kinship as being the basis by which the villagers determine the relationship. An Mbuti who has only temporarily changed allegiance (and at this point I should make it clear that permanent changes are by no means taking place every day) may continue to respect his permanent allegiance, even to the point of sending his hereditary *kpara* occasional gifts of meat or honey. If he changes his allegiance permanently, however, it will be because of some major disagreement, rather than simply because of a temporary shift of residence on either side, and in that case all previous bonds are broken and the Mbuti will leave it up to the villagers to settle the matter between them.

In the belief that kinship is of as vital concern to the Mbuti as it is to themselves, and carries the same indissoluble obligations and rights, the villagers seek to reinforce their relationship with the Mbuti by bringing them as closely into the village kinship system as possible. This is sometimes done by direct intermarriage, a male villager taking an Mbuti wife, but never the reverse. In this case the offspring are considered in every respect as villagers, by both Mbuti and the villagers themselves, but the wife is still Mbuti, with relatives in the forest, and therefore in a good position to attract meat and honey. But it can be seen that it may also cause a further conflict of interest, as it will attract to the villager's household a number of Mbuti relatives who technically may owe allegiance to other villagers, yet who cannot be debarred from showing concern for their sister. In such a case the Mbuti relatives are entitled, and indeed expected, to use the appropriate kinship terminology and follow the appropriate behavior patterns. It is difficult to see what attracts the Mbuti girl to such a union except the politically advantageous position in which it places her. Unfortunately, little is known of the extent to which she stays in the village, or to which she takes advantage of her ability to slip into the forest unpursued and rejoin her band from time to time.

However, this is considered a selfish and antisocial way of attracting Mbuti adherents, and it is only countenanced by other villagers if it is done because the villager concerned is unable, for one reason or another, to acquire a villager wife. More generally the villagers try to introduce the Mbuti into their own kinship framework by insisting not only on the myth of hereditary ownership, but by positing a parallel relationship, a *kpara* referring to his Mbuti as his "children," but not allowing them sibling status with his real children.

As their "father" he then claims the right to concern himself with all their domestic problems, and most particularly with marriage. For an Mbuti boy to marry an utterly unrelated Mbuti girl owned by his *kpara's* brother, for instance, would be considered by the villagers as incestuous, and prohibited. It could only take place if either the boy or girl changed allegiance. Marriage between the Mbuti, then, becomes a matter of major concern to the villagers, who will not only provide all the necessary ritual for the Mbuti but who will also have to negotiate between themselves, just as if it were a village marriage, the *kpara* of the groom paying appropriate wealth to the *kpara* of the bride. In every respect the *kpara* act as parents, except that it is as if they were considering a less important line of children by some very inferior wife. In 1957–58 the wealth paid by one villager to another for an Mbuti wife for his own Mbuti "child" was about a tenth of what he would have to pay for a villager wife for his real child.

The matter is one of some concern, because a wealthy villager might "own" or claim to own a hundred or more Mbuti, and his only assurance against bankruptcy is an insistence upon his hereditary rights over the offspring of his male Mbuti, and his right to demand wealth from other villagers whose Mbuti married his own Mbuti girls. Considerable conflict arose between villagers as a result, because while the Mbuti accepted the feasting and their share of the wealth, they did not accept any of the obligations, and according to their own custom of betrothal and marriage they did not consider the marriage final until a child had been born. At any time before then, without asking leave of anyone, Mbuti or villager, they were free to separate. I have known it to happen for Mbuti youngsters to go through the entire village marriage ceremony simply for the sake of the feasting, considering their relationship as no more than a mild flirtation. In either case the premature separation involves their respective *kpara* in restitution proceedings, which even if successful will still leave a net loss to the extent, at least, of a feast that may have involved a hundred or more Mbuti and villagers for up to three days.

This, together with the fact that a union that is considered as incestuous by the one group is not necessarily considered incestuous by the other, is sufficient to indicate the incompatibility of the two systems, which is only heightened if we attempt to correlate either kinship system, that of the villagers or that of the Mbuti, with the economic exchange system.

By extending the parallel still further, however, the villagers make their final attempt to gain some effective measure of control over the Mbuti and resolve the inherent conflicts through supernatural sanctions. And once again they are thwarted by a number of factors, one being that the Mbuti continue to adopt the outer form of the village customs with the utmost readiness, but do not adopt the system. Whereas, for the villagers, the total social structure is an integrated whole consisting of a number of institutions interrelated in a definite manner, for the Mbuti, in the village context, the same institutions are adopted but by no means interrelated in the same manner. The relationship between kinship and leadership, as we have seen, does not apply to the Mbuti. Their *capita* is elected rather than descended, and his whole meaning and purpose are correspondingly different. The *capita* has absolutely nothing to do, among the Mbuti, with the maintenance of law and order, and in no way symbolizes the common origin of the male members of the band.

So also, for the Mbuti, is the economic exchange system unrelated to either the kinship or the political systems in the village context. The exchange relationships may run directly counter to all those prescribed by the various political and kinship institutions the Mbuti have equally adopted.

Their apparent readiness to participate in village institutions, if not in the system, however, leaves the Mbuti open to yet another line of attack. Unable to enforce any of the control that would normally derive from the adoption of their socio-politico-economic institutions, the villagers open their magico-religious institutions to the Mbuti, and thus seek to place them under supernatural control—the

control of the specifically village supernatural. Indeed the villagers are
obliged to do this, in consonance with the rest of their system, for
to admit someone to the kinship system without admitting them to
the ancestral cult would be a contradiction in terms. But not so for
the Mbuti. The most sacred of the village institutions is completely
divorced, in the Mbuti system, from any other adopted village institution. It is, like the other institutions, adopted for what it offers in
itself, and if it is related to anything, it is related only to the economic
aspect of the Mbuti/Villager relationship.

CHAPTER 5

The Notion of Supernatural Control

THE VILLAGE SUPERNATURAL

We have already seen something of villager participation in Mbuti marriage arrangements, but only from the aspect of kinship. From this point of view the villagers hope to be able to control, to some extent, the movement and residence patterns of the Mbuti, and to support the myth of hereditary ownership. From another point of view, however, villager participation in the marriage of their Mbuti necessarily introduces the Mbuti to the village magico-religious system, through the ritual that consecrates the marriage as well as through the absorption of the Mbuti, in this way, into the village kinship structure. It might also be pointed out in passing that as far as the villagers are concerned, marriages between their Mbuti are of as much political importance as their own marriages, in regulating relationships between one village and another, one segment of the tribe and another. Insofar as our primary concern is with the Mbuti, however, this political aspect does not directly concern us here.

Marriage is only one village ritual adopted by the Mbuti, and in considering any such adoption we have to keep in mind the structural aspects of ritual in the village social system and, in particular, the relationship between ritual and kinship. It is in light of structure that the villager side of the Mbuti/Villager relationship is comprehensible, the attempt to include the Mbuti within the village framework being an attempt to secure some measure of control over them. That is not to say that the motive of control is necessarily responsible for the inclusion, but it is certainly openly acknowledged by villagers and has some bearing on their attitudes.

At the same time we must be aware that on the Mbuti side there is the knowledge that the villagers are seeking to gain control. There is a considered element of risk involved in accepting certain institu-

tions, even in the strictest village context, but it is outweighed by
what at first seems little more than a lively desire to have all the advantages of village life with none of the disadvantages. Again, it is
only through an examination of the interrelationship of the institutions adopted by the Mbuti, and their relationship with the
indigenous Mbuti social system, that we can arrive at any true understanding of the apparent process of acculturation.

The attempt by the villagers to assert supernatural control is structurally the most significant, for it involves elements with which the
Mbuti have no institutionalized means of dealing. Political pressure
the Mbuti can counter by changing allegiance; economic pressure
can also be countered, by reverting to the always available pure hunting and gathering economy; as we shall see in the next section, pressure through absorption into the village kinship system is repelled
quite simply by the maintenance of an opposed kinship system.
However, the Mbuti have no magic with which to counter magic,
no witchcraft or sorcery with which to counter witchcraft and sorcery.
They do have belief with which to counter belief, but it is part of
the belief of both Mbuti and villagers that in a war between the gods,
no man can safely predict the outcome. It is in this situation that
the villagers do manage to effect some extent of control, but it is
also in this context that they come up against the ultimate bedrock
of opposition.

Let us look at the various ways in which the magico-religious life
of the villagers impinges upon that of the Mbuti, and the extent to
which it exerts some measure of control over the hunters and gatherers. Fully recognizing that a clear division of the subject matter is
difficult, if not impossible, to make, we nonetheless have to attempt
such a division for the purposes of discussion. There is a great deal
of overlapping, but nonetheless at the extremes, in this case, the division used here between magic and religion is legitimate.

By *magic* I refer to activities involving, on the part of the African,
villager or Mbuti, a conviction in the pragmatic relationship between a cause and an effect which, in terms of Western science, is
not demonstrable. The term in its usual sense has meaning only as
far as we are concerned, for as far as the Africans here are concerned,
magical activities are as scientifically valid as any other. They may not
always be able to explain the exact way in which the effect is related
to the cause, any more than everyone who drives a motorcar can
explain the mechanism. Indeed, the corresponding term "medicine"

is usually applied by the African to causal relationships he does not understand but which he still believes to be pragmatic. The mechanism exists, just as surely for the African as for the motorist. Whereas the term "magic" implies, for the Westerner, supernatural intervention, its African counterpart, for villagers and Mbuti alike, has virtually no such connotation. Some "magical" activities are not given any special term other than that for the activity itself. Those that are classified apart as a special type of activity are thought of as *curative*, and the classificatory term indicates effective function, not supernatural intervention. It is in this sense that we use the word, and in this sense alone that it should here be understood.

Witchcraft, on the other hand, introduces other elements, although it is still basically thought of as a scientifically explicable phenomenon, involving certain supernatural powers conveyed by the possession of witchcraft substance, something that can be touched and seen but, being located in the entrails (details as to exactly where, and what it looks like, vary), cannot be removed except at death. But whereas the existence of the powers is explained by the substance, the nature of the powers themselves is inexplicable, therefore supernatural.

Sorcery is akin to witchcraft only in that it involves the possession of similar powers. But whereas with witchcraft the powers depend upon the existence of witchcraft substance in the body of the witch and are controlled by that substance, the powers of the sorcerer come to him, or her, through the exertion of willpower, and are therefore controllable by the individual. A witch acts only as such when forced to do so by the substance. A sorcerer acts as such when he wishes to, for whatever purpose he chooses. There is, naturally, a complete terminological distinction between the two in the various local languages: in the lingua franca of the area, KiNgwana, the term *chawi* is used for witch, *lozi* is used for sorcerer. These terms do not necessarily correspond in their usage to the same terms in other Bantu languages, and there is a significant difference between village and Mbuti usages of each term. Needless to say, in that an individual possessing witchcraft substance is not directly answerable for his actions, however grave, he is not considered antisocial. But as a sorcerer directs his power for individual ends, he *is* considered antisocial, and is therefore culpable.

Religion, as used here, refers to the realm of belief where there is no attempt to explain supernatural powers in terms of empirical experience and natural life. There is no practical cause—the cause itself is supernatural. I include various *rites de passage* under religion because such rites involve a thoroughgoing belief in the supernatural. The nature of the supernatural, however, varies greatly as seen by Mbuti and as seen by villagers. Both peoples, however, do have a belief in the supernatural; that is, scientifically nonexplicable powers that are invested in another class of beings, without form or substance, which we call *spiritual*. It is belief in these spiritual beings that is the essence of what we here call religion.

CURATIVE MAGIC

As indicated above, we are not here in the least concerned with acts, of either the Mbuti or the villagers, simply because they involve an assumed but scientifically false connection between cause and effect. We use the term "magic" as a translation of the native term, which groups together divers curative activities in the belief that all are equally scientific. Thus the penicillin that cures a sore is magic just as much as the antelope horn that cures a spell of bad hunting.

In trying to assess how far the village world impinges on the forest world in this respect, then, we have to see what situations there are for which the Mbuti have no cure and which they wish to cure, and for which the villagers do have a cure. Or, indeed, we must look to see if the reverse situation exists.

When I say there is little magic in the forest world of the Mbuti, I mean that there are few curative activities, and for the very simple reason that there are relatively few situations that require curing. For most Mbuti who have reached adolescence the life expectancy is good, as is the expectancy of good health. For most minor physiological disorders the Mbuti seem to have effective remedies, some of which are cited in Appendix II together with details of the botanical identification of the plants, wherever I was able to be sure, or reasonably sure, that these were the only plants used. Such remedies cover not only the mild fevers, aches and pains, and sicknesses that may come the way of the Mbuti, but they also cover accidental injury such as may be incurred by falling on a spear, by being attacked by a wild animal, bitten by a snake, stung by bees, or by falling from a tree, breaking or twisting an arm or leg. Such injuries, however, occur remarkably seldom.

For these particular curative activities the Mbuti are acknowledged as being masters, and their help is constantly being sought by villagers, not so well versed in forest lore. It has been shown, however, that where the Mbuti see a remedy that is more effective than theirs, such as modern drugs (only in some cases are these apparently superior), they will eventually seek them. Insofar as local dispensaries were run by villagers, the Mbuti had to rely on the villagers for such drugs. I do not consider this an instance of dependence, however, as up to the end of my last field trip the Mbuti would only seek such help when they were in the village; in the forest they found their own remedies adequate. Even more, when sickness or injury befell them in the village, the common reaction was to return to the forest.

But here we may note a significant difference in attitude to magic, or curative activity. Childbirth is a time which is thought of by both Mbuti and villagers as being attended by the possibility of danger, at least. The Mbuti think in terms of physical danger, and they have precautions that they take in the diet and behavior of the expectant mother before birth, and apparently effective knowledge of midwifery, including recognized ways of dealing with difficult births. After birth there are known cures for any weakness the infant or mother might show. What is lacking, among the Mbuti, is precisely what is dominant among the villagers: a felt need for protection against the supernatural.

A village mother and child will both have, according to how wealthy the family is, a number of potions to drink (which may or may not have medical significance, but are thought of as being protective) and divers charms to wear. The protection is thought to be necessary against *unknown* dangers. The difference between the two peoples is in the extent of this unknown. An Mbuti infant will have a vine bracelet or belt tied to it almost immediately after birth, and a small piece of wood or two will be fixed to the vine. It is stated that the vine and the wood convey to the child the health and strength of the forest. There is no apparent concern for any supernatural dangers, and no precautionary steps taken.

From the village point of view the lack of such measures involves the child and possibly the mother in great danger, and out of self-concern as much as out of concern for the Mbuti, the villagers proffer charms in abundance to expectant mothers and newborn children. However, the need is only felt by the villagers, not by the Mbuti.

This is precisely the difference we find when we seek other situations for which only the villagers have a cure—they are situations in which only the villagers *need* a cure. There are a number of such minor crises. Even if the action appears to be protective, it is still basically curative. For instance, theft is common in villages, and villagers have a number of magical cures for theft that prevent it by curing the situation that might give rise to this antisocial act. This may seem like an academic quibble, justifying the inclusion of protective magic under the definition of magic as curative activity, but it is more basic than that. If the Mbuti saw themselves in a future context they might be interested in protection, but one of their characteristics is to think in terms of the present. Theft is not a part of their behavior toward each other; there is nothing they have that the villagers can steal from them, so there is no immediate situation to be cured. But the danger of poor hunting is more real.

For the hunt the Mbuti themselves have divers cures, but mostly of a sympathetic nature and, considering the importance of the hunt, remarkably few. The villagers, on the other hand, have a great number of cures to offer, and if convenient the Mbuti accept them. But once again the question is one of need. From his experience the hunter sees no need to concern himself with the future: it is rare that the hunting is so poor that he goes hungry. It is rare indeed even that there could not be a surplus to trade with the villagers. But lack of meat for trade is always excused by a plea of bad hunting. In fact, the Mbuti even go further and point to the fact that they have no elaborate cures for bad hunting, so how can the villagers blame them for not bringing in meat? The villager then supplies the cures, and if these do not work he will even be told by the Mbuti that it must be witchcraft, and asked to call out a diviner. I know of three cases where Mbuti have been trained by villagers to divine witchcraft and are believed, by villagers, to be highly effective. But once again there is no question of dependence.

Other situations that need curing and that may be cured by empirical (i.e., "magical") means available to villagers alone include poor weather, attack by lightning, attack by a witch, or by the spirits of the forest (*keti*). The cures consist of divers charms and fetish bundles, but they are considered as effective only by the villagers. The Mbuti recognize man's inability to control the weather, though they have a small amount of very simple sympathetic weather magic; lightning strikes where it will, though again fires are covered by the Mbuti during a storm in case the flames attract lightning. As for attack by a witch, their attitude is somewhat ambivalent, but they do not place much faith in a charm against a witch's power, if such power exists; their own remedy is retreat to the forest, where there are no witches. They do not believe in the existence of malevolent *keti*, or spirits, as do the villagers.

In the realm of curative magic, then, the villager has nothing to offer that the Mbuti needs, and has no means of utilizing magic or exclusive village knowledge of magical techniques to control the Mbuti.

WITCHCRAFT

If it were not for their own misconception of village witchcraft, the Mbuti would be at no disadvantage through their own lack of it. As it is, however, they tend to confuse witchcraft and sorcery, and consequently find themselves dealing with a phenomenon totally outside their forest-world experience—conscious malevolence.

Their confusion is visible in their constant usage of the terms associated with sorcery, even when only witchcraft is implied. The forest hunters are aware of the theoretical difference, but simply do not believe in the existence of witchcraft substance. They are unwilling enough to believe in malevolent supernatural powers, but events combine to persuade them to belief.

Unlike magic, which applies to natural phenomena, witchcraft and sorcery deal necessarily with the supernatural, and create their own need for protection. But whereas the villagers, in their acceptance of the theory of witchcraft substance, can happily accept a fetish bundle as adequate protection, the Mbuti, seeing the whole thing as malevolent sorcery, cannot believe that a bundle of sticks and bones is going to afford much help. Looking at witchcraft—and sorcery—as something belonging essentially to the village world, however, they do have recourse in flight to the forest, where, in their experience, these supernatural powers cannot easily reach. In the village world they can find no protection, and can only hope for an end to the underlying hostility.

Thus witchcraft, which among the villagers is essentially a mechanism for social control, being a concept employed usefully to bring to light hidden sources of dispute and to publicly shame trouble-makers, inadvertently gives the villagers a weapon against the Mbuti, while at the same time it drives the Mbuti both literally back into the forest, and metaphorically into further dependence upon the forest.

Witchcraft being such an important part of their own lives, the villagers are unable to conceive how the Mbuti can survive without knowledge of the necessary procedures, and as in other instances, they assume control of appropriate situations and provide the procedure. Upon death in a village, for example, the cause of death must be determined, and the cause is usually believed by the villagers to be witchcraft or sorcery. If they do not discover the cause, the witch or sorcerer may continue to kill. The Mbuti have no knowledge of divination of this kind, so it is done for them by the villagers, and the villagers believe that this places the Mbuti in a dependent position. In fact of course it does not, because the Mbuti believe in natural causes rather than supernatural.

Similarly the Mbuti have no need for the concept of witchcraft to enable them to exert social control. They have their own procedures in this respect, but nonetheless they do sometimes use the village concept of witchcraft to regulate relationships with the village, still denying any belief in "witchcraft substance." They are aware, then, of the social value of witchcraft.

VILLAGE SORCERY

While from the Mbuti point of view sorcery is effectively synonymous with witchcraft, from the village point of view sorcery, being quite different, is by its very nature more directly related to the problem of exerting control over the Mbuti. No villager will admit to being a sorcerer, but there is nothing particularly reprehensible in a villager claiming to hire a sorcerer to curse an Mbuti. All he does in fact is to say that he has had a curse laid. (He may go to the local doctor and persuade him to take action, but in that case his action is legal and is not technically "sorcery," though the net result is much the same.) The curse, alleged or actual, is sometimes followed by the sickness or death of the person cursed.[1] But even if it is not, sooner or later some disaster will come to the family or band of the person cursed, and the villagers will claim that this is the result of the curse.

Insofar as the Mbuti consider the two worlds as being apart, and do not feel bound by their own code of forest behavior to behave in

---

[1] I have known three young Mbuti who were cursed for not having fulfilled a bargain with an Ngwana villager and died within a few months.

that way toward the villagers, who are like animals, they also are forced to recognize that the villagers may feel similarly released from laws that would otherwise prevent them from using sorcery as a means of revenge. The villagers, in point of fact, usually deny actually using sorcery, even against the Mbuti, but they admit to using the threat of it. They do, however, use the doctor, who also has access to supernatural powers for the social good, but this involves religion rather than witchcraft or sorcery. It is mentioned here because the Mbuti considers the power, not the agent. Be it witch, sorcerer or doctor, it makes no difference; the Mbuti still has no recourse but flight.

Even flight, however, will not entirely remove the sneaking fear that persists despite expressed disbelief in these supernatural powers. And that power is perhaps no small factor in effectively giving the villagers some measure of control, though the villagers happily do not realize it. They simply believe in the efficacy of their magic, and of their supernatural powers.

The extent of the control that comes this way is difficult to measure, and it has to be balanced against the extent to which the situation drives the Mbuti into an even greater reliance upon their forest world, separating the two worlds still further. It certainly can be seen to operate effectively in inducing reluctant Mbuti to fulfill specific bargains. I did not come across any instances where the actual or threatened use of supernatural powers was invoked to control the normal course of the exchange relationship. But there were a number of instances over a twelve-month period in which Epulu villagers invoked supernatural powers to revenge themselves against Mbuti who had behaved with particular irresponsibility.

Three of the cases were of alleged sorcery. Sefu of Epulu village claimed that two Mbuti had accepted beans from him and had not sent him the meat they had promised in return. He said he had employed a sorcerer to make the Mbuti bleed to death if they did not give him the meat. But he lost courage when he thought that the administrator might get to hear of it, and he recanted. The Mbuti concerned sent him a token amount of meat and the matter was con-. sidered as settled.

André, headman of the village known by the name of his late father, Effundi Somali, claimed to have himself invoked supernatural aid against an Mbuti who refused to pay him money received by him when he captured a live okapi and brought it to the government *sta-*

tion de chasse. This curse, which was of leprosy, was never lifted, to my knowledge, and caused some uneasiness among the Mbuti but mainly anger. So far it has not been effective, either in obtaining the money for André or in bringing leprosy to the Mbuti.

The other case involved the headman of the nearby Ngwana village, who claimed that three Mbuti from the Epulu band had taken a sack of rice from him and had promised meat in return but never sent it. He allegedly employed a sorcerer to curse the Mbuti to death if they did not send the meat. Within a matter of three months all three had died. Two died evidently of stomach disorders that might have been due to or aggravated by poison, which is sometimes used by the Ngwana; the third man died a long way off in the forest under conditions that would make it unlikely that the death was due to poison, though quite likely it was due in part to fear. All three were young and healthy.

There were almost certainly other instances that I did not hear of, where it was claimed that sorcery had actually been used. There were innumerable instances when it was threatened, and also innumerable instances of accusations of witchcraft involving Mbuti. In fact, talk of village witchcraft and sorcery was among the major topics of conversation in forest camps, particularly just prior to and following a visit to the village. Although the Mbuti had no beliefs of their own concerning the manipulation of such supernatural powers, and although they were reluctant to believe that it was more than either a hoax or, as most of them put it, the mere stupidity (*mbafu*) of the villagers, it nonetheless occupied their thoughts. The death or sickness that inevitably followed a curse, happening sooner or later to someone in the same family, was generally accepted by the Mbuti as coincidental no matter how hard the villagers tried to relate it to the curse; but the occasional exceptional instance, such as that quoted, when the three Mbuti died within three months, was enough to cause serious doubt and fear.

CHAPTER 6

Village Religion

NKUMBI

Both villagers and Mbuti have notions concerning spirits and spiritual intervention, and associated religious systems. Once again, however, even where the facts coincide, the systems do not. One of the major differences is the lack of ritual ceremony among the Mbuti and the importance of it among the villagers. Thus, though manhood is every bit as important to the Mbuti as to the villagers, there is no formal Mbuti initiation ritual. And although marriage is considered just as sacred, and is recognized by the Mbuti as having profound social implications, it takes place in the forest in an apparently utterly casual manner without any ceremony or ritual joining of the boy and girl or of their families. The ritual attitude of Mbuti and villagers toward death again is totally different.

But in the lack of ceremony the villagers once again see a chance for acting as intermediaries, as though this made them indispensable. The Mbuti are continually being subjected to one or another ritual ceremony at the hands of the villagers, even when the affair is entirely domestic and apparently does not in any way directly concern the villagers.

According to the notion of hereditary ownership, of course, the villagers also have a responsibility, and by virtually assimilating or, better, adopting the Mbuti into the villager tribe they are obliged to adopt them also into the religious system. The parallel kinship system, while never opening the way to complete integration, nonetheless demands an extension of the parallelism in all directions. The villagers have no qualms about this, and it is certainly no indication of friendly intimacy, for in this way they hope to secure the inferior status of the Mbuti not only in the present but also in the afterlife. At the same time the villagers believe they have found another source of control over their wayward servants.

Of all the various *rites de passage* practiced by the villagers, and to which they are forced to introduce the Mbuti, none probably is so important as the *nkumbi* initiation of the boys into manhood. Among the Bantu tribes this is practiced with circumcision, among the Sudanic it is without circumcision, though there is a tendency among some Sudanic tribes situated close to the Bantu, such as the Lesé bordering on the Bira, to adopt the custom, one village at a time.

The major purpose of the *nkumbi*, as stated by the tribes that practice it (I refer mainly to the Forest Bira here), is to fit the youths as men, to make them men in the eyes of the ancestors. A boy who does not undergo the *nkumbi* is denied access to the ancestors after death, and during his life has the status of a child. Boys between the ages of eight and twelve, generally between nine and eleven, are eligible for the ceremony, which now takes place once every three years and lasts for two or more months. The traditional time element has been completely upset by the administration, which, together with the missionaries, has tried to discourage the whole institution. But the *nkumbi* initiation has remained as the only way to achieve adult status within the tribe. I have seen an entire *nkumbi* ceremony, including circumcision, held for a boy who died just prior to being initiated.

Effectively the *nkumbi* also unites a few neighboring villages as a single political unit, and affords an opportunity though the system of *karé* blood brotherhood, of cementing specific political bonds. It also effectively unites those tribes who practice circumcision in opposition to those who do not practice it, and it determines certain lines of marriage prohibition.

One such line, of course, divides the circumcised from the uncircumcised, and theoretically marriage between a Bira and a Lesé would be unthinkable. The only cases known to me allegedly happened during war, captive women being taken as wives. But equally theoretically these prohibitions should apply to the Mbuti who, according to the practice of their *kpara*, not having any of their own, either do or do not suffer circumcision at village hands. As we shall see, however, forest territorial organization is no respecter of village tribalism, and band composition is fluid, to say the least. Consequently, in any one band one can by no means be sure that all the men are circumcised, and the question is never raised. Further than that, there is no objection to marriage, among the Mbuti, between a family whose *kpara* circumcises and one whose *kpara* does not. Such marriages would certainly not be countenanced by the *kpara* concerned. This is only one indication of the lack of respect with which the Mbuti view the *nkumbi*, and it is important that this be understood at the outset. The structural implications of the *nkumbi* as they apply to the villagers in no way apply to the Mbuti. I had graphic evidence of this when following recently initiated Mbuti youths back to their forest hunting camp at the conclusion of the two-month ceremony. They had just been acclaimed as men by the villagers, and allowed to take their place as men in the village *baraza*, or meeting place. But their first act on entering the hunting camp was to sit on the laps of their mothers as an indication that they still considered themselves as children in the forest world. I might further mention that the Mbuti, who in the forest consecrate every activity of major importance with a special type of song, have no song whatsoever for the occasion of the *nkumbi*. Further arguments are given elsewhere (Turnbull, 1957[2]). Here we are concerned with villager attempts to secure control, and it is only necessary to indicate the two different attitudes to the *nkumbi*, and its evidently different significance for the Mbuti in the forest world.

However the Mbuti might deny the village attitude to the *nkumbi*, and the villagers are aware that such denial does take place, the villagers nonetheless see a number of advantages accruing to them in their admission of the Mbuti to the tribal initiation ceremony.

First, as the *nkumbi* fits a youth to go to the ancestors after death, the ceremony serves as an introduction of the Mbuti to the afterworld of the village. By undergoing the *nkumbi* they equally are fitted to go, after death, to the world of the village ancestors. But it is made plain throughout that the status relationship remains unchanged. Mbuti and village boys are circumcised alternately on the day of the cutting, which opens the ceremony proper. The Mbuti boy is generally sent first—"to clean the knife"—and throughout he is made, in innumerable ways, to recognize that in village eyes he is inferior to the village boys.

KARÉ

The pairs of boys, one Mbuti and one villager, whose blood has been allowed to mingle, are called *karé*. The degree of formality with which the *karé* relationship is solemnized varies considerably from village to village, and depends to some extent upon the proportion of Mbuti to village boys. In some cases the Mbuti's *kpara* may choose him as *karé* to his own son, and in other cases he may see some advantage in having his Mbuti form a *karé* pact with another villager, as this forms an economic and political link, then, between the two villagers. It seems that, generally, *karé* brotherhood is formed between Mbuti and their *kpara's* patrikin, however. It is believed that this places the two in an indissoluble politico-economic relationship for the rest of their lives, a relationship of subordination as far as the Mbuti is concerned, and one that will persist into the afterlife of the same individuals.

The villager concepts of afterlife are not clearly defined, but it is accepted without question that individuals continue to exist after death and may, if qualified by initiation and by adherence throughout life to the tribal code of behavior, join the ancestors, who live together much as they did in the present world, and continue to concern themselves with the present world. It is also accepted without question that there must be Mbuti in the afterworld, just as there are in the present. If one asks why must there be Mbuti, the invariable answer is in terms of the economic dependence of the villagers upon the Mbuti in the present world, the assumption being that the same needs will exist in the afterworld. But the economic relationship is the most easily expressed and recognized, however mistakenly, and is not necessarily therefore the most important. The political relationship is also recognized, though not quite so easily expressed because of the greater incompatibility of the systems of the two peoples. But there is also a ritual relationship which is certainly as powerful as the others, if not more so, and it is just as much a part of the *karé* pact as are the economic and political aspects.

Karé partners are expected to trade with each other, though not necessarily exclusively. This allows for the formation of *karé* brotherhood between individuals who are not in a *kpara*/Mbuti relationship, and is an attempt on the part of the villager to regularize the situation should his Mbuti join a band trading with a neighboring village. To have a *kpara* in one village and a *karé* in another, strategically chosen, is considered equally advantageous by Mbuti and villager. As far as the Mbuti is concerned it provides him with two groups of people who feel under some kind of an obligation toward him, and who need him. As far as the *kpara* is concerned it gives him someone he can effectively claim against should his Mbuti decide to trade in that direction. As far as the villager *karé* is concerned it is another Mbuti to his credit, increasing his prestige and also somewhat increasing his trading opportunities. The trade is mainly thought of in terms of meat and labor on the side of the Mbuti, village foods, clothes and tobacco on the side of the villager. A fairly friendly relationship does sometimes develop between two *karé*, who, regardless of the status differentiation, undergo the whole *nkumbi* together, suffering the same ordeals side by side, and are perhaps more united by age than they are separated by the status differentiation.

The political aspects of *karé* brotherhood reinforce the economics, not only serving as a basis for compensation against a migrant Mbuti, but also for extending the *karé* relationship to link the Mbuti's *kpara* with the village boy's father. The relationship is primarily between individuals, but it nonetheless creates felt obligations between the families involved, and one family of villagers may invoke the help of another family in a dispute, through an Mbuti *karé* link. The kinship ramifications of *karé* brotherhood are still far from clear from the village point of view, and it seems that the introduction of the Mbuti to the system may have somewhat disorganized the traditional system. For the Mbuti there is no connection between *karé* and kinship, and effectively there can be none among the villagers. If there were, then the formation of a *karé* tie between *kpara* and their own Mbuti would be incestuous, and the formation of such ties with unrelated families, conceived of as a sibling relationship, would effectively prohibit marriage in that direction and create an impossibly confused dual kinship system. Yet *karé* do refer to each other sometimes as "brother," and take advantage of their thus extended kinship relations.

The religious aspects of *karé* brotherhood are far less easy to define, and far less easy for the investigator to determine because they are seldom, if ever, discussed. I have never heard such a discussion, unless I instigated it, except on the occasion of the death of a villager. On the death of an Mbuti it is generally only the other aspects of the *karé* relationship that are discussed, involving liability for funerary expenses, compensation for outstanding obligations, divination of the cause of death. But when a villager dies the Mbuti *karé* is introduced into the heart of the funerary ritual, having to perform divers functions such as beating the villager's wives, leading an attack upon all close kin of the deceased, conveniently clustered together for the purpose, "to drive away evil," as the villagers explained it among themselves and to me. The Mbuti *karé* is also made responsible for providing certain foods for the deceased and, I believe, certain herbs with which the body of the villager is treated before burial. Owing to my somewhat peripheral relationship with the villagers I was not allowed to witness the more intimate rituals when the *karé* Mbuti was closeted with the deceased on one occasion for about three hours, on another occasion for one hour. Nor was I able to elicit much from the Mbuti, who said that they knew nothing about it, and only did what they were told to do by the villagers. When asked what that was, they repeated the above information, which was as much as I had gathered from the villagers, and no more except a few colorful and imaginative details about the appearance and odor of the corpse. This being clearly something better investigated from the villager side, I did not press the matter. It seems sufficiently well established, however, that the ritual connection between *karé* is considerable as seen by the villagers, and this was borne out on one occasion when an important Bira noble died and the entire funeral ceremony, including the burial, was held up for a day and a half because of the non-appearance of the dead man's Mbuti *karé*. On this occasion the Mbuti eventually arrived on the run carrying a spear, loudly shouting his complaints at being brought from the forest for such stupidity (again the term *mbafu*). There were several hundred villagers assembled, and the Mbuti ran through them to the compound of the deceased. He evidently knew in advance what was expected, and broke his way in to the closed hut where the widows were wailing. There was great concern among the villagers because he took his spear with him, and they said he might kill the women, but they did nothing to prevent him. Happily there was a full complement of widows at the subsequent burial.

The villagers recognize that they cannot force the Mbuti *karé* to fulfill their obligations by political or economic pressure, but they now have another weapon. By the act of ritual circumcision, according to tribal lore, the Mbuti are placed in a direct relationship with the tribal village ancestors, and by the *karé* bond each Mbuti is placed in a direct relationship with the protective spirits that look after the welfare of their respective individual villager partners. Every step of the *nkumbi* reinforces the authority of the tribal ancestors, through the supernatural powers at their disposal, over the Mbuti as well as over the villager initiates. Failure to fulfill "kinship" or *karé* obligations on the part of the Mbuti cannot be dealt with by the legal mechanisms available to the villagers, but it can now be countered by supernatural sanctions. Villager lore defines the Mbuti responsibili-

ties to villagers, and villager supernatural sanctions enforce fulfillment.

From the Mbuti point of view, however, the whole *nkumbi* is
mbafu (stupid) and *bulé* (empty), and so are the sanctions. The
initiates and their "fathers" who attend them during the ceremony
take every opportunity to mock the procedure (Turnbull, 1957[2]),
and as stated earlier the *nkumbi* in no way alters the status of the
initiates back in their forest world, where they are still regarded as
children. In all the *nkumbi* that I have witnessed in different parts
of the forest, among different tribes, with varying proportions of
Mbuti/Villager initiates, and under divers degrees of severity of village control, I have not seen one indication of genuine respect or belief on the part of the Mbuti, and not one instance of the initiation
having the slightest structural relationship to the Mbuti forest world.

Yet by undergoing the *nkumbi* the Mbuti place themselves in a
position of ritual inferiority and subordination to the villagers. They
do not have any ritual specialists of their own to perform the *nkumbi*,
so are wholly dependent upon the village doctors. As the *nkumbi*
only perpetuates the status differential, it gives the Mbuti knowledge
of tribal lore but does not grant them access to mastery of the lore.
Not being full kin, but only adopted, parallel kin, the Mbuti can never
qualify as ritual specialists, and are therefore at once forced by the
nkumbi into participation in innumerable other tribal rituals, and
at the same time denied any measure of ritual control and placed in a
position of still greater dependence upon the villagers.

Once again the villagers cannot conceive of life without the necessary ritual observations, and in a sense they feel an obligation to
provide these services for the Mbuti, but the Mbuti avoids actual dependence by adopting only the outer form of the institution, not the
system. Insofar as we are discussing the village world, however,
from the villager's point of view the *nkumbi* places the Mbuti in the
greatest possible condition of dependence by creating an obligation to
take part in a ritual life in which he will need village ritual specialists.
It also provides the villagers with the surest method of control,
through supernatural sanctions. The villagers have such belief in these
sanctions that they are content to allow the Mbuti to get away with
much trickery, convinced that sooner or later the score will be evened
and restitution made.

Having drawn the Mbuti into the world of the village supernatural,
because it *is* of the village, the villagers feel they have established

ultimate if not immediate control. It is more difficult to see what the Mbuti get out of it, except for certain economic advantages which are meant to be reciprocal. Looking at it briefly from the Mbuti point of view, however, we see that the advantages are perhaps more real than those accruing to the villagers. For the villagers are bound by their own sanctions, and therefore the Mbuti can make demands of his *karé* with reasonable assurance that they will be met. Also, he can now expect a succession of relatively lavish ceremonies to be prepared for him as he goes through life, at the expense of his *karé* and *kpara*. The feasting involved may seem a trivial gain for the Mbuti, but in fact it is one of their major sources of entertainment and relaxation. The *nkumbi* extends the Mbuti's economic and political horizons just as it does those of the villagers, and the Mbuti know how to reap the advantages, just as they know how to avoid most of the disadvantages. This avoidance in fact forms one of the important features of the over-all structure of their society.

One final advantage that should be mentioned, though its importance is perhaps more personal than social, is that only by participation in the *nkumbi,* or its equivalent among tribes with other forms of initiation into manhood, can the Mbuti become a man in the eyes of the villagers. There is a strongly paternalistic attitude held by villagers toward their Mbuti that is resented by the hunters, who consider themselves more manly than the villagers. The *nkumbi* at least offers them an opportunity for proving their manliness to the villagers, and it sometimes develops into a contest between the Mbuti and the village initiates. And only by participation in the *nkumbi* can the Mbuti acquire the right to be addressed as adults, admitted to the adult *baraza,* and accorded other adult privileges when in the village.

ELIMA

The villagers do not attempt to exert supernatural control through the women, as they do through the men. While the Mbuti men have nothing comparable to the *nkumbi* initiation of the villagers, the Mbuti women, in the forest world, do have a recognizable and formal way of acknowledging the puberty of a girl. They give it the same name as the villagers (the Bira call it *elima,* the Lesé *peipa*) and in its outer form it appears roughly similar; the occasion at least is the same, the first appearance in a girl of menstrual blood. But there the similarity ends.

Be that as it may, the villagers do not take nearly as much interest in the puberty of the Mbuti girls as they do in the puberty of the boys. The Mbuti generally seem to hold part of their *elima* festivals in the forest, and the closing part in the village. In this way they are able to pursue their own way through the festival without interference, claiming a feast at village expense only when the forest festival is virtually ended. Village interest in the *elima* while it is in the forest is not manifest in any practical way, although a particularly fond *kpara's* wife might send out an occasional gift of plantains or manioc. But when the *elima* moves to the village there is invariably some conflict, because the closing phase of the Mbuti *elima* is particularly untraditional in the eyes of the villagers (as well it might be, for in fact it is probably a totally different tradition) and offensive to their tribal lore. In particular in recent years, there has been a tendency for Mbuti girls to imitate the boy's *nkumbi*, of which they are supposed to know almost nothing. They display an intimate knowledge of the most jealously guarded secrets, and there have been, throughout the Ndaka and Bira tribal areas, instances of *elima* girls adopting both the costumes of the boy initiates and some of their behavior.

In 1958 the Epulu band went so far that both the Bira and the Ndaka chiefs and ritual specialists joined in complaint, and threatened the *elima* girls (the two candidates and their companions, known jointly as the *bamelima*) with a death curse if they did not desist. The girls were upset because they claimed that they had merely adopted the boys' costume because it was so much prettier than the traditional costume approved by villagers for village *elima* girls. And was not the whole idea to look pretty? Of course from the village point of view the whole idea was to behave as one defiled, and this is one of several indications of the total difference between the two attitudes to the event of puberty.

We shall see that the Mbuti attitude is that a girl's first menstrual period is an indication of her readiness for motherhood, and is therefore a time for great and public rejoicing (see Turnbull, 1960[1]). It is also a time when boys and girls should get together and think about settling down in marriage, so it is a time for experimentation. The girls are expected, during the last stages of the festival, to look their best at all times, and they paint and decorate and dress themselves to excellent effect. They flaunt themselves in public, to the increased dismay of the villagers.

The villagers regard the appearance of menstrual blood as a disaster, and as the inauguration of a time of great danger for the girl, her family and, by extension, the whole tribe. She is considered as unclean, and is rigorously secluded and abased. Her family has to undertake a series of purification rituals ending in a feast (the part of the ceremony for which the Mbuti solicit "help"). They also have to discover the cause of the blood, which is believed by the Plains Bira and still by a number of the Forest Bira to be due to intercourse. The girl is questioned as to who caused the blood, and she names the youth on whom she has set her heart. He may acknowledge the blame, whether or not he ever had intercourse with her, and can then resolve the unclean situation by marrying her. If his wishes are otherwise he can deny her accusation and she will have to try elsewhere. The girl's parents will guide her accusations as they think necessary, but the actual extent to which the village *elima* leads thus directly into marriage seems to vary. Sometimes it is sufficient to secure admission of guilt and payment in lieu of marriage. But the villagers seldom try to follow an Mbuti *elima* through its full course; their major concern is that the impurity of the *elima* girls should not touch them. The provision of the final feast gives them an opportunity, which they do not always take, for supervising the ritual purification of the girls by bathing, the cleansing of the *elima* house, and the ritual disposal of all clothing and bedding and utensils used by the *bamelima*. The latter they do generally supervise, as the Mbuti are notoriously loath to part with perfectly good clothing or bedding for such *bulé* reasons, and will try to avoid having them destroyed.

If anything, the *elima* sets the villagers and the Mbuti apart, rather than offering any means for drawing them closer together. This is perhaps because while the *nkumbi* involves the village ancestors and is in honor of them, and secures their blessing, the village *elima* involves malevolent spirits more than it involves the ancestors. And as far as the villagers are concerned, evil spirits emanate from the forest. The *elima* offers no opportunity to the villagers for placing Mbuti girls under the control of the ancestral spirits; at the most, it offers them a responsibility for freeing them from contamination by the evil spirits. They sometimes voice the opinion that the Mbuti are in league with those spirits emanating from the forest, and rigorously avoid any contact with an Mbuti *elima*.

MARRIAGE

Marriage, as we have already seen, may involve the Mbuti in village ritual, and even if their Mbuti claim to have been married in the forest according to their own rites, the villagers try to insist on a village ceremony. Their concern is that the marriage shall be protected, as in village society, against disruption. As the Mbuti not only have no system of paying bride wealth but have no wealth that could be paid, the villagers are obliged to supply the wealth they deem necessary to help stabilize the marriage. They say that a marriage without wealth will not last. But as with the *nkumbi*, they feel that the major safeguard they secure by putting the Mbuti through the village ritual is that the marriage then becomes the concern of the tribal ancestors and subject to supernatural sanctions, all of which operate in the interests of the villagers.

[An important part of the village ceremony formalizing a marriage between two Mbuti is the admonition given by a number of villagers to both groom and bride, reminding them of their old obligations and telling them of the new.] The bride is introduced to her husband's *kpara* and his wife, and is told exactly what the wife expects of her; at the same time she is reminded of her own *kpara* and admonished not to forget where her "relatives" live. In fact, the place that would be occupied by the parents of the bride and groom in a normal village ceremony are, when two Mbuti are being married, occupied by the *kpara*. Each admonition generally ends with a reminder that the tribal ancestors of the villagers have been invoked for their blessings, and the tribe has provided generous feasts for all the relatives of the bride and groom, and wealth to boot, so any infidelity or any breach of the bond will call down supernatural wrath upon the (Mbuti) families of all those concerned.

In the various crises that may face the couple now, it will be all the more important for the villagers to take the necessary ritual precautions, and to investigate any calamity for evidence of witchcraft. [Mbuti marriages tend to be somewhat unstable until the first child is born, and indeed are not considered as marriages by the Mbuti until then, separation and the formation of new unions being the rule rather than the exception.] The villagers tend to suspect that witchcraft is at work, sometimes suspecting an Mbuti, sometimes another villager. Bad hunting and sickness are considered to be due to witchcraft or to a breach of marital taboos, as indeed are any disasters, natural or unnatural, that befall the couple. The Mbuti, not having any traditional means of divination, are considered by the villagers to be dependent on them for help, though a few Mbuti have learned the art and become quite highly respected by the villagers. Sometimes if villagers come to hear of a marital dispute within a band, they will try to settle it by reference to divination, and if so the Mbuti appear to accept the settlement without question, in the village, but in no way allow it to impinge upon the reality of the situation in the forest. So once again the only dependency that exists is in the minds of the villagers.

DEATH

Even when it comes to the greatest crisis of all, death, the Mbuti seem to accept all the externals of village ritual but none of the implications. The invariable accusation of witchcraft and the equally invariable mention of supernatural sanctions as an alternative cause of death are made to remind the Mbuti not to falter in fulfilling their obligations to their *kpara*. Village insistence upon the unnatural causes of death serves to sow enough seeds of doubt in the mind of the Mbuti to cause at least momentary fear.

The actual ritual of burial is conducted under strict village supervision, the necessary payments being made by the *kpara*. The *kpara* and his family, as well as many other villagers, attend personally in the procession to the grave, and the *kpara* is almost certain to take a prominent part in the subsequent discussion as to the cause of the death and be present at the divination, if one is held. But whereas the Mbuti generally subject themselves to village ritual with the best of grace, they become quickly impatient following the burial of the dead and sometimes simply walk out of the *baraza* where the cause of death is being determined, leaving it entirely to the villagers to decide whatever pleases them. The village preoccupation with death and its unnatural causes disquiets the Mbuti, and when an Mbuti dies in a village there is frequently voiced suspicion that somehow the village is responsible; maybe one of the old curses is at work, perhaps a neglected *kpara* is employing a sorcerer to seek revenge, or, more likely, it is impersonally simply the village itself that caused the death.

Among themselves the Mbuti do not bother to settle the question, if they ask it, but if they feel that the village is to blame in some undefined way, they do not hesitate to return at once to the forest. On the other hand, if they consider the death perfectly natural, they do not want to be bothered with a senseless preoccupation with causes. They know that in the course of the discussion the villagers will find opportunity to raise a number of issues better forgotten, such as unfulfilled obligations, and they are also uneasy at keeping the name of the dead person alive, in this way, for longer than is necessary. [The forest procedure would simply be to bury the body, probably by pulling the hut down on top of it, then to abandon the camp and build a new one, never again mentioning the dead person by name.]

On one occasion already cited (p. 10), an Mbuti funeral party returning from the grave converted itself into a wedding party. On another occasion, when the Mbuti were in a particularly festive mood and were bent on a long stay in the village, they played along with the witch-hunt even to the point of suggesting a second diviner from another village to check the findings of the first, stretching the proceedings out in this way for nearly a week. This meant that all the "mourners" (and Mbuti from villages up to twenty miles away came to this funeral) had to be fed for that long by the villagers. When the final act was done and the diviner had pointed out the witch that had "caused" the death, the Mbuti became annoyed that the villagers said something would have to be done about it, talking about a propitiation and a cleansing ceremony, with restitution. When the Mbuti saw they could not talk the villagers out of these less popular final rites, they returned to the forest, taking the "witch" with them.

On the few occasions on which I have seen the Mbuti apparently go through with the act until the very end—that is, divining the witch, accusing him or her, trying the case, giving judgment and going through the necessary cleansing rituals and actually making the necessary restitutive payments—it was when they already had a grievance against a certain person and chose this way of expressing it. On each such occasion there was not, among the Mbuti, the slightest thought that the "witch" actually had anything to do with the death. On two occasions the accused was a woman singularly well equipped to appear as a witch, her face being almost entirely eaten away by yaws. She was actually extremely well liked, but nonetheless she belonged to the volatile Cephu family who were always joining and breaking away from the main band, and she was very loud in her comments about that main band. Further, her husband, Aberi, normally also well liked, was particularly quick-tempered and a disturbing element.

He was the only one I ever knew who fought with his brother, and his wife was the cause of that fight. (Aberi was also one of the three to die following the curse of the Ngwana villager).

On another occasion the witch was also a woman, a rather crotchety, interfering old lady who was in the difficult position of being both a mother and a mother-in-law as well as a grandmother in the same camp. Her son, Amabosu, had exchanged sisters with Ekianga, and all of them lived in the same band. As Ekianga was an individualistic Mbuti with three wives, the situation was one fraught with difficulties, and old Sau's outspoken championship of her daughter as against Ekianga's two older wives did not help.

Sau was also the one chosen as witch in the mock trial after which the villagers attempted to detain her and the Mbuti carried her off with them to the forest.

[Evidently even in the village, regarded with suspicion and fear as it is, the Mbuti are not prepared to accept the real implications of witchcraft, so they see no need for the associated ceremonies.] But they do sometimes make use of the villager institution to settle their own dissociated grievances in their own way.

THE VILLAGE *MOLIMO* MOURNING CEREMONY

The funerary rituals and the divination of the cause of death are only part of the village ceremony attendant upon death. There follows a period of mourning that varies in length according to the status of the deceased and the wealth of his survivors, and that is terminated by final cleansing ceremonies and a feast for all mourners who have stayed the course, which generally means the immediate patrikin. During the mourning period, the patrikin are obliged to perform certain ceremonies to protect the deceased and help him on his way to join the ancestors. This ritual is known to the Bira by the name *molimo*. When talking in KiNgwana they call it *essumba* or *ishumba*, although it is quite different from the Ngwana ceremony of that name. The Bira *molimo* involves the use of a "singing" pot called *tete*, which is used to create a noise in imitation of the clan totem of the deceased, and of the leopard who is respected by all Bira. Exact details of the ritual are not known. I was not allowed to attend village *molimo* ceremonies because my close association with the Mbuti in the forest was considered as evidence of antipathy, if not of hostility. But from a number of different sources which I investigated as thoroughly as possible, it seems that among both Bira and Ndaka, and I believe also among the Lesé, death is believed to put fellow clansmen of the deceased in great danger from the *keti*, or evil spirits. The object of the *molimo* is twofold, then; it must help the deceased on his way, giving him what protection it can, and it must protect the living, who will be in a state of ritual danger throughout the period of mourning.

During that period the *molimo* meets regularly, at nighttime, in the house of the senior surviving member of the clan, in whose possession the *tete* is held. Only adult male clansmen are admitted, and the sound of the *tete* is the audible evidence of the invisible presence of their totemic guardian spirit. Specially prepared food is offered to the spirit, and the rest is eaten by the men. No women are allowed to participate in any way, even by cooking the food, according to all informants. However, I had been told the same thing about the Mbuti and found it to be different, and do not accept this information without some reservation. It would seem, though, that women generally are excluded from the *molimo* of the villagers, and indeed it really is no concern of theirs.

During the proceedings, which may last an hour or so, the men wail and call out the name and/or the kinship term of address of the deceased; his praises are recited and he is commended to the ancestral spirits. At the same time, the praises of the surviving clan members are similarly recited, and mention is made of the way in which they have upheld tribal lore and observed all the rules of clan exogamy, and have increased the number of attendant Mbuti. Continued protection for the living is requested, particularly for the period of mourning. Apparently no Mbuti take part in this part of the ceremony, though there seemed to be some disagreement over this and my impression was that the associated Mbuti are not prohibited from attending, but effectively seldom, if ever, do.

Upon the death of an Mbuti the *kpara* will not only oversee the burial and funerary ceremonies and divination, he will also want to hear announced the calling together of the men of the *molimo*. Sometimes he will leave it at that, but if the Mbuti continue to stay in the village and hold any *molimo* meetings in their village camp, the *kpara* may attend one or two meetings. It is very noticeable that when he does, the meeting runs a completely different course, centering around some erotic dancing by the younger men and a small amount of singing. The *molimo* trumpet, which is the Mbuti counterpart of the villager *tete*, may be heard growling in a noncommittal manner, as if uncertain which clan totem to imitate from the diversity of clans undoubtedly represented at the Mbuti *molimo* fire. It seems that the most common sound for the instrument to make under such circumstances is the growl of a leopard, which safely covers all clans, Mbuti and villager.

However, the villagers are not made welcome, and if it were any but the *kpara* or his representative the *molimo* would be abandoned the moment a villager approached. As it is, on the few occasions when I have seen a *kpara* attend, he was not offered any food or any other inducement to stay, the *molimo* trumpet remained out of sight the whole time and only growled indistinctly once or twice; the singing was sporadic and only the young men were active, dancing around the fire.

The Mbuti said that the villagers were afraid and would not in any case be likely to come near; the *kpara* only did it because he felt obliged to. In all cases of which I have any experience, except two instances where a brief *molimo* was held in a village camp for an Mbuti child who died there, the Mbuti *molimo* is held at nighttime in the forest, where interference from the village would be unthinkable. As with the *elima*, however, the closing stages are often held in the village, this being meant to coincide with the end of the official period of mourning and therefore the signal for a feast to be supplied by the villagers.

It does seem significant, nonetheless, that the Mbuti should sing any *molimo* songs in the village camp, for normally they refuse to sing any of their true forest songs when in the village. However, they are sung infrequently, with marked restraint, and widely separated by long snatches of songs that I never heard in the forest or, unfortunately, in the villages. The latter bore a distinct resemblance to certain songs taught during the *nkumbi*, and some were undoubtedly variants on *nkumbi* songs. The only information I could get was they were not "songs of the forest" but were "songs of the village." The villagers confirmed that they heard the Mbuti sometimes singing village *molimo* songs, and surprise was expressed that they would sing anything else, for everything else was *bulé*, empty.

The connection between the *molimo*, as performed by the Mbuti in the village, and the *nkumbi* was made all the more evident when on one *molimo* occasion the two members of the *kpara*'s family stood up and performed a dance only seen otherwise in the initiation camp.

On another occasion the *kpara* himself did exactly the same thing. In the first instance the *kpara* was Ndaka, in the second, Bira. The villagers evidently believe that whatever *molimo* ritual the Mbuti have, it was learned from the village, if badly learned and performed with illegitimate variations. As with the *elima*, perhaps also for fear of exposure to the malevolent forest spirits, the villagers do not seek to interfere too much with Mbuti *molimo* celebrations. We shall see that these celebrations are quite divorced from the village *molimo*, regardless of whether or not the origin of the two was common. Also, we shall see that the Mbuti *molimo* has none of the connections that evidently exist between the village *molimo* and the *nkumbi*.

As with the *elima*, the villagers limit the extent of their interest to ensuring the removal, by village-supplied procedure, of the last taints of uncleanliness. This they do, again in conjunction with a feast, turning a blind eye to the fact that as many as a dozen different Mbuti "clans" may be represented at what is supposed to be a closed clan feast.

The extent to which the villagers believe they assert supernatural control over the Mbuti does not coincide at all with the extent to which they effectively do exert such control, for the reason that must now be sufficiently obvious; no matter how many or what manner of village institutions the Mbuti adopt, they are adopted into a pre-existing system and no longer have the same interrelationships they do in the village system. The two systems are kept irreconcilably apart by what has in effect been emerging throughout—the existence of two completely different sets of values.

Yet the villagers are not entirely victims of their own *mbafu*, as the Mbuti would have it. There is little else they could do, and the adoption of the Mbuti into one aspect of village social structure would indeed be *bulé* without their adoption into the total structure. The villagers are consistent and logical, and above all it must be remembered that in their own eyes they have achieved what they set out to achieve—control. They believe that ultimate control is theirs because of the force of the supernatural powers on their side, and in point of fact, although it does not work quite the way they think, the concept of supernatural power does give them a small measure of control to the extent that it creates fear.

But what is also achieved is the creation of a myth that completely regularizes the whole situation, as far as the villagers are concerned, affording them an institutionalized means of dealing with every possible situation, retaining at all times the village position of superiority over the Mbuti. But it is a myth which at the same time satisfies the needs of the Mbuti, affording them precisely the freedom of which the villagers seek to deprive them, enabling them to rationalize the situation in their own favor and to their own advantage. We shall shortly see how this takes place.

CHAPTER 7

Flux and Instability

Not yet having examined the forest context, we cannot completely dispose of the question of economic dependence or interdependence. At the moment, it appears that the Mbuti do not need the villagers except for luxuries which may in time become necessities, and it equally seems that the villagers do not need the Mbuti except as laborers on the plantations, in particular with the cotton harvest, and this is a very recent need introduced by Belgian administration. The most that one can say about the economic aspect of the relationship is that it appears to be one of mutual convenience. The villagers *could* hunt (and in areas where there are few or no Mbuti, they do) but they prefer not to go into the forest if it can be avoided. The Mbuti *could* live successfully off the forest at their indigenous level of technology, but trade with the villagers makes life that much easier.

If we look carefully at daily life in any village, the economic aspect of the relationship fades even further into the background. Mbuti can occasionally be seen bringing in from the forest meat or other forest products needed by the villagers, such as the *fito* saplings and phrynium leaves for their houses. More often they will be seen helping with odd domestic chores, such as fetching water or firewood, house-building, or guarding plantations. Mbuti women help the village women pound manioc and to thresh and winnow the locally grown dry rice. They also help the village women carry loads of plantains to and from the market.

But mostly, if any Mbuti are to be seen at all, they will be seen lazing on the *baraza* of their *kpara*, being fed and offered ends of cigarettes, or bribed with liquor to put on a dance that all the villagers will come to watch. Such dances are wild and erotic, accompanied by anything from one to three or four drums, never by song. It is also possible to see Mbuti scrounging food from villagers

other than their own *kpara* and, when not successful, simply stealing
what they want. If they are caught they are scolded by their *kpara*
and that is generally all. If more fuss is made than that, all the Mbuti
are likely to pack up and return to the forest within hours. But whatever Mbuti may be seen engaged in whatever activity, they can be
seen only as individuals in relationship to a particular villager at that
particular moment, unrelated to other villagers and other Mbuti, unless they are included in the same activity. Only in the village camp
of the Mbuti, usually at the edge of the plantation, do they form a
society, but the interpersonal relationships observable even in a village camp bear little resemblance to relationships in the more strictly
village context.

The situation becomes more understandable in light of the expressed Mbuti attitude to their own place in the village world. They
refer to the village as being a place for good hunting and good eating.
Hunting requires cunning, and particularly when dealing with a
"tricky" animal such as the villager, say the Mbuti. The word for
"trickery" means more than "clever," it has connotations of supernatural power. So the Mbuti, when hunting in the village, use appropriate tactics, just as they do in the forest. Carrying wood and
fetching water, building houses and pounding manioc, are all part
of those tactics, and may perhaps be likened to the net with which
the Mbuti trap the forest animals.

This Mbuti attitude to the relationship not only fits with the theory that there is, in effect, no necessary economic interdependence,
but it also fits well with the suggestion of *apparent* structural incompatibility. Mbuti talk of "eating" the villagers, and indeed the
villagers also talk, with some asperity, of being eaten. In Mbuti
thought, however, it is rather more literal than it may seem, for the
villagers are not only referred to as animals, a common term of abuse,
but they are considered as animals. And when one eats an animal one
merely consumes its substance, one does not thereby assume its form
or its pattern of behavior.

Even supposing that there was a necessary economic interdependence, the daily life of the village in no way reveals any sense of economic urgency. Even in times of crisis, such as the cotton harvest,
powerful chiefs like Kachui may evidently find themselves deserted
by the Mbuti and forced to make out on their own. But if there were
a true economic dependence, then there would have to be a workable
economic system, with an associated system of social control; and

we have already seen that in place of system and control there is, apparently, only flux and instability that militate *against* system and control.

By flux I refer to the fact that the Mbuti appear to adopt village institutions but not the village system of interrelationships. In this way there is a disconnectedness in the village context of the Mbuti that enables both sides to refer to whichever institution is convenient at the moment to establish a relationship of the moment. Thus an Mbuti may be asked to help one villager on the ground of their *karé* relationship, and expected by another to help because of the hereditary *kpara* relationship. Considerations of simple economic exchange between the same Mbuti and still other villagers may override either of the above considerations at another moment. Thus the Mbuti has a number of possible ways in which he can link himself with the village and the villagers, at different and distinct times. The converse also applies, and if a villager finds his hereditary claims ineffective he may call on other Mbuti because of the *karé* relationship, and so forth.

In view of the nomadic nature of the hunting band and, as we shall see, of its composition, this "system" of flux is the only one that could possibly pertain. But it leads inevitably to instability because of the consequent lack of any one system of control. In the same way that the Mbuti can hop from one conflicting set of relationships to another, so he can hop from one system of control to another. By Mbuti rejection of the total village system and by what proves to be an opposition of a totally different set of values, the villager ultimately is denied virtually all control, and the Mbuti similarly is denied any absolute security in his relationships with the villagers.

However, the loss of control is more serious to the villagers than is the loss of security to the Mbuti, and it is also more complete, for the villagers are themselves bound by the supernatural sanctions through which they vainly attempt to impose control upon the Mbuti. The whole situation is incompatible with the notion of economic interdependence, yet there is no denying the actual relationship between the two groups of people. Nor can one deny that within a framework of flux and instability, the relationship is persistent, so there must be some system. If that system is so evidently unrelated to economic factors, we have to look elsewhere for its focal point.

There are not all that many basic relationships that can exist between two peoples in a context such as this. Apart from one of symbiosis, implying interdependence, there could be political subjugation, such as existed, say, between the Tussi and the Hutu. But that is plainly not the case here. The villagers themselves admit their inability to exert physical force to bend the Mbuti to their will, for the Mbuti always have the ultimate escape of flight to the sanctuary of the forest. The villagers are completely unequipped to pursue the Mbuti into the forest, and never attempt it. They are incapable of even finding the Mbuti if the hunters wish not to be found. And, as we have seen, there is no effective political mechanism for maintaining any kind of political relationship, let alone one of superordination/subordination.

Another possible relationship would be one of assimilation, such as occurred among the Ganda of East Africa, where two different peoples merged, as did their two different economies. At the present there is no question of actual assimilation, but the existence of linguistic and institutional similarities certainly indicates an interchange of ideas, at least. But it is, at the moment, an interchange of outward forms only, and not of the accompanying systems and structure. And while a great deal of intimacy is expressed, in action as in word, between the two groups, there is also a great deal of expressed opposition, and sometimes hostility.

The intermarriage between Mbuti girls and village men and the attempted absorption of the Mbuti into the village kinship system may be considered as steps toward assimilation, but if so they are very tentative and preliminary steps, and as such need not concern us here. Indeed we shall find that there are other indications of the reverse process, of separation. There is no question of physical separation in the sense of the expulsion of one group by the other, but a perfectly valid alternative relationship left to us for consideration is one of ideological separation accompanied by a mutually accepted territorial separation—a form of indigenous apartheid.

This in fact seems to be the case, for in common conversation, as in action, both groups distinguish the village and the village people from the forest and the forest people. The Mbuti effectively are the only group to cross the territorial boundaries, and the ideological boundaries remain inviolate on both sides. When the Mbuti cross into the village world they leave the forest behind them, and with it they leave their forest social system. Forest values cannot be so easily left behind, but in the village world they are dormant, and do not come into play until the two worlds begin to impinge upon each other.

Thus the economic, kinship and political relationships that bind the Mbuti together as a society in the forest do not pertain in the village, and consequently the society disintegrates as such. An example can be had by comparing plans of the forest hunting camps with plans of the village camps over the same period (see Plan 2). It will be seen that there is virtually no correspondence, and that while each successive forest camp (approximately one a month) shows a significant change in structure related to the constant process of fission and fusion and of fragmentation, the village camps show no such pattern. At first they seem much more stable, but that is due at least in part to the fact that the actual camp is more permanent in nature, being occupied for much shorter periods of time. Also, such camps are sometimes built in imitation of the real villages, the houses being made smaller, though of the same semi-permanent mud and wattle construction. It is only the physical disposition that remains constant, however, and that only for as long as the physical camp remains unchanged. This may be for as long as a year or more. During that time the composition of the village camp is constantly changing, according to no discernible pattern, and certainly none related to the composition of the forest camp.

The Mbuti living in a village camp can no longer be considered as a band. Indeed, there are times when the village camp may be fully occupied, as if by a band, but in fact by Mbuti who have nothing more immediately in common than their intent to "eat" those particular villagers. Even considerations of kinship and of age break down, though nuclear families tend to continue to live together. A nuclear family will not co-operate within itself in the same way, however, as it would in a hunting camp; nor, most certainly, will it co-operate with other nuclear families. There is not even the necessity for a wife to cook her husband a meal, as he can always scrounge one from a villager. Whether he does so or not is purely a domestic issue between himself and his family and, as seen, because of the flux that pertains, different members of the same family could choose to establish village relationships, each by invoking a different context— the one karé, the other kpara, another economic exchange—so even three brothers technically "owned" by the same villager could find themselves attached to three different villagers, possibly living in three different houses (when in the village, the Mbuti sometimes

sleep in the *baraza* of the villagers rather than in the village camp).
The nuclear family is further disrupted by the fact that a wife may
well seize the opportunity of being in the village to leave her husband
and visit her own *kpara* in another village.

Men and women of quite different ages who would normally, in
the forest, be separated for most aspects of daily life may find themselves thrown together. Young and old are quite likely to find themselves eating together on the same *baraza*, helping to build the same
house, even joining in the same erotic dance. Sex differentiations that
pertain in the forest do not necessarily pertain in the village, where,
for instance, Mbuti men do the housebuilding, not the women, and
where the women are most effectively the "hunters" and food pro-
ducers.

It is only, as stated, when the two worlds of the forest and the
village impinge upon each other that the Mbuti in the village camp
show any sense of identity as a unit. Those who belong to the same
hunting band will then cluster together around the same campfire,
and if the issue involves a return to the forest, then quickly the village
camp begins to assume, so far as possible, the composition and characteristics of a forest camp. Forest relationships between individuals
and families are gradually reestablished, and at the same time village
relationships are gradually abandoned. This inevitably meets with
concerted opposition on the part of the villagers, who offer threats
and bribes to maintain the precarious and temporary relationship just
established. But with no effective means of control there is nothing
they can do but accept the departure of "their" Mbuti with as much
good grace as they can muster. Those who are wise make presents of
plantains and manioc. Those who do not are likely to have their
plantations robbed.

The imminence of a mass return of Mbuti to the forest is frequently marked a night or two before it takes place by the singing
in the village camp of hunting songs or, on special occasions, of the
lesser *molimo* songs, late at night when all the villagers will have retired. This is a sure sign that the forest world is asserting itself, for
forest songs are generally considered as sacred, and not to be profaned
by performance in the village. They would never be sung in the true
village, and only in the Mbuti village camp when they wish to convert
the context to a forest context. The forest, it must be remembered,
is physically always within sight and, perhaps more important as far
as song is concerned, within earshot. It may, indeed, be no more than

a few yards away, and some village camps, depending upon the circumstances, are actually built still in the shade of the forest, out of sight of the village and its plantations.

But granted this separation of the two worlds, and the fact that when the band (or part of it) comes to the village it disintegrates as such, and if we accept the lack of any economic necessity or political force by which we could explain the relationship, we still have to answer the question as to why a relationship exists and what its true nature is.

This can best be answered after we have seen the nature of the forest world, but it can already be seen that the meeting of the two peoples is somewhat like the meeting of two polar opposites that are irresistibly drawn together. And indeed, such magnetic links between opposites are the only true ones we have found. The point at which the forest and the village truly meet, the focal point of the relationship between the two peoples, is not economic or political, but religious. The nature of the meeting is one of opposition, and this opposition is most clearly expressed in the mutually antagonistic systems of values. Although we have only concerned ourselves with the village world to this point, we have already seen the strength of the village fear of the forest, resulting in their unwillingness to enter it and their consequent "dependence" upon the Mbuti for necessary forest products. This fear is expressed in religious terms by reference to the hostile forest spirits, and the general antagonism of the forest to the village world, witnessed by its reluctance to support village crops. Insofar as the villagers recognize the Mbuti as a forest people they believe them to be somehow aligned with the forest spirits, and therefore to be placated. That does not prevent the villagers from attempting, while placating, to extend some form of control over the Mbuti. Indeed they seem far more concerned about this than they are about the small amount of meat or labor they manage to extract from the Mbuti (see Table 3 for an example of "economic" exchange).

The Mbuti most nearly fall under village control through their own fear of the village (which by its very nature is not only not "of the forest" but is actively hostile to the forest), and through their fear of the powers the villagers claim to have over the supernatural, by witchcraft and sorcery. Quite apart from the historic genesis of the Mbuti/Villager relationship, the very antagonism of their ways of life, together with their territorial propinquity, would be enough to demand that they come to some kind of terms and establish some kind of mechanism for dealing with the threat that each feels.

We have seen how the villagers attempt to deal with the situation by asserting control over the Mbuti through the adoption of the Mbuti into the village social system, thus placing them under the supernatural sanctions of village society. We have also seen that the Mbuti evade such control, though we have not exactly seen how, for at the moment the success of their evasion seems to lie in the rejection of system, in a flux and instability that alone would lead to chaos. In examining the forest society of the Mbuti now, however, we shall see how this flux and apparent instability is in fact a structural factor, and that while the villagers are constantly attempting to absorb the Mbuti into their village social system, the Mbuti have evolved a social system of their own which, while still permitting their traditional hunting and gathering existence, takes this new village factor into consideration and, so to speak, by opposing, ends it. For the Mbuti forest system seems almost expressly designed to run counter to the village system, and, by opposing it at every point of possible structural contact, it makes any structural relationship except one of opposition quite impossible.

Thus in examining the forest system of the Mbuti we have to remember that the same institution may well have a double function; the one of maintaining cohesion with the forest world, the other of maintaining opposition with the world outside. And insofar as the invasion of the village tribes is relatively recent, this is a system that is still evolving. All the more so because the successive waves of the invasion, followed by the advent of the Arab slave traders and finally by the arrival of the Belgians, have all wrought sudden and drastic changes in the nature of village life and on the village settlement pattern. There may indeed be some institutions that are newly evolved and the purpose of which is directed primarily at maintaining the relationship of opposition between forest and village. Others are in the process of adaptation, notably the Mbuti *molimo*, where the forest system of values has its deepest roots and where, consequently, their opposition to village values must be most forcefully expressed. And some institutions appear to be in a state of atrophy.

We are, then, very clearly going to be studying a society in the process of change. The structure that will emerge, involving a disconcerting lack of emphasis on kinship, is not necessarily or even probably characteristic of hunting and gathering societies, and should certainly not be taken as such. It should only be considered as a system that maintains, in its basic respects, a hunting and gathering tradition, while also maintaining, as completely as possible, a physiological and ideological separation from a hostile village system.

PART THREE

THE FOREST WORLD

CHAPTER 8

The Band

TERRITORY

Before we can begin to understand what the Mbuti band is, we have to understand the notion of territory, which is effectively the only concept through which the band can be defined. Insofar as the band is the largest effective political unit, so the widest territorial boundaries that are recognized are those separating each band from the others. As will be seen, there is a current tendency for all Mbuti bands to recognize a loose unity to bind them in common opposition to the villagers, and in this context they will define a correspondingly wider territory, the forest, in which the villagers are regarded as trespassers. At the other end of the scale, the nuclear family has no territorial claims except those held jointly with other families of the same band. An individual may stake his claim to a tree that he knows or believes will yield honey, or to one that promises to provide good bark for making into cloth. A common way of showing that the tree is claimed is by tying a vine around the trunk at shoulder height.

A claim thus made by no means gives the individual or his family exclusive ownership of the tree or exclusive rights to its produce, however. It merely conveys the right for that individual to have the first opportunity for collecting the honey or for cutting the bark. When the honey is collected or the bark cut, it is done collectively and the claimant is subject to all the usual rules governing the sharing of forest produce. He will have precedence of choice and his share will be larger. If he is not on hand when the honey is ready, however, and if he does not signify his intention to come to claim it, his right is forfeited. It may be seen that the advantage accruing from this slight departure from the norm of joint band ownership of the territory and its produce is in no way great enough to detract from the central value of communal territory, but at the same time it is sufficiently great to provide some incentive for individual effort and, much more important, it also provides some incentive for a wandering member of a band to return to his home territory at least once a year, for the honey season.[1]

The territory of any band is always ample for its needs. That is perhaps the safest way of defining the size of band territory. Never, in any part of the forest, have I come across any complaint of the insufficiency of a hunting territory, in terms of either size or produce. Nor are there sufficient instances of trespass to indicate that any band suffers from inadequate natural resources. In every case that I have investigated the band has been able to define its boundaries by citing rivers, streams, mountain ridges, ravines, caves, or other locally well-known natural landmarks. These boundaries generally extend one day's march in one direction, three days' march in the other. The shorter base is invariably parallel to the line, a trail or road, connecting two villages, though it may well overlap it. A "day's march" is the way the Mbuti generally define distance, and in practice this means that the first day in from the base line is the longest distance, extending perhaps as far as thirty miles. Beyond this the territory is less intensively traveled, the trails are more difficult to follow, and the third day in may represent only ten or fifteen miles. The base line, similarly, is comparatively short, being perhaps the least hunted as it is the closest to the village. Also, as the forest in this area will have been penetrated by villagers in search of building materials, it is generally much more difficult to traverse than the virgin forest a mile or so further in.

In using this measure of time and distance, the Mbuti do not think of how far a single hunter could travel in a day, but rather how far the whole band could travel, as if shifting camp. A single man could travel almost twice the distance. This is a small point, but serves as an indication of the way in which the Mbuti see the world around them, in terms of the potentiality of the whole band.

The territory of the Epulu band (Map 6) was defined by a series of rivers: the Harama, the Itoro, and the Epulu to the northeast, the east and the south, and by the small Nepussi and a series of hills and caves to the west. As usual, the innermost boundary was the least

[1] This also seems to be the season when bark-cloth manufacture is at its height, perhaps largely because more time is available during this season. But bark cloth is made throughout the year, and fresh sources of the best barks are always eagerly sought and claimed.

clearly defined, opening northward into a large central area unclaimed by anyone.

The topography of the Epulu territory is similar to that of most other bands, though without the steep, mountainous ridges that occur slightly further east. The ground is gently undulating, as thickly forested on the hilltops as in the valleys, though the vegetation is much denser along the banks of streams and rivers. It is almost impossible to walk more than a few hundred yards without having to cross a small stream, and after a particularly violent and prolonged rainfall there are areas that become temporarily flooded and the larger streams may become uncrossable torrents. But normally there is little difficulty in traveling from one extreme of the area to another. There are no swamps, the ground is clear of the tangled undergrowth that characterizes old plantation sites, and all but the largest streams are either shallow enough, in places, to be forded or are bridged at intervals by fallen trees. Nowhere do the Mbuti need to build bridges, and nowhere do they do so except in the village context.[2] It is a simple fact that rivers that are too wide to be bridged by a fallen tree are relatively far and few between, and therefore form convenient natural boundaries. There is neither the desire nor the need to cross such rivers. A certain mistrust of large bodies of water strengthens the efficacy of rivers as boundaries, just as the few superstitions to be found among the Mbuti mostly relate to ravines, caves, streams or hills that form other boundaries.

The abundance of game and vegetable food may be taken for

[2] The famous "pygmy" bridge and the spectacular technique of crossing a river by swinging on a vine from one side to the other were taught to the Mbuti, not without difficulty, by an enterprising movie-maker. Patrick Putnam was asked to assist as interpreter, but refused. His first wife, however, went to watch the proceedings. The same group of pygmies retained some knowledge of the technique, and obligingly repeated the act for subsequent "documentary" film units. They are the only group with the knowledge, though they are now less proficient. A more recent movie-maker had to sling a wire hawser across the river and suspend the vine swing from its midpoint. A simple mathematical calculation will reveal the impossibility of the swinging technique, even disregarding the area behind the swing that would have to be cleared, a task in itself beyond Mbuti technology. Assuming the fulcrum is over one bank, and the branches into which the pygmy is to swing are directly over the far bank (a generous assumption), and assuming that the pygmy can be drawn back far enough to swing up to a 45-degree angle at the far end of his swing, the maximum width that can be crossed is three-quarters of the height of the swing. In practical experiment among the Mbuti, I found that effectively half the height of the swing was the maximum horizontal distance that could be so traversed. This would mean that to cross a river a mere hundred yards in width, the fulcrum would have to be some 600 feet up, demanding a tree approaching the height of the Eiffel Tower. Conversely, a swing of the maximum normally practicable length of 60 feet would enable a pygmy to span a stream a mere 30 feet across. Pygmies generally have rather more sense, in such matters, than movie-makers.

granted in any part of the forest, except possibly that small triangle bounded by the three roads joining the administrative centers of Mambasa, Irumu and Beni (Map 4), where the roads and the heavy concentration of foreign settlements, coffee plantations, hospitals, missions and mines have considerably affected the natural resources and the natural patterns of game migration. There is no economic need for trespass. Each territory is large enough for a band to roam within it for year after year, never twice occupying the same camp site, never exhausting its supplies of food or the materials needed for shelter and clothing and the rest of the minimal Mbuti material culture.

All of which is not to say that boundaries are not crossed. They are crossed, either when hunters commit trespass or when individuals or families visit relatives in other bands. In the case of trespass, a band of hunters may pursue game across a boundary stream, particularly if it is one of the more prized animals. An elephant would almost certainly be pursued, but it is understood that the band whose territory is so violated has certain rights to the spoils. Such trespass is considered excusable under these conditions. Generally, however, a band will never hunt near its boundaries if the neighboring band is in the vicinity of the same boundary.

The only cases of uncondoned trespass known to me are rare instances when a band has found itself short of honey during the brief honey season, and has invaded its neighbor's territory and actually set up temporary camp there. This was considered inexcusable only because permission was not first sought.

If trespass is rare, boundaries are being crossed frequently for the approved purpose of visiting relatives, consanguineal or affinal. Individuals or whole families sometimes wander in this way until they are several territories distant from their home territory. By "home territory" an Mbuti would mean the territory in which he most habitually hunted, and in which he has established certain claims to honey or bark trees. He would be unlikely to attempt to define it in terms of clan or lineage concepts; that is, he would refer to the territory rather than to the band. This habitual exchange of visits is, in fact, the major social communication that exists between one band and another, but it also has a secondary economic significance: a band that becomes too large for convenience may split, a part of it going to join another band that has perhaps fallen below the optimum economic size. The major purpose of interband visits is the extension of the social horizon, particularly necessary in view of the preferred territorial exogamy. When the Mbuti say that they like to "marry far," they think primarily in terms of spatial distance, on the assumption that this will provide the necessary kinship distance. Thus territory is used, in the absence of a formalized kinship system, to express and maintain the necessary degree of exogamy. Territory is also used as the concept by which men and women define "home," and it is through territorial membership that any individual has such rights as he has. Above all, it is the territory which has bounds, not the band.

COMPOSITION

Both archer and net-hunter bands exhibit the greatest complexity in composition, particularly when large, but also sometimes even when fragmented into the smallest segments. The Epulu band, over the course of a year, was made up of twenty-seven patrilineages sharing seven totems, although the largest single camp contained only twenty-six family huts. Of these twenty-seven lineages, each of which has a name (possibly in imitation of village clan names) and a totem, only two are divided into more than one totemic group: the Puemi respect the leopard or the chimpanzee, the Bokelé respect the leopard or the buffalo or a rare antelope. The Puemi and the Bokelé alone, then, may be considered as clans, and even they only with reservation, for though each totemic group of the Bokelé (or the Puemi) claims to be related to the other through a distant ancestor, the ancestor remains unnamed and is never invoked, and it is admitted that intermarriage might take place. There is no record of such intermarriage, and certainly the lineage is exogamous. In the accompanying plans these totemic subgroups, then, are considered and represented as separate lineages.

For three large camps (over twenty huts[3]) made by the Epulu band within a twelve-month period, the following is the breakdown, giving the number of patrilineages and lineage totems represented in each camp, counting the husband, widower or rare bachelor hut-owner on the one hand, the wife or widow on the other, and counting only those living and present at the time:

[3] A hut is normally occupied by a nuclear family, but may sometimes be occupied only by a bachelor, widower or widow. Also, rarely, a married son and his wife may stay temporarily in the hut of either parents (more likely the parents of the son). By and large, however, a hut represents an economic unit owning no more than one net.

	Male Members		Female Members	
Camp 3a – in 26 huts, there were	13 lin.	5 tot.	9 lin.	6 tot.
3b – 22	10	5	10	6
3c – 22	12	5	11	5

When the band fragmented into small camps, the picture was not far different:

	Male Members		Female Members	
Camp 3d – in 9 huts, there were	5 lin.	5 tot.	5 lin.	4 tot.
3e – 9	5	3	6	3
3f – 6	4	4	4	3
3g – 3	2	1	3	3

Apart from the totemic subdivisions of the Puemi and Bokelé, the lineages all intermarry freely and do not consider themselves related to each other in any way whatsoever other than as affines.

The camp plans (Plans 3a–g) indicate the extent to which the lineages maintained their separate identities in the above camps. If we consider the lineages of both the husband and wife, we can see a slight tendency for women to build the family huts so that men of the same lineage will be near each other. The significance of this is dubious, and the rest of camp life does not indicate lineage to be of any particular interest, although in disputes lineage members tend to support each other, but not necessarily.

With other bands of net-hunters and also with archers the situation seems similar, though there is some tendency, perhaps, for the lineage divisions to be more visible in archer camps (see Plans 4a–m). I was not able to stay long enough in these other camps to thoroughly verify the genealogies, however, or to observe what changes took place from camp to camp. The material is all the more interesting, nonetheless, in that in the first instance I was always told that the camp consisted of one "clan" (using the village terminology), yet they did not deny the possibility of marriage within that unit.[4] This is another indication of how difficult are the conditions of work among the Mbuti, when they are constantly using words that have definite and very specific significance when used by the villagers, but which may have a completely general and other meaning among the Mbuti. The

---

[4] "Clan" terminology is used freely by the Mbuti when talking to villagers. It is rarely used in the forest, and was used to me only in response to my genealogical inquiries.

figures for six net-hunter bands and seven archer bands, where I am
most certain of the genealogies, are as follows:

NET-HUNTERS		Total No. of Lineages	Members Male	Female
In Camp 4a there were 28 huts,		10	5 lin.	9 lin.
4b	18	3	3	3
4c	16	5	5	5
4d	13	7	5	5
4e	11	5	4	3
4f	8	5	4	4

ARCHERS				
In Camp 4g there were 25 huts,		8	6 lin.	6 lin.
4h	11	3	2	3
4i	10	4	3	2
4j	10	6	4	4
4k	9	3	2	3
4l	6	3	2	2
4m	5	3	1	2

Owing to the difficulty of ascertaining the lineage membership of
the women, the above figures, for them, are probably minimal. I also
found it difficult to be certain of the totemic observances elsewhere
than among the Epulu band, where I had ample opportunity for cross-
checking, but the proportions elsewhere appeared similar—in any band
you would expect to find each lineage sharing its totem with one other
lineage. The plans of the above camps (Plans 4a–m) indicate the
possibility of greater lineage solidarity among the archers, if we are
to judge by the disposition of the huts, but the significance of the
lineage did not appear much different. Structurally it seemed of little
importance.

We cannot arrive at any immediate conclusions from these examples of camp composition beyond the Epulu, but drawn as they
are from bands selected for study at random, at the extremities of
the forest as well as in its center, they at least indicate that the Epulu
situation is not unique. Returning to the Epulu band, then, we are
left with the fact that even a cursory glance indicates clearly a certain
lack of lineage interest as manifest in the physical arrangement of the
hunting camps. It certainly indicates that the band as a whole in no
way and at no time resembles a patrilineage in its composition. With

this in mind we shall go on to discover the nature and extent of lineage participation in band activity, but the nonlineal nature of the corporate unit—i.e., the band or sub-band—has first to be examined in another context.

FRAGMENTATION, FISSION AND FUSION

We have already mentioned that the band may be large or small, that it may be established in a single large camp or in a number of smaller camps. In examining the process of fission and fusion, it is plain that lineage considerations are by no means paramount, but that, if anything, there is some effort to maintain nonlineal composition even in the smaller camps. That is to say, there is at least a consciousness of lineage and an apparently felt need to maintain some kind of balance between lineages. Whereas the process of fission and fusion—the division of the band into small segments, each with its own hunting camp within the hunting territory, and the eventual realignment of the band as a single unit—is systematic, it is not without an element of the less systematic process of fragmentation that takes place within any single camp, large or small, and which starts the day the camp is first established.

The whole shifting complex is best understood by looking at the camp plans at the end of the book. As each hut represents a married couple with or without unmarried children, Plans 5 and 6, respectively, show the lineage groupings according to male and female membership for the camp named *apa* Lelo. *Apa* Lelo was one of the larger camps and is as typical as any. Plan 7 shows the significant changes made in the direction in which the huts faced as the camp took shape, day by day.

On looking at Plans 5 and 6 it is evident that not only does the shape of the natural clearing lend itself to the division of the camp into sections, but that these sections show as much consideration for affinal as for consanguineal ties. Plan 7 shows how the natural divisions offered by the clearing were made plainer by the addition of screens to hut entrances, or by rebuilding huts so as to face them in different directions. The fallen tree trunk and a clump of undergrowth are also utilized, and in other camps such undergrowth was eventually cleared if the reason for making use of it disappeared.

When we examine the camp, section by section, it will be seen again that lineage is only one of many factors in determining the social groupings within the camp. Plan 8 offers a dramatic example of the kind of major change that can take place in any one camp, and of the kind of change that may lead to ultimate fission, and that is certainly likely to determine one of the lines of cleavage when fission does take place. The change was brought about by the arrival of a controversial sometime member of the band, Cephu.[5]

The camp was already settled at optimum-to-maximum size when, on the fifth day, Cephu arrived. He used to migrate from his natal band to this one, and was not overly welcome in either. He arrived by stealth with his father's brother's son, and their families pitched their belongings in a small clearing near the main camp. They were joined by a member of the important Puemi clan of the main camp, whose wife was friendly with Cephu's womenfolk. Their camp established, they opened a trail leading directly into the main camp. The various reactions, seen in Plan 7, effected a consolidation of the southwest corner of the main camp and caused a rift between two sets of brothers: M and N (N having joined Cephu while M pointedly rebuilt a new hut in the main camp), and D and I, D setting up with Cephu, his brother I and nephew J refusing to leave the main camp and join him.

Even more important, the consolidation of the southwest and, to some extent, the southeast corner of the main camp involved the southward realignment of S, T and U, S and U being highly influential elders, T being one of the greatest hunters. T and U were members of one section of the dominant Puemi clan, the other section being localized in the north part of the camp.

Plans 9 and 10 illustrate the rather more radical change that may take place, effecting a temporary consolidation of lineages. Such changes within a camp are extremely rare however—in this case the consolidation was of the lineages concerned in a vital dispute against one of their members, the same controversial Cephu guilty of a serious hunting crime. Table 4 gives the relevant kinship structure for this particular camp, and Table 5 gives the complete list of lineages, as far as I could trace them, with indications as to which individuals were effective members of the Epulu band during the year.

[5] I use personal names that were used in the forest, though some Mbuti use different names when in the village. It is perhaps significant that Cephu is a common name among the ill-considered Ngwana, and that Cephu's children were also mostly known by villager names or even by European names, such as "Teresa," currently in vogue among the villagers. Any one Mbuti might be known by as many as four names, certainly two or three. The names used here correspond to those used elsewhere (Turnbull, 1961) from which source some additional information on the personalities involved may be gleaned.

When the camp is first set up, the framework of the huts is completed, but they are probably only partly roofed. The greater the distance between camps, the later the band arrives and the less opportunity there is to complete the building that day. Sometimes shelter is sought overnight at an old camp site on the way. But however advanced the work may be on the first day, subtle changes take place for the next two days, during which time lagging members of the band will have arrived.

The first to reach the site choose any location they wish for their family hut, the choice being left almost entirely to the women. Men, women and children co-operate in the necessary work of clearing and of cutting and collecting the saplings and phrynium roofing leaves (*mongongo*). Women build the huts, sharing the supply of saplings and leaves as necessary, and helping each other with the building if darkness is approaching or if rain threatens. Such help seems to follow lines of friendship rather than of kinship, as does the grouping of the huts themselves.

For instance, the tight cluster at the north end of the camp (Plans 5 and 7) was brought about because of the death of Balekimito, an old and respected lady who was a member of the Puemi/leopard lineage, but married into the Bomasua/buffalo lineage. Both lineages were jointly holding the *molimo* festival for the dead lady, and the *kumamolimo* (*molimo* hearth) was placed in the center of their rather exclusive cluster. The presence of two male and two female members of another lineage, the Bokelé/buffalo, should be noted, however, as an instance of the strength of affinal ties (the same thing being evident at the southern end of the camp).

However, the Puemi and the Bokelé were the only ones in that part of the camp to arrive on the first day. They built their huts facing equally toward each other and toward the *kumamolimo*. When Ekianga, member of the Bomasua and son of the dead lady, arrived the next day with two of his three wives, there was an immediate change in all the huts. When Amabosu (β) saw Ekianga (B) occupy the hut built by his youngest wife, Amabosu's sister, he took action. His own wife, who was Ekianga's sister, built an extension to the house facing it almost directly away from her brother, looking right into the entrance to the hut of Ausu (α), her husband's kinsman. The reason was that Amabosu felt Ekianga should not be sleeping with his youngest wife at that time, and wanted to show his displeasure. Ausu, not wanting to take sides, carefully projected the entrance to his hut so that it no longer looked directly at Amabosu's, which would have been taken as indicating extreme intimacy, but instead faced narrowly across to the hut of his wife's uncle (C), Masisi; Masisi's son's wife (D), who was not only kin to Ekianga's young wife but close friends with her, promptly added to her hut, despite her husband's protests, and faced it boldly toward Ekianga. Ekianga's young wife, Kamaikan, responded the next day by facing her hut in the direction of her friend, at the same time deflecting it away from her co-wife's hut, Arobanai (A), next door. Arobanai had on the day of her arrival made an addition facing toward Kamaikan as a conciliatory gesture, but in face of this rebuff she turned the entrance of her hut away again. Meanwhile Masisi's lineal cousin, Manyalibo, made no effort to enter the dispute, but rather turned slightly toward the rest of the camp. Masisi contented himself with completing the entrance to his hut on the second day, leaving it facing the way it was. An extension he built several days later, as did Ausu, was merely to provide separate accommodation for young girls who were approaching puberty.

In the rest of the camp similar petty jealousies and hostilities brought about similar clusterings. Njobo (W-1A), for instance, was an unusually dominating personality, and was consequently accorded, or took, the position of *capita*, representing the band in all matters concerning the village. But he was unwise enough to try and assert the same authority in the forest, and the over-all layout of the camp shows clearly how he and his sister's son, Asuku (W-3A), whom he favored, were ostracized. His wife Masamba (X) built my hut for me, as women sometimes do for adult bachelor kinsmen, to one side, and another hut for strangers on the other side. Maipé (G), the son of another of Njobo's sisters, was the only one to allow his hut to remain facing toward Njobo. After Njobo had left, Nikiabo (H) joined the camp and Masamba built his hut for him, facing toward her own, saying she needed a friend. Makubasi (U), a prominent hunter and a member of the same clan as Njobo, but of a different lineage, turned his hut away on the second day, isolating Njobo in the middle of the clearing. At this, Njobo and his nephew, Asuku, joined their huts together, using only one entrance facing across to Njobo's other nephew, Maipé. When Makubasi's father, Tungana (T), arrived on the third day, he built his hut so that one entrance nominally faced toward Njobo, but it was generally covered and the other entrance faced clearly into the southwestern section of the camp.

Arriving on the same day as old Tungana came Moké, who built a large rectangular hut (S) in the center of Tungana's section. The two men claimed kinship with each other, Tungana allegedly having on his mother's side the same great-grandfather as Moké. Endeku, who was a son-in-law of Moké, was also a renowned clown, and the hut he built was wide open on two sides, so that it was little more than a roof. It stood close to Moké's hut and was an effective link between that cluster and the southern cluster, which included some members of Cephu's sub-band. Endeku's hearth became a gathering place for the southern part of the camp, just as the *kumamolimo* did for the north. Njobo and Asuku were received politely at either, but not with any enthusiasm. When Njelu and Betuli (M and L) arrived on the second day and, because of their mutual affinal relationship, built their huts close together, their neighbor Masimongo (K) turned his hut away for no evident reason at all. Betuli reacted by turning his back on Masimongo, joining his hut to Njelu's. One day later Njelu built a new hut a few yards away, still facing it toward Betuli, however. He said he did not like his "sister" so close to him. Actually, Betuli's wife was of the same clan as Njelu, but of a different lineage. Although Njelu's wife, kin of Pangia (P) and Betuli, had left him, Njelu always preferred to move and camp with his affines, even though they usually camped with Cephu, who was somewhat in conflict with Njelu's own, Puemi clan. At the time the camp was built, Cephu was not present, but most of the Cephu sub-band members occupied the southern part of *apa* Lelo together. With them were Kelemoké and Masalito (J and I), who were members of Cephu's own lineage, but who preferred to camp with the main camp, whereas Cephu usually made a sub-camp of his own.

When Cephu arrived, three days after the establishment of the main camp, he built a camp (Plan 8) of his own a short distance away, then connected it to the main camp by a narrow trail. The trail leading from the sub-camp to the village was closed after some protest, as it effectively offered a second point of entry to the main camp from the village, through Cephu's camp. In the same camp as Cephu (FF) were two others—his kinsman, Masalito's older brother Abeli (DD), and Njelu's older brother, Toko (BB), who moved from the main camp the moment Cephu arrived. For some reason, at this point, Njelu moved back to his old hut adjoining Betuli. It was only a few yards further from Cephu's camp, but it was a significant few yards. Njelu and Toko had married two patrilineal cousins, so Toko's wife was, like Pangia and Betuli, a member of the lineage that nor-mally associated with Cephu. Three days later, however, two more female kinsmen of Toko arrived, also members of the rival Puemi/chimpanzee lineage, and they too joined Cephu's camp. The two camps had effectively divided two sets of brothers, indicating much more sharply than the more subtle divisions within the main camp the extent to which lineage values may be counteracted and even superseded by other values.

In the following chapters we shall see more of the kind of petty disputes and hostilities that bring about this shifting of alliances, and the gradual fragmentation of a camp into distinct sections. It should suffice for the moment to have this one example of a single camp in a state of flux from the first day of its existence, and to know that this flux, whatever its cause, cut directly across unilineal descent group-ings as conceived by the villagers.

Apart from the personal, unpredictable causes for constantly chang-ing alliances, there are other factors that can always be relied on to introduce change into a camp, cutting across unilineal descent lines and causing further change in its balance. Visits from affines and to affines are one such factor; such visits sometimes become permanent, as can be seen in the composition of this particular band. Visits to neighboring villages may also affect the balance of its internal sec-tions as, apart from the major co-operative activity of the hunt, there are other activities calling for co-operation of only a few people, and such smaller co-operative units almost invariably fall within the sec-tions that divide the camp. If a section becomes depleted because some of its members have gone visiting, it may be forced to co-operate with another section in activities such as gathering, collecting fire-wood and building materials, repairing nets, and so forth.

Not having seen an archer *begbe* beat-hunt camp, which approxi-mates in size, as in hunting technique, to the normal net-hunting camp, I can supply no material for comparison of the process of frag-mentation. The smaller, and for the archers more normal, camps are similar, however, and exhibit the same tendencies but with less em-phasis. This may possibly be related to the fact that the smaller camps involve food-getting technologies that do not call for large-scale co-operation, but which demand the co-operation of two or three adults. Thus such divisions as may appear on the formation of such a camp tend to be rather more stable, and with the archers they are certainly

more related to the demands of economic co-operation than to any
other factor.

But however stable a camp may become after the initial fragmentation, that fragmentation is but an indication of the more systematic
processes of fission or fusion that come into play each time a camp
moves. Plan 11 gives the layouts of each camp built by the Epulu
band for a period of over a year, and the cyclic process is quite clear.
For the net-hunters a large camp is normally advantageous, although
beyond a certain point a net-hunt becomes unwieldy. But once a
year comes the honey season, when hunting is of secondary importance, and it is more advantageous for the band to be split into two
or more sub-camps, thus tapping the territory's honey resources
more effectively.

The series of camp plans shown indicates how the process of fragmentation as observed at work within *apa* Lelo is continued and
sharpened with the building of each new camp. Sites are even chosen
because they afford greater privacy between the various sections, thus
minimizing any serious disputes that are in progress. Some interpersonal hostilities will persist, however, and it is these and not lineal relationships that are reflected in the final fission, when the camp
divides into a number of independent camps, or sub-bands, each going
its own way. If the dispute is serious, one or another sub-band may
go off to another territory, and seek to join up with that band. This
was in fact Cephu's situation. During the honey season he left the
Epulu territory and went back to his home territory to claim his honey
trees. But that territory was occupied by a large band where Cephu's
hunting chances were no greater than those of anyone else, and this
was not to Cephu's liking. Cephu tried to carve out a territory for
himself, between his own band and the Epulu band, but he was always being forced by sheer economics to join the one or the other.
He could never induce enough men to camp with him to set up an
effective independent net-hunt. For this a minimum of seven is generally required, and Cephu could seldom raise above six.

So the monthly change of camp is an opportunity not only for a
diplomatic rearrangement of the layout, minimizing latent hostilities, but it is also an opportunity for improving the economic strength
of the band by either adding to it or subtracting from it.

The honey season itself is a last opportunity for old hostilities to
fade away, and the complete separation of the sub-bands into camps
many miles apart generally resolves most sources of friction. If dis-

agreement persists, however, then when the honey season ends and the band is forced to resume net-hunting, and therefore has to rejoin its forces in the common interest of an effective net-hunt, one or another of the dissident segments will join up with another band in another territory. It is said that it would not stay within the same territory and hunt there, even if it were numerically strong enough.

Thus we can say that the composition of each camp is ad hoc, responding to the needs of the moment rather than to any preconceived plan, or to any notion derived from tradition. The lines of division are never the same; the reasons for division are nearly always personal. The system does not lie here, then, but rather in the economy, which favors a unified camp for the major part of the year and a divided camp for a brief two months or so. The complete break and freedom of separate association allowed by the honey season (which is also a particularly bountiful season as far as vegetable foods are concerned) is, in fact, what makes practical this otherwise apparently unsystematic flux. That the flux has a function we shall shortly see.

For the archers much the same process pertains. The economics work in reverse, however, for the *begbe* season is made an occasion for the entire band to gather together. Normally, throughout the year, the band is divided into three or four small sub-bands, all within their common territory. Tracking and ambushing and using the bow and arrow do not call for co-operation among more than two or three or four men. A large camp of, say, twenty-four men would then have at least six hunting parties setting off each day, and this would necessarily mean frequent changes of camp. A small camp, however, sending out two parties in opposite directions, can remain in the same area for a long time without scaring the game away. There are few occasions for members of different sub-bands to get together during this time, except for casual visits. Once a year the whole band unites, however, for the communal beat-hunt known as *begbe*. The mechanism for convening the whole band and the exact time of year this takes place, if there is a special time of year, are not clear either in the literature or from my own records. Each archer band I visited, however, assured me that it was near the honey season, and I suspect before the honey season.

However, the essential remains the same. Among the archers, as among the net-hunters, there is a process of fission followed by fusion —or perhaps, in the case of the archers, it would be better to say there is a process of fusion followed by fission. We now have to try and discover, at least for the net-hunters of Epulu, what is the structure of this process.

We have seen that the band is plainly a nonlineal entity; it cannot even truly be called bilateral, as descent is not counted on either side for practical purposes.[6] Lineages are known, and these are always patrilineages, but they seem to have little economic, political or even religious significance. The only time the lineage is mentioned with any frequency is when discussing the merits or otherwise of a proposed marriage, and then it is not the lineage name that is usually mentioned, but rather the names and relationships of the individuals concerned, their parents and grandparents. It can be seen from the plans, in any case, that the process of fission and fusion under discussion is not one that supports the integrity of unilineal descent groups, but rather one that cuts across such groups.

Nor can the nonlineal nature of the band or the flux of band composition be attributed solely to the ecology. The situation is comparable between the archers and the net-hunters, and yet each of these groups practices a different hunting technique, and the process of fission and fusion takes an opposite direction. Either the archers or the net-hunters could, in fact, operate perfectly efficiently without all the internal movement that we have seen, and they may very well once have operated as patrilineal bands. While in no way supporting those who suggest that band composition is due to local ecology, it is undeniable that there is an interest in lineage, evident in the attempt to balance lineages and prevent lineage dominance. Further, the camp plans indicate a general tendency toward lineage solidarity, particularly in times of crisis. For instance, with reference to Plans 9 and 10, the normally unsystematic camp plan that pertained (9) was abruptly altered and became divided along strict lineage lines when one of the sub-band members, Cephu himself, committed the unforgivable crime of placing his net in front of others during the hunt. The only significant relationship of the flux to forest life is that it enables the band to respond to changes in environmental conditions by altering its size. It must also be admitted that it is

---

[6] Some misunderstanding may arise owing to different usages of descent-system terminology. Some schools of thought consider "bilateral" as synonymous with "cognatic," and hold that the terms include all affines and do not imply any differences in the method of tracing descent. To such an extent, perhaps the Mbuti band may be termed bilateral or cognatic, but to me, and I believe to others, both terms imply one kind of descent *system* or another, placing an emphasis on lineage that is not characteristic of the Mbuti band and therefore to be eschewed.

1. The village of Epulu, shady but constantly threatened by the encroachments of
the forest.

2. The village headman's *baraza*, used for receiving visitors and holding public discussions.

3. An abandoned village, overgrown in a few months.

4. Mbuti girl helps village woman pound manioc in shade of plantain tree.

5. Mbuti women and girls rest as they bring roofing leaves into village for village houses.

6. Mbuti men help villager build a new house, having cut and fetched the saplings for him.

7. Mbuti youths, in clothes provided by their *kpara*, are fed as part of their "payment."

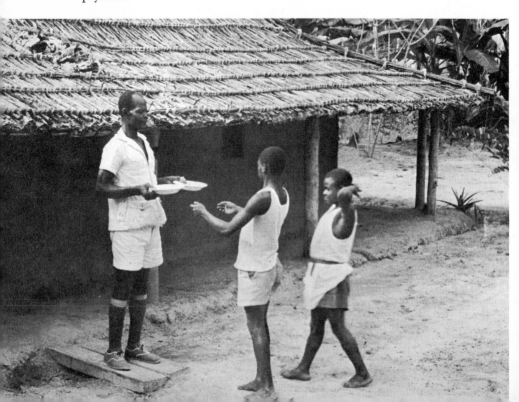

8. This village camp of the Mbuti at Epulu was built in imitation of the main village. It soon became fouled and was abandoned, succeeding village camps being built in the forest at the edge of the plantations.

9. The Mbuti village *baraza* was never completed, and remained marked only by four posts.

10. While in the village camp, an Mbuti mother borrows or steals many luxuries too bulky or heavy to carry with her into the forest. Of the mortar and pestle, stool, metal cooking vessels, enamel bowls and bottle of palm oil, she will probably return to the forest with only one vessel.

11. An Mbuti hunter amuses himself in the village by playing a village-made zither.

12. Mbuti women may take part in a hoop dance while in the village, but traditional forest songs and dances are forbidden outside the forest. Note the body decoration on the leg of the woman to the rear; the dye is obtained from the gardenia fruit.

13. A village wedding is arranged for the Mbuti hunter Makubasi. Here his bride, flanked by two sisters, stands in the middle of the village on banana-leaf cushions, fanned by her *kpara*'s sister. By arranging such marriages, the villagers hope to maintain some control over the Mbuti they believe they "inherit."

14. The *nkumbi* initiation is another means by which villagers attempt to control the Mbuti. The initial dance here, with the sacred *makata* sticks, is led by the traditional doctor, Sabani, at the village of Eboyo. Mbuti and villagers take part jointly in the festivities, but the Mbuti are excluded from all ritual roles.

15. Village women of Epulu dance to celebrate an approaching *nkumbi* during which only Mbuti boys will be initiated, owing to lack of village boys of the right age.

16. A boy, just circumcised, is comforted by an Mbuti hunter. This would be considered a lasting shame by either a village boy or an adult, but the Mbuti see no shame in acknowledging and healing pain.

important, for both net-hunters and archers, that a hunter should know well the habits of those who are near him on the hunt. Insofar as children learn to hunt mostly but by no means entirely from their fathers, it is obvious that brothers are likely to be most familiar with each other's hunting techniques, and will thus make the best hunting partners. But against this work many other practices, such as communal hunting games for all children, regardless of relationship, and the frequency of adoption, and of assimilation of adult strangers into the band.

If we cannot find any explanation for the flux and instability that seem characteristic of the band in terms of kinship or economy, or indeed in terms of any aspect of forest life, both become immediately meaningful in considering the relationship between the band and the village. Without going into this in detail at the moment, it must already be evident that the system, or lack of it, must be unhappily confusing for the patrilineal patrilocal villagers, who claim both lineal and territorial rights over Mbuti bands. For as we have seen, a band does not maintain any kind of unilineal integrity even within a single camp, let alone from one camp to the next. And owing to the wider flux, caused by the constant process of fission and fusion, the band has merely territorial reference and cannot be said to apply to specific individuals or lineages. A lineage such as Cephu's may be in the Epulu territory one month and in Ebiani the next. So with every lineage, as with every individual, there is an infinity of territories to which he may move if it pleases him, and the system, such as it is, encourages such movement to the point that no villager can ever be sure of what Mbuti lineages are hunting in "his" territory. Let us leave it for the moment, then, that at least one possible structural result of the combination of the nonlineal nature of the band and its tendency to flux is the counteraction of the village system, rendering the villagers' lineal and territorial claims impractical of assertion.

THE FAMILY

It would of course, be ridiculous to deny that there is any system of kinship, but it is certain that the kinship system does not have the same importance as a focal point of social control as it may in other African societies. To my mind this is undeniably linked to the ad hoc nature of the society, with its almost complete lack of concern for the past, as for the future. This is something we shall discover in

the economic and political life, and even in the religious life of the
Mbuti, who are supremely concerned with the present.

The effective kinship terminology at once reflects the situation,
which only becomes confused when any attempt is made to relate the
terms to their usage in village society. It distinguishes generations
rather than kin, and cuts indiscriminately across actual kinship boundaries. Through its effective organization of the band into age groups,
it emphasizes the economic basis of band unity rather than any kinship bonds. The only terms in general usage in the Epulu region, and
among the Mbuti bands to the east-west extremes of the Bira-speaking
net-hunting territory, are as follows:

Grandparent:	*tata*	for address and reference
Father:	*epa*	for address and reference
Mother:	*ema*	for address and reference
Sibling:	*apua'i* or *moko*	for address and reference

(*apua'i* is used rather than *moko*, though its connotation is one of
close friendship)

Child:	*miki*	for address or reference

Except at the parental level, there is generally no sex differentiation. At times it seems that *taté* is used for grandmother, *tata* for
grandfather. Similarly, *amua'i* is a possible variant to denote a female sibling. But as frequently, if not more so, and more consistently,
I found *tata* and *apua'i* used for either sex. Differentiation is also
made, if necessary, by adding the terms used for boy or girl—*moko* or
kali, respectively. Thus *miki a moko* is a boy child; *miki a kali* is a girl
child. There is also a way of distinguishing the younger from the
older: *vomia* is older, *motoa* is younger, but the Mbuti generally only
couple these designations to kinship terms in direct imitation of the
village usage and only in village contexts.

Bira terminology, with minor dialectal variations, is similar to the
above, but with the addition of terms such as *noko* for mother's
brother; *kola* for father's sister; *om-epa* and *mot-epa* for the older and
younger brother of the father; and *om-ema* and *mot-ema* for the older
and younger sister of the mother. The Bira call an older brother
homioné, an older sister *alwané*, and a younger brother or sister
simply *moto*. The Mbuti normally refer to their father's sister simply
as *ema* ("mother"), but if trying to refer to her for the benefit of

villagers, instead of using the appropriate village term, *kola*, they are apt to bring in the concept of relative age and specify *alwa'e na epa* or *moto e na epa*. For, not themselves distinguishing between cross and parallel relationships, the Mbuti see that the villagers refer to their mother's sisters according to their relative age (*om-ema* or *mot-ema*), and to the Mbuti this age differential is of recognizable significance.

In their own usage, however, their father's sisters and their mother's sisters are all equally *ema*, as are indeed any unrelated females who fall into that age group. So with other terms, for with the Mbuti age rather than kinship is the determining factor. I have known a man with a brother much younger than he refer to him as *miki*, and the younger brother refer to his older brother as *epa*. The older brother at that time was a married man and a great hunter; the younger brother was single and not yet a net-owner and not a great hunter. Their activities were therefore different, and each assumed the "kinship" term that included him in his appropriate economic age group.

There are appropriate corresponding structural differences between villagers and Mbuti; for instance, an orphaned child among the villagers is taken in by his father's brothers, with precedence being given to the older brother. Among the Mbuti a child may be adopted by any "father" or "mother," which effectively means anyone of the same age group as his biological parents. Generally a boy or girl goes to live with his mother and her natal family if his father dies, and stays with his father, living with one of his father's married brothers, if his mother dies. This is assuming that the marriage has been patrilocal; if it has been matrilocal, as it frequently is, the reverse applies. But in every case there is great freedom of choice, and each instance is decided according to the context of the moment.

It is plain, then, that the personal terminology of the Mbuti stresses their relative age and economic status rather than their kinship, and both for address and reference it is used mostly in economic contexts, personal names being most widely used in other contexts. The only time that biological kinship becomes an important factor in discussion is in connection with sex and marriage. Relationships are then spelled out and traced through the "stomachs" from which the individuals concerned are born. People who are related through the stomachs of their mother or of their father's mother may not marry or have extramarital sexual relationships. This is the one and only stated and observed rule of incest, and although genealogical memories are short, never rising further than two above ego, it is adequate in preventing the marriage of first cousins.[7] This seems to be about the limit of the intended restriction, as at this level flirtation, accompanied by sexual intercourse, may take place with only nominal disapproval. The disapproval becomes more loudly voiced if the young couple seem to be forming too strong an affection for each other, such as would normally lead to marriage.

There is some expressed disapproval, of about the same degree of seriousness, if children of the same social mother, but not of the same stomach, flirt with each other, but such flirtations happen.

I found it impossible to discover a single admitted instance of incest closer than between first cousins, but there is some evident restraint between brothers and sisters, none between mothers and sons, little between fathers and daughters. To swear at someone by accusing them of having sex with their parent is mild; it is more serious to accuse them of having sex with their sibling of one stomach. Worst of all is to accuse someone of having sex with her or his spouse. (The degree of freedom between sons and mothers may be seen in the fact that a mother gives strength to her children, if they are ill, by sleeping in the same bed with them. This is sometimes done between a mother and her adult son, so long as he is unmarried, without occasioning any comment.)

Together with this lack of emphasis on the biological aspects of kinship and the accompanying generational system of terminology goes a lack of formal restrictions on behavior between different kin categories, and a marked unwillingness to clearly define kin relationships between individuals. One suspects at times that the apparent shortness of genealogical memory is almost deliberate, for not only would such memory have no use, it would, in fact, undermine the whole delicate balance of social relationships among the Mbuti.

AGE GROUPS

Table 6 shows quite clearly the effective difference between the village system and the system of the Mbuti, granting that they both share the same terminology. The fact that among the Mbuti all mem-

7 It is often stated generally that one marries nobody related through either the father's or the mother's line, but in special situations the restriction is narrowed down as given here.

bers of each age level may be *apua'i* to each other doubly underlines
the importance of this age grouping as a structural principle of their
society, because it not only effectively allies members of the same
age group, but it cuts across any unilineal descent pattern. Even
though, if pressed, any one *apua'i* can and will trace his relationship
to almost any other, through either cognatic or affinal lines, among
themselves this is never done. The functions of the age group, also,
have little to do with kinship.

The age group forms the next unit above the nuclear family, each
having its own functions and its own sphere of authority. Above the
age group one might consider the band to be divided into alliances
of age groups, though their function would be less easy to define.
However, such alliances do take place, generally in major disputes,
where youths and children might ally against hunters and elders. Char-
acteristically, disputes concerning premarital sexual activity, betrothal
and *bopi* (playground) activity are the major occasions for such alliances. But the same element may be seen at work during the religious *molimo* festival, where the group of adult men that sing around
a fire at night may divide the hearth into two or three fires. The unmarried youths nearly always have one fire for themselves around
which they dance their erotic dances; the hunters (the younger married men) may have a fire of their own, or they may join the *mangesé*,
the elders, men who are no longer as active in the hunt as they used
to be.

Young married couples are held responsible for reproduction, but
only to a limited extent for the rearing and education of their children, for beyond the age of three or four a child becomes the responsibility of the band as a whole. As an economic unit the family is
divided into the appropriate age groups as a co-operative part of the
total band. Effectively much of its economic activity is directly for its
own individual benefit, but there is nearly always some sharing even
when there is no necessity for sharing, to emphasize the communal
rights to forest produce. As a political unit the family only has internal jurisdiction of the most minimal kind. The punishment of a
wife or a child, or the complaint of a child about its parents, quickly
becomes a matter for communal discussion. As a religious unit the
family is of little significance indeed. But every nuclear family is expected to participate in religious festivals, as symbolized when the
molimo hearth is made up by taking embers from every family hearth,
and when a camp is moved each family carefully takes an ember from

its own hearth to kindle its own fire in the new camp. The responsibility of members of a nuclear family in times of crisis, such as birth, puberty, marriage and death, does not differ much from the responsibility of the band as a whole, the difference being one of degree or intensity.

The age group functions as a major institution of education, instructing the group junior to it in its ways, preparing it for advance to the next, their own, level. Thus the care and education of children rests largely with youths and the oldest of the elders. Youths and hunters depend on each other in the joint hunting and gathering activities, the youths learning from their mothers and fathers all they will soon need to know as hunters themselves. Hunters gradually associate more and more with the *mangesé* (literally, "the great ones") around the evening fires, to listen to the talk of the elders and, in time, to participate.

As an economic unit the age group is of supreme importance. Children scavenge and help supply their own needs through fishing, trapping, snaring and any other forms of collecting or hunting within their means. In this they may at times be helped by the youths. The youths are of vital importance to the hunt, the girls acting as beaters with their mothers, and also collecting, while the boys stand guard at the extremities of the circle of nets, having assisted in setting up the nets. Youths may also be expected to perform a number of chores such as fetching wood and water into the camp. The hunters are the prime unit responsible for the sustenance of the band; the *mangesé* are absolved from such responsibilities and may expect to be fed, housed and clothed by the younger age groups.

Politically each age group has informal jurisdiction over its members, utilizing ridicule and ostracism, sometimes driving a member to seek acceptance in the lower age level, or justification by the upper. For a lower age level to ridicule or ostracize a member of a higher level is a supreme condemnation and a most powerful sanction. Further, it will be seen that part of the *molimo* festival is a morning tour of the camp by the youths, carrying the *molimo* trumpet and disguised by leaves and branches, at which time they single out the hut of any troublemaker, however young or old, and threaten to tear it to pieces. Even if there is no such troublemaker, the youths will go from hut to hut stripping a few leaves off the roof of each, causing other minor damage, simply representing the accepted principle of authority, of law and order.

Youths also have considerable say in the settling of any dispute concerning betrothal, though ultimately it is the *mangesé* who decide such matters. The hunters control all activities concerning the hunt and the movement of camp. The *mangesé* act as general arbiters and are effectively a court of final appeal, their age entitling them to unquestioning respect. Particularly in matters concerning betrothal are the *mangesé* consulted, for their genealogical memory can be stretched to suit the occasion. And in the *molimo* festival, as in the *elima,* they share the honors with the youths: the hunters have to do most of the work, supplying the food and cooking it for the nightly or daily feasting, but the singing and dancing, which are central to the festivals, are led by the *mangesé* and the youths.

In matters concerning relationship with other bands, the band as a whole, rather than any age group or association of age groups, decides the issue. On such occasions even children will sit by and take part.

We have already mentioned some of the religious functions of the age groups, in association with their political functions, and it will be seen that the two are closely interconnected. It might just be pointed out here that in a *molimo* festival held for the death of an Mbuti, age-group and band membership take precedence over family membership. The youths will lead the dancing, and the leading youth will lead because he is the best dancer, not because he is related to the dead person. Similarly with the singing led by the *mangesé.* The *molimo* horn may be supplied by anyone. The person who sings into it is generally a youth, though sometimes a young hunter, again regardless of kinship but on account of his renown and ability as a singer.

Considering the very clear roles of the age groups, and their comprehensive nature, it is plain that any unilineal system of descent would be highly disruptive. The loose laws of marriage and adoption, which are permissive rather than prescriptive, preferential or prohibitive, and the nonlineal nature of band composition allow for the flexibility that is obviously necessary to maintain the proper balance of recruitment into each age group.

Although a bilateral recognition of descent does exist and is sometimes utilized to provide the necessary balance of power, it can still hardly be dignified by the term "lineage system." Owing to the nonlineal, territorial nature of band composition, and the frequency of sister exchange, nuclear families may divide or remain united, regardless of lineage, depending upon the context. Affinal ties are considered just as legitimate, and used just as frequently in balancing power and in determining allegiance as cognatic ties. In this way security is guaranteed to any individual because of the number of recognized social groups to which he can claim membership. This ambivalence is again an important structural principle, and is certainly manifest in the social groupings observable in the building of successive hunting camps.

If age rather than kinship fixes one's place within the band, then, we have to consider how a band maintains any sense of continuity from one generation to the next. There is the alliance of age groups and the educational role of age groups which provide some degree of continuity, but this would not be sufficient in view of what we have said about the shifting composition of the band. It is undoubtedly territory that gives the band its identity as such and enables that identity to persist, and it is to his territory, as to his age group, rather than to any kin group, that an Mbuti owes allegiance.

Kinship is recognized in assessing problems of inheritance, but with so little to inherit the problems are minimal. In general a man's belongings are divided among his sons or, if his sons are too young, they are held in trust for them by his brothers. Similarly with a woman's belongings. Kinship may also be used to maintain an economic balance, just as it may be used to maintain a political balance, by advancing claims to the spoils of a hunt on the ground of kinship, or indeed by advancing claims for the adoption of children. But again, as such claims are advanced on grounds of both cognatic and affinal ties, the principles of unilineal descent are directly contradicted.

In fact the nuclear family is best regarded as one of a number of cells that make up the totality of the band, each cell reflecting the same basic structure as the band itself. Within the family the factors of territory and age also play a part, the locality of the hut symbolizing the unity of the family and its separateness from others, the age differential dividing the family in activity, authority and allegiance. Even fission and fusion are a part of family life, as children are apt to leave their natal family any time after they reach the age of three or four, and either be adopted by or simply live for a while with another family in the same band; or they may be adopted by a family in another band and go to live there, even if their parents continue living together in their home band. Such separations within the band do not affect their relationship with other members of their family of the same age group, and on maturity and marriage the old nuclear family sometimes reaffirms itself as an extended family. The old parents may build a separate hut adjoining the huts of their married children, or even live in the hut of one of their offspring, who will probably build an extension for the purpose. But during adolescence children may well be separated from their biological parents by both time and space. Similarly in adulthood there is not infrequently friction between brothers, sometimes leading to fission within the band.

Finally, in connection with the importance of age as a structural principle, it should be pointed out that the lack of a unilineal system of descent among the Mbuti is associated with a lack of any developed form of ancestor worship. Practices associated with death will be dealt with more fully later; here it need only be said that far from remembering the dead by word or action, the main objective seems to be to forget them. They may never be referred to again, particularly by name, and there is no memorial maintained in their honor, no marked or tended grave site. However, they are by the same token not feared, and insofar as they are remembered at all they are remembered with affection. The concern of the Mbuti is almost exclusively with the present. This is not to say that they deny a past or a future, either in this life or the next; it is merely to say that they believe that by a correct fulfillment of the present, the past and the future will take care of themselves. This correlates with the age-group system and with the dominance and prestige of the two middle groups, the youths and the hunters, for in their hands lies the fulfillment of the present.

CHAPTER 9

The Life Cycle

DAILY LIFE

The life of the nuclear family is so closely interwoven with that of the band that it is not always easy or possible to separate which activities and occasions are the concern of which. The difference is only one of degree, for even the most insignificant and routine action in the daily life of the family is potentially of major concern to the band as a whole. Thus a man seeking to borrow his brother's pipe may provide the occasion for a petty jealousy to flare up and divide the brothers, if not the camp (this case is quoted in full in the section on Government). In fact, in a society where there is no formal legal institution for the redress of wrongs, individuals resort to self-help and forcibly bring their case to public attention by deliberately provoking an incident. It is important then that there should be a pattern of behavior that is generally accepted, and which covers every conceivable activity so that there may be some direction and constancy in the ensuing discussion. The degree of "general acceptance" is of course not of such rigidity as to preclude the flexibility necessary for the pursuit of justice. But beneath the evident ambivalence there is a recognizable pattern of things that should or should not be done. This pattern is sometimes most plain in matters that seem most trivial, such as the insistence that embers that fall from the fire should not simply be scooped or pushed back, but should be picked up and placed on top of the fire; the feeling that anyone passing through a stream should wash himself, or at least a part of himself, even if he crossed another turn of the same stream a few yards back. If anyone is silent and untalkative, this is considered unusual and unfortunate. If one trips up accidentally, or stumbles even while crossing the camp, without harming anyone or anything, there is a distinct air of reproach among the onlookers. Such patterns of generally accepted behavior are contradicted every day without necessarily causing any mention, but in the event of anything more serious happening later, the earlier incidents will be recalled and made into an issue that successfully embroils, ultimately, the entire camp.

But more curious than this slight emphasis on normal, or mildly abnormal and trivial patterns is the lack of emphasis at times where one would have thought the occasion to be of major concern to the band. Birth and marriage, for instance, provoke little comment, and concern primarily the nuclear families and not the band. The relationship between these particular attitudes and the nonlineal and fluid composition of the band is plain. The constant movement of families from one band to another, alone, opens up different and important avenues for recruitment that has the advantage of being selective.

With this in mind, let us look first at the daily life of the Mbuti, briefly, for it is of little structural significance, then at the life cycle.

Among both net-hunters and archers five days out of seven are likely to include some hunting. Even though it would be possible for the Mbuti to kill a surplus of game and dry the meat and store it for their own future use, as indeed they do for the benefit of the villagers, such measures are no more to their taste than to their advantage. On a hunting day the family rises at dawn, the mother and her older daughters who are at the age of puberty go to the stream to wash themselves and bring back water for drinking and cooking. The menfolk go to a different part of the stream, and generally slightly later. The older men might be excessively lazy and use the water brought back for drinking as bath water.

While the women cook the light morning meal and set food aside for taking with them on the hunt, the men shake out and inspect their nets, bows and arrows, their sons helping them or simply looking on. If the forest is dry, the hunt may start leaving within an hour of dawn, otherwise it may not leave until midday. Usually it sets off about two hours after sunrise and may return anytime between midday and dusk. There is no particular order for leaving the camp, but the youths usually go ahead, and not far away they light a fire at the base of a small tree, as an invocation to the forest for a good hunt. Men and women alike stop by the fire on their way, but with no ceremony. It does serve, however, as a place for a more cordial exchange of greetings than generally takes place in the still sleepy camp.

Back in the camp some old grandparents, or maybe only a handful of youths, will be left in charge of the camp and of any children that elect to stay behind. Any child old enough to make the decision does so himself. If his parents do not want to be bothered with him he has a wide range of classificatory mothers and fathers to call on, or if he is old enough he will simply join his own age group and set off with them. Girls always go with the women; boys go with their fathers, youths may go with their fathers or on their own. If a father has a particularly long net he may welcome an extra spear or bow and arrow nearby, and his adolescent sons serve in this capacity.

The hunt is described more fully in Chapter Ten. Here it is only necessary to point out that among the net-hunters, where a net is owned by married men or by extremely rare, gifted bachelor hunters (youths), the hunt effectively divides itself into nuclear family groups but not into nuclear families, for each family, during the hunt, is itself divided by age and sex. The family-owned nets stretch out in a long semicircle, end to end, and the women act as beaters, forming a corresponding semicircle opposite. But each net is utterly dependent on the others, as is each beater, and it is the co-operative aspect of the age group that is emphasized, rather than the distinctness of each family. The division of spoils similarly stresses band rather than family values, and the hunting songs and dances that take place after, and sometimes before, the hunt further illustrate that the hunt is considered an affair of the band as a whole.

When the hunt returns to camp there is immediate excitement as those who stayed behind crowd around for tales of all that happened, and maybe for a few tidbits of raw meat. In the confusion, men and women alike, but particularly women, may be seen furtively concealing some of their spoils under the leaves of their roofs, or in empty pots nearby. For although there will have been some sharing on the scene, there is always more back in the camp, and family loyalty is not that subject to band loyalty that there is no cheating.

The food is prepared and cooked right away, and while this is being done a hunting dance may take place, in which men and women and children all take part. This dance is frequently imitative of hunting activities, with older people taking the part of the animals hunted. Any unusual event of the day's hunt may be reenacted, and this is also an occasion where the sanction of ridicule may be applied to any hunter, male or female, who is considered to have been unsatisfactory. It is not uncommon for a husband to lead a dance ridiculing a wife who, through her laziness as a beater, spoiled his chances.

Women are equally quick to ridicule the menfolk when there is justification.

This is also a time favored by youths for slipping off into the forest with their girl friends for some not very quiet lovemaking. Although lovemaking is not performed openly, no great attempt is made to conceal it. The general feeling is that if surprised in the act, one simply says hello (*karibu*) politely and expects the intruder to continue on his way. Fathers, and mothers too, refer to the nuisance of a flirtatious son or daughter whom they might surprise in this way. The parent pretends to see nothing in such a case, and the youths claim, with more bravado than truth perhaps, not to be unduly disturbed unless they are making love to a relative.

Lovemaking generally takes place in the forest, though there is no fixed rule. It is thought somewhat exciting to make love in a hut, but not very healthy. There are preferences that individuals have for making love near a stream, or in a splash of sunlight, or in the dark depths of the forest. It is evidently a purely aesthetic consideration, and I have heard a number of youths who stated that the best time was while hunting. But moonlight evidently attracts a great number, and I have met several who talk, with great poetry, of the joys of masturbation when alone in the moonlight. On three rare occasions I have seen different individuals dancing, by themselves, in the moonlight and in the forest, away from the camp. The intimacy between the individual and the forest—one might almost say the act of making love to the forest—was expressed by one Mbuti who said, when I questioned him as to why he was dancing alone, that he was dancing with the forest, dancing with the moon. He then continued his dance with the utmost unconcern.

Not all lovemaking is quite so romantic, however, and when boys and girls are following a trail together, the procession may degenerate into a good-humored but undeniably lusty orgy. A boy may rip off a girl's outer bark cloth, if he can catch her, but he may never have intercourse with her without her permission. I know of no cases of rape, though boys often talk about their intentions of forcing reluctant maidens to their will.

There are no formal bachelor huts, but many camps have informal variants. They are sometimes built for an older youth by his mother, or they may be taken over by adolescent boys or girls when the occupant leaves for some reason. In such huts, and even out in the open, around the campfire, it is usual to see not only youths but also married men sleeping together. The two age groups do not mix, but among themselves members of the same sex think nothing of sleeping close to each other and deriving mild sexual satisfaction from the physical contact. They state very carefully rules as to how to lie, with legs thrown backwards around the other's legs, or even around his hips or waist, and they say one may entwine legs while lying front to front, though it is not considered good to hold each other too closely with the arms. The thought of any sexual intercourse taking place, however, is greeted with apparent horror, and homosexuality is never alluded to except as a great insult, under the most dire provocation. There is, however, a dance in which the sexes are effectively reversed, and which is danced with the utmost humor, but the role of which I could never exactly determine. The dance, *ekokomea*, is dealt with later in the context in which it occurs; namely, at the time of the *molimo* festival.

If a considerable amount of sexual liberty is allowed the youths, a fair amount is at least said to be taken by the younger married hunters. I have not, however, been able to record a single instance of a marital dispute involving the band that arose out of infidelity on either side. There are few restrictions on sexual intercourse, though the villagers state many on behalf of the Mbuti. The married hunters, as do the youths, regard the hunt as an opportune time for activity of this kind. At menstruation, which is a time when a village woman is under the strictest ritual prohibitions, the Mbuti attitude is that it all depends on whether or not you want children, as this is when conception is most likely to take place. There are those who enjoy sex at this time, and those who find it distasteful. The only restriction is that a wife should inform her husband, or a girl her boy friend, that she is "with blood" so that he will know.

Immediately following childbirth is a rather vague period, sometimes stated as days, sometimes more grandiosely as years, when intercourse is forbidden. Unfortunately I was able to follow up only on three instances of childbirth, but in each of these the Mbuti fathers did exactly what they said they would do; two of them refrained from intercourse with their wives for about a year, during which time they flirted with as many girls as they liked, and did not deny open gossip that they were "sleeping around." This is the generally accepted pattern, the reason being given that a woman can only feed one child at a time, so she must not become pregnant again until her last child is weaned. This may be from one to three years. If during that time her milk dries up and the child is given to someone else to feed, or if it is weaned early, then intercourse is apparently resumed. The third father, however, while acknowledging this to be the accepted pattern, began sleeping with his wife again within a month. This he did even though he had the rare advantage for an Mbuti of having two other wives. His action caused a major dispute. (See p. 207 seq.)

During pregnancy there are no restrictions; sexual activity in early pregnancy is believed to hurry matters along, and during the latter stages is merely considered uncomfortable, and possibly physically injurious to the child and mother.

As the evening settles in, nuclear families sit around their family hearths outside the huts, talking across the camp at each other until they go inside to sleep, or simply lie down to sleep by the fire (the women nearly always sleep inside, but youths and men frequently sleep on their hunting nets either by their own fire or by a central fire). Even when families have retired inside their huts, conversation continues between them. If there is any singing, other than of lullabies, the camp divides into age groups, each building its own fire. Unless there is an *elima* or *molimo* festival, there is no marked division between the sexes.

On retiring for the night family hearths are brought inside the huts, and any central fires are also brought inside unless someone is sleeping by them. When a central fire is broken up, each family tends to take an ember and add it to their own hearth. A fire is not left untended at night. During the night a man may awaken and stoke up a fire, warming himself by the blaze. At such times, when cold, the Mbuti smoke particularly heavily, and as a result they sometimes fall unconscious. They may fall into the fire and suffer serious burns, occasionally fatal, and this is one of the few generally cited causes of accidental death—other than falling from a tree.

On days when the hunt stays in the camp, because of rain or because some dispute has caused a rift, both men and women attend to specific chores. Men repair and add to their nets and make new bows and arrows; the women roll twine and work at basketry. Both may make and decorate bark cloth, a major activity on such a day. A good part of the day is always given to singing, dancing, playing games and storytelling. There is a constant shifting from family groupings to age groupings, but mealtime is the only time when there is a definite emphasis on the nuclear family. Even then, male youths, hunters and elders may take their food to a central fire and eat there with their fellows. There is no set mealtime, and any one person eating alone is likely to attract his friends, who will expect to share his food. Only if a family is eating together by their hearth will they be undisturbed.

Infants are allowed to crawl all over the camp, and will be picked up and fondled by anyone, and even fed, if old enough. If they get in the way, or crawl into a fire, they are picked up roughly by an arm or a leg, slapped hard and brought back to their mother's hut. Even at this age their education begins, a concentrated effort being made to teach them erotic dancing before they can properly walk.

Children have a *bopi* (playground) of their own, separated from the camp by a short trail. It is frequently by a stream in which the youngsters can splash and swim. If they make too much noise, however, they are severely criticized, and it is not thought good for them to spend too much time in the water. They have a number of games that are mainly for amusement, such as spinning tops, swinging on vines, and climbing on trees until they bend to the ground, then jumping off. But even these games teach quickness of reaction and body control. Other games are more strictly imitative of adult activities, and are a primary means of educating the children. They may be played alone or with the help of youths or elders, occasionally of the hunters. Generally, however, parents fondle their children rather than play with them.

From the time they can walk both girls and boys play "house." They wander off from the camp, though never out of earshot, collect the necessary saplings and leaves, and return making the pretense of carrying a heavy load. The girl then goes through the motions of preparing the leaves and sharpening the ends of the saplings while the boy, with a tiny bow and arrow, goes off hunting. While his "wife," as he calls her, sticks the saplings in the ground and makes a rather crude imitation of a hut frame, then covering it with the leaves, the "husband" is busy catching some kind of food—either a rat, if he is skillful enough with his bow, or else some slow game such as snails and grubs. If he is unsuccessful the two may go off together and, unlike adults, fish. If this is unsuccessful the boy will say he is going to "the village" and that they will "eat the villagers." He then creeps into the camp and steals a morsel of village food, a banana or manioc root, from wherever he can find it. The food is cooked and eaten together, and the young couple lie down together and pretend to make love.

Another important imitative game is the hunt, in which a youth or an elder pretends to be an antelope, sometimes with another pretending to be a leopard. An old piece of a real hunting net is used, and once again every action is gone through in almost exact imitation of a real hunt. The antelope and the leopard move erratically and unexpectedly to test the reactions of the children, and any child who fails to react properly is laughed out of the game. The game continues up to the ensnarement of the antelope in the net, then abruptly ends and starts again. Different localities in or around the camp are chosen for these mock hunts, to show the necessity for varying the hunting technique. If any Mbuti are keeping chickens for the villagers (this is often done when a camp is near a village, as the villagers have reasons for wishing to conceal their wealth), the chickens often become the quarry.

Girls imitate their mothers by carrying a stick of rough wood as a baby, perhaps in a tiny hide sling. Any girls large enough to carry a real baby do so. They make miniature carrying baskets and go off with other girls on gathering expeditions, always returning with some real food either found in the forest or begged or stolen from the camp. With their hunting and fishing activities as well as this gathering, the children make a small contribution to the food economy even at this age. They also learn not only to rely on their fellow age mates for help in food-getting activities, but to share with them. The sharing is largely left to the girl's decision.

The boys also learn to live and work with their fellows of different families rather than with their nuclear family, and will often be far more intimate with an unrelated boy of the same age than with a brother much older or younger. They play many games that develop quickness of eye and co-ordination of the body, such as the spear practice, where one boy stands in the middle with a large forest fruit at the end of a six foot vine which he swings around him, trailing the fruit about twelve inches above the ground. The other boys stand in a circle around him, their fire-hardened spears poised. As the fruit passes them they throw their spears at it. If they miss they have to dash in to retrieve their spears while the fruit continues to swing around, and other spears continue to be thrown. If a spear hits its mark and holds firm, the boy in the center tries to dislodge it by bouncing the fruit on the ground as he swings it around. This is an additional hazard for the others, as the spear may come flying out at them. Youths join the older children at this game, but never in a supervisory capacity.

Youths may also join the children on their swings in the *bopi*, and will almost certainly build their swings for them, climbing high up into adjacent trees to drape a long liana between them. They then teach the younger children the wild somersaulting games on these swings that are particularly characteristic of the honey season. On the other side the youths equally often join the hunters but, again, always as a separate group, sometimes participating fully, but still as youths. And as youths they continue the process already begun in childhood, of growing more away from their nuclear families and together as an age group. Their hunting and scavenging abilities are greater, and they sometimes even maintain a self-sufficient food economy. As youths they are allowed to stay up at night, instead of retiring with their mothers, and they build their own fire near the hunters' fire and cook their own food and sing and dance, sometimes with the hunters and elders, sometimes separately.

As youths they are also given increasing responsibility, especially in the economic life of the band. They may listen to the discussions of the hunters and elders, but even if they make comments, as they do, they are not readily listened to unless it is a matter pertaining to their age group. Then they are required to be able to voice their opinions and cite precedents. They are expected to show an adult sense of responsibility in matters concerning sex and marriage, and although they may flirt quite openly and even audaciously, they never "play house," and not until after the *elima* will a girl again show her favor by cooking for a boy. Then it is tantamount to an admission of betrothal.

After marriage a boy acquires a net. It may be made for him by his mother, or his father may give him part of his net to which he will add, with his wife's help. He has already demonstrated his hunting prowess or he would not be married, but now he is a full hunter with additional responsibilities. Whereas economic activity is shared between the hunters and youths, it is the hunters who ultimately make the decisions concerning camp life, and about the hunt. Where to go for the daily hunt, when to move camp, to what region, how to deal with threats of physical danger, and how to surmount physical problems; such are the questions the hunter has to face. They all concern the band as a whole. Nonphysical dangers and problems—that is to say, moral, psychological and spiritual issues, those that affect the nuclear family often before the band—these are more the concern of the elders. As we are here considering the normal run of daily life we are leaving aside special occasions such as the *elima* and *molimo* festivals, which are primarily religious in nature, but in which the hunters and youths play their own distinct parts together with the elders.

The hunters are generally in the middle of any dispute that occurs, but in a serious dispute it is more likely to be an elder that will be able to effect a settlement. It is, however, the disputes of the hunters that establish the lines along which fission and fusion will take place, and the elders have little influence over this process, nor do they even seem to wish to influence it. They content themselves by using the respect that is accorded them to maintain some kind of balance between the band factions. It is the hunters who initiate both fission and fusion, and who are thus responsible for the composition of the band. Relationships with neighboring bands and with the villagers, insofar as they are determined by band movement, are also largely in their hands, and in this sense the hunters may be considered the political leaders of the band. In this the women are almost, if not fully, the equals of the men.

The hunter's life is the most active and arduous, and this may in part be responsible for his somewhat disputatious nature. In elderhood there is a chance to relax. There is no shame in an elder having his children bring him back food, and in any case he may be needed to keep an eye on the camp while the hunt is away. It is an age group to which a man or a woman resigns himself with some reluctance, but in which he soon finds considerable satisfaction. He is able to intervene in disputes without fear of physical violence, for one thing, and often does so with enjoyment. The elder is undoubtedly the arbiter, though by no means the only source of solution. From his position of immunity he is able to interfere in the most private and domestic affairs of anyone. Whereas a hunter solves his problems empirically, answering facts with facts, the elder solves those that face him with considered opinion, drawing from a lifetime of experience. A hunter would be laughed at if he could not support an opinion with fact. An elder is never expected to do so, and is consequently admirably fitted to deal with moral and spiritual matters. It is, however, opinion that he offers, not judgment. He will concern himself in questions of the upbringing of children, of their puberty and of their marriage. At any time of major crisis the elder will play the resolving part, though the hunter may initiate the action. Thus the *elima* and the *molimo*, which are crisis festivals, are initiated by the hunters, but it is the elders who control them and give them their spiritual quality. It is the elders who act not only as arbiters between the members of the band, but between the band and the forest, between this life and the next. Even in the most ordinary run of everyday life there is seldom a day that does not demand from one elder or another, man or woman, some opinion that will be couched in terms like "such and such is good for (or pleasing to) the forest," or "this makes my spirit (*roho*) feel good."

The greatest departures from daily life occur when the band visits the village, or when a villager visits the band. In either case it is as though the whole social structure of the Mbuti were suddenly changed. A single individual becomes, all at once, a chief. Age groups break up and nuclear families come to the fore. The only central fire will be that of the "chief." But as this is not part of the forest world, exceptions occur within the forest context only rarely. There is seldom any disaster such as the invasion of a camp by elephant, though it happens sometimes. Hunting is generally more than adequate throughout the year. But though hunger does sometimes come to the Mbuti, starvation is unknown. Sickness is not uncommon, but is rarely serious. Throughout the year daily life goes its usual way interrupted only by major, inevitable crises of the life cycle.

BIRTH

Birth is the first crisis of life, and among the Mbuti it is, as elsewhere, not without its attendant dangers. Though no statistics are available, it is the opinion of villagers and Mbuti, and of many Europeans, doctors and otherwise, who know both communities, that infant mortality is appreciably less among the Mbuti, and sterility less common. This may be due to the fact that their relative isolation has defended the Mbuti against the venereal diseases widespread among the villagers. Be that as it may, there is no doubt that the Mbuti evidently feel less need for concern at childbirth. This applies to both the nuclear family and to the band. There is absolutely no formal recognition on the part of the band, and only the barest of interest. Considering the fluid and nonlineal composition of the band this is not surprising, particularly since, for this type of band, birth is only one form of recruitment, and by no means the most sure or effective. The only indication of band interest in birth is the prohibition against married women procuring abortions, which are known and sometimes practiced among the unmarried girls, though rarely.

As far as the nuclear family is concerned the event arouses considerable happiness, and the mother's female age mates may gather with her to sing a few *elima* songs to celebrate the blessing of motherhood; a childless woman is regarded as the most unfortunate of beings. A few of the younger youths may show some interest, as the new child will before long become their responsibility for protection and instruction. After a few days, when the child is brought freely into the open, the hunters and elders will fondle it and compliment the parents. The father is as proud as the mother, and just as likely to carry the child around to show it off.

Medical precautions are minimal. The mother is likely to be off on the hunt, or on the trail somewhere when birth takes place; there is no lessening of activity for her during pregnancy. Childbirth is said to be effected easily, with complications only rarely happening. Any woman may act as midwife; the father should not be present. If there is delay the expectant mother may be massaged to help delivery, or she may be brought away from the camp into the forest, and sat close to a tree against which she pulls with a vine rope. Within two hours of delivery, if birth took place in the camp, the mother is apt to appear in the doorway of her hut, with a bundle wrapped in bark cloth held in her arms. Within the same period of time, if birth took place on the trail, she will continue her journey.

Although the father is not present at the birth in person, it must be one of his arrow blades, or formerly a wooden or leaf knife made by him, that will cut the umbilical cord. The blade is kept with the cord until the child is old enough to make a bundle of them both, take them to a stream and bury them where they will get carried away by the next flood waters.

There is also knowledge of a custom of couvade, though I did not find anyone who had practiced it. If the birth is slow, the father takes off all his clothes and his sister-in-law washes and rubs him. She then goes to the place of labor, and when the child is born returns to the father, who must make a token gift before he can clothe himself again.

The father, and the mother's brother, if he is in the camp, cut special vines daily and sprinkle their juices over both the baby and the mother, "to make them strong." Some of these vines contain so much juice that when cut they have to be bent, with both ends upward so that the liquid will not be lost. Sometimes they are cut into chunks and soaked in water that is used for washing the infant.

A third precaution that is taken is to tie a vine bracelet around one of the infant's wrists, or around his waist. A small piece of wood may be roughly threaded to the vine, and the stated function is again to give the infant strength, except that with specific reference to the wood, it is frequently said that it "gives the child the strength of the forest."

With regard to preferences among the women as to where they give birth, it varies. But there is unanimity that if there is any difficulty at all, then the right thing to do is to go off away from the camp and into the forest, which will "help." The forest appears quite clearly as helper and protector in the vine and wooden medicines and charms, and in the scarification that will take place at the first sign of sickness. Even with adults this is done: the skin is cut in a number of small slits with an arrow, and some of the flesh is gouged out. The ashes prepared from forest woods and plants are made into a paste with spittle and rubbed into the wounds. When the skin grows back, the black ash is still visible beneath, and is regarded as a source of the strength and health and happiness that derive from the forest.

Both parents are under food restrictions until the baby is old enough to crawl, the main one and the only general one being that they must not eat meat. The father may go hunting, but any meat that falls into his net is divided among the others. More often he stays away from the hunt, sending his net out with some youth. However, somewhere between one and two months after birth, and when the family net has made a particularly successful catch, the father will usually announce that he is eating meat again.

The only other restriction placed on the nuclear family by the crisis of birth is the restraint placed on the father, who is forbidden to have sexual intercourse with the mother as long as she is breast-feeding the child. The restriction is quite definitely linked by the Mbuti to the supply of milk, which is also given as the reason for their rather mild aversion to twins. I know of no record of twins who both survived into adulthood, and it is stated that one of them invariably dies. It is also stated that no woman would feed a child at each breast, and I understand that if twins are born, one is simply not fed by the mother, and is taken away and buried by her friends. But there is no fear of twins, and no ritual in connection with their birth or death.

Finally it may be remarked that whereas in many African societies, including those of the neighboring villagers, birth fixes the social position of an individual through the structural ramifications of kinship, among the Mbuti it achieves the same end, to a less fixed degree, by placing the individual in a specific age group and relating the infant to a specific locality. The child might not be reared in that locality, but the fact will remain valid as a claim to band membership throughout his or her life. Adoption is often agreed upon in order that a child, or even an adult, may return to his natal band, regardless of what kin remain to him there.[1]

It will also be noticed that in the absence of the magical and supernatural protections that are sought for a newly born child among the villagers nearby, there is a lack of concern with the possibility of disaster, and only a concern that the child should be strong. Insofar as this strength is conveyed by washing the baby with the juice of forest vines, tattooing it with forest ashes, and binding it with forest symbols, this may be regarded as sympathetic magic. But it is better regarded as the beginning of a lifetime of close intimacy between the Mbuti and the forest, an intimacy that may or may not give the physical strength it is believed to convey, but that is undoubtedly responsible for the cohesive social strength found in this one omnipresent, omnipotent symbol of Mbuti unity, the forest.

The absence of formal ritual protection and of the invocation of supernatural aid and attention at birth is the first clear indication that for the Mbuti the norm is the good, and that this goodness derives directly from the forest, physically and spiritually. Although birth is primarily the affair of the nuclear family, all members of the band share the pleasure and the pride of the parents, concern themselves with the welfare and education of the child according to the functions of the different age groups, but they do not see that it is necessary to make of birth what we might here call a "spiritual" occasion. In referring to childbirth the men and women alike say, simply, that "it is the work of women, it is what they are for." There is nothing abnormal about the event, nor is there any expectancy of danger or complication, and so the band does not see that it is necessary to intervene with a formal religious festival.

[1] See Table 11 for examples of adoptions of boys and girls among net-hunters.

PUBERTY: THE *ELIMA*

At the next crisis in the life cycle, however, it is the band rather than the nuclear family that takes charge. By early childhood the child has already grown away from its family to some extent, and become more a member of an age group cutting across kinship lines. At puberty the boy or girl may not even be living with kin any more, let alone in the nuclear family. But even if they are, the band takes control of the situation. It is an occasion that concerns the band as such, for adolescence leads into marriage, and marriage will inevitably bring about a significant change in the economic structure of the band. A member of the band may leave it, or a new member may join it, or, if the marriage is within the band, then at least there will still be an additional net, and a change in the hunting and gathering pattern and perhaps in interfamily alliances. The process of fission and fusion might also be affected by the political implications of the marriage. The *elima* is best regarded as a premarital festival. It does not necessarily lead directly into a marriage that is marriage in the sense of a final, childbearing union. It is rather a preparation for marriage, an opportunity for the youngsters to find suitable partners. It does not even have to end in betrothal, so there cannot be said to be a functional connection between *elima* and marriage.

The arrival at puberty among boys being somewhat less easy to determine, the signal for an *elima* is the first appearance of menstrual blood in a young girl. This is something that fills the local villagers with horror, and with fear of evil influences against which they take elaborate ritual precautions to protect themselves. These precautions are costly and inconvenient, and the girl who has brought both shame and annoyance to her family is hidden and treated harshly. There are elaborate cleansing ceremonies for the girl and her family. Among the Mbuti, however, the appearance of menstrual blood is a sign that the girl is now a potential mother, and it is consequently a signal for rejoicing and for preparation for motherhood. Thus an integral part of the festival is the selection of suitable potential husbands. Such selection demands that the boys prove their manhood, since it cannot be proven as simply as is the womanhood of the girl. In this sense, then, the *elima* is a joint initiation of boys and girls into adulthood. Having dealt with it in descriptive form elsewhere (Turnbull, 1960[1]), I shall keep the description here to those essentials concerned with the structural implications of the *elima*.

The fact that it is not an individual family affair, to be concealed with shame as best possible, is doubly emphasized when two girls in a band, of quite different lineages, "see the blood" within a few days of each other. There will then be a joint *elima*. And there is also the selection by the girl or girls of the *bamelima*, the friends she likes and wants to accompany her for the duration of the festival, living with her in the *elima* hut. They will be drawn from her female age mates, and may or may not already have had their own *elima*. If they have not yet seen the blood, participation in their friend's *elima* will excuse them from having one of their own when the time comes. If a girl sees the blood, and a close friend thinks she is about to see it as well, the *elima* will be delayed, perhaps for several weeks.

As with birth, this life-cycle crisis does not evoke any sense of need for urgent ritual action, protective or otherwise. Its significance is of a different order. It is regarded as essentially natural and therefore good. Also as with birth, the personal importance of the occasion leads to an establishment of personal contact with the forest, a reification of the direct bond between the individual and the forest world; but the social importance of puberty for the band is recognized, so the band as such takes certain measures, both social and ritual, to mark the occasion.

The girl or girls with blood are expected to keep to their homes and an extension may be built onto one of their huts, or onto that of any friend or relative who is willing to house the *bamelima*. Every *elima* girl with blood has to choose a personal assistant, and the choice is left entirely to her, and again may fall on a relative, though more often it is a very close friend, of the same age group. They then invite other friends to join them in the *elima* hut, when it is ready. The assistants share such restrictions as are placed upon the *elima* girls, except that they are more free to leave the hut unaccompanied. There are few restrictions anyway, it seems, and they are mainly concerned with maintaining adherence to the schedule of instruction and activities. There are some minor food prohibitions, based on the personal taboos of the *elima* girls and their assistants, which in turn are based on their individual reactions to these foods as young children. If a certain food makes a child sick it may be forbidden to him until puberty, when he may try it again and abandon the taboo if it no longer affects him adversely. Sometimes, but not always, there is an injunction against eating meat, and this seems to be when the *elima* activities are affecting the hunt and the supply of game.

The rest of the *bamelima* are merely expected to be in attendance, and come and go as they please.

In the very lack of restrictions we can see that the Mbuti do not regard the *bamelima* to be in any ritual condition of danger or impurity. At such times as they are free to be among other band members in the camp they behave perfectly normally, playing with young children, fondling babies, sitting by family hearths, and so forth. But they eat separately and wash separately, so we might say that at least they are in a condition of ritual respect.

To begin with, the *bamelima* spend most of their time either inside the hut or else off with an instructress, in the forest. Inside the hut they are taught the songs of the *elima* by any older women who care to take part in the instruction. In the forest, I was told by a number of women, young and old, the girls are instructed in the arts of motherhood. This presumably includes such aspects of sexual life as are still unknown to them, which are probably few, but also use of the various herbs and treatments that a woman must know to insure fertility, an abundance of milk, easy childbirth, and abortion if necessary.

Girls say that certain of the *elima* songs are taught them in the forest rather than in the hut, and as the festival progresses less and less time is spent in the hut, and more in the forest. For the festival is said "to rejoice the forest," to make it happy and glad. If the girls are not singing well they are told the forest will be displeased. If they are dejected they are asked if they want the forest to be sad. Everyone is expected to be happy, and as the *bamelima* go through the forest they sing to it. As with so many of the other songs of the Mbuti, the *elima* songs are either wordless, being just plays on vowel sounds, or else the words are slight and without any evident significance, such as "Ibu is a dog," "Let's get leaves," and "Oh, the mud!" Other songs sung by the *bamelima* toward the end of the festival, when they sing in public in the camp, are rather different, making rather more sense and being distinctly spicy in nature.

But the songs that are considered as true *elima* songs and which conform to a musical style of their own, are evidently sacred. When they are sung in the forest, they are sung *to* the forest. A phrase is cast at the forest and an echo is awaited before the girls continue. Even an individual girl, usually the one with blood, will sing in this way to the forest. If the *elima* happens to be in a village camp, as it sometimes is for part of its duration, the girls will still go away off into the forest to sing their songs. The older men and women say that the festival should be held entirely in the forest, but the younger Mbuti point out that it is an occasion for rejoicing and feasting, and so it is much better to be near a village and eat off the villagers. Even when doing that, however, one is likely to come across broken saplings stuck in the ground alongside a trail many hours from the village camp, showing that the *bamelima* passed by there, "rejoicing the forest." Sometimes they may be heard in their peculiar antiphony with the forest, at other times the saplings appear swiftly and silently a few yards from an Mbuti youth as a sign that the *bamelima* are nearby and should not be disturbed. Sometimes youths, thinking they have left the *bamelima* safely in their hut in a village camp, are hours off in the forest in their usual boisterous, noisy way, and will find themselves attacked and chased by the girls, armed with sticks and whips.

Usually the girls are all together, but every now and then one of the *elima* girls and her assistant will go off together into the forest, and stay there for half a day or more. At such times the others sit around looking dejected, and complain of being deserted. The older women then say that they should not complain, that it is good for the girl to go away sometimes and "converse with the forest."

As at birth, there is a certain amount of decoration of the body with what might be considered as forest charms, and toward the end of the festival the girls paint each other with a white forest clay. The personification of the forest, and the frequency with which it is referred to, and the way in which this is done as though its personality were an ordinary matter of fact are another indication of the intense personal importance of the forest in the life of the Mbuti, of its character as a parent, a friend, and a lover, the provider of all things. But it cannot be interpreted as forest worship, for to the Mbuti it is simply a matter of fact.

One thing that is particularly interesting in consideration of the *bamelima* is that while it is very clearly an age group, it does two things. It does not deny individuality to the *elima* girl, who in fact is constantly displaying it and often causing friction as a result, but it effectively consolidates an age group that might otherwise have been rather lacking in cohesion. Girl's activities are, on the whole, less cooperative in nature than those of boys, and whereas boys are clearly formed into co-operative groups before arriving at puberty, this is not quite so with the girls. But by the end of the festival bonds have been forged between the *bamelima* that will never be broken and that will provide a firm basis for co-operative activity throughout their lives.

The other thing achieved is that there seems to be at least a temporary obliteration of the bonds of the nuclear family. The nuclear family has no particular responsibility toward the festival, though they will generally contribute more food than others and may offer shelter, and it has absolutely no authority. Further, although relations between brother and sister are free at all times, it is worth noting that in the *elima* house the girls sleep with the boys of their choice openly and without shame, though their own brothers may be among the boys sleeping with other girls beside them. It is difficult, however, to determine whether or not sexual intercourse, which is permissible at this time, openly takes place under such conditions. I am told that it does.

Neither do kinship considerations seem to play any important role, and certainly no predetermined role, in the instruction of the girls. The only roles that are distinguishable as such are the provider of the *elima* hut, the mother of the *elima*, the father of the *elima*, the assistants and the rest of the *bamelima*.

Of these, the *bamelima* are without question an age group with no kinship considerations. The assistants are primarily close friends and confidantes of the *elima* girls, and seem likely to be related distantly, but there are no stated preferences concerning this. It is said that the father of the *elima* does not have to be a relative at all; his job is to use force, if necessary, to stop the somewhat violent altercations that break out among the attendant youths or between them and the *bamelima*. It is said that the mother of the *elima* is usually an elderly relative of the parental or grandparental level, and that the provider of the hut can be anyone willing to put up with the noise. Table 7a shows the kin relationship between these various roles and the *elima* girls in an *elima* held among the Epulu Mbuti at the end of 1957 and into the beginning of 1958. It also shows the relationship of those senior girls who took the most prominent part in the instruction of the *bamelima*. Tables 7b–d show the same relationships on three other occasions among other net-hunting bands.

Instruction, as already mentioned, is in song, and in such of the arts of motherhood as are yet unknown to the girls. The instructors, apart from the mother of the *elima*, are senior members of the same generation as the *bamelima*, and mostly married, or else they are elders. Like the "mother," their role is also that of chaperone, however, for the second most important activity, after song, is the selection of and sleeping with lovers.

Sexual experimentation is certainly a major element in the *elima*, but it is combined with a very definite move to widen the social horizons of the girls, and to direct their attentions into what the parental and grandparental generations consider proper directions. There are also certain rules about intercourse in the *elima* hut. The senior girls, or instructors, and the "mother" guide the *bamelima* in all this. Their decisions are never questioned, and never discussed by the rest of the band. It is not until the latter stages of the festival that the parental generation takes an active part in the proceedings.

The widening of horizons is achieved by taking the girls to visit neighboring bands. On such visits they may stay for only a day, or for several nights, depending on whether the girls find suitable lovers. It is considered important by everyone that the *elima* house should be a place of what is best translated as enthusiastic lovemaking. At first it is modest in scale, and, depending on the composition of the band, is likely to take place early on and within the ordinary hunting camp. The boys who will enter the *elima* hut will be the younger ones, not likely to be serious suitors. They may enter only if they are invited by a girl, and the girl is forbidden to invite anyone related to her on her father's side or closely related on her mother's side. Effectively that means any descendant of the father's father or of the mother's mother; the children of any of the father's brothers or sisters or half brothers or half sisters, and the children of any of the mother's full brothers or sisters. Invitation is made by the girl, who whips the boy of her choice. The girls come out of their hut at regular intervals, during the day to begin with, armed with pliable young saplings. They seek out and soundly beat whatever boys lawfully take their fancy, if they can catch them.

Any boy so whipped is under an obligation, whether he likes it or not, to enter the *elima* hut later that day. When he does so he is subject to a further beating by the *bamelima*, and even then may not be invited to sleep with the girl who first selected him. Unless she gives him permission, he may not sleep with her. And if she allows him to lie with her, he again has to have her permission before intercourse can take place. The men say that once they lie down with a girl, however, if they want her they take her by surprise, when petting her, and force her to their will.

In intercourse the only restriction I could discover was some rather vaguely stated prohibition on a boy holding his partner in his arms. Some adults say that this prevents conception, others say that the girls take contraceptive medicines. Whatever the reason, there is no documented or even reported case of pregnancy arising out of intercourse in an *elima* hut.

The *elima* is given wide publicity (unlike the villager practice) and young men from neighboring bands are expected to come and participate. If they are whipped during a visit to their band by the *bamelima*, then they are obliged to return the visit. The latter part of the festival is the time when prospective suitors are sought, though there is still no feeling that betrothal must necessarily result. At this time even the younger married men may enter the *elima* hut, though they will sleep with the senior girls rather than with the *bamelima*. It is nothing unusual for the husband of the provider of the house to do this, nor for an elder brother of one of the *elima* girls themselves. But at this time the younger boys are kept out.

Access to the hut may still be had by being whipped, but now there is an additional possibility. In the late afternoons the mothers gather outside the hut, with their carrying baskets, and with a good supply of sticks and stones and any other suitable ammunition. Any youth that wishes to declare his affection for one of the girls is free to attempt to enter the hut, but he must run the gauntlet of the women, who are perfectly capable of beating him soundly and even of throwing him in a river if they do not consider him suitable. Depending upon how well they favor him they will let him pass with anything from token to stiff resistance. If the resistance is stiff the suitor may use his bow and fire fruit peel or small pebbles with it, and fight the women back in this way. When the women become particularly aggressive the youths make a combined attack.

Minor injuries are frequently sustained, and the Mbuti say that in the old days the "war" used to be real, with arrows used instead of peelings. The important thing is that it is still impossible for a youth to enter the *elima* hut, at this stage of the festival, if the older women decide against it for any reason.[2]

Once inside he still has to face the girls, and the same conditions as before pertain except that if he is allowed to sleep with a girl and

[2] The drama not only appears like a reenactment of the proverbial "marriage by capture," but some Mbuti say that they used to have to fight and carry off their brides in this manner.

have intercourse with her, he must then stay in the *elima* hut until the end of the festival, and he will be considered as her betrothed. There is no doubt that the girls are, like their mothers, anxious to find suitable lovers who may become their betrothed, and it would indeed only be a particularly flirtatious girl who did not hope that her *elima* would end in betrothal. During the first weeks the girls have ample opportunity for experimentation, and it may be assumed that such experimentation began even before the festival began. But in the last two weeks they are looking for a future husband, and they take great pains to paint their bodies and make themselves beautiful for their evening appearances outside the *elima* hut.

These occasions are formal presentations of the girls as adults. For the first time they sing the *elima* songs and dance before the entire band, and for the first time the youths who are considered as suitable candidates sit together and join in the singing with the girls. Each youth will try to catch the attention of the girl of his choice, and each girl will try to respond, but the occasion is a serious one, and the mothers, who sit with the girls and separate them from the youths, sharply reprove anyone who is caught flirting. When the singing is over, the girls are shepherded back into their hut, and unless they come out in an attack with their whips, no boy may enter.

The length of the festival is anything from one to two months, and it ends without regard to the successful betrothal or otherwise of the *elima* girls. The girls are taken to a nearby stream in the early hours of one morning, and wash themselves carefully a number of times. I have heard them refer to this as "washing the blood," but this is also a village expression for the ritual purification of a menstruating woman, and it is impossible to be sure of the exact significance of the term for the Mbuti until more material is available. The washing, however, is unlike that of village ritual washing, being completely informal, the *elima* girls washing together with all the others, eating and drinking in between sessions of swimming and splashing and playing in the water. When it is over they return to the camp, rub their bodies with oil, sing and dance in public as much or as little as they like and without adult supervision. They continue to stay together throughout the day as a group, but in the evening they disperse to their individual homesteads. For the next few days this is repeated, without the washing, and then the camp returns to normal.

If a betrothal has been effected, the boy will wait for a suitable opportunity, then make the proper approach to the girl's parents, asking for permission for her to live with him. He will already have proved his manhood by running the gauntlet and by sleeping with the girl, and the fact that he has succeeded in these endeavors is alone proof of his acceptance. He now only has to prove himself as a hunter, and the act of betrothal is sealed by his killing one of the larger antelope and presenting it to the girl's parents, perhaps also with some other gifts, such as a bow and arrows, bark cloth, or a machete.

The girl then goes to live with him, unless it is considered preferable, probably on grounds of band size, for the boy to join the girl's band. In either case, or if they both belong to the same band, the girl simply builds a hut without any ceremony, and they live in it. No particular note is made of the occasion, though there may be a few jokes made at their expense, and they will be allowed considerable freedom from camp routine for a few days. No further change in status takes place until the girl becomes pregnant, at which time we might consider that the betrothal becomes effective as marriage. Separation before this takes place is perfectly possible and likely, and takes place without any comment, difficulty or restitution. Separation later, after childbirth, is more rare. If a couple have lived together for a long time (over a year) without having children, they will also be considered as married. This is unusual, however, for the object of marriage is in good part to have children, and if a couple fails, each will accuse the other of sterility and seek a new partner.

In seeking a partner who has not slept with him in the *elima* hut, a boy goes through the same procedure, except that the band will be called on to give its approval, and the prospective union will be discussed, elders having the most say. If he is refused, and if he and the girl are persistent, they may elope, joining another band. In this case that other band will be expected to provide a girl in exchange, for the system, such as it is, is one of sister exchange in the widest classificatory sense of the term. It frequently does take place between full brothers and sisters, but equally frequently there is no attempt to effect exchange so long as the married couple remains within the band. If the marriage is out of the band, then any return marriage, regardless of kinship, is considered to restore the balance. Again, in view of the constant fluctuation in band composition, it would be of no advantage for any more formal system to pertain.

MARRIAGE

Betrothal and marriage among the Mbuti, then, are permissive. Prescriptions and prohibitions are minimal, and even preferences are not dominant. But permission of the band or bands involved is required. In giving assent a band does not concern itself with the niceties of the kinship relationships involved, nor with the question of reciprocal obligations and privileges, except for the question of sister exchange. While not expecting an immediate exchange to be made, or even asking for a suitable future exchange partner to be named, the band bears this reciprocal obligation in mind and will demand that it be fulfilled the moment such fulfillment becomes necessary to band composition.

Considerations in approving a betrothal or marriage are personal and economic, and to a lesser extent political. The affections of the two individuals concerned is of the utmost concern to everyone, for great mutual affection is considered to lead to a "real marriage" rather than an "empty marriage"; that is to say, affection is thought to carry the desire for children, and will so bring stability to the marriage. But the band is also concerned with the character of any individual, male or female, who will join them through marriage. A boy wishing to marry a notorious flirt and bring her to live with him is likely to meet considerable opposition, and may have to go to live with her band. In that case they will consider how faithful he is likely to be, or whether he will find he prefers his own territory to his wife, and will abandon her to return to his own band. In the general discussion that takes place when a betrothal or marriage is proposed these are the kinds of issues discussed, together with the personal habits of the newcomer —cleanliness, laziness, talkativeness and noisiness.

The hunting and gathering abilities of the individuals are also discussed, first to decide whether they are able to look after themselves, and second in relationship to the band economy. As with personal considerations, the discussion is of particular importance if one or the other of the proposed partners is a newcomer. If the marriage is within a band the same discussion takes place, but because both partners are known well the problem is much simpler and arouses less argument. There may still be differences of opinion, however, as to whether the couple are likely to have a real marriage or an empty one.

The band will also discuss the question of residence. If the band is

small it will wish a boy to stay or a girl to bring her husband to live
with her. If the band is large, however, it will prefer to lose a member.
If the marriage is within the band, and the band is large, the couple
may still go to join another band, the choice of which being determined by size again, more than by any other consideration. The
presence of friends or relatives and knowledge of the territory are important but secondary considerations. This question of residence falls
primarily upon the hunters to decide; the elders have little to say.

DEATH

In death, the final crisis of the life cycle, we again see a lack of emphasis on kinship, though once more perhaps we should bear in mind
that the contact between the Mbuti and the villagers has undoubtedly affected not only kinship and ritual terminology, but also kinship
relations and ritual practice. Be that as it may, in the present context,
death is of immediate concern to both the nuclear family and the
whole band. For the nuclear family, and for other members of the
family who have during their lives been close to the deceased person,
it is an occasion for grief. This grief is freely expressed by young and
old together, and may at times become apparently uncontrollable.
In the same way that the Mbuti are given to excessive bursts of laughter, often developing into near hysteria, so when they weep they do so
with what amounts almost to violence. Children of the deceased,
without regard to age or sex, begin weeping the moment they hear
the news of death, or as soon as a sick person indicates that he is not
going to live much longer. If news of sickness or death reaches a relative some distance away, the relative will shout and yell rather than
weep, and will continue this way until he reaches the camp where the
sick person is lying. Immediately on entering the camp he will burst
into tears, and wailing loudly will enter the hut and throw himself on
the ground at the bedside of the dying person. Sometimes a close relative will injure himself with self-inflicted knife wounds, or by tying
a halter around his neck and trying to strangle himself. Others pay
little attention to these demonstrations of grief and I have never seen
any serious injury result. Elders look on, however, with some disapproval, and will intervene if there is any danger of such injury.

The rest of the adults in the band will sit around outside their huts,
watching the wailers run in and out of the sick person's hut, and while
they themselves are likely to be serious and upset they are also likely

to make jokes at any excess of zeal on the part of any mourner. Young children continue playing as though nothing were going on; youths sit morosely by themselves, or wander off into the forest on foraging expeditions.

The moment death occurs there is a renewed burst of wailing, then the camp begins to quiet down. In the forest the practice is to scratch a shallow hole in the floor of the hut and bury the deceased person there, pulling the hut down over the grave. The camp is then abandoned, nothing being left to indicate the grave site, nothing being buried with the body except maybe a few very personal belongings such as bark cloth, bracelet or necklace. All other property is divided before the camp is abandoned. If death takes place in a village, then the Mbuti leave the funeral arrangements in the hands of the villagers.

If death occurs suddenly, the same procedure applies except that the period of wailing is shorter. In either case burial takes place the same day, if enough daylight is left, or as early as possible the following day. During burial, either in the village or in the forest, there is likely to be a final outburst of wailing from the relatives, particularly female, and some may try to throw themselves into the grave. In the village the eldest son is the chief mourner, and is supported by either a friend or another relative, younger or older.

In the village the entire band takes part in the burial procession, and those who dig the grave, under villager supervision, are youths and not necessarily connected in any way with the deceased, other than by band membership. They laugh and joke, sometimes even when the body is being lowered into the grave. Mbuti elders only take exception to this if they see that it is annoying the villagers. On the other hand if the formal wailing becomes too loud and enthusiastic, as the villagers like it to be, the elders object strongly. Particularly do they object to excessive demonstrations of grief from anyone who is not a close relative. Their main objective, it seems, is to restore "quiet" to the camp as soon as possible. The moment burial is over only the genuine sobbing of the immediate family is permitted in the forest, and this may be heard coming from their huts at any time of the day or night, never in public. In the village, however, there is still an obligatory mourning period, and about three times each day, for about two or three days, sporadic formal wailing breaks out in the village camp.

If a child dies the grief is less widespread, and in the case of a very small child the camp may not even be abandoned; only one hut will be pulled down and deserted. The child may even be buried within

two or three yards of the hut, which in that case continues to be occupied. The main difference between the death of a child and that of
an adult is that the death of an adult is likely to be made into an occasion for a *molimo* festival; a child's death is seldom marked in this
way, and if at all then only briefly.

Because the *molimo* has more to do with life than death it is dealt
with separately in the section on religious life of the Mbuti. Here it
should simply be noted that it coincides with the efforts of the elders
to restore normality as quickly as possible. While personal grief is
recognized and allowed, it is still resented and every effort is made to
minimize it by those not so directly concerned. The majority of the
band make every attempt to maintain a normal daily routine, and to
ignore the death as far as possible. The *molimo* itself calls for vigorous
hunting during the daytime, and equally vigorous singing and dancing
at night. It involves the entire band except the children and through
its very emphasis on life it reinforces band solidarity. Through the
sheer pleasure found in *molimo* activities personal grief is lessened,
and through the symbolic nature of some of the songs and dances the
despair that death could otherwise awaken is averted. Death is acknowledged, in the *molimo* fire dance, as inevitable and as being uncon-
nected with any unnatural force. The *molimo* songs stress that if
death occurs it must occur at the will of the forest, and since the forest is good then death must be good. The *molimo*, however, goes
beyond a mere acceptance of death, and many of the songs and dances
are sheer expressions of joy in life, and the stated objective of the
molimo is to make the forest happy, "to rejoice the forest."

Thus death affects the nuclear family through the personal nature
of the loss, and it is the duty of the nuclear family, in the forest context, to dispose of the dead. They are prevented by the rest of the
band from giving way to any prolonged exhibition of grief, and in
any case by the time death takes place much of their grief has been
spent in the last moments of sickness. The family may be aided by
others in the burial, though help is not generally needed. But from
that moment on, the band takes charge of the situation and concen-
trates on restoring the normality of life. The extent to which the
molimo is a band affair rather than the affair of the nuclear family
concerned will be seen later. It will also be seen, then, how death is
made into an occasion for reaffirming the bonds of age groups, and
for establishing their distinct responsibilities.

If life begins, for the Mbuti, with little fanfare, it ends with one of the most dramatic festivals possible. The *molimo* is not concerned with the death of the individual, nor with securing safe passage for the soul, but rather with affirming a belief in life and in the continuity of life and in the continuity of the band, despite the fact of death.

It seems, from inquiry in all parts of the forest, that there were many different ways of burying the dead and that no uniform custom existed; rather that, as now, each band had its own preferences. The most common method now, and apparently in the past, is simply to pull the hut down over the corpse, the body having been buried in a shallow pit dug in the ground or simply left on the bed, covered with leaves. In some bands the hut is then burned, in others it is left, but the general practice is to move camp at once. If it is too late to move that day, the family concerned will sleep out in the open until they are able to build a new hut in the next camp.

On some occasions bodies are buried up in trees, and in the southeastern region of net-hunters this is how the Mbuti say they dispose of dead lepers. Nearly all Mbuti say that in the old days they buried their dead in holes in the ground, filling the holes in afterward so that the animals would not find the bodies. Today it is usual, throughout the forest, to wash the body before disposing of it in any of these ways. But this, and other practices such as scenting the corpse, wrapping it in a cloth if one is available, raising and lowering it three times before burial, and orienting the body in its resting place, vary according to the practices of the local villagers, and are almost certainly to a large extent borrowed from them. The Mbuti seem impatient and unconcerned about such details, and if they attend to them they do so only perfunctorily. They are particularly reluctant to allow anything of any possible value to be buried with a body, and if the burial takes place in a village and the villagers insist on using cloths and sleeping mats, the Mbuti will do their best to retrieve these unseen, at the last moment.

Similarly, head-shaving seems to be of little significance to the Mbuti, though they frequently do shave when a member of the band dies. But, unlike the villagers, they are not consistent in the practice, and they leave their hair lying around where it has fallen to the ground, whereas the villagers are scrupulously careful to collect their own hair cuttings, which they take off into the forest, or to a stream, and secretly hide.

The explanation given for self-mortification is that all the immediate family feel responsible, to some extent, for a death in their midst. Family members also openly comment on all the things they should have done for the dead person but did not do. At times when one individual is particularly repentant, such as one old lady I saw who tied a noose around her neck, others will assist her. In this case the old lady was attacked by her own family, some of whom jumped on top of her, beating her to the ground, others grabbing the rope and tugging it, tightening the noose around her neck. There was never any question, however, that this was anything but a histrionic display. On a different occasion, when another old lady started stabbing herself with a knife, the band looked on unconcernedly because even when the blood was flowing freely they knew she would come to no harm; she was merely scratching the skin.

By contrast there is no actual attempt to lay the blame for death at any individual's door. The occasion may be made one for blaming people for not having behaved as they should have behaved, but death itself is accepted by the Mbuti as being perfectly natural. It does not seem to be thought of as unclean or contaminating, and there is no purification ritual, or any ritual to speed the soul of the departed on its way. On one occasion a procession of Mbuti returning from the burial of one of their band proceeded directly to the wedding of another member. The nuclear family concerned is under no restrictions, only under heavy pressure to forget the death as soon as possible. In wailing, instead of using the dead person's name the mourners will refer to him as "You who died in the morning," referring to whatever time the death took place. Those in the band not immediately related will not refer to the dead person even in this indirect way.

In various parts of the forest there are tales of a custom whereby female relatives of a dead man used to close the trails leading to the camp and guard them, wailing and singing. Anyone wishing to pass had to pay by leaving an arrow in a piece of soft wood left there for the purpose. Among the Budo, in the north, this is known as *unai*, and the net-hunters in that region call it *butuma*. They say that while the girls are wailing and singing the men are silent. After a week the girls stop and the men take over and sing joyful songs. The women's job is "to remember," they say, the men's "to forget." The Budo and Mbuti insist this is an old Mbuti custom. (Among the Epulu Mbuti it is certainly true that most of the wailing is done by women, but it is not formalized in this way.)

Among the Lesé the same custom is known as *ofa*. They say their women wailed for two or three months, and during this time the men became bitter and went far away until they had killed and eaten someone. Their bitterness then left them and they returned and the *ofa* ended. The Mbuti archers in this region deny they do this, but agree that it is a woman's job to wail. A man's job is to hunt. A man will say, "We are glad you are dead, now you can guide us to good hunting." (The Epulu net-hunters claim to say the same thing when the *molimo* is over.) Some Lesé refer to the same custom as *chachima*.

Over to the east, I found that the Plains Bira have a similar custom called *masoso*. Among the Forest Bira it seems to be a part of what they call their *molimo*. Again the women of the family are expected to wail formally and to exact tribute from visitors coming to the village of the deceased. The men argue about problems of inheritance, and conduct the burial and purification rituals.

Among all the villagers it is stressed that any such death ritual concerns only the family of the deceased. Whatever other similarities there may be between their practices and those of the Mbuti in this connection, a restriction on participation along kinship lines is not one of them. For the Mbuti a death is mourned and grieved by any who have reason for feeling a personal loss. This means primarily the immediate family and age mates. These are the people responsible for the disposal of the body, though others will help if help is needed. The band as a whole reacts to the loss however, and it is the responsibility of the band as a whole to celebrate the death in such a way as to restore the normality of life. This is the *molimo*.[3]

[3] The wider structural significance of the *molimo* is discussed in the last two chapters, "Principles of Organization."

CHAPTER 10

The Economy

THE BAND AS AN ECONOMIC UNIT

We have seen the limited importance of the family in the lineage context, and that the band itself can only be defined, as a persisting entity, in terms of territory. Its composition and size fluctuate in response to a number of factors, among which the current economic context is of undoubted importance, regulating the size to a large extent, but also sometimes affecting the composition. We can clearly say that the band is not a unilineal institution, as seen in our camp plans for both archers and net-hunters, and in many instances even if we consider the band as a bilateral unit, lineage considerations appear to be minimal in determining its composition.

We now consider the territorial band as an economic unit. When discussing the Mbuti/Villager relationship (p. 33 *seq.*), we assumed that there was no economic necessity involved in Mbuti dependence on the villagers for plantation foods or village utensils. This is the first point to be considered here, in order to justify our treating the band as an economic unit without reference to village economy.

To begin with, it can be clearly stated that nowhere in the Ituri, except possibly in the triangle bounded by the three roads linking Beni, Irumu and Mambasa, have I ever come across a hunting band suffering from any shortage of forest foods, unless the band was at that time camped near the village. Further, in the heart of the forest I have come across many bands that are too many days away from the nearest village to maintain any kind of supply line, and that have existed solely on forest foods for from three to six months, with ease. It has been obvious, however, that in those bands there was considerable hankering for the luxuries supplied by the village, and there is no doubt that in time these luxuries will become necessities, given a continuation of the situation.

The very fact alone that each band has clearly defined boundaries and that each hunting territory borders on two or three others may be taken as an indication of the self-sufficiency of the over-all region and of each territory. Were such fixed and adjacent boundaries to exist with the accepted and generally practiced custom of non-trespass, then where each territory was not self-sufficient trespass or warfare would be bound to occur, and there would have to be some institutionalized manner of dealing with the situation. Mbuti society has no institutional means of dealing with any such situation, nor is there any indication that it ever has had either the institutions or the need for them. The social organization, such as it is, indicates that each band within its territory is to the largest possible extent independent of its neighbors in terms of politics and economics. It might indeed be argued that territorial self-sufficiency, and consequent territorial demarcation, were achieved only with the advent of the village tribes and their plantations. There is, however, not the slightest evidence for this, and the evident abundance of the forest is a strong counterargument.

At all times of year there is in the forest an abundant supply of mushrooms, roots, berries, nuts and herbs, some fruits and some leafy vegetables. The very fact that the Mbuti exchange meat for plantation foods and villager utensils indicates that there is at least ample meat for Mbuti needs, with a surplus for trade. And again it is worth noting the fact that the Mbuti themselves equate hunger with noise and laziness, both perfectly rational explanations of poor hunting and gathering.[1] On those rare occasions when the hunting, even far off in the forest, really is poor, it is considered exceptional enough to call out the *molimo* society, normally reserved for death.

As far as items of material culture are concerned, we have probably indicated sufficiently (p. 33 *seq.*) the extent of Mbuti dependence upon the village, and the degree of its necessity. It is more significant and telling to look at the structural aspects of the economic relationship. Here we immediately see that the structure is very heavily one-sided. From the village point of view it is perfectly clear-cut, depending on the two alleged institutions of *karé* blood brotherhood and hereditary ownership, although, owing to the constant flux in

[1] The equation of hunger and death is a common one to the Mbuti, who say "Hunger kills me" instead of "I am hungry." But the symbolism goes deeper, and a surfeit of food is considered the sine qua non of a *molimo* death festival—the primary focus of which is not on death but on the continuity of life.

band composition, these institutions have little direct economic application. However, they do serve as a means by which any villager
may assert a claim of any Mbuti. Villagers frequently enter into
agreements and become involved in disputes with each other as a
result, but nonetheless a villager whose *karé* or hereditary Mbuti is
supplying another villager with meat may demand either compensation, a share, or rights to the services of one of his fellow-villager's
Mbuti.

This, however, is still from the villager point of view. From the
Mbuti point of view the only relevant factors are strictly economic:
they will exchange meat and their services whenever it suits them, for
whatever goods suit them, with whichever villager suits them. The
subsequent complications due to any breach of *karé* or kinship considerations does not affect them in any way. Owing to the variable
nature of Mbuti wants and the whimsical nature of his behavior when
dealing with villagers, there can be no attempt to establish any kind
of equivalent rates of exchange.

Whereas with the villagers the exchange is institutionalized and
integrated with the over-all social structure, with the Mbuti it is not.
It is in the realm of individual and nonformalized behavior, not even
necessarily linking the various members of a nuclear family. Since the
exchange almost invariably takes place in the village, this may be
taken as an indication of the breakdown of forest bonds among Mbuti
living in a village. This fact is extended when, rarely, a villager visits
a forest camp in the hopes of insuring at least an immediate and temporary supply of meat. His very presence, if permitted, changes the
context from forest to village, and the hunting band becomes, with
respect to the visiting villager, a village band, with corresponding
social relations. The Mbuti only permit such visits if it is to their advantage, and even then they conceal with ease the game they catch
daily and only give the villager what they wish to give.[2]

In view of the absence of any necessary dependence of the Mbuti
upon the villager, for food or material, and even more in absence of
any mutually accepted institutional relationship, we may regard such
exchange as takes place with the village as having little or no bearing
on the structure of the Mbuti forest economy, and we need consider it

[2] Villagers consider it perfectly legitimate to cross their own territorial boundaries to
visit any of "their" Mbuti who might be in someone else's village area, providing the
visit is to a forest camp. This is one of several indications that the villagers clearly
acknowledge the forest as belonging to the Mbuti; the offering of the firstfruits of a new
plantation is another.

no further, except to point again to the obvious potential relationship between hunting technology and village exchange, the net-hunters being more easily able to acquire an excess of meat than the archers. However, it is difficult to ascertain just how far this relationship is effectual, for even the net-hunters maintain minimal exchange with the villagers, and only on the same nonformalized individual basis. There is rather more likelihood among the archers for there to exist a *capita* or *sultani* who will convey to his fellow-Mbuti the wishes of the villagers although he has no authority to take any other action, and this may be seen as being due, in part at least, to the less productive technology of the archers, and in part to the greater prevalence of fragmentation into small sub-bands.

DIVISION OF LABOR

There is little to say about the division of labor in Mbuti society, but most important is the fact that there is no religious belief or ritual practice that relates any activity to any one sex, nor is there any consecration of those everyday tasks that normally fall into the jurisdiction of one sex or the other. This, of course, is what might be expected from the personal terminology, which differentiates the sexes clearly only at the parental level. Basically men hunt and make hunting equipment, and organize the *molimo* festivals. The women gather vegetable foods and other forest produce, build the huts, prepare and cook the food; they organize the *elima* festival. Men make bark cloth, women make baskets. Children take part in all the economic activities. But women help make the nets, and they invariably make the twine from which the nets are made. Among the net-hunters the women, girls and young children act as beaters and are thus an integral part of the hunt, as they are among the archers in the archer *begbe* hunt. Men of both archer and net-hunter bands have no hesitation in gathering mushrooms and other vegetable foods when they have the opportunity. In both groups it is primarily and almost exclusively the men who gather the honey, for women seldom climb trees.

Women take part in the *molimo* and, although it is a small part, it is a highly significant one. The *elima*, though organized by the women and stemming from the maturation of a girl, is of equal importance to the male youths who play a vital role in the festival. All in all, sex does not seem to be of any particular significance in determining the structure of Mbuti economic activity. Of far greater significance is age,

although once again the general pattern in no way implies an invariable rule.

Infants sometimes accompany their mother on her activities, or
are left in camp in the charge of youths or elders of either sex.

Children who do not stay in the *bopi* to play or to imitate adult activities accompany their parents according to sex; however, boys who
cannot do much more than walk will, on the hunt, be more likely to
accompany their mother. Children up to the age of puberty frequently
prepare meals for themselves, not only in the process of "playing
house" but also when together as a group. They go together to the
streams to fish or crab, to the forest to gather and maybe to hunt for
small or slow game, and together they cook and eat these foods. Older
children may also co-operate in building a bachelor hut, though more
often they will occupy one that has been abandoned, if they want one
at all. But even before puberty they are beginning to help on the hunt,
the girls with the beating and the boys with guarding the extremities
of the nets.

After puberty the activities of youths are temporarily closer to those
of their parents, causing some friction and disaffection, particularly
between fathers and sons. The sibling groups, however, are reunited;
youths now have activities and responsibilities comparable to those
of their older married brothers and sisters. It is the younger married
couples and the older youths who are primarily responsible for hunting and gathering, not only for food but also for the other material
necessities of life, such as saplings and leaves for the huts, bark for
clothing, wood for the fires. It is also this age group that manufac-
tures, without any other form of specialization, the entire limited
range of artifacts that constitutes Mbuti material culture.

The older couples, widows and widowers, retire with regret but
without shame or stigma from communal life, and to the end they
will act in divers useful ways, in particular looking after children left
in the camp while the rest of the band is off on the hunt. Older people
also spend a great deal of their time making the twine used in hunting
nets, plaiting vine belts and preparing food. They can expect to be fed
by the rest of the band, regardless of its kinship composition, and at
the same time they are free to undertake whatever individual hunting
and gathering they can. The sick or crippled enjoy similar status, being also unable to keep up with the rigors of the hunt. That such
people are regarded as a potential danger to society is seen in the
legends of old and crippled people who die or who disappear or who

become spirits, but there is no evidence of the old or crippled actually being treated with anything but a care and respect that, judging from appearances, derives more from affection and a sense of responsibility (not unmixed with a certain amount of rare forethought) rather than from fear.

HUNTING TECHNIQUES

The iron tools available to the Mbuti since the inception of their relationship with the village tribes have not, apparently, tempted them to develop their hunting technology. They do not dig pits or make traps, nor do they erect spear-falls, techniques employed by the villagers. To make their traditional technology more efficient, however, the Mbuti do use iron blades for their spears, axes, knives and arrow blades. The spear blade makes the hunting of elephants much easier, though old Mbuti assert that they used to kill elephants with fire-hardened wooden spears. The knives and machetes undoubtedly make the cutting of leaves, saplings and vines much quicker and easier, and the honey ax affords simple access to beehives deep within hollow branches or tree trunks. The arrow tip is used more by the archers than by the net-hunters, it seems, but both groups rely primarily on poisoned arrows. The bows of neither group are large or efficient, accuracy is made doubly difficult by the limited vision of the forest environment, and hunters often aim at a sound or a movement of leaves rather than by sight of the actual quarry. With the poisoned arrow even a light graze will bring down the quarry, whereas with the metal-tipped arrow direct impact on a vital spot is essential. Even so, so chancy is Mbuti archery that throughout the forest the practice is to hold a handful of arrows in the hand that holds the bow; this enables them to be drawn and fired with remarkable rapidity. Naturally many are lost, but the loss of a poisoned arrow is of far less economic significance than the loss of a metal tip.

Traditional hunting techniques include archery, net-hunting and spear hunting, and occasional snaring (usually by youths, sometimes by old men). Nets vary in length from one to three hundred feet, and are about four feet in height. Seven small nets, together with beaters, might form a circle of over one hundred yards in diameter. Any area smaller than this would be impractical, as the game would be scared away before the nets could be set up and the beaters get in place. Even seven nets of average length would only form a circle barely two hundred yards across. However, thirty nets would form a circle, with beaters, which in diameter could be as much as a mile. Such a large area becomes difficult to control and dangerous. Since it is customary for nets to be owned only by married men, and exceptionally by a bachelor who has proved himself as a particularly fine hunter, it can be seen that a net-hunting band, to be an efficient economic unit, must be limited to between six or seven and thirty nuclear families.

Insofar as brothers tend to learn to hunt from their father they make ideal hunting partners, and frequently stand in line in the hunt. It is important to know the habits of the hunter next to you, as he will be hidden by the undergrowth and his movements must be anticipated before shooting an arrow or throwing a spear in the direction of any game. Even when game falls into a net there is still danger, since the smallest antelope is vicious when trapped, and the larger animals capable of inflicting serious injury with their teeth and horns. A trapped animal has to be killed as quickly as possible, and anyone nearby will run to the spot with his spear at the ready. Injuries resulting to Mbuti in the resultant melee are not frequent, but when they occur it is almost always between two people who do not commonly hunt close to each other, and who have misjudged each other's movements.

However, there is no rule about brothers setting up their nets next to each other; the order of nets is determined primarily by age, the older hunters occupying the center of the semicircle of nets, the younger hunters at the fringes (conveniently separating fathers from their older sons, with whom there may be some rivalry). A young man is much more likely to choose to hunt beside an unrelated friend of the same age than beside a brother who is much older or younger than he is. A dispute in camp may upset the customary order, but generally the order, once established, remains fairly constant except for the retirement of older men from the center, and the movement inward from the younger men at the extremities. Temporary visitors to the camp usually hunt near the ends of the semicircle, but older men will probably be invited to join those in the center.

Magic associated with the net-hunt is slight. If rain threatens there are a few hunters who will try to blow the rain away by allowing moss to fall from their fingers while they blow at it and wave their arms in the direction they wish the clouds to go. Sometimes a whistle is blown, with the same arm-waving. If rain comes despite these activities, there is generally laughter, and the "magician" shrugs his shoulders as though he expected as much. Rather more serious is a medicine called, in the Epulu district, *anjo*. It is a paste made from the heart, brain and eyes, sometimes from other parts as well, of some highly prized game. The paste is charred and placed inside the horn of that animal, which is then inverted and stuck in the ground, usually near the family hearth. The paste is put on the body, most often the forehead, of the hunter and of members of his family. Sometimes it is even offered to privileged friends. It is believed to convey to the hunter the senses of the animal so that he will be able to deceive the animal as well as foresee his movements. However, the use of this individual magic is considered antisocial in many bands, particularly if it appears to be attended by success at the cost of others in the band. It may cause disputes, and then generally all such medicine is collected and burned.

By far the most significant magico-religious acts connected with the hunt are more of the order of religion than of magic. One is the hunting song (with or without dance), and the other is the hunting fire. The song or the dance may precede or follow a hunt. It is distinct from any other form of song or dance. The song form is rather complex and demands co-operation in a manner comparable to that demanded in the hunt itself. The dance is suggestively imitative of a successful hunt, but is by no means mere mime. Like the song form, the choreography is quite distinct, and is not used in any other context.

The hunting fire in the southern part of the net-hunting area takes the form of a fire lit near the trail just before the hunt sets out in the morning. It is generally lit by youths, always at the base of a young tree. When blazing it is covered with leaves, so the heavy smoke is given off. Men and women, as they pass by the fire on their way to the hunt, may stop to gossip, or they may pay no attention. I have not seen or heard of any accompanying ritual or invocation, the only explanation ever stated being that the fire is to rejoice the forest, and it would seem to have the same primary purpose as song and dance, that of attracting the attention of the forest. It is certainly believed that the fire will insure the protection of the Mbuti and help toward success in the hunt.

Further north, another form of hunting fire is used, associated with rather more ritual. There the net-hunters build the fire within the camp, whereas in the south it is always just outside. The fire is surrounded by a vine that is carefully staked into the ground by V-shaped twigs. Within the circle long twigs, clean of bark, sometimes simply burned to create a pattern, are stuck into the ground pointing in the direction the hunt is to take place. Any animal caught is brought back and placed within the circle before being divided.

There is undoubtedly village influence to be found in some of the more elaborate magical practices. The Mbuti themselves consider *anjo* as village magic, also the magic sticks within the hunting-fire circle. The fire, however, is used everywhere, and regardless of any other accompanying ritual, there is no ritual attitude toward it other than the belief that it will secure the attention, hence the blessing, of the protective forest.

One clear example of village influence is that in any village context the Mbuti are likely to state sexual taboos connected with the hunt. These vary according to the village tribal custom, and may involve prohibition of sexual intercourse before the hunt, either as a permanent rule (which would be inconvenient for people who hunt almost daily) or for special occasions or classes of people. A menstruating woman and her husband are forbidden to take part in the hunt, according to some village customs. A pregnant woman may be under restrictions, as may be her husband, and childbirth involves further restrictions among many village tribes. To all such customary practices the Mbuti gladly pay lip service. In the forest, however, forest values prevail, and I have come across no sexual taboos associated directly with the hunt. Indeed, the hunt is considered by many, married and unmarried, as an excellent and exciting time to slip away into the bush and copulate. But sexual activity is above everything else a matter of personal taste. If a pregnant woman stays in camp, it is more likely because she feels unwell. If a father stays behind with his wife and her newborn child, it is probably because he wishes to be with them, though there are sometimes stated prohibitions on hunting or eating meat until the family net traps a large antelope. This will be made the occasion for lifting the taboo and for naming the child.

However, it is impossible to discover any consistent pattern of actual behavior, the only consistency appearing in stated behavior, and this relates directly to local village custom, which is based on the belief that the forest is ritually dangerous, unclean. Any villager in a position of crisis, such as becoming pregnant, being born, suffering from sickness or even injury, during menstruation or while near

17. A forest camp (a corner of apa Lelo) is far removed from the dust and dirt and heat of the village. When the Mbuti tire of the village, they can escape to the forest and build a camp such as this in a matter of a few hours.

18. Apa Kadiketu, showing Ekianga's village-style hut, where he lived with his controversial youngest wife.

19. In one of Cephu's camps, Aberi talks to his family. His wife, her face ravaged by yaws, holds their youngest child in a sling of fresh-painted bark cloth.

20. Cephu the troublemaker, but also Cephu the great storyteller.

death, will be kept well clear of the forest, whose malign influence could adversely affect the outcome of the crisis.

While the net-hunt divides the band into nuclear-family units insofar as each net clearly belongs to a nuclear family, there is no particular order for setting out on the hunt. Nuclear families may split up right at the beginning, children joining their age mates, women going off together, the menfolk forming clusters of friends or brothers, in much the order in which they will hunt. It is always decided the night before, by common discussion and consent, where the hunt is to take place, and everyone makes his way there of his own accord, generally passing by the hunting fire on the way. On arrival the women will already be mostly separated from the men, and invisibly take up their stations while the men silently stretch their nets out through the undergrowth, supporting them on the foliage, the ends of each net being tied to those on either side of it.

The hunters generally take up their stand near the center of their net, but the practice varies according to their relationship with their hunting neighbors, and also according to whether they have any sons with them at the net. When the extremes are ready (the setting up begins in the middle of the semicircle) a signal is given to the women, who immediately start closing in from their opposing semicircle, beating the ground with branches, shouting, yelling and hooting. The men remain concealed until the very last moment. They always lie in wait behind the nets, and will only cross into the circle to go to someone's assistance when game is caught. Game is not generally shot at or speared until it is in the net or until it shows signs of escaping. It is then that the Mbuti must know the likely whereabouts of all his fellows, as the strophanthus poison used most widely is as deadly to human beings as to animals.[3]

Once an animal is killed, and each cast of the nets may bring in several animals, it is taken by the wife of the lucky net-owner and put into her carrying basket, to be shared out on return to the camp. If the animal is a large one, and too heavy to put in a basket, either one

[3] When the poison is prepared, one test for its strength is to make a slight cut in the forearm and to allow the blood to trickle down for an inch. The poisoned wooden tip of an arrow is then touched to the blood below the wound. If, as the Mbuti say, the poison "walks up the arm," they claim to feel a tickling sensation and hurriedly wipe the blood away. If the poison does not "walk up the arm" it is not strong enough. So wary are the Mbuti of poisoned arrows that they carry them thoroughly sheathed in a bundle of leaves, in case they accidentally scratch themselves. Also, when they have fired and lost a poisoned arrow, they may spend a considerable time trying to find it rather than leave it as a possible danger to other hunters.

of the youths will put it across his shoulders and take it back to the
camp, or it will be divided on the spot. Such division, however, is not
considered final, and further sharing may be demanded on return to
the camp if the hunt was not fully rewarding.

The system of sharing is nowhere the same, and the frequent interchange of visitors between hunting bands renders sharing even more
complex. Each band, however, will state certain rules, and will not hesitate to override them in order to bring about the recognized goal—
equitable distribution of the spoils, with special consideration for the
owner of the successful net and for anyone who contributed to the kill
by using or lending his spear, and so forth. Elders and children are
allocated certain parts of each animal, and this helps to insure that
these nonhunters are cared for adequately, though their friends and
kin will always provide them with more if needed. If the hunt is so
successful that game falls into every net, then there will be no sharing, though there may be exchange simply for the sake of preferences
of taste.

This is not to say that sharing takes place without any dispute or
acrimony. On the contrary, the arguments that ensue when the hunt
returns to camp are frequently long and loud, and appear to be almost deliberately sought. One such example is when someone will
invoke the rules of sharing of another band, where perhaps she or he
may have a relative. Indeed it is remarkably seldom that the Mbuti
will admit to having had a completely successful hunt. As a result, the
return of the hunters is the inevitable signal for personal grievances,
however far out of context, to be aired and expressed in terms of sharing rights. There is no formal settlement of the dispute, but invariably
there is a compromise and there will be an exchange, at least, if not a
sharing. This is undoubtedly an important outlet for petty hostilities
and jealousies, which are automatically kept well within bounds by
the very fact that, whatever the nature of the original dispute, it is
made to relate to the hunt. No dispute can be allowed to threaten the
co-operative pattern of the hunt, for subsistence depends completely
upon the continuation of such close co-operation. This is of course
particularly true among the net-hunters, whose hunting technology
demands larger bands and closer and more constant co-operation
between band members.

Following is an example of different rules for the distribution of
game:

NET-HUNTERS

Area	Portion of body	Given to
Epulu	Head	Elders, for wisdom
	Back	Male hunters, for strength
	Private parts	Children, to help them grow
	Shoulder, liver, heart	Owners of net, spear, and others who helped in kill
Wamba	Head	Sister or sister-in-law, or to dog if it helped in kill
	Back and forelegs	Shared all around
	Private parts	Owner of net
	Rear legs, liver, chest	Owner of net and those who helped in kill
	Stomach	Elders
Biasiku	Head	Women, or to owner of dog if it helped in kill
	Back	The woman who carried the animal back to camp
	Private parts	Children (who also get other intestines)
	Forelegs and liver	Net-owner and helpers
	Rear legs	Net-owner and helpers
	Stomach	Women
	Chest	Net-owner

ARCHERS

Area	Portion of body	Given to
Kilo	Head	Owner of dog
	Chest, legs, liver, heart	Owner of dog
	Back	Divided among all
	Rump	Elders, particularly to dog-owner's father, who will then further share it
	Stomach	Anyone who might have gone ahead and first put up the game

Area	Portion of body	Given to
Nduye	Head	Women
	Back and legs	Shared all around
	Private parts	Dog-owner (who will give them to the dog)
	Intestines	Shared all around
	Stomach	Elders
Biasa	Head	Owner of dog
	Chest and legs	Shared all around
	Back	Dog-owner
	Private parts	Children and elders
	Stomach	Elders

It will be seen that the only element the various systems have in common is in the selection of certain categories of people. Women are separated from the men among all three net-hunting bands and one archer band. The net-owner corresponds to the archer dog-owner. Elders are singled out everywhere except at Biasiku, where the hunters said they would be obliged to give the elders whatever they wanted. Children figure in two net-hunting bands, and only in one archer band, where they are coupled with elders.

The only kinship relations specified are "sister and sister-in-law," which can perhaps be better interpreted simply as "women," among the Wamba net-hunters, and "dog-owner's father" at the Kilo archer camp, where the hunters were insistent that the rump would be given to the father, if alive, for him to divide among the other elders as he thought fit. In practice, however, sometimes using a village system of kinship obligations, the Mbuti men and women will make claims on grounds of kinship. In any case, as stated, the actual sharing generally is accomplished to suit the needs of the moment rather than to satisfy any system, stated or otherwise.

The net-hunt can then be seen not only as a determining factor on the size of the band but also as a major mechanism for insuring cooperation of band members, and for allowing daily expression of internal hostilities and providing for their resolution through the highly fluid "system" of sharing. While the net-hunt expresses the importance of the nuclear family in that the nuclear family is the basic hunting unit (the father owning the net, the mother beating toward it, the children standing guard at the net or at the fringes of the hunt), nonetheless the nuclear family is divided in the hunt, and both men and women are forced to co-operate with their neighbors, who may or may not be kin. The hunt above all is not an individual affair but involves the band as a whole, as is borne out in the ultimate disposition of the spoils.

That the net-hunt is regarded as a matter of importance to the forest, regarding the forest in a religious sense, is evidenced by the hunting fire, the song and the dance, rather than by any elaborate ritual, purification, or sexual taboo. The close relationship between the hunt as an economic activity and the hunt as a religious act is seen in the widespread custom of rubbing ashes from charred forest woods into the skin, sometimes slitting the skin first to achieve permanent tattoo marks. This is stated to secure the protection of the forest.

Whereas I was never able to secure confirmation of Schebesta's description of food offerings being made to the forest, except through villager informants, there is very definitely a strongly felt and stated urge to use every part of the animal, and never to kill more than is necessary for the band's needs for the day. This in fact may be one reason why the Mbuti are so reluctant to kill an excess of game and preserve it for exchange with the villagers. There is no expression of joy in the capturing and killing of an animal, though the excitement still runs strongly. The moment of killing is best described as a moment of intense compassion and reverence. The fun that is sometimes subsequently made of the dead animal, particularly by the youths, appears to be almost a nervous reaction, and there is an element of fear in their behavior. On the other hand, a bird caught alive may deliberately be toyed with, its feathers singed off over the fire while it is still fluttering and squawking until it is finally burned or suffocated to death. This again is usually done by youths who take the same nervous pleasure in the act; very rarely a young hunter may absent-mindedly do the same thing. Older hunters and elders generally disapprove, but do not interfere.

The respect seems to be not for animal life but for the game as a gift of the forest, and a gift that may be withheld if abused by waste. It is further considered that good hunting is essential to the success of either an *elima* or a *molimo* festival, and during such festivals certain hunts are devoted expressly to supplying the festival with food.

Among the archers, the system of sharing game and the respect for game are comparable in their political and religious connotations:

magic seems to be somewhat more prevalent. Further, although archery does not demand a relatively large co-operative band as does net-hunting, and although for most of the year the archers seem to be split into small bands of maybe only three or so nuclear families, the band is actually comparable in size and composition, and manifests its unity once a year for the annual *begbe* beat-hunt.

The *begbe* is remarkably like the net-hunt in technique and in social function. The major difference is the absence of nets, which makes for a much smaller circle for the same number of participants. Seven nuclear families could successfully hunt with nets; they could never form a *begbe* hunt. By the same token, more than thirty families could easily participate in *begbe* without inconvenience or danger, and if we define the archer band by stated territorial boundaries, and consider its composition as consisting of those who hunt within those boundaries during the year and form the communal *begbe* hunt once a year, then the average size of the archer band is probably larger than that of the net-hunting band.

The *begbe* demands large numbers; the men form a tight semicircle, each man well within sight of the next, the women and children forming a similarly tight semicircle opposite. The men are armed with bows and arrows, and with spears; the women make petards, which when beaten on the ground make a sharp, explosive sound. When the circle is complete, the women beat toward the men, who try to kill the animals before they break through their ranks, a procedure that is considerably more hazardous than the net-hunt, where the hunters can afford to wait until the game is at least temporarily held up by the net.

Among the archers the *begbe* is referred to as the beginning of the new year, and the hunt coincides, it seems, with the honey season, which for the net-hunters is similarly the beginning, or the end, of the year. During this season, then, the archer band is consolidated and co-operative, though it seldom builds a single camp. Rather, there may be from three to five large camps, but built close to each other (within earshot) and connected by trails. This, however, is the one time of year when the band does meet and hunt as such, though even at this time there is no central authority.

For the rest of the year the band is broken up into smaller units, each one economically and politically independent of the other. These sections may vary in size from two or three nuclear families to as many as ten, or temporarily even a few more. Generally an archer camp contains from three to six families. In the same way that among the net-hunters the smaller camps built during the honey season show rather more evidence of patrilineal bonds, so do the smaller archer camps. They are still by no means exclusively patrilineal-patrilocal units however, and although respect is paid to the lineage head, it is no more than would be paid to any elder. Indeed, even the small camps are frequently composite to an extent that lineal authority would be unworkable. As we shall see for the net-hunters, authority is widely dispersed through the different age groups, for different activities.

The archers make use of the dog to a far greater extent than do the net-hunters, who only use it incidentally (particularly elders who go off on their own with bow and arrows). The common practice is for three or so hunters to lie in wait, possibly concealed up in trees, near an animal trail. They will entice game with antelope calls, and shoot at it when it has come between them. Dogs are used more by single men or men hunting in pairs, who prefer to track rather than to ambush. Women do not participate in the hunt, and go off on their own, but never singly, to gather.

If one such minimal section of the band is not having successful hunting or gathering, its first step will be, as with any hunting camp, to abandon the site and move elsewhere. However, with the territory split up among a number of similar sections, the freedom of choice is not as great as among the net-hunters, where the band is encamped as a single unit and may move anywhere else within the territory without hindrance. Consequently one section may join temporarily with another. Alternatively, it may send to another and ask for a share of their spoils. Generally, however, contact between one section and another is more for purposes of socialization, as the forest is no less abundant here than in the region of the net-hunters, and the same axiom holds good—a hungry camp is a lazy camp.

Each section is free to move where it will and cannot claim any right to any particular subterritory, and although it happens, it is considered bad form to camp too close to another section without asking permission simply because they have found good hunting. It frequently happens that hunters from different sections find themselves hunting in the same area between their two camps, and in that case they either separate or else they join up, depending on the nature of the game present.

The presence of elephants may be made an occasion for two or more sections to join together temporarily, and the archers share the same two techniques of elephant hunting that are used by the net-hunters. Some hunters like to make a kill on their own, not so much to gain status, for such status is virtually meaningless, but for personal satisfaction. They will trail an elephant, then run up underneath it and jab their spear several times into its belly, aiming at the bladder. If they see urine spurt out they know the elephant will die in a day or so, and they will return to their camp, which will pack up and trail the dying elephant and build a new camp around it.

Alternatively, four or five Mbuti will lie in wait, and when an elephant appears one will stand out on the trail in front of it so that it stops. At that moment one who is concealed behind will run out and slice the tendon of one of the rear heels. The elephant will spin around, partially immobilized, whereupon another concealed strategically will run out and slice the other tendon. The elephant can then be killed at leisure, though still not with ease.

The killing of an elephant will inevitably bring other sections of the band to the scene, and the meat will be shared among all. The moment it is finished, however, the band will again split up and remain this way for the rest of the year. Thus the *begbe*, during the honey season, remains the only time when the band assembles as such for the purposes of acting together as an economic unit. It is unlikely that more than one elephant will be killed during the year; the maximum I know of in one territory is three, and this was considered highly exceptional. Further, although elephant hunting may result in the assembly of a number of sections, or even of the total band, it does not involve communal activity.

Neither the archers nor the net-hunters, despite the abundance of wildlife around them, acknowledge many totemic restrictions, though they could well do so without suffering. But the very abundance also renders it unnecessary to have institutionalized methods of insuring even distribution. Among the villagers, whose supply of meat depends almost entirely on the Mbuti and is consequently unpredictable and erratic, totemic observances are common and rigidly enforced, and can be seen to affect distribution to some extent, as the totemic animals include those most frequently caught.

Such totemic observances among the Mbuti that do not derive from individual allergies are associated with membership in the patrilineal lineage. The animals so respected are without exception those least frequently killed, hunted or eaten. By far the most widespread totem is the leopard, and even those who do not have the leopard as their clan totem, and can therefore lawfully kill the animal, say they would never eat the meat. Some give the reason that the leopard eats human beings, and in this way anyone eating a leopard is also eating human flesh. Whereas insofar as clans themselves are suspect as being possibly of village origin, so are the totems, and indeed totemic observance itself. But there is no doubt that the leopard is throughout the forest considered by the Mbuti as having supernatural connotations. More of this will be seen when we discuss the *molimo*, the men's religious association, which is active primarily at the time of death of a member of the hunting band. The derivation of the term is unknown, and it has no translation, but *moli* is the word used by the same Mbuti for the leopard. The animal is considered beautiful because of the grace of its movements, and in this context it is likened to a dancer. It is respected for its power and skill as a hunter. It is feared for the way it brings death, to animals or human beings, swiftly and silently and inevitably. There are many who do not claim the leopard as their totem, but who nonetheless would not even touch a dead leopard, let alone kill one or eat it.

The chimpanzee and the buffalo are probably the next two most commonly given totems, and they are also animals that have the least possible interest among Mbuti as a source of food. The chimpanzee because, they say, it is nearly human, and the buffalo simply because it is such bad eating. Other Mbuti who may eat these animals seldom do. Buffalo is tough and unpleasant-tasting, they say, and is eaten only if there is nothing else. Also, any sensible Mbuti will seek to get out of a buffalo's way rather than to challenge and kill it. There is no merit in killing a buffalo, as there is in killing an elephant. To seek one out is considered a foolishness, the mark of a stupid and conceited hunter. To be attacked by one and to escape are considered a sign of good luck; if the buffalo is killed in defense, however, that only brings incidental fame. If, as sometimes happens, a buffalo is constantly making a nuisance of itself in a particular part of the territory that cannot always be avoided, and presents a real danger to hunters and gatherers, then five or six of the great hunters will set out to kill it, with considerable trepidation. It is above all an animal to be avoided for every possible practical reason.

The chimpanzee, on the other hand, is avoided for more personal reasons, largely associated with its semihuman appearance. Someone who does not like to eat chimpanzee will also be likely to refuse to eat any monkey. Sometimes older men will eat chimpanzee, and this seems to be more so among the archers than the net-hunters. Certainly, chimpanzees are more likely prey for the archer than the net-hunter.

Other animals stated as clan totems are similarly either undesirable for good practical reasons, or so rare that their exclusion is of little practical significance.

Restrictions sometimes cited as "totemic" by the Mbuti, and which include the more common and desirable game, have proven in my experience to be not totemic at all, but due to personal allergies. Any food that makes a child sick will be forbidden to it until it grows older. At puberty (i.e., when he or she is old enough to participate in the *elima*) he may try that food again, and either continue the restriction or abandon it, according to the results. Again at marriage he may try it. From then on he is unlikely to make any further attempts, though nothing is to stop him. There are plenty of alternatives, and exchange on grounds of taste is about as frequent as economic sharing. There is certainly nothing hereditary about such restrictions.

Apart from this, the Mbuti make ample use of the game offered by the forest. Their technology, limited by the same environment to nets, bows and arrows, spears and vine snares, is more than adequate for their subsistence. Perhaps some measure of the sufficiency of supply is the fact that little effort is made to tap the more difficult sources of food, such as the fowl and monkeys that throng the upper branches of the trees. An even more surprising rejection of a much easier source is the rejection of fish. Fish of many kinds fill the forest streams and rivers, and are caught with the utmost ease, yet they are considered as food fit only for children.

On the other hand certain ants, termites, snails and grubs are considered as delicacies and eagerly sought, though these are probably more properly considered under gathering.

GATHERING

Gathering among both net-hunters and archers is similar, and although primarily the concern of the women, there is no shame in a man gathering any vegetable foods he may come across. The gathering of termites, grubs and so forth is equally practiced by men and women.

The foods most commonly gathered for daily consumption are

mushrooms, of which there are many edible varieties at any one time throughout the year; the sweet *itaba* and similar roots, which are found by following its telltale vine along the ground, then grubbing with a stick for the roots at the end; nuts, of which there are again many varieties at any time of year; and divers berries. There are also succulent fruits and a few leafy vegetables, though the latter seem rarely used except as herbs. However, they are likened by the Mbuti to the village manioc top, which is cooked as a spinach, and perhaps it is because of the availability of manioc tops and their more pleasant taste that the indigenous vegetable is falling into disuse.

Among the net-hunters, gathering takes place during the course of the net-hunt, on the way to and from the hunt, and between each cast of the nets. Women carry baskets on their backs, with a bark tumpline over their foreheads, as do their young daughters. In the same way that the boys form an age group during the hunt, so do the girls. The boys split into two sections and guard each extremity of their hunting semicircle; likewise the girls split into two groups and beat at each end of the semicircle of beaters. Only the older boys and girls are expected to act as adults, and even they need not necessarily act with their parents. The girls go off on foraging parties on their own, and women go off in twos and threes to do their gathering. There is no recognizable kinship pattern, at least among the Epulu band, to these gathering associations. Women or girls who gather together are likely to be friends of approximately the same age; that is about the only generalization possible.

Men, not having baskets with them, are less able to gather effectively, but if they pass a bank of mushrooms they will pick whatever they can carry without encumbering themselves, and they will send the younger boys back to camp with their arms full.

Gathering, then, is a much more individual affair than hunting among the net-hunters. Even among the archers, where the women are not required on the hunt, they only go off in twos or threes to gather, and the same freedom is allowed for the men to gather whenever they have the opportunity. The spoils are similarly regarded much more as individual property than as communal, though sharing does take place.

There are no rituals and no magic associated with gathering, but insofar as it is primarily a woman's occupation, *elima* songs are frequently sung on gathering expeditions. As with hunting songs, the *elima* songs are designed to attract the attention of the forest deity,

and since the forest is benevolent the songs thus are thought to secure protection. In point of fact they do, for the throaty chorus of
even two or three Mbuti women is enough to scare away any game.
When not singing the women beat their hands together, shout or talk
loudly to each other, for the same purpose. I know of only one woman
injured while gathering. She was alone, which was the first mistake,
and the first question asked when news came back to camp that she
had been attacked by a buffalo was the apparently surprising one,
"Was she not singing?" She was not, nor was she "talking to the
forest," and that was her second mistake, the consequence of which
was death. The Mbuti are practical enough to recognize the "noise"
value of song, but they see more in it than that.

When the Mbuti are near a source of plantation foods and can
acquire them by one means or another, then their daily diet is largely
vegetable. The meal taken before going hunting and the snack on the
hunt are both likely to be entirely vegetarian, meat being eaten only
at the evening meal. Even then it may be served with one or another
vegetable. Even when the Mbuti are far away from a supply of village
foods and living entirely on the forest they still rely heavily on vegetable foods, and gathering must be considered at least equally important
with hunting as a subsistence activity. From what I was able to see,
this is true among the archers as well as among the net-hunters. It is
also true that throughout the forest the supply of forest vegetable
foods, though varying, is constant and sufficient, frequently ample. If
there is any time when there is a greater abundance than at other
times, it is during the honey season.

HONEY

Falling approximately in the middle of our calendar year, and lasting a full two months, the honey season is of vital importance to the
Mbuti not only from a nutritional point of view but structurally.
We have already seen how at this time the net-hunting bands split up
into minimal sections, separating hostile or factious elements and
consolidating existing friendships, so that when the band re-forms it
will have resolved most of the internal dissensions built up over the
previous year, on the whole reaffirming old loyalties but always asserting some that are new. The archer band, normally segmented, joins
together during the honey season in what is essentially the same
process. It is significant that the honey season should be marked

among the Mbuti by a special type of song, musically distinct from the other types, and by a ritual dance involving ritual use of fire. I have seen this dance throughout the forest, and heard the same distinctive honey song, the latter being made all the more distinct by the use of special wooden clappers called *ngbengbe* by the net-hunters of the Epulu region, *epopo* or *koko* by the archers further east.

Many different kinds of honey are recognized, and each has its own distinctive taste. All that I tasted were exceptionally sweet except for the *apuma* honey, which is very liquid and highly fermented by the time it is collected late in the season. Most honey is found high up in boles in the upper branches of the tallest trees. This is always collected by men and youths who can climb trees, unless the diameter is too great, simply by exerting lateral pressure on the trunk with their arms while they move their feet up, pulling themselves close to the trunk with a jerk as they move their arms up. If a tree is too wide to climb this way, they may loop a vine around it, holding the ends with their hands, or they may climb a smaller tree nearby and jump across where the branches meet higher up. Hollow trunks or branches are used by bees as hives.

Other honey is found a few feet above ground level, again in a hollow tree trunk, and this is the only kind of honey, except for the rare *sundu*, which is found in the ground, that a woman may collect.

The actual collecting procedure is the same. If the entrance to the hive is small, it has to be widened with an ax. Then a leaf tube in which there are smoldering embers is introduced into the hole, and by blowing through the other end, the Mbuti fills the hive with smoke and drives out the bees. Most of the bees do not sting at all, and those that do sting do not seem to cause any great pain. Even before they have all left the hive the collector puts his arm in and pulls out handfuls of honey, eating it on the spot, sharing it with friends who may be helping him. When they have had their fill they throw down what is left to those waiting below. If by themselves, they fill a special bark honey container or a basket lined with leaves, and bring the rest back to camp. There it is shared by all, either being eaten in the comb or warmed in leaf containers over the fire. If it is full of white maggots it is particularly prized, and will almost certainly be warmed to loosen the honey until the maggots wriggle, at which point it is consumed with relish.

If the honey is very dirty, full of rotten bark or leaf mold, it is wrapped in a leaf container and immersed in water. When it is pulled out the liquid that drains from it (*kombo*) is caught in leaf cups and drunk. Never is any honey wasted, never is it kept or used in the preparation of other foods; what is not consumed on the spot is eaten or drunk the moment it is brought back into camp.

There is a craving for honey during the season that never seems to be satisfied. No amount of alternative foods, even meat, can reduce this passion for honey. Each band has its own way of listening for the telltale sound of bees swarming. Among some, a leaf is rubbed between the hands, which are then rubbed across the forehead to enable the hunter to see the bees high up in their hives. I found this practice among the eastern archers. Elsewhere, throughout the net-hunting region and also among the western archers, at least, the chameleon (*ameuli*) is believed to lead the Mbuti to honey by uttering a long-drawn-out throaty cry. Chameleons, however, are not known to be capable of making any such noise, and the noted ornithologist Dr. James Chapin claims to have tracked this weird sound down to the *Sarothrura elegans*, a bird with a skinny pouch in its neck that enables it to give an unbroken wail lasting fifteen seconds or more.

But most noticeable among a people who take the success of hunting and gathering so much for granted is the presence of honey-collecting magic, and an inordinate emphasis on song and dance, legend-telling and other recreational activities. There is no doubt that whatever else it may be, the honey season is also a festive season where celebration is the order of the day, even at the cost of a relatively empty stomach.

Some activities are purely recreational, such as spinning tops made of nut sections, and gambling with dried seeds thrown on the ground to make up a total number that is a multiple of four. Others are educational, and in particular the honey swing is for training youngsters in agility at heights, as are the informal contests at climbing dangling vines. The honey swing is suspended from two high branches, so that it has a long, powerful arc. The youths line up and one jumps into the bend of the vine that forms the seat and sets the swing in motion. As the swing moves backwards, a youth runs forward, catching onto the side of the vine, giving it added momentum. As it carries him off the ground, he throws his legs forward and up over his head and into the swing just as the previous occupant jumps to the ground.

The younger children also play with smaller swings, and they have their own game of climbing saplings until there are so many of them that the young tree bends to the ground. The children then leap to the ground, and any who are timid or slow get whisked back into the air again as the sapling rebounds, and are much laughed at for their failure.

The tug-of-war separates the sexes, and although it is primarily an adult game, youths and children sometimes join in. However, it is likely to become rough, and youngsters are not encouraged. A man may, and sometimes does, pull on the side of the women, to make a better match, but he may also go to their side as if to help and then start pulling in the opposite direction. It is then up to the women to decide whether they are better off continuing to pull, or whether it is worth their while for two or three of them to attack the man. They themselves will sometimes leave their side and go to the men's side and simply try and pull them away from the vine rope. No restrictions were evident, and each contest continued until the complete collapse of one side or the other. If anything, among the Epulu net-hunters the women seemed to win more frequently. An immense amount of energy was dissipated in this way, yet one tug-of-war would follow another for sometimes as long as an hour.

The division of sexes visible in this contest, and the same implied symbolic conflict, was also visible in the *ekokomea* dance which I saw among the Epulu net-hunters during two honey seasons; but I have also seen the dance in the same band during the course of a *molimo* festival. I found it to be known among all other bands I visited, though I never actually saw it practiced among the archers. With these other bands it is said to be danced on occasions of great importance to the band, such occasions not being specified.

Ekokomea involves a reversal of the sexes, and everyone from the oldest to the youngest may take part. Usually the children follow the youths and adults and imitate the dance on their own. Women put heavy objects in the bark cloth between their legs and stride along in a way that emphasizes the swinging motion of their "genitalia." The men indicate their assumed female sex by performing divers actions typical only of women, often pretending to clean their private parts as women do. Both men and women, but mainly men, may take a leaf or a small strip of bark cloth or skin, make a slit in it, and proudly display it, occasionally putting a finger through the slit so as to leave the symbolism in no doubt.

The dance begins spontaneously, without preparation, with two or three individuals assuming the reversed roles and marching in line from hut to hut, singing, "*Ekokomes.*" No satisfactory translation of the word was ever given to me; it simply refers to an elbow, a chicken or a fallen tree, according to pronunciation. It is pronounced all ways, and all forms of translation are given, stories being invented ad lib to explain the dance.

As people come out of their huts or leave their hearths to join in the line, the movements get more and more suggestive and rhythmic, and when the line is complete couples will break away and dance into the center and there imitate the act of copulation according to their reversed roles, while the others dance around, singing and laughing loudly. Each couple tries to outdo the others in exaggeration and suggestiveness, and just about every conceivable abnormal situation is imitated, dogs, chickens, children, even infants being dragged into the act if they are within reach.

The end of the dance is the usual near-hysterical laughter that is brought on by any form of exaggerated mime or storytelling, with the dancers rolling on the ground and clapping their hands to show their amusement. As soon as this has subsided the dance is likely to start all over again for a second or even a third time.

Ekokomea, however, is by no means danced every day, even during the honey season; more than once or twice a week would be rather frequent. It is similar during the *molimo*. So throughout the year the dance is not likely to take place in any one band more than a dozen times. This is one dance that I have seen danced both in the forest and in the village. It is never danced by the villagers, who regard it as a sign of Mbuti depravity, but who nonetheless watch it with the greatest pleasure. The older Mbuti say it would not be danced in the village, but even to them either its exact significance is not clear or else it is something they were unwilling to discuss.

Much more directly connected with the honey season is a mimetic dance in which the men enact the honey gatherers, the women the bees. The men form a line and dance around the camp as though going through the forest looking and listening for bees. Parallel to them, and sometimes on the verge of the camp or even in the forest, is a line of women. The men sing a honey song, the women buzz like bees. When the men pretend they find the honey and are about to take it, the women descend on them and beat the burning embers they carry above the men's heads so that the sparks fall on them—stinging them like bees, they say. This is often followed by a good-natured fight which may develop either into the tug-of-war or *ekokomea*.

Because of the rarity of ritual performances there is one which should be mentioned here, though it seems unique and known only to net-hunters as far as I could ascertain. The ritual involves the building of a fire, with much greater care and concern than the hunting fire or the *molimo* fire, and it is believed specifically that the correct performance of this ritual will lead the Mbuti to honey and/or bring the bees, and their honey, closer to the Mbuti. A full description is given in the section on religion and magic (pp. 231–33). Here it need only be said that the preparations, including the digging of small trenches for water and the use of special woods and leaves, are designed to give the maximum amount of smoke. The lighting of the fire is accompanied by blowing on the *madé*[4] (efe: *segbe*) whistles, through which water is first poured.

All being taken into consideration, the relative lack of magic or ritual associated with food quest, the lack of interest shown in certain readily available forms of food supply such as fish, and the lack of food taboos all confirm the abundance of forest foods and the adequacy of Mbuti technology. This is important in considering the over-all economic system.

ECONOMIC ASPECTS OF TERRITORY

While the environment does not, through areas of shortage or abundance, determine the location of hunting bands, it does provide natural boundaries which form convenient borders between each hunting band. The total territory is more than ample for the total population, and the even distribution of game and vegetable foods means that there are no preferential areas that might make for rivalry between one band and the next. There is, in any case, a safety factor in that the bands are arranged side by side, in several vast circles, in the center of each of which the boundaries are so loosely drawn that there is effectively a no-man's-land, in which anyone may hunt and where bands occasionally, though rarely, may come in contact with each other.

The only territory to be considered, then, is that of the individual hunting band. This is again, in all cases except possibly the area

[4] The *madé* is a conical pipe, open at both ends, made of two hollowed-out cross-sections cut lengthwise, bound together either by *nkusa* twine or by strips of vine. The pouring of water, which is comparable to the pouring of water through the *molimo* trumpet (see Chapter 14) may have ritual significance, but is explained invariably and unhesitatingly as being necessary simply to get a better sound. It swells the wood and binds the sections closer to each other.

bounded by Beni, Mambasa, and Irumu, more than sufficient for the economic needs of any band, however large. The size of the band is determined more by hunting technology than by territorial food-producing capacity, but each territory does provide, within itself, a means of regulating the internal movement of the band or its subsections.

Game, while not migratory in the wider sense, nonetheless tends to move about from one part of the forest to another nearby part, as it temporarily exhausts one area of supply after another. The game itself is in this respect comparable to the band, which similarly is forced to move, not only as it gathers out an area but also as it hunts it out. The same topographical barriers that provide natural boundaries to the Mbuti also often provide natural boundaries to the game, and so in any one hunting territory there is a definite pattern to the movement of both Mbuti and game, the one following the other. The Mbuti may break the pattern either by eating village foods or by abandoning one section of their territory for another, for there may be several "game territories" within one hunting territory.

There are then general economic aspects of territory that influence the movement and division of the hunting band, but they in no way compel it into one specific pattern or another. Far more important is the simple fact of the ample economic self-sufficiency of each hunting territory, and the fact that this is a factor recognized, appreciated and utilized by the Mbuti.

ECONOMIC RELATIONSHIPS BETWEEN HUNTING BANDS

It is only extremely rarely that one band has any kind of economic relationship with its neighbors, and the nature of the relationship depends entirely on the context. As already observed, while there is a recognized custom of not crossing into another band's territory, this may be done if that band is nowhere in the vicinity. The likelihood of this happening depends on the nature of the boundary (how easily it may be traversed) and the nature of the quarry. It is unlikely that any but the most desirable game would be pursued. If such game is caught, however, then a share of it is due to the band in whose territory it was killed. While it would be unusual for one band to inform another of such good fortune, if discovered there is no hesitation at sharing in the prescribed way.

The movement of bees seems to be somewhat less even than that of game in the Ituri Forest, and it sometimes happens during the honey season that one hunting territory may have a glut of honey while a neighboring territory has a scarcity. In that case the less fortunate band will either poach, and hope not to get caught and so have to share, or else it will ask permission to camp on foreign territory. In the latter case there will probably be an exchange of residents between the two bands, the host band thus being able to insure its rights. (As often as not, due to the composite nature of the bands, the encroaching band will have among its female or even its male members a relative, if not an original member, of the resident band. However, the loyalty of such individuals is divided, and is generally given to their present hunting band; otherwise undiscovered poaching would be impossible.)

The camps are generally as far apart as possible, unless the encroaching band is small, or a mere subsection that is tentatively seeking a re-alignment with the resident band. Similarly with hunting, joint hunting camps are exceptional, and to my own knowledge occur only if there is a common desire to hunt elephants which may be in one or both territories. The purpose of such joint hunts generally involves village economics, in particular the supply of ivory to the villagers. In itself elephant-hunting demands only a handful of men at the most, and more than one dead elephant would be an *embarras de richesses*, to say the least.

It is not surprising, then, that there are no institutionalized means of regulating economic relationships between bands. Such co-operation as does occur is completely outside the normal economic frame of reference. There is certainly no exchange of goods or food between bands, except insofar as a visiting family generally brings with it some meat, honey, nuts or mushrooms to share with their hosts. Each territory not only provides a sufficiency of food but an equally ample sufficiency of all the other material necessities of life.

The only true economic relationship that persists between bands is concerned with maintaining each territorial band at its optimum economic strength of composition. The overenlargement of one band and the diminution of another leads to a relocation of some of the families of the larger band in the territory of the smaller. Owing to the constant flux in composition, however, this is only a temporary relationship between two temporary populations, and does not involve any reciprocal rights or obligations, the increased efficiency of each band being the reward of each.

ECONOMIC RELATIONSHIPS BETWEEN BAND AND VILLAGE

This has already been dealt with to some extent, and has been seen to involve a question of mutual convenience rather than of economic necessity. What needs to be emphasized, perhaps, is that there can in effect be an effective economic relationship only between a territorial band and a territorial village, without regard to the composition of either. The territorial village is likely to be far more consistent in composition, moving less frequently, less far and less at random than the band, and above all following a clearly patrilineal/patrilocal system of descent and marriage. Any village, then, may be said to be in an economic relationship with any hunting band whose territory includes that village. In addition, it may have a relationship with other bands whose territories are sufficiently close to allow easy exchange.

The band is similarly in relationship with a village or villages according to territorial considerations. Within that band each individual will also have personal-exchange relationships with his villager *karé* brother, with his *kpara*, and with any other individual villager in the local village if neither his *karé* nor his *kpara* are there. He may maintain any, all or none of these individual relationships as it pleases him; there is no institutional means of compelling him one way or the other from either the band or the village. He decides entirely in terms of his own needs, those of his family and the general needs of the band. If he finds himself in conflict with the band then he either forms a subsection with two or three others or he goes to visit another band. Generally, however, a band tolerates complete individualism in this respect. The obligation to share, however, does not apply to village foods. Any Mbuti who does not enter into an exchange relationship with a villager, or who does not steal what he wants, goes without unless his relatives or friends voluntarily offer him of their own.

The decision of the individual Mbuti often shows rather more forethought than is shown or called for in his other economic activities. The probable length of absence of or from his *karé* or *kpara* is taken into consideration. If an Mbuti has a particularly generous exchange partner, he will, in that partner's absence, maintain at least nominal exchange with his partner's next of kin. If his partner is within a day's walk or two he may visit him briefly, bringing a suitable gift of meat with him. Even on returning to his *kpara's* village, an Mbuti may maintain exchange with a generous villager elsewhere.

There is no system of equivalents, only the obligation to reciprocate. Indeed it is doubtful if we can really even talk of it as theft when the Mbuti raid a plantation and carry off what they want, back to the forest, without leaving anything for the villagers, whom they may or may not even know. The villagers recognize their need of the Mbuti if they are to be spared the necessity of going into the forest themselves. They also recognize that the territory, even that on which the village and plantation are built, was formerly, and in a sense still is, all Mbuti territory, and that they therefore have special privileges. When a raid takes place, the established villagers assume that a reciprocal presentation of forest foods, other forest products, or of service will be made at a future date.

On the village side, *karé* and *kpara* relationships may well operate and persist over long periods of time if the individuals are wise and just. If they are not, then the same relationships, in village society, afford an institutional means of regulating the situation with any other villagers with whom the Mbuti may take up. Among the Mbuti no such considerations or mechanisms pertain.

In the latter days of Belgian administration, when increasing demands were made upon the villagers to produce certain cash crops and to supply labor, the villagers found themselves in correspondingly greater need of Mbuti labor to help them with their plantation work. Demands would be made of a whole band to come and camp near the plantation for several weeks on end, to help with the sowing or the harvesting. The demand would be made by the village chief or headman to the appointed *"capita"* or *"sultani"*[5] of the Mbuti band. Once notified, the band then decided the matter by common discussion, any dissenters being free to leave and go their own way without any attached stigma. The considerations involved in arriving at a decision were entirely practical and material, and a decision always stood ready to be reversed at a moment's notice if it was found not to be in the favor of the band.

The work entailed on the plantation in no way involved groups comparable to those formed in hunting or gathering activities; consequently in the village a different set of interpersonal relationships

[5] These terms derive from the Belgians and the Arab slave traders, respectively.

exists among the Mbuti, and mutual obligations that exist in the forest are no longer practicable and so are no longer considered as binding. Generally there is a fractioning into individual family or even smaller elements, each individual or family having a villager exchange partner. However, some villagers with larger and more productive plantations, or with other assets (such as the blacksmith), may attract a number of Mbuti who thus form a temporary co-operative group while in the village. Any such bonds formed are purely of the moment and in that context, and are shed immediately on return to the forest. For the moment, however, they are real and binding, falling under village sanctions and even to some extent subject to village jurisdiction. To this latter, however, the Mbuti only submit so far as it is convenient. In a case of inter-Mbuti dispute in the village context, the litigants are likely, for personal and individual reasons, to accept villager arbitration. In the case of a dispute between an Mbuti and a villager, however, it will be the convenience of the band that is considered as well as that of the individual.

ECONOMIC AUTHORITY

Such organization as exists for economic purposes arises in direct response to the immediate demands of the present context. It is constant only as long as the context is constant, and any continuity derives from contextual continuity, not from any hardening of traditional arteries or inherited patterns of leadership or behavior. The only structural aspects of the economy that persist in other realms are those related to the principles of territory and age.

Ecological and technological considerations determine the general pattern of subsistence activities, hunting and gathering; this pattern is modified according to the desire of the Mbuti for village luxuries or to the pressure put upon them by their villager neighbors. As any of these considerations changes, so does the pattern. There is no attempt to control or dominate either the geographical or human environment.

Insofar as organization is in the nature of a response, then, leadership is minimal, in the economic realm. All major decisions are taken by common consent, as in other realms of Mbuti life. Men and women have equal say, hunting and gathering being equally important to the economy. Young married couples and youths have the most to say, being the most active hunters and gatherers, but while ability as a hunter carries some weight, too much ability may lead to ridicule. That is, a man who displays himself as a great hunter, and boasts of his achievements too loudly, is somewhat distrusted, and any attempt on his part to use his reputation to gain more say than others will lead immediately to ridicule.

One other consideration determines the extent of influence of a man or woman in economic matters, and that is their knowledge of the territory. Thus, no matter how deserving of respect as hunters, a visiting Mbuti family who do not know the territory well will have little to say regardless of their kinship, age or other considerations. They will nonetheless be expected to take part in discussions.

It is not possible to talk of organization of economic relations with other bands, for such relationships are so rare and diverse. And insofar as the exchange relationship between the Mbuti and the villagers is an individual one, there is little call for organization or leadership there either. When there is call for a joint decision concerning the village, even if it does not directly concern hunting and gathering but, say, the desire of the villagers for entertainment for a wedding feast, or for harvest labor in the plantations, it is still treated by the Mbuti as a hunting issue and it is the same people, the younger married couples, who have the most say. It is made clear in Mbuti discussions concerning a projected move to a village camp that, for them, the village is regarded as another hunting ground. A move villageward of the whole band is to be considered in terms of the amount of energy and the nature of the effort to be expended, and of the consequent, prospective rewards.

The same pattern of organization and leadership pertains only in the making of the decision, however. From the moment of arrival in the village, the band ceases to operate as such and will only assemble for general discussion, in the forest manner, when contemplating a return to the forest, or if it is deemed profitable to organize a hunt for the specific intent of securing meat for the villagers.

It is only in the village, then, that the nuclear family can really be considered as a separate economic identity (this is particularly true of the net-hunters, rather less so for the archers). In the realm of forest subsistence the individual and the family are subordinated to the band or, perhaps better, become immersed in the band, for they almost lose their identity. Family membership is of no consequence in determining economic responsibility; age and territoriality are the more important factors. Any tendency toward charismatic leadership is countered by ridicule, and any persistence on the part of the hunter may lead to his being given the job of representing the

band to the village as its *capita* or *sultani*. In the Epulu band, Njobo
was an undisputed great hunter, knew the territory as well as anyone
and had killed four elephants single-handed. He was a good enough
Mbuti not to attempt to dominate any hunting discussion in the
forest, merely to take a normal part. If he ever appeared to be overly
aggressive or insistent he was shouted down and ridiculed, although
highly popular. He was also the one chosen to represent the band to
the villagers. Ekianga, on the other hand, was less generally popular
and was the source of some friction, having three wives (one the sister of another prominent member of the band), but he was a fine
hunter, endowed with exceptional physical stamina, and he too knew
the territory well. Even at the height of his unpopularity he was one
of the most effective "leaders" of the hunt. So was Nikiabo, a youth
who had achieved some notoriety by killing a buffalo when barely out
of childhood. Although a bachelor, he had a net of his own and took
a prominent part in all hunting discussions. Makubasi, a young married hunter, was also accorded special respect because of his hunting
prowess and his physical strength, combined with his knowledge of
the territory. But while these four can be singled out as exceptional,
they could either separately or together be outvoted by the rest of the
hunters. On such occasions they were compelled either to give their
assent to the popular decision or to refrain from joining the hunt that
day. None of them had the slightest authority over any others. Nor
was any moral pressure brought to bear in influencing a decision
through personal considerations or respect. The only such moral consideration ever mentioned was that when the band arrived at a decision, it was considered "good," and that it would "please the forest."
Anyone not associating himself with the decision was, then, likely to
displease the forest, and this was considered "bad." Any individual
intent on strengthening his own argument might appeal to the forest
on grounds that his point of view was "good" and "pleasing"; only
the ultimate general decision, however, would determine the validity
of his claim.

Finally, it has to be pointed out that while the forest is appealed to
almost as an arbiter, and is considered as imposing the standards and
even the leadership, which all Mbuti follow, this only holds good in
the forest, where the forest directly "feeds its children." Once in the
village, actions concerning the village are never judged by whether or
not they are pleasing to the forest; a totally different set of values
pertains.

CHAPTER 11

Government: Internal

INTERNAL RELATIONSHIPS

Before attempting to understand the over-all system of government in Mbuti society, it is necessary to distinguish between different fields of authority, for each field of activity has its own leaders, drawn from a particular segment of the community. It is in this way that authority is dispersed throughout the band; every adult is accorded special respect in one field or another, but none can claim respect in all fields. Individual authority is unthinkable, and not only are there no chiefs or headmen in Mbuti society; there are not even any councils of elders or any ritual specialists such as prophets or diviners. Such adults as have respect in any particular field at any particular moment do not even have any authority; they can merely claim to be heard. Their decision is likely to be given general assent and, as in economic matters, that decision is then said to be "good," and "pleasing" to the forest. The forest personified as a benevolent divinity remains as the only recognized authority, one which sometimes expresses its feelings with unmistakable clarity; an excessive storm, falling trees, poor hunting and ill health may all be taken as signs of displeasure, while good weather and good health and good hunting are indications that all is well. But often the forest remains silent. Then the Mbuti have to sound its feelings out through discussion. Dreams may be taken into account, but there is no question of waiting for visible signs of the forest's pleasure. The delegation of authority is clear; the decision of the whole band, the very fact of unanimity, is sufficient sign of the favor of the forest. There is always diversity of opinion, freely expressed, but prolonged disagreement is considered as "noise," and offensive to the forest. Unanimity, therefore, is a powerful and positive value, equated with the opposite to noise— quiet, or *ekimi*.

The various fields in which we can speak of authority fall into three main categories—economic, ritual, and legal. In the first two, by authority is meant prominence of activity and participation in discussion in what is, generally, a normal situation. In the last category, legal, the situation is abnormal, one of dispute, and by authority is meant prominence in the settling of that dispute. Nowhere does it have any validity unless backed by common assent. Yet it is more than mere influence, for in each field certain classes of individuals are recognized as having the right and ability to interpret the pleasure of the forest.

Table 8 indicates the distribution of this "authority" throughout the band. It will be seen that it is evenly divided between the sexes and among all adult age levels; only the children are not accorded any authority except among themselves. Further, authority is located at one age level or another or with the nuclear family, with few exceptions. For the life crises (excluding birth), authority is divided between the youths and the elders. Youths and elders also share responsibility for the camp while the hunt is away, even if some of the hunters remain behind.

There are many examples of Mbuti who have appeared in the role of leader vis-à-vis the village, but as their authority was nil in relation to forest life, they need not concern us here. Their only function in the forest, other than their normal role as hunters, was to communicate the wishes of the one group of people to the other.

The only individual who might be recognized as occupying a special political position in the life of the hunting band, on any ground other than age, is the camp clown. He is usually a hunter, and his position is unofficial, depending on his abilities as an actor and a clown. He is not appointed, and there is no special name for him or his position. However, every band seems to have its clown. His function is to act as a buff between disputants, deflecting the more serious disputes away from their original sources, absolving other individuals of blame by accepting it himself. Frequently he will end a dispute simply through the use of ridicule, and although such ridicule may be taken as a form of judgment, the essential point is that once again its objective is to divert attention from the source of the dispute and also to divert blame from anyone who is clearly in the wrong. The major concern of all, except possibly the prime disputants, is that the dispute shall be ended, and frequently by creating or reviving another, lesser dispute the clown brings the disputants into the same frame of mind.

Everyone recognizes that the slightest rift in the band can lead directly to hunger through failure in economic co-operation.

The clown, however, never passes judgment or exerts authority (except through ridicule); he is better considered, in this role, as a professional scapegoat, a person outwardly not deserving respect or authority. Because of his antics, and the Mbuti love of mime, he is popular, but the blame he takes upon himself is often expressed with feeling, and it is only his ability to turn ridicule upon himself and to laugh at himself that rescues him from what would otherwise be constant opprobrium. His status as a hunter is unaffected by his role as a clown, and depends solely on merit.

There is one type of person, however, and there were two examples in the Epulu band, who leans toward the assumption of individual authority. Every Mbuti is nothing if not a powerful individualist who expresses his opinions with force and clarity. But he generally does not claim any support for his opinions other than his own experience and ability. Some men, because of exceptional hunting skill, may come to resent it when their views are disregarded, but if they try to force those views they are very promptly subjected to ridicule. Ekianga and Njobo were two such hunters in the Epulu band. Ekianga was constantly being ridiculed for his matrimonial difficulties (he was a rare Mbuti, with three wives, living in the same camp with his in-laws by sister exchange). Even his elder sister ridiculed him at times. Njobo was sometimes rather unkindly ridiculed for infertility. Out of four successive wives he only managed to sire one child, a son, who became crippled in adolescence with tuberculosis of the leg. His current wife had given birth to a daughter who out of politeness was generally accepted as Njobo's, though all the evidence pointed in other directions. He was, at least, accredited as the social father.

Of the two, Ekianga probably had the more influence in the band, and his unique position as a polygamist was undoubtedly related to both his prowess and his pride. There is, however, no parallel with the situation acutely described by Lévi-Strauss (1955, pp. 325–39) for the Nambikwara. Ekianga was indeed a potential leader, but the band did not derive its major characteristics from him. Still less was generosity demanded of him (in return for his three wives), and by no means was his undoubted dynamism contrasted by a passivity of the rest of the band. Nonetheless, his three wives and all the consequent "noise" were accepted by the band, and although it was not spoken of as an exchange, it was expected of Ekianga that he would be a particular asset in the hunt. This was his world. He had little or no interest in the village.

Njobo, on the other hand, was excellent at dealing with the village and seemingly enjoyed it, for brief periods. He was much closer to the Nambikwara, who "delights in responsibility" and who "finds enough reward in those burdens that their fellows shy away from" (ibid). Although his wives were successive, it is worth mentioning that his penultimate wife, mother of his crippled son, was not remarried and was still considered by all, including Njobo, as his senior wife. Although she lived with her natal band, she sometimes visited Njobo (particularly when he was in the village), and he also visited her, at which times they acted in all respects like man and wife. Njobo refused to allow her to live with him in the forest hunting camps.

Njobo's father, Biyonga, had not been outstanding in any way. He had been dead a number of years, and nobody seemed to remember him for any particular qualities.[1] Njobo, on the other hand, was among the finest hunters, and unique in having killed, single-handed, four elephants. He had also participated in successful communal elephant and buffalo hunts, and apart from being a hunter of the utmost courage, he was also a man of the utmost integrity. He possessed, in abundance, all those qualities the Mbuti admire most except a good singing voice. He himself was modest, and usually self-effacing in the hunting camp. He came to the fore in relations with the village, and frequently acted as "headman" of the band in that respect. However, if ever he spoke too loudly in camp, he was either shouted down or laughed at; ridicule he accepted and even welcomed. I only heard him make a retort once, when reference was made to his son's inability to walk without a stick. He said, "It is never good for one man to talk too much, particularly if he is right. But if an Mbuti has something to say, what else can he do?"

Njobo had no brothers, but his sisters had produced a number of children, several of whom, married and single, were members of the same band. The only sister who was in the band was a widow, and her children were elsewhere. She acted as mother to all her nephews and nieces, among which were two youths, cousins to each other, and each recently married. When Njobo was away from the band for a

[1] Although there was a general reluctance to mention the dead by name, or even to talk about them, there was no rigid prohibition. It was a question more of there being no particular occasion for such mention. If Biyonga had been exceptional in any way, it would certainly have arisen sooner or later in ordinary conversation, and equally certainly in response to questioning.

number of months with his son, these two nephews moved in. Normally they were not resident. Asuku brought not only his wife but also his father. He insisted on Njobo's wife looking after them, building their hut and so forth. Although Asuku was not liked, he would have been tolerated had he not tried to assume the status of Njobo, but this assumption moved him into an age group to which he did not belong, and he was consequently always being shouted down.

On one such occasion, Asuku was annoyed at the hunt for not leaving as soon as he would have liked. He strode up and down, telling everyone that they were lazy. When they shouted him down, he told them he was Njobo's son, so "I *am* Njobo, and this is Njobo's camp." When he was ignored he then turned from one great hunter to the other, and they all ignored him except one, who placed a stick on the ground at Asuku's feet and said, "There is a stick; if you are so big, pick it up and hit me." Asuku then turned to the elders, and Moké, the most influential of all, laughed in his face. At this, Asuku entered his hut and stayed inside for the whole day until dark.

On another occasion Asuku tried to say that his net was Njobo's net, and he was therefore entitled to Njobo's position in the hunt and should not be out on the fringes. He had chosen a time when his mother, Njobo's sister, was visiting, and the hunters did not want to make a dispute of the matter in front of her, out of respect for Njobo. However, one of them, Njobo's paternal cousin Manyalibo, went up to Asuku and said that if Asuku wanted that position it would mean setting his net next to him, and if that happened he would set up his net alone rather than stay in the hunt. This temporarily checked Asuku, and that evening old Moké gathered the senior hunters around him and, for once not smiling, he raised his arm and pointed across the camp to Asuku. This is considered a grave indictment, and the whole camp fell silent. Moké, very quietly, and talking as if only to the hunters but never lowering his arm or taking his eyes off Asuku, said, "That is a completely bad man. I have been watching and I have seen with my eyes, and my spirit [*roho*] makes me speak. He makes noise all the time, and he is the cause of all the noise in the camp. I would like to throw him out forever. But he is a relative of Njobo, and we should wait and see—and watch. That person is a child and has no right to share conversation with men. He is not of us. He comes from far off. I don't like people from far off. They are bad for any camp; they kill any camp completely." He then changed his attention and pointed at Ekianga, the other hunter of renown, the man with a troublesome trio of wives, himself a frequent cause of friction in the camp. Shaking his finger at Ekianga, Moké said, "And that is a man, completely clean. He pleases my spirit [roho] very much."

After the evening meal Moké stood in the middle of the camp and pointed to the hearth of each great hunter and male elder in turn, naming them, and saying, "This is my man, this is my hearth, for it is his hearth; but it is not Asuku's." He even pointed over to Cephu's camp, and included Cephu. He then went back to his hut, leaving Asuku at the central fire with two elders.

Despite this display of disaffection, however, Asuku remained on. He had not only been pointed at, but named in public, and another had been named as good while he had been named as bad—a double disgrace. Ridicule, after this, was pointless, and although everyone wanted to be rid of Asuku, their respect for Njobo, coupled with Njobo's continued absence, prevented them from doing more than ignoring the offender as far as possible. After some three months, however, Asuku began to frequent the village for long periods. Although this meant he was at least not in the camp, which was thereby much improved, the hunters found this the ultimate insult and disloyalty. When he refused a summons to return to the hunting camp, old Moké once again stood in midcamp, an honored position from which any Mbuti, young or old, is free to claim the attention of everyone. He said that since now Asuku had become a villager, he was no longer an Mbuti, no longer "ours"; he belonged far away, very far away indeed. Pointing to the central fire in the section of the camp that included Njobo's wife and three great hunters, and divers others both related and unrelated, he said, "This is a matter of the forest. This is our hearth. It is Njobo's hearth. It is not Asuku's hearth. He belongs in the village or completely and absolutely far away."

There were murmurs of assent from everyone, and Moké looked around to each individual hearth, asking, "Is my spirit [roho] right?" Agreement was unanimous, though subdued, and Moké simply said, "Asi-to"—"It is finished." The next day word was sent by a youth to Asuku's father, in the territory of Effundi Somali, a few miles on the far side of the Epulu. I was told that the youth simply gave a verbatim account of what had happened. Asuku never returned to the Epulu band, and left the village, returning to his father's territory.

His cousin, Mbaaka, was not such a stranger in the band, but soon after his marriage, and some six months after the Asuku episode, he began more and more frequently to talk from midcamp. Like Asuku, he complained about laziness and bad hunting, common enough complaints but seldom aired from midcamp. When he began to claim special attention by virtue of being Njobo's "son," however, he was promptly ridiculed. People stopped listening to him, even from mid-camp, and dared him to name them—a procedure that commands attention. Even unmarried youths called out, "Your noise will kill us all," and children began to imitate his whining voice. Masisi, a cousin of Njobo and, with Manyalibo, about to move from the status of hunter to that of elder, took Mbaaka aside at one point and talked to him quietly, recalling what had happened to Asuku.

Seeing that Mbaaka at last had begun to listen to reason, his brother, who up till then had never interfered, made a loud and rude joke that brought the whole camp down with laughter, then said, "Everyone is crazy—I'm going to sleep," and promptly went to sleep. Masisi then returned to midcamp with Mbaaka and said that if any-one else tried to be funny he would turn himself into a villager and bewitch everyone. A youth took up the thread and said that the vil-lage was responsible for all the noise anyway, because his girl friend never listened to him any more and was a bad cook (a typical pygmaean non sequitur). This rather forced good humor persisted throughout the next day, with the women telling jokes and laughing loudly the moment the conversation drifted in the direction of Mbaaka's former complaints. There were a few more remarks to the effect that the village was indeed responsible for all the noise, and the rest of Mbaaka's stay (two further months) was unmarred by any repeated claims to privilege through kinship to Njobo.

It is plain, then, that while any movement toward individual au-thority, conscious or otherwise, is sharply countered, and while in-dividual authority is virtually nil, there is nonetheless a clear basic framework to support the values of the hunting band. There is the division of leadership, according to field, throughout the entire band, yet there is the midcamp site from which anyone may harangue all present. Although he has no means of compelling attention, it is gen-erally accorded, and may be further compelled by pointing to or nam-ing the individuals concerned. Further it is plain that the elders, in-cluding those hunters whose position is being gradually taken over by their children, act as final arbitrators, always careful to stress that what they say is a matter of their opinion, or of their heart. Only when unanimity is beyond question is an opinion or an action considered "pleasing to the forest." Asuku had placed himself, physically and morally, beyond the forest.

In the two instances cited so far, although the kin relationship of Asuku and Mbaaka to Njobo was the source of their claim to special privileges, this was recognized as a village attitude, and a valid village argument. It is noteworthy that the details of the relationship were never spelled out once, except by Asuku and Mbaaka. The attitude of all the Mbuti was one of respect for Njobo, but of equal recognition of all those who shared the same central hearth, including some who were not even affines. It was stated very clearly by Moké that though Asuku was a member of the band by virtue of having shared the same hearth, he had no more privileges than anyone else of that hearth, and was under the same obligations of respect and responsibility to his elders.

There was one other elder who could claim the same respect as Moké, by reason of age, and that was Tungana. But Moké had the added advantages of being a widower and virtually unrelated to anyone in the band. He claimed fictitious relationship with Tungana, it being said that the same foster mother fed them both, and he frequently gave Tungana's "clan" name as being his own. Clan names were seldom mentioned in disputes, except in a village context, and even then they in fact referred to a unit that was either nonlineal or cognatic, and not confined to one clan. Rather than differentiate between lineal units, the Mbuti used the concept of the hearth (*kuma*). Each family had its own hearth, but there were also several central hearths, each shared by a number of families.

Each camp, except the smallest, was distinguished by several such central hearths, effectively breaking the camp into subcamps that usually revealed a line of fission or fusion, but which frequently ran counter to all kinship considerations. As far as the Epulu band was concerned (and I believe this to be true of many other bands), authority was again, as with other aspects of life, more associated with age and territory than with kinship. Each section of the camp was, in a limited sense, a political unit, and sometimes disputes would remain confined to one section without spreading to others. A man could invoke kinship or friendship to go to the aid of a disputant in another section, if he wished, but somebody like Moké was even more free to wander wherever he liked. The rules of self-help among the Mbuti are quite simple. It is perfectly proper to hit someone with anything wooden; it is not at all proper to draw blood, nor to hit anyone on the forehead, which is considered a dangerous spot. In the frequent marital disputes, any man who hits his wife on the head or in the face promptly loses any sympathy he might have had from his fellows. A dispute that follows such lines almost invariably ends with an elder, male or female, physically interposing himself between the disputants, who then revert to hurling abuse which becomes more and more exaggerated until it is so humorous that even they join in the laughter. Alternatively they may lapse into a sulk, which will last for the rest of the day and through the evening, but will be gone in ample time for the next day's hunt to take place as though nothing had happened.

If a dispute becomes widened in scope, however (and this is generally achieved by one of the disputants naming someone, either in his own support or as a supporter of his antagonist), it will ultimately involve the entire subsection of the camp, and quite possibly the whole camp. In either case the process is the same. Whatever the cause of the dispute, it is still regarded as essentially the concern of the individuals concerned. Rather than attempt a probably impossible reconciliation of the excited participants, the rest of the band joins in an effort to divert attention away from the actual cause of the dispute. If this fails, they attempt to dissipate the blame by raising all sorts of minor but associated disputes, so that a number of people become involved. If blame still seems inescapable, the camp clown is likely to try and take it on himself, or else it will be put upon him by the others. The disputants, in my experience, accept this device as a genuine solution. There is no attempt whatsoever, nor have I heard of it in other bands, to make any restitution other than verbal.

As already mentioned, a dispute may be stopped simply by making life intolerable for the disputants by miming them and throwing them into ridicule. If these measures fail and the dispute persists, the hunting automatically suffers, and if no reconciliation is effected, the band splits, either forming two subsections or remaining as a single band, with the splinter section joining another band, at least temporarily.

Not only is the attachment of blame avoided or dissipated as rigorously as possible, and restitution largely ignored, but punishment is almost completely unknown. There are one or two instances where a youth might be thrashed by communal decision, but they are rare and foreign to Mbuti nature. Closer to an indigenous system of punishment is the morning rampage of the youths' section of the *molimo* society. Disguised behind leafy branches they charge through the camp with the *molimo* trumpet on their shoulders, and attack the huts of any truly recalcitrant offenders. Even then, as a token of the responsibility of the entire camp, the youths attack *every* hut to some extent, taking a token leaf from every hut. And still in keeping with the notion of dissipating the blame, they are likely to give the worst beating to the hut of the disputant who is least to blame.

There are two threats that form the ultimate sanctions against the most serious offenses. One is the threat of ostracism, for such crimes as incest, and this is spoken of as leaving the matter to the forest. Ostracism means refusing membership in the band. If one band does this, other bands are likely to follow suit, and the offender will be left alone in the forest, and alone he will die. The other threat is the direct threat of death, but this is reserved among the Epulu Mbuti and other net-hunting bands uniquely for the crime of failure on the part of an adult male to sing (a crime sometimes conversely described as sleeping) during the *molimo* festival. The sacred singing takes place late at night, and its efficacy depends on participation of all the men and youths. It is said that anyone found sleeping (the only conceivable reason for not singing) would be killed with two spears in the stomach and buried beneath the *molimo* hearth. The women would simply be told he had gone away, or been taken by a leopard, and he would never be referred to again.

The different ways of dealing with a dispute depend so much upon the context rather than upon the precise nature of the dispute that the legal process can best be illustrated by citing a number of cases. It will immediately be apparent that in the vast majority of instances there was no visible conclusion to the disputes at all; they evaporated as quickly as they arose. There were few instances where anything resembling a general opinion was expressed, and even fewer where any positive action was taken. The cases that follow, then, are classified according to the most common causes of dispute. Of such causes food and sex are by far the most common. Territorial disputes are confined to married couples with different territorial affiliations, but whereas food disputes are also largely found among the young (married) hunters, they are by no means always marital, but often between unrelated hunters or their wives, and occasionally among youths. Disputes concerning sex involve both the young married couples and youths, as do the everyday disputes over apparently meaningless trivia. Such disputes I have put in a class by themselves, though wherever a deeper underlying dispute was known to have lain behind an apparently trivial dispute, it has been classified accordingly.

DISPUTES CONCERNING FOOD

1. A mortar was borrowed by Njobo's sister, Teningbengé, from Amaloku, Amabosu's wife. There is no kin relationship. Teningbengé's subsequent cooking did not please her son (Maipé, actually her nephew), who complained that the mortar must have been dirty. Amaloku, who by then had retrieved the mortar, said that on the contrary it was the food put into the mortar that was dirty, and not the mortar itself. Maipé promptly seized a log of wood and started fighting with Amabosu. Amaloku and Teningbengé fought with sticks. Amabosu's mother, Sau, joined the fight, against her daughter-in-law's oldest sister, old Asofalinda. The dispute remained thus confined and was watched with much enthusiasm and laughter by the rest of the camp until Ekianga, brother to Amaloku and Asofalinda, stepped in and stopped the fighting by seizing the sticks and logs and throwing them away. Everyone returned to his hut and continued the evening meal.

2. Masisi, a great hunter, complained that the hunting was bad and said the band should move to the village and eat there. His cousin, Manyalibo, moved to midcamp and began a tirade against Masisi and everyone else for always complaining there was not enough food. He cited ten antelope caught that morning as evidence of the good hunting, and said that everyone should be happy and should be making the forest happy by singing, with so much food. And if they wanted more food they should hunt more and make the hunt even better. He said that if Masisi's noise continued he was going to leave.

Moké then took his place and quietly told everyone that nobody should leave for anywhere, that nobody could deny that the hunt was reasonably good, and that therefore the forest was pleased. If they moved or made too much noise it would be displeased. The forest would be happy if the whole band were to set out the next day on the biggest hunt of all. Then when the weather was better (it had been raining for some days, always a cause of discontent and discomfort) and nobody was making a noise, the whole band could move wherever it liked (knowing that in such a mood it would move further away from the village, and thus further away from a source of friction).

There was no singing, but it was done as Moké suggested. Murmurs of assent came from all over camp, with both Masisi and Manyalibo agreeing loudly.

3. Particularly at the beginning of the honey season, when tendencies to fission are already well marked, disputes over food, particularly over hunger attributable to poor hunting, are made occasions for enlarging the rift between the camp segments. Thus one day old Tungana's younger son, named after his distant relative Njobo, came flying back from the hunt in hot pursuit of his wife, Nakoranja. Nakoranja, much to everyone's surprise, had lost her bark cloth and was holding a leaf in front of her private parts, occasionally removing it to emphasize her cry of "I am naked!"

Having made her point she disappeared into her hut and modestly continued her description as to how her husband had torn her bark cloth off to shame her because she wanted to join her "sister" (who was a member of another segment), Ekianga's youngest wife. Young Njobo, standing outside the hut, told the camp that his wife was useless on the hunt, that she could not run as fast as even the slowest animal and let them all escape. Now they had no food and they would be hungry all day. Evidently she could not run as fast as her husband either, for he had caught her and given her a sound beating, ripping off her bark cloth when she tried to escape. He did not deny this, and Nakoranja said that this entitled her to pack up and leave.

Evidently this was something that had been brewing for some time, and when the hunt came back and it was seen that the dispute was forming along the line of fission, Tungana intervened and said that there was no sense in everyone making so much noise, that the next day he and his wife were going to leave for the village, and that young Njobo and Nakoranja were coming with them to look after them. The discussion immediately turned to the dangers of the trail, with the two segments siding with each other in common and equally insincere but polite opposition to Tungana's suggestion.

4. At a later stage, when fission became inevitable, discontent being so high that the sections were not uniting in the hunt and therefore not getting any meat, old Moké intervened. He stood in midcamp and harangued each section in turn, facing it and naming its members. He emphasized that this was the honey season and that hunting should be stopped anyway, and everyone go to the forest in search of

their honey trees, "you in this direction, you in that." But Moké did an unusual thing. He said it was all right for the camp to split, but it would displease the forest if it split badly, and it *was* splitting badly (*"apa ndaso aké sinana"*). Tungana had gone to the village; Masisi, siding with Tungana but not wanting to join him, was planning to go east, Ekianga to the north; Cephu was going to leave the territory altogether; and Manyalibo's head "walked without sense" (said in KiNgwana: *"kichwa yaké a na tembela wazi-wazi"*) and he didn't know where he was going. This was all bad. For this was one camp, it was Kolongo's.

Kolongo had been dead some three years, and the names of the dead are rarely mentioned. The whole camp fell silent, and very quietly Moké recounted the history of the friendship between Kolongo and Njobo, and how they used to hunt together and kill lots of elephant and catch lots of antelope and how they always had full stomachs. "Kolongo never allowed noise, Njobo never allowed noise. Now there is nothing but noise, and we are hungry. Kolongo is dead, but that person there, Ekianga [Kolongo's younger brother] that person is now Kolongo. Njobo is not here, but that person and that person [Manyalibo and Masisi were indicated but not named] are Njobo. Let us all go our own ways and get lots of honey and sing honey songs and dance honey dances, then come back to one camp as before and hunt again."

The immediate bickering was stopped, and everyone agreed loudly that Moké was indeed right. But as it turned out Manyalibo made Moké's speech an excuse for siding with Ekianga in a hunting-honey camp, and a deep rift opened up between the hitherto inseparable cousins, Manyalibo and Masisi. Moké threw his lot in with Ekianga, in an effort to dissuade them from any grosser sacrilege, with exhortations to Masisi to make a good camp and gather lots of honey. Ekianga's eldest sister, her daughter, and Njobo's wife and some of his nephews and nieces joined Masisi, as did a young married nephew of Cephu, Kelemoké. Others joined Tungana, who prudently moved close to the village, where he could, by virtue of his age, claim gifts of food from all the sections and from his village *kpara*.

5. During the honey season, with the band divided into four sections, Masisi and Manyalibo were again at odds. Manyalibo, with Ekianga and Moké and old Tungana, among others, formed a powerful section at the far northern extreme of the territory, and offended Masisi's much smaller section by continuing to hunt. Masisi argued

that this was not customary during the honey season, and was displeasing to the forest. He also added that as his section was too small to hunt, Manyalibo was under an obligation to send him a share of all the meat caught by his part of the band. At the same time he set about trying to encourage the usually unwanted Cephu to join him, and swell his section to an economic hunting size. Cephu, always unpredictable, refused, though he agreed to send three nets as a token of goodwill. He never did. These communications were made through a series of visits made by Kelemoké, Cephu's nephew, between the three sections. The fourth section was in the village, and did not enter the dispute.

Two neighboring bands, hearing[2] that (a) the Epulu territory was exceptionally well endowed with honey that year, and that (b) Masisi was looking for reinforcement, took advantage of the situation to trespass judicially in the southeastern extreme of the territory, well away from all the others. Their overtures, made in the one instance by a meeting on neutral ground, and in the other by a personal visit to Masisi's camp by Herafu, a distant affine, were coldly rejected, and they were told to leave the territory or there would be war. In each case they responded that the territory was not Masisi's, and that in any case they had rights to the territory through affinal ties. They added that in view of the surplus of honey Masisi was offending the forest by trying to steal it all for himself.

This put Masisi very much in the wrong. He then raised an issue, long known, to divert attention from himself. He pointed out to his own section that Manyalibo's camp had a drying rack in it, sure indication that he was trading with the village. This was a major crime, and two youths went to investigate. They found it indeed to be so, and without much argument Manyalibo offered them food to take back to Masisi. After a great deal of further argument, and threats by the youths that they would tell the rest of the villagers of what appeared to be a secret alliance between two of their members and Manyalibo's section, the youths were allowed to take all the meat they could see, and Manyalibo promised to send a net to his "brother" so he could hunt for himself. Two days later he did this. Attracted by the meat, Cephu sent two of his section to join Masisi, and eventually joined himself. The rift between Masisi and Manyalibo, however, remained, and they did not re-form in the same camp again that

2 News of this kind travels between bands via the villages, and through the constant exchange of visits between cognates and friends.

year. While Manyalibo's crime was serious enough, desecrating the forest in the honey season by hunting for the villagers, Masisi's was equally, if not more, serious, in his attitude to the trespassing bands. The night before Cephu joined him, Masisi was made the subject of discussion, from the middle of his own camp, by several youths and young hunters. They all asserted the right of their in-laws to enter their own territory, to hunt or gather honey, whether they were wanted or not. They agreed that permission should have been asked first, but that in light of the surplus of honey in the forest it was hardly necessary. The discussion ended by everyone agreeing that all the noise[3] of the past weeks was plainly the fault of the villagers who wanted the meat that caused the rift to begin with. This decision was followed by a plea from Masisi for much singing to make the forest happy again. The honey songs were immediately taken up with renewed vigor, and Masisi was prominent in maintaining them right to the end of the honey season.

6. Largely through preoccupation with Cephu, Manyalibo and Herafu, with the Effundi Somali band and now yet another trespassing band from the neighboring Eboyo territory, Masisi's camp had several days with little honey and little food of any kind. All men in the group took turns in stating their complaints from midcamp, each promising to find out who was responsible and threatening to name them. On the fourth successive day of such "noise," the singing having deteriorated, much to the disgust of the youths and the women, Masisi was particularly irritable and began a long harangue about how bad the whole thing was, including his present camp, and saying that he could name those who were responsible for it all being bad, but instead he was going to name those who must go out the next day and collect lots of honey and make it well again. He then named all the hunters. But he continued arguing and, getting more and more irate, began to imply that those he had just named were in fact those responsible. There were growing murmurs of protest, which only excited Masisi further, and there would almost certainly have been a fight had it not been for the intervention of the youths and the young women. Two of the women and one youth seized the *ngbengbe*,

---

[3] "Noise" is a direct translation of the word *akami* in the local dialect of KiBira, or *kelelé* in KiNgwana. It is used in ordinary parlance, but always with an unfavorable connotation. It is given special significance by adding the comment that noise is bad (*sinana*). This is tantamount to a moral judgment, invoking the supernatural sanctions of the forest, for noise is also said to kill the forest (*akami a mu ndura*), just as it is said to kill the hunt (*akami a mu mukira*).

wooden clappers used only for the accompaniment of honey songs, and started clapping them vigorously while singing. Masisi found the competition too strong, shrugged his shoulders, chased the women away and, taking a pair of *ngbengbe* himself, joined in the singing.

The next day the men and the older youths went honey gathering and brought back enough honey to send some as a gift to Cephu.

7. Laziness is highly criticized among the Mbuti, and is always related to hunger. It is one of the few qualities (noisy hunting is another, "blindness" in the honey season a third) that is countered by public assertion, in mime, dance and song, of the opposite value. One morning, shortly after dawn, there were murmurings of discontent because of the dampness of the forest, and suggestions that there was enough food in camp to allow for a day without hunting. One of the older hunter's wives stalked out into the center of the camp and began an elaborate wordless mime, showing that she was not going to be lazy and stay behind and play and dance "empty" games and dances. She was going to take her husband's spear and go off and hunt (she reenacted a successful hunt) and return with lots of food and share it all around and make her *roho* good and make the forest happy. Then when *she* sang and danced, it would not be empty.

It was a good show, and the whole camp looked on and laughed, then went hunting.

8. One morning, at the beginning of the honey season, a number of hunters set out, as usual, at scattered intervals. Several seemed to be staying behind, so I also remained. After about half an hour the hunters returned, one by one throwing their nets on the ground in the center of the camp. When they were all back, a bachelor youth who had gone with them began a tirade against the hunters who had stayed behind. Hearing his voice, and wondering why he was taking such a prominent part in a hunting issue, women began sleepily coming out of their huts. It was evident that too many had decided to stay home, and the hunt had not had enough beaters. The youth, Pepei, not only criticized the women as lazy animals for not coming on the hunt but also criticized the rest of the hunters, pointing out they had been even too lazy to send their sons with their nets, and had left people like himself, an orphaned youth, to do the work of men.

The hunters had nothing to say, but the women responded vigorously that they were not going to carry nets and spears for the men, they had work of their own to do, and that if enough youths had gone there would have been enough beaters. As usual the women were loud in their complaint, and two of the hunters who had stayed behind with their nets now joined the side of Pepei and said that they had not gone because the women made so much noise, all the game was scared away and the hunt would have been empty anyway. Even Cephu had meat (a highly dramatic statement, for Cephu was usually meatless, or considered so), and the neighboring Lesé pygmies had meat, and everyone knew what poor hunters they were. But we were all starving because everyone was lazy.

The discussion went on for about an hour, it being made an excuse to raise all manner of minor sources of discontent. The hunt did not go off again, but in the afternoon there was a big hunting dance, and the next day the women made a special show of setting out, carrying their husbands' nets and spears, at least until they were out of the camp.

9. While many of the disputes concerning food arise out of general shortage or dissatisfaction, usually owing to poor hunting, and are made occasion for bringing up almost any topic, they are more often made occasion for criticizing specific groups. Thus children will find themselves criticized for making too much noise in their playground, or for splashing too loudly in the stream and so frightening the game away. Youths are accused of idling and playing with girls on the fringes of the hunt instead of guarding the edges against escaping game. Women are blamed for being lazy or inefficient as beaters, men for relying too much on women "who have other work to do." Elders are blamed for not keeping the camp quiet while the hunt is away, and always the whole camp is blamed for causing poor hunting by not singing and dancing properly.

There are innumerable petty squabbles over division of food, but these are always settled by those concerned. Never once have I seen such a squabble become an affair for the whole band to discuss. The only cases of disputes concerning food that have centered around specific individuals, and have not been mere expressions of marital disharmony, have concerned hunting "crimes." These are few and far between, and rather than accuse someone of being a poor hunter it is more often just pointed out that his net is always empty. There was one occasion, however, on which Cephu set his net up inside the hunting circle, therefore in a better position to catch the game being driven in by the beaters. A full description of this is given elsewhere (Turnbull, 1961, Chapter 5). Its essentials are as follows:

Cephu was neither a very good nor a very popular hunter, and it may be that he was afforded less cooperation by his fellow hunters as a result. Toward the end of a particularly unsuccessful day, Cephu slipped off and set his net up where it would catch the first wave of animals put up by the beat. He was caught with his spoils, however, and when back in camp there was a gathering of all the youths and hunters and elders (except Moké) at the *kumamolimo* (hearth of the *molimo*), to which Cephu was summoned by calling his name across to the small camp he had built for himself. He was named in the most uncomplimentary terms, and when he finally came to defend himself he was subjected to indignities, even by the youths and children. He was openly accused of stealing food from his fellow Mbuti, and this was something only animals did (note that the anger was of the band at someone having stolen from the band; this to the Mbuti is true theft). All manner of other grievances were brought up against Cephu, particularly his lack of participation in the *molimo* for Balekimito, Ekianga's mother, paternal aunt to Manyalibo and Masisi. Cephu responded that Balekimito was not his mother, and this was the trap into which he had been led. By saying this he disclaimed membership of the hearth, and so his theft became more logical but his act even more reprehensible. Finding himself now both a thief and an outsider, Cephu broke down and offered to return all the meat he had caught. The hunters went with him and stripped not only his hut but those of the three other families in Cephu's camp, leaving Cephu complaining that he would die.

That evening, however, Masisi slipped over in the dark with a peace offering of cooked food[4] and not long afterward Cephu made his way to the *kumamolimo* and joined in the singing for his "mother," Balekimito. This was one of the very rare occasions when a dispute was ended by what might be considered as direct retributive and punitive action by the band.

10. This is not to say that theft of food never takes place. It would be a rare Mbuti woman who did not conceal a portion of the catch in case she was forced to share with others, and occasionally a bachelor like Pepei, with a reputation for being somewhat *wazi-wazi*, was caught stealing a small quantity of food from a cooking pot or from

[4] Prestation is an important though unformalized part of Mbuti life, and a major means of establishing social relationships. Any property except the most personal items, such as used bark cloth, bows and spears, are likely to change hands, and even these personal items may be offered or sought.

someone's hut.[5] The woman would be roundly criticized, and maybe named. Pepei was either ridiculed or caught by other youths and given a mild thrashing with a thorny branch. But that did not stop Pepei, and at one time he was becoming such a nuisance that there was considerable discussion as to how to deal with him.

One morning a leg of meat was found missing from a rack where it had been smoked in readiness for a visit to the village. The owner of the rack had been one of Pepei's most outspoken critics, Makubasi, a son of old Tungana. Pepei, incidentally, was a discriminating thief, and he was generally tolerated because his thefts frequently operated as unofficial sanctions against people who had incurred public disapproval for some reason or another. However, Makubasi was a highly respected member of the band, and Pepei had overstepped himself by committing a theft that could not be construed as a mark of disapproval of some mild misdemeanor on someone else's part, but that was plainly an act of personal vengeance. Instead of thrashing him, Makubasi simply pulled down his meat rack, tumbling it into the fire below and burning it along with what was left of the meat. It was a dramatic gesture, and although his wife was seen to sneak some of the meat out of the fire before it was consumed, it was an effective move.

Makubasi's mother collected all the meat she and Tungana had, brought it over and threw it on the ground in front of Pepei's house, saying it was a gift for animals and insects, and for Pepei to eat it if he wanted. This was too much for Pepei, who started crying and saying how terrible it was to be an orphan. Everyone ignored him and for the rest of the day not a word was spoken to him. The meat lay rotting outside his hut, where it remained until consumed by animals and insects.

That evening, again at dark, a peace offering of cooked food was brought to Pepei by Sau, the old "witch" from whom he most frequently stole. Thus did Sau, like Masisi, restore harmony and *ekimi* (quiet) to the camp.

[5] The acknowledgment of theft as a crime might well be taken in support of Nippold's (1954) contention that, together with other hunters and gatherers, the African pygmies, and the Mbuti in particular, have a highly developed sense of private property. It is a debatable point, and largely a semantic problem, and if labored too much only obscures the essential structural fact that regardless of the extent to which property is "privately" owned (and if it is, where are any corresponding patterns, let alone laws, of inheritance?), the obligation to share is an important recognized value, recognized in practice (cf., constant reciprocal prestations). There is frequent show of reluctance, but

11. Sau was the mother of Amabosu, who had exchanged sisters with Ekianga. Sau was regarded by the villagers as a dangerous witch, a role she filled with zeal and which the Mbuti found useful in two ways. It provided them with a scapegoat in the forest just as it was a handy excuse for any misadventure in the village. In either situation the latent dramatic possibilities appealed enormously to the old lady's histrionic susceptibilities. One day Sau asked the wife of Mbaaka, a nephew of Njobo, for some food. She was refused. That night she did a little dance in front of Mbaaka's hut, her usual way of showing her displeasure. The next day, on the hunt, Masisi's son was about to run in bare-handed to catch a sharp-toothed *sindula* (chevrotain), but Amabosu persuaded him to take his spear. He did so, and then collided with Mbaaka, spearing him in the side.

There was actually some bad feeling between Amabosu and Mbaaka, and in case this was brought up (making it seem that Amabosu had deliberately caused his injury) the discussion of the incident was quickly turned to the refusal of Mbaaka's wife to give Sau food. She thus became the prime target for blame, with Sau acting as a secondary scapegoat, being criticized for dancing her "bad dance" outside Mbaaka's hut. In case anyone should take it too seriously, Manyalibo promptly started making fun of Sau's dance, flapping his hands to imitate Sau's pendent breasts. This was taken up by the children, who would not be content until Sau herself gave a demonstration.

That evening several hunters stood in midcamp[6] and said what a good camp it was, and commented on the good hunting. No further word was said about the spearing, except in the village, where the respective *kpara* went to the tribunal to effect reconciliation (between themselves) and blood payment. Amabosu's *kpara* agreed to pay sixty francs to Mbaaka's *kpara*, Masisi's *kpara* paying only forty. This news caused great hilarity in the camp, and the comment that villagers were animals, always "eating" each other. Between the Mbuti themselves I could find no evidence of blood payment of any kind, though any incident involving the drawing of blood is bound to provoke discus-

---

failure to share in time of need is considered a far greater crime than is petty (i.e., individual) theft.

[6] The importance of the "midcamp" position is that it defines the viewpoint of the person talking. An individual talking from his own hearth talks as an individual. If he talks from midcamp he is taking a band rather than an individual point of view. Similarly the *kumamolimo* is central, but more restricted in area and viewpoint, being used as a vantage point to discuss with the whole band matters pertaining to the *molimo*.

sion, during which any latent dispute might be aired. I could not definitely trace any heightening of reciprocal prestations between the individuals concerned, but it could have taken place in divers ways without my knowing it.

12. A number of disputes arising over food indicate trivial domestic disagreements, and seldom reach major proportions. A wife is late in cooking her husband's food, or cooks it badly; he spills some precious oil or fails to catch any game on the hunt. Such disagreements are confined almost entirely to the younger married couples, and they usually settle them by beating each other. If the beating gets too severe then the older women intervene, slapping both boys and girls soundly. If a marital dispute is more serious it may still emerge through a trivial incident in the hopes that it will be settled peacefully. If it is ignored, or mistaken as another petty squabble, then a more serious incident has to be created.

Baumbao, Tungana's eldest son, was having trouble with his wife, Tabakali. She was frequently away, back with her parents, and was suspected of having innumerable liaisons with other men. Baumbao said that this was particularly bad because of the *molimo* that was going on at the time. She had changed her hearth when she married him, and was now a member of this hearth, and she had to contribute to the *molimo*. He first brought the issue up simply by accusing her of cooking badly, and slapping her so hard that an old widow intervened, hitting Baumbao on the back with a burning log. Then everyone agreed that Tabakali was indeed a bad cook but that Baumbao knew that when he married her.

Baumbao took drastic measures. He took down the baskets full of offerings to the *molimo* from the *molimo* hearth, uprooted the sticks and the vine marking the site, and threw the lot onto the ground. While doing this he was busily saying that the *molimo* was empty. He said he had dreamed that his dead sister, Beselinda (naming her), had appeared to him in a dream and told him it was time someone made a good *molimo* trumpet and stopped using drainpipes.[7] She told him to make one and, having made it, to use it and then keep it carefully and not let it rot. He had done this and had been supplying

---

[7] As described elsewhere (Turnbull, 1961), the Mbuti on one occasion made use of some metal drainpiping they found in the local administrative center. Recognizing its musical potentialities, they stole two lengths and used them as *molimo* trumpets. Everyone agreed that the main thing was that the sound was undeniably good, but the more conservative elements strongly felt the lack of the identity between the conventional trumpet (made of a forest wood) and the forest itself.

the food for the festivities, but nobody was helping him. At this point, instead of naming his wife, he named another sister, living in the same camp, and said that she had not done her part. He added, as an afterthought, that his own wife was equally responsible, and stepped down.

Moké took his place and began a long harangue, telling the camp that the *molimo* was nothing to play with, that it was big and it was dangerous, and it could kill you. He pointed out that there had been no singing for two days and two nights, because of rain, and that indeed the *molimo* had become empty. The men should have built a hut for the *molimo*. But even so it was bad for Baumbao to take down the baskets. These should have been kept full; an empty *molimo* basket is bad for the forest. Moké then turned to Baumbao and said, "Your wife is one of us, she belongs to this hearth; it is for you to see that she keeps the basket full." Baumbao then stalked off in a temper, and Eyalo, his sister's husband, said that Baumbao never dreamed of anything but his wife's bad cooking and the whole *molimo* was empty and he was not going to contribute to an empty *molimo*, nor was his wife.

Moké replied, "Empty or not empty, that is the *molimo* hearth and it has to be looked after as long as it is there." He left, and a number of youths began to restore the sticks that had held the baskets, and then carried the baskets around from hut to hut, collecting offerings from each one. That night there was some singing, and for the next few nights. Then the festival was brought to an end. It was noticeable, however, that Tabakali was constantly being helped by her youngest sister-in-law both in collecting food for the *molimo* basket, and in cooking it.

DISPUTES CONCERNING SEX

13. There is a great deal of latitude in any Mbuti band on the sexual behavior of its members, but there are certain things that are known to cause offense. One is the playing with the private parts of a woman in front of her kin or her husband. One morning the camp clown, Matungi, was playing in this manner with Kengé's half sister, married to Kokoyo and mother of two children. Kengé was nearby and took great offense, and said that if Matungi wanted to play with the girl elsewhere that was all right, but not in front of her brother. Matungi replied by becoming even more intimate, whereupon

Kengé called out loudly that the only kind of person who would do that was one whose mother's private parts were smelly.

Matungi leapt into the center of the camp and challenged Kengé to a fight. Kengé refused, until called a coward. He and Matungi then each raised one foot against the other, and grappled. At this point the older men intervened and pulled them apart. By then it was time to go hunting, and the incident was forgotten.

14. Two of the most popular people in the band were Moké and Mayuma. The one was a widower, the other a widow. Mayuma wanted desperately to marry Moké, and as fond as he was of her, he equally desperately wanted to remain single. He had reared one family, he said, and had grandchildren, and that was enough. He wanted quiet, and women were noise.

But everyone else thought it would be a good match, and they plotted to help Mayuma. They tried to shame Moké into sleeping with her, at least, by getting her to ask him publicly to do just that. Moké refused.

Shortly afterward Mayuma became ill, and Moké was blamed. It was recalled by Mayuma's kin that after her husband had died, Moké had slept with her and offered her marriage. Now his refusal to fulfill that promise had brought about her illness.

Moké sat and listened, then restated his reasons for not wanting to marry Mayuma, but said that nonetheless he was very fond of her and would help to feed her and make her well. This was accepted, but it was still considered that thwarted love is a very bad thing, and nobody should deliberately mislead another in such matters.

15. Sexual relations between unmarried youngsters are countenanced happily unless they approach the rather hazy realm of incest, or unless they create a disturbance. Parents were constantly complaining of the noise their children made while engaged upon amorous expeditions; they preferred being able to turn a deaf ear. One youth went too far when he called out from inside his girl friend's hut to the group outside (which included her parents), and begged them to continue singing because "it is so sweet to [make love] to song, just like in the *elima* hut." His phrase for lovemaking was somewhat intimately descriptive, and brought cries of protest and his immediate ejection from the hut.

There are numerous other examples where parents become enraged simply at having their attention forced. Manyalibo's daughter, Mebapepé, was courted by all and sundry, and it was not this that

upset her father so much as all the accompanying noise. In particular
he was irate when waked up by a suitor crawling over him in the
middle of the night to get at his daughter. In this instance he gave
chase, and woke the whole camp up with a harangue from midcamp.
The accused's reply was effective—that if he had made noise and
wakened Manyalibo, it was not as bad as Manyalibo's noise, which
had awakened the whole camp for nothing.

16. By and large all that the parents can complain about in the
sexual life of their children is the noise. If the noise becomes too much,
however, it then becomes a matter for the band.

Such a matter became the affair between Appiamomba, nephew
of Njobo, and Mebapepé, Manyalibo's flighty daughter. The situation
was aggravated by the relationship between the two lovers, Appiamomba's mother being descended in the male line from the allegedly
same great-grandfather as Manyalibo. When accused of being of the
same clan (using the village term) as Mebapepé, Appiamomba denied it and said they shared different hearths. He was then asked, "You
cannot deny your mother was a Mupuemi; then so are you."[8] However, his argument about being of a different hearth carried weight,
the more so as Njobo was not at this time in the same section of
the camp as Manyalibo, and had not been for nearly a year.

One night Manyalibo's adopted son, Madyadya, chased Appiamomba away and called on the other youths to beat the offender.
The others demanded what offense had been committed; there had
been no noise. This was the beginning of a major argument which
quickly spread all over the camp. Manyalibo went to the midcamp
site and said, "Appiamomba is my child and he does not listen to
me. Mebapepé is my child and she does not listen. My children are
sleeping together and this is bad, for they are making noise all the

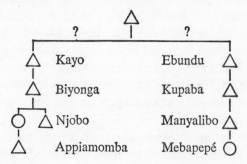

[8] An example of a common confusion concerning lineal descent among the Mbuti.

time. They sleep together every night. Why do they not make up their minds and get married? Then Madyadya can have Appiamomba's sister for wife and there will be no more noise."

The next day the issue was taken up by the elders, who gathered together and called on Appiamomba and Mebapepé to say what they wanted. The question of relationship was quickly dismissed by Tungana saying that nobody knew whether Kayo and Ebundu were brothers or not; who was alive to know, so what did it matter? It was "completely far away." The only question remaining was one of intent, and all the elders agreed that the children had been troubling their parents and spoiling the hunt with their noise, and that they must make up their minds and either get married or stop playing around. Appiamomba seemed unsure and said he would ask Mebapepé in his own time. Mebapepé, under pressure, denied that she loved Appiamomba and said she did not want to marry him at all, or indeed have anything else to do with him. She burst into tears and ran to a friend's house.

This relieved the tension somewhat, but Tungana brought up the fact that there were far too many young people around who should be married, and he started naming them. Each in turn began to state his case, but various jealousies quickly came to the surface, and fighting broke out among the youths and their girl friends. Tungana and Moké shrugged their shoulders and retired to their huts, sitting outside and watching with interest. The parents mostly left the scene completely, Manyalibo loudly complaining that the noise would kill him completely. Ekianga remained and tried to restore order, but quickly became involved himself. He shouted for Kengé to get a stick and beat some of the youths away. Kengé shouted back, "Later," and ran to join the other uninvolved youths on a hillock, to get a better view.

By evening the fight had ended, and everyone was too exhausted to renew any discussion. Moké and Tungana suggested it might be good to break camp and go and visit the village for a few days. Kengé said he thought this was an excellent idea, for then all the girls could sleep with the village men and that would keep them quiet for a time. He diverted the conversation to a discussion of village sex techniques, and the camp quickly regained its good humor. The next day half the band left for the village, the rest going further off into the forest. Without exception, the five young couples in question were divided by this move, though nobody referred to the fact.

17. A recently married Mbuti girl, while in the village, slept with a

villager. On returning to the hunting camp the first youth she met (Pepei, totally unrelated) beat her up severely, throwing her to the ground, holding her by one arm and kicking her. Nobody intervened, even her parents, and not a word was said about the incident.

That evening Pepei complained to the camp that no girls would sleep with him because he was an orphan, but when he began to make allusions indicating that this was one reason why he beat up the girl, Moké broke in and said that the only reason girls didn't sleep with Pepei was that he was so old. He was about nineteen.

18. It is seldom that within a camp a girl will go after one of the married men as blatantly as did Biyokenama, one of Tungana's daughters. Moreover, Biyokenama's father was distantly related to Masisi, the father of her lover, Ageronga. One morning she went so far as to follow Ageronga down to the section of the stream where the men bathed, taking off her cloth as she went. Ageronga's wife, Ambelema, a husky maiden, went in pursuit, hurling abuse. Biyokenama was heard yelling that Ambelema had no business suggesting such dreadful things; how could anyone think that she, Biyo, would flirt with her "brother"? But Ambelema had seen enough and began fighting. Tough as she was, she lost three teeth and came running back to the camp in tears. Biyokenama prudently took off for the village.

Everyone waited for Ageronga, who eventually came wandering in and went up to Biyokenama's mother and said he wanted three hundred francs, one for each tooth her daughter had taken from his wife. He said Biyokenama followed him without reason, that he wanted nothing to do with her, that she was a nuisance. Nobody believed this, but it was clearly a statement of loyalty, and sympathy swung to his side. It was agreed, in a discussion in which mainly youths took part, that Ambelema should not have said such dreadful things to Biyokenama, that even if true they were better not said; but the blame was more firmly placed on Biyokenama, and her mother was urged to take better care of her in future.

19. Marital disputes that are overheard but not deliberately forced on the attention of the band are ignored for the most part. If they are noisy and keep people awake, there may be complaints or there may be some ridicule. Certainly a fight going on between husband and wife inside a hut is followed with zest by all the youths and some of the younger married couples. These may even stand around watching

the hut shake, ready to catch whoever comes flying out first and prevent further damage.

Sometimes after such a squabble the young man and wife will equally loudly make up, so that everyone can hear, and will then emerge from the hut hand in hand and walk up and down the camp in ostentatious amity. This is considered a very good thing.

The custom of sister exchange, and the lack of any system of patrilocal residence, however, lead to conflicts of loyalties, and brothers or sisters find themselves drawn into disputes that are not strictly theirs. Ekianga was the cause of one such situation that continued for months, manifesting itself in a whole series of apparently unrelated disputes.

He had three wives, the youngest of which, Kamaikan, was the sister of Amabosu. Amabosu's wife, Amaloku, was in turn Ekianga's sister. Kamaikan was not only the youngest of the wives but by far the prettiest, and Ekianga ignored his marital obligations to the other two wives, even to the point of retaining favored portions of the game for Kamaikan. And only with Kamaikan would he sleep.

The other two wives responded in different ways. The oldest, Arobanai, ostentatiously built her own house and did nothing for Ekianga's. She said she was finished with her husband; if he wouldn't sleep with her she would sleep with his child. She phrased this in a way that made it sound rather incestuous as a form of insult, but everyone agreed that it was good for her to keep herself and her children out of Ekianga's hut.

Loku, the middle wife, had no children, and she retaliated simply by occasionally going off to join another band and letting it be known that she was available for temporary liaisons, owing to her husband's incapacity. This again was a blow at Ekianga's vital spot, his pride. But still he slept on with Kamaikan.

When Kamaikan became pregnant, Loku and Arobanai both rejoined Ekianga, thinking this was surely their chance. But when a boy was born, Ekianga still showed no signs of changing his ways. Arobanai brought her complaint to the band by striding up and down the camp listing all her grievances against her husband, one after the other. Moké came out and agreed that it was bad but that it was something that should be settled by them, and not made an issue for everyone else. But Amabosu now felt he had to intervene, and he sided with Arobanai, saying that Ekianga was doing a bad and dangerous thing continuing to sleep with Kamaikan. Everyone agreed that after giving birth a woman should be left alone for a while, and that her belly should not become big again until her child became big.

One of the many fights that occurred because of this relationship is described in *The Forest People* (Turnbull, 1961), at the end of Chapter 6. There it is seen that Amabosu sided with his sister, and consequently shared what everyone agreed was at least partly her guilt. Arobanai and Amabosu's mother, Sau, were the two who intervened to stop the fight when it began to get beyond bounds.

Amabosu, who intervened to help his sister, now found himself associated with her in her obstinate disregard of public opinion, so he ignored her and contented himself with continuing, from time to time, to make uncomplimentary remarks about her husband. This created a strain between Amabosu and his wife, Ekianga's sister, and while Sau became the protectress of her daughter-in-law, Arobanai became the protectress of her young co-wife.

One night Arobanai grumbled loud and long throughout the small hours until, about an hour before dawn, she came out into midcamp and woke everyone up with a torrent of abuse that was delivered with such vigor and evident sincerity that men came tumbling out of their huts holding their spears, ready for a large-scale fight. Arobanai had named just about everyone in the camp for some kind of offense, all of which contributed, she said, to Ekianga's delinquency. To emphasize her points she clapped her hands each time and pointed. Masisi tried to quiet her down by imitating her and laughing at her, but all but a few were too sleepy to see much humor in the situation, and when he saw he was not achieving anything he abruptly told Arobanai to "close her teeth" and then walked away. Ekianga came out of his hut and also quietly tried to pacify his irate wife, but was equally unsuccessful. Others tried similarly and made equally little impression. Sleep was impossible, and everyone sat around huddled over their family hearth, cold and miserable, listening to the still undiminished flow of invective. Occasionally a finely turned phrase brought some nervous laughter, but on the whole Arobanai was not going after dramatic effect, she was merely cataloguing all the disturbances of the past few months and laying them at her husband's door. After over an hour of nonstop tirade Arobanai began to wind up her argument with an indictment of both Kamaikan and Amabosu. Kamaikan could have resisted Ekianga's attentions, she said, and she added that she had resisted them often enough herself. But Kamaikan had either given in or had actually encouraged Ekianga, and Amabosu had supported her. This brought a mild cry of protest from Amabosu, and hearing it Arobanai rounded on him and asked him whether or not he was an Mbuti, for he had not behaved like one. What did it matter whether he was out of the same stomach as Kamaikan or not, were they not all *apua'i* (the term of friendship that covers brothers, sisters and age mates)? And was it not more important whether something was right or wrong than whose stomach who came from?

Finding this an unexpectedly dramatic declaration, and one which made Moké visibly sit up, and almost certainly feeling somewhat fatigued, Arobanai suddenly stopped and brightly said that she was going to get some sleep, the rest could do as they pleased. As she strode into her hut Moké came over and stirred at the central fire. Not addressing anyone in particular he said that this thing had gone on long enough, and that he did not want to hear another word about it. He said that if disputes continued they would kill the camp completely and absolutely, that the forest would refuse to accept the band and would send all its hunts back empty. And what Ekianga did was a matter for him to think about, for if he continued sleeping with Kamaikan it would almost certainly kill their child, and that would again displease the forest. He ended by saying, still staring carefully at the fire, "It is no longer a matter for us, it is a matter for the forest."

20. A month or so later Kamaikan's young son became ill. Arobanai was not in the camp at the time, but Loku was. Nobody mentioned Moké's warning that the boy would become ill if Ekianga continued sleeping with Kamaikan (as he did), and Amabosu was shouted down when he appeared about to say something to this effect. He changed his mind and went over to Loku, and said that she was to blame; she would have to cure the child by cicatrizing it. In the village this is tantamount to an accusation of sorcery, cicatrization being an admission of unknowing guilt by which the accused at the same time absolves himself and does all that is possible to negate the curse. The Mbuti know the belief and the custom, and sometimes, as in a case like this, they follow the custom without following the belief. Loku put up the expected resistance to the idea, and Amabosu chased her with a stick. The youths and hunters followed the show with enjoyment, and Manyalibo made jokes about nobody daring to come near him because he was the biggest sorcerer of all. Eventually Loku

feigned to run into a tree and fall unconscious. She was carried into Cephu's hut, where she stayed until the next day. Then, in a very matter-of-fact way, she emerged, went over to Ekianga's hut and picked up the sick boy. In front of the few who cared to look she made a few incisions with an arrow tip. The boy seemed better, and Loku happily played with him. Ekianga came and inquired how her head was where she hit the tree, and persuaded her to go and lie down. They disappeared into the hut together and that settled the matter. Manyalibo pointed to the hut and observed that it was shaking somewhat. "Sorcery, indeed!" was his comment as he turned his back to go into his own hut.

Ekianga settled down, from then onward dividing his attentions equally among his three wives, though seldom again was there a camp when all three were with him at the same time.

DISPUTES CONCERNING TERRITORY

21. There were only four such disputes that I recorded during an entire year, all of them slight and apparently indicative of marital disagreements; that is, excluding discussions as to whether or not to break camp and go to the village, a stock suggestion and a good arguing point whenever another issue turns up that is better avoided. Once, however, when such a suggestion was seriously made and the general opinion seemed to be that it was time for a move to the village, an elderly widow, Nakwanji, came out of her hut and harangued the band from midcamp. She said that a child had been born in that camp and that the child was well. Its food was there, in that camp and in that part of the forest, and it should not be taken from its food. Everyone agreed except Tungana, who said perhaps they could compromise and go halfway to the village and make a new camp there. Nakwanji was insistent and said no, this was the child's forest and this was where it must stay as long as it remained well and happy.

22. During the big rift in the honey season, Moké was up in the northern part of the territory with Ekianga and Manyalibo. Isa, his son, and Isa's wife, Pikenasona, were at Masisi's camp staying with Njobo's wife. Partly because of the noise Masisi made every evening, and partly because he wanted to be with his father, Isa kept insisting that Pikenasona leave and journey with him to the north. His wife, Njobo's niece, and therefore much at home in Masisi's camp, refused to go. Asofalinda, Ekianga's sister, told Isa it would be bad to go, as it

is bad to split a camp because of blood. Usually the metaphor of "stomach" is used in such cases to express kinship, but it was plain that this was what Asofalinda meant.

Masisi joined in and said that all members of a camp were of one hearth, regardless of stomach, and they belonged to the hearth; so Isa belonged to this hearth and his father to that. Until the next move of camps that was how it should be. Isa capitulated and continued to stay on.

23 and 24. Mbaaka fell from a tree and broke his arm. While incapacitated in this way, his recently acquired wife took off to join Cephu, who had invited a number of his Lesé-speaking in-laws to hunt in the western borders of the Epulu territory. When Mbaaka was well enough he went to Cephu's camp and brought her back. On arrival back in the camp, he threw her to the ground and said he had brought back rubbish, and he didn't know why. His wife got up and sat down in the door of the hut, upright and rigid, in a posture widely used by Mbuti women to show their utmost displeasure. Mbaaka told her to get his supper but she ignored him. His pleas and threats fell on deaf ears, and even when he slapped her once she barely moved. Masisi's wife eventually brought over some food and put it down between them. Mbaaka offered some to his wife but she pretended not to see it, so in a burst of temper he ate all he could and threw the rest away behind the hut. His wife found this too much to bear, and went inside the hut sobbing. She sat upright still, holding a tiny oil lamp in her hand. Mbaaka went in after her and knocked the oil lamp out of her grasp. She promptly picked it up, and this was repeated several times. Eventually she gave up and, still not saying a word, lay down. Mbaaka, trying hard to make peace, lay down beside her, but no sooner was he down than his wife sat up again, and remained bolt upright for the next two hours.

25. Meanwhile there was a diversion. Kengé and his wife were also having a squabble. Kengé, only indirectly connected with Njobo's family as an affine, was a person of some consequence because, although boastful, it was said he knew the forest better than any other Mbuti, and although he liked village life as well as any, he was not one for any display of individual authority. Roused by Mbaaka's having to go all the way to Cephu's camp to fetch back his wife, Kengé said that all wives were a lot of trouble, his own included. She was empty. "She cannot even speak; when she opens her mouth she just makes noises. She is an animal."

Everyone was tired of disputes in the camp, and they turned on
Kengé and told him it was he who was a bad husband. He promptly
said, "I shall tell my mother; I shall tell her everything, and she will
come here." His mother was notoriously argumentative, and the
thought of having another disputant on their hands was too much.
There were unanimous shouts of disapproval, whereupon Kengé said,
"So you let the Lesé Mbuti join empty Cephu in our territory, Cephu
who always hunts against us and should be turned out completely
and forever, yet you do not want your own mother-in-law to come
and live with you. What kind of Mbuti are you?" He went inside his
hut and after a few muffled cries and sounds of blows, there were
other sounds, less offensive, and in a half hour or so Kengé and his
wife came out together, making a great show of friendliness, peering
into Mbaaka's hut and laughing loudly at them for fighting so much.

DISPUTES CONCERNING TRIVIA

A headache, a hungry stomach, a painful leg, a leaking hut or a
damp forest—almost any kind of discomfort is likely to make an
Mbuti irritable, and he will pick a quarrel with ease and readiness so
that he can make his heart feel better, as they say. It is known to be
bad to keep things concealed, so there is no particular disgrace in
voicing suspicions and revealing antagonisms, particularly if it is done
quietly. Few, however, managed to make their heart feel better without creating a great deal of noise and making everyone else feel considerably worse.

Most such disputes, and there were likely to be several every day,
died as they began, in complete indecision. The following are typical
instances:

26. A small girl, playing in imitation of the boy's *nkumbi*, play-
fully whipped some of the men, including her uncle, Masalito. Masalito was enraged and hit her, which started a fight between his age
mates—that is, the young hunters.

27. Pepei fought another youth with sticks because the other told
him to beat the *banja* sticks, and Pepei said he was not a woman to
be ordered around. Tungana's wife then beat Pepei, saying that women
do not get ordered around, only children, and that is why nobody
will marry him.

28. Kengé beat his sister because she caught cold.

29. A girl returning from the village related how there was an

administrator there who took her photograph. Masisi demanded the money, and the girl said she did not ask for any. Masisi's wife said the girl was a fool, that she could have got fifty francs. In fact, she was a thief because she deprived everyone of cigarettes. The girl was still standing up where she arrived in camp, and Masisi's wife went up and forced her to sit down, and thrust her private parts into the girl's face as a gesture of contempt. The girl's parents said nothing.

30. A man burped loudly during the evening meal, and brought forth insults from all sides that would have developed into a fight had Moké not taken the *banja* sticks and started beating them, a sign for the *molimo* singing to begin.

31. A girl, decorated with leaves stuck in her bark cloth, was dancing vigorously and some of the leaves kept falling out. She blamed the younger children and started beating them until they fled, crying. Nobody interfered.

32. Amabosu, for no known reason, refused to allow his wife to move the fire from their hearth when changing camp. She went to her brother's hut and sat there sulking for nearly a whole day. Amabosu, fed by his mother, paid no attention.

33. Occasionally, however, even the most trivial origins can lead to a serious and lasting rift. Such a dispute, described more fully in *The Forest People* (Chapter 6), involved two brothers, Aberi and Masalito. It started when Masalito went to visit his brother on a rainy day. Masalito was in the main camp, Aberi in Cephu's camp. Aberi was asleep, and his wife insulted Masalito twice, first by refusing to smoke the same pipe, second by offering him an old and dirty pipe-stem to take back to the main camp with him. This led to a fight between the two brothers which was temporarily healed by the force of ridicule levelled against Aberi, and further subdued by the action of the *molimo* in beating Masalito's hut as a sign of the displeasure of the forest.

However, the bad feeling remained, if hidden, until Aberi's death.

DISPUTES CONCERNING THEFT

Theft, apart from the kind practiced by Pepei, was unknown except in the village context. Sometimes when Pepei was caught he was thrashed; on the other hand, sometimes he was tolerantly laughed at and allowed to go his way. There was once, however, a curious case that was never settled.

34. During a hunt Ekianga's unmarried niece, Ekimanji, had charge of his two spears and lost these together with her own basket, full of meat. Her story was that she was standing about, waiting for the rest to join up after a beat, when she had to answer a call of nature. She went a few yards away, and on return found the two spears and the basket gone. She called out, and Masalito, who was nearby, came running over. She asked him to stand there while she went and searched, which she did. She could find no traces. He also searched, and neither could he. It then began to rain and they returned to camp.

The next day the hunt went back to the spot and searched all over but found nothing. They even repeated the hunt in the same spot, casting the nets and beating toward them. Nobody offered any suggestions as to what could have happened, other than that they must have been taken. Not a single individual was hinted at directly or indirectly. One of the hunters suggested it was a villager, for Mbuti don't steal, but everyone knew that no villager was anywhere about in the forest during the hunt. However, the explanation, weak as it was, was better than none and, if not accepted, it was certainly not denied. The matter was not mentioned again.

DISPUTES CONCERNING THE VILLAGE

35. It might be thought that the village would be a common source of dispute. Far from being so, the village most frequently occurs in disputes as above, as a means of ending a dispute without settling the blame on any Mbuti and thus hastening the process of fission. Even money is assimilated into the forest pattern of distribution of food, insofar as it is ever brought into the forest (see 29, above). The only real dispute over money in my records was because the money was received for a spear which had been stolen from one villager and sold back to another, and it was difficult to assess the correct apportionment of the "game" (a hundred francs) between the "hunters."

The village, however, was often being blamed for ill health, and with frequent justification, for sanitation, which was no problem for the Mbuti in the forest, was a major one in the village. The village also frequently took the blame for poor hunting, particularly if some individual or some group in the band (e.g., the women who did not beat) seemed to be genuinely to blame.

One dispute of major proportions, and one of the few which occasioned direct action, did, however, have its cause in the village. The village itself was being pressed by the administration to increase its productivity at the same time that it was being pressed to supply the administration with more labor. In turn the villagers tried to press the Mbuti into supplying them with more food. Accustomed to a bare subsistence economy, the Mbuti could never quite see the necessity, nor did they altogether feel it was right or that it would be pleasing to the forest. Their belief, as far as I could determine, was not so much that they would be punished by the forest, but rather that the hunt would "be closed," that they would not get the unlawful surplus, that they might not even get enough for themselves.

To counter this the villagers offered divers kinds of medicine[9] for use in the forest, and agreed to make even more powerful medicine in the village. Sometimes the villagers offer to come into the forest, with a ritual specialist, to make medicine. The Mbuti tend to allow this, as it is profitable to them. Occasionally, however, the habit lingers, and whether or not *anjo* was originally a village or an Mbuti custom, it is now considered as a village trick, and disliked as such. *Anjo* is made by taking an antelope horn and filling it with a paste made from special parts of the antelope, charred black. This paste is then applied with a stick to the body of the hunter, to convey to him the senses of the animal.

This custom could sit perfectly well among the archers, where hunting is on a more individual basis. But among the net-hunters its use was taken as a sign of desire for personal gain above communal gain. On one occasion, when the hunting was not particularly good, *anjo* horns were rounded up from all over the camp, eight in all, and destroyed in the central fire. There was some protest from the owners, but not much. It was generally agreed that this made everyone the same, and that was how things should be.

From all the above, and from the rest of the disputes recorded in my notes, totalling 124, not counting the petty daily squabbles of no apparent import other than as an indication of bad temper, one of the most significant features is the small number of cases in which any

---

9 Among these medicines is that encouraged by the Arab slave traders in search of ivory, specifically to give success in the elephant hunt. Known as *esumba*, *ishumba*, and divers other spellings, it is sometimes confused with a love medicine of the same name, and even more frequently with the *molimo* of the Mbuti, the word *essumba* or *lusumba* being used to describe the Mbuti *molimo* when speaking in KiNgwana, language of the Arabized Bantu tribe. It is perfectly possible that the two practices became intermingled, both, from the Mbuti point of view, being concerned with the pleasure of the forest.

attempt is made to settle the issue in question one way or the other, even verbally, and the equally small number in which direct action is taken. The percentages are given as follows:

DISPUTE	Number Recorded	Number of Decisions or Judgments made	Instances of Positive Action
Food	67	5 (7.5%)	4 (5.9%)
Sex	37	4 (10.8%)	5 (13.5%)
Village	11	1 (9.1%)	1 (9.1%)
Theft	5	3 (60%)	
Territory	4		3 (75%)

These figures indicate the greatest degree of decision, either by the passing of opinions (judgments) or by the taking of action, in the least frequent types of dispute.

In the most common disputes of all, those arising out of trivia and having no particular direction and no specific purpose, it is only about one in a hundred that comes to a head in a way that calls for action or decision, such as the case of the two brothers (34). Such disputes gave frequent opportunity for the voicing of opinions on almost any matter, and acted as a mechanism by which most incipient disputes of a more serious nature were detected and aired before they grew to major proportions.

An examination of all the recorded disputes shows that without a doubt there are forces working toward order in Mbuti society, despite its unformalized nature and the absence of political or legal "systems." Such forces include the compelling demands of the stomach, which suffers directly from any dispute that interrupts the hunting and gathering economy, as any major dispute will; the weight of public opinion, expressed verbally, or through ridicule or mime, or in action such as thrashing (rare, and only for youths) or ostracism and exile. These are the negative forces against antisocial behavior. There are equally positive forces toward social behavior, including the esteem of one's age mates and elders, the affection of children, the contentment of a full stomach and, perhaps above all, the belief in the personal benevolence of the forest.[10] The positive aspect of the

[10] Fortune (1935) describes a parallel situation among the Manus, who, like the Mbuti, respect morality beyond the pressures of social sanctions. Fortune claims that the religious sanctions provide a socially established way of keeping the social sentiment "quick," and of bringing offenders to book without seeming to be personal. The latter aspect of religious sanctions is probably more vital for the Mbuti, where any dispute is

forest as an incentive toward good behavior is far more important
and far more strong than its negative aspect as a deterrent against
bad behavior.

---

likely to be highly disruptive but where disputes nonetheless occur. Any personal intervention or judgment would only be likely to lead to further disputes. The impersonal
nature of the forest as arbitrator and judge maintains the impersonality of the laws; or
if the forest is considered as endowed with personality, it is a spiritual personality and
owes no more allegiance to one Mbuti than to another, and so is still impersonal in this
context.

CHAPTER 12

Government: External

BAND TO BAND

Marriage

As already seen, the occasions calling for political relationships between one band and another in the forest context are minimal. Insofar as bands can be considered to exist only with respect to forest hunting territory, they cease to exist as political units when in the village, and there even the little interband relationship that pertains in the forest disappears completely.

There are basically only three areas of relationship, two of which might be considered formal, or institutional—marriage and trespass. The third, probably the most important structurally, is the interfamily visit. In all three areas there are no recognized or set patterns, each instance being conducted according to the context of the moment. But it will be seen at once that the relationships involved are once again along age lines. Marriage involves an interchange and a relationship between the elders of one band and the elders of another, between the youths of the one and the youths of the other. Trespass involves the hunters. Interfamilial exchange generally involves the older hunters, in my experience, or young married individuals who want on occasion to visit their parents and friends in their old band.

If marriage is contemplated between two youths of different bands, it will be the result of their having met through interfamilial exchange, or while in the village. There will have been an exchange of visits between the individuals, and when their intentions are made known it is likely, but by no means inevitable, that the family of each will visit the other's band in turn, building their hut close to that of their child's future in-laws.

The propriety of the marriage will have been discussed within each band, primarily by the elders; there is no exchange of this kind between the elders of the two bands unless there is some extraordinary complication, such as the adamant objection of the parental age level of one band or the other. If this happens, then two or three elders, male or female, come to visit the elders of the other band, and when the visit is over they will return, taking with them two or three elders to discuss the issue with their band. There is no privilege attached in such exchanges to either band because of sex; any privilege there might be depends upon the question of territory. Thus the band where the young couple is expected to live and hunt, regardless of whether their child is the bride or the groom, is considered as privileged, and consequently is to an undefined extent under obligation to the other band. However, as the question of residence is primarily an economic factor, depending on the relative sizes of the bands, it is generally settled to mutual satisfaction, and residence is not, in itself, a frequent cause of conflict.

Elders may be called upon to interact between two bands if the balance of sister exchange is becoming disproportionate. However, this too is essentially a question of economic balance and is only called to count if a band needs to strengthen itself. Again the issue of locality is more important in determining the matter than is the issue of sex. That is to say, in Mbuti society "sister exchange" can also, under certain circumstances, be regarded as "brother exchange," although insofar as patrilocality is the more usual pattern, so is "sister exchange" more appropriate. However, a band that needs strengthening and has just received a bride for one of its members may conceivably demand that the other band execute the rest of the exchange and provide a groom for one of their girls. They can then insist that he come to live with them. The fact that they have gained by both marriages is excused because of their economic situation.

However regarded, the exchange system is so loose that it is easily adaptable as a mechanism for maintaining hunting bands at economic strength. To this end the hunters have some voice, but it is an issue that is too clear-cut even to call for discussion, and once the issue is considered on grounds other than band size—i.e., the propriety of the marriage or exchange balance—it is in the hands of the elders. But even more is it all in the hands of the two individuals concerned, for although a serious depletion in the size of the band can induce hunters and elders alike to bring great pressure on its youths to marry, they cannot force such marriage. Interfamilial exchange, after all, is a perfectly simple method of increasing band strength, at least temporarily, and is considerably easier to arrange than a reluctant marriage. It can be seen, then, that the kinds of relationship existing between bands for the regulation of marriage are necessarily flexible. More important, marriage between bands provides a formal relationship between the nuclear families concerned and so provides also a basis for interfamilial exchange between those bands. To have such an exchange relationship, on a familial level, is of much more importance than wider political ties to a band which only on the rarest of occasions may need to act in concert, as a band, with the other band.

Trespass

Each hunting territory being economically self-sufficient, there is generally no need for economic cooperation. Boundaries are frequently natural features that restrict effectively the movement of both the hunters and the game, so trespass is also restricted. However, if following especially prized game, hunters will follow it across such boundaries with little or no hesitation. It is even said that if a band's territory is exceptionally unproductive, the band may move into a corner of its neighbor's territory, the furthest removed from wherever that band is camped at the time.

It is understood that in the case of pursuit of quarry a portion of the game will be sent to the resident band. It is equally understood that, if moving into someone else's territory, they should be notified and their permission sought. If either of these provisions is not maintained it may lead to friction, and a delegation of hunters from the offended band will visit the others in their camp, perhaps even staying with them for a few days. The question of who forms such a delegation is again largely an economic matter, for the members have to be drawn from the hunters, and the home band will obviously be unwilling to decrease its hunting efficiency to any significant extent. There is the stated possibility of a resort to fighting with wooden clubs; in one instance a few young hotheads suggested using spears, but this appeared to be more a figure of speech to indicate extreme anger, and was promptly rejected by the older hunters. I have, in any case, come across not a solitary instance of such open hostilities taking place between two bands. The visiting hunters are received with respect, and the trespassing hunters generally say that they intend to fulfill their obligations and, as a sign of good faith, offer to send out a hunt so their visitors can bring meat back to their band. If the host band insists that the others leave their territory, this will be done, but such action is rare, for it creates a barrier against interfamilial exchange.

If there is exceptionally good hunting in one territory and poor in another, and the bands are each small, they may temporarily join as one band. If they decide to cooperate in pursuit of a special hunt, this is achieved in much the same way that segments of a single band rejoin after the honey season. Indeed, during the honey season (among the net-hunters), each section of the band thinks and moves in terms of its specific section of the band territory, and if feelings run high between sections, infringement of section boundaries is considered just as much trespass as if it had occurred between two bands. In the same way that such segments, at the end of the honey season, gradually camp closer to each other, so two bands wishing to cooperate may approach each other.

Instances of cooperation, however, are even more rare than instances of trespass, and even though both may be regarded as formal, there is no special mechanism for dealing with them, and their influence in determining relationships between bands is negligible.

Interfamily Exchange

Although the above two areas of contact and interband relationship may be considered as formal, being institutionalized to at least some extent, there being a recognizable process of relationship though the outer form changes with the context, neither area is of as much effectiveness, in extent or degree, in determining interband relationships as the persistence with which families exchange visits. But such visits are so utterly unpredictable and circumstantial that there is not even the small amount of discernible process to be seen in the other areas. Whereas negotiations concerning betrothal or trespass at least involve recognizable elements of each band and act in response to a given stimuli, there is no saying when any given family, or how much of it, is going to decide to pack up and visit friends or relatives in another band. Nor do the families themselves generally express any other reason than that their "heart" wants it. No interference is offered by the rest of the band; indeed, there is generally no comment at all, unless their absence becomes prolonged beyond the duration of one camp—approximately a month.

The reasons for which a family might move out of one band and into another, for a temporary visit, are many and varied. Some have already been mentioned, and it should be reiterated that the freedom of individual families to detach and attach themselves more or less at will is of the greatest importance in the maintenance of bands at optimum strength, this consideration overriding any other considerations of residence, and apparently governing the system of sister exchange itself. But the band has absolutely no control over the nuclear family if it chooses to assert itself as such in this way. There are no direct bonds tying the family to other families, or to the band; the only influence the band can exert is between members of the same age group. This may result in only a part of the family moving, though when a family does decide to act in concert it usually does so despite any amount of opposition.

Whatever the purpose of the visit, whether it is in answer to a request to help swell the size of a small band, or whether it be part of an exchange of betrothal courtesies, a desire to see old friends and relatives, sheer whim, or of course displeasure with their own band, a family that visits another band is effecting a relationship between those two bands. Their very presence in the territory of another band entitles any member of the host band, regardless of kinship, to pay a return visit, then or at any time in the future.

To a certain extent even individuals visiting in the same way create the same kind of relationship between their own bands and the bands they visit. There is no particular term that distinguishes bands related in this way, and the Mbuti all say that in effect they could always find an excuse, if they wanted it, to visit any band anywhere in the forest—"relatives (friends) are everywhere." But generally there are preferred areas of visitation. Cephu, for instance, was criticized for visiting with the band immediately to the west of the Epulu band. But there was no way of preventing him from doing this, nor even from inviting some of them into the Epulu territory. Generally the exchange relationship exists between bands removed several times, spatially. This corresponds to the stated preferential marriage pattern, it being considered bad to marry into the immediately adjoining bands. However, in case of trespass, if a dispute ensues, an exchange relationship is sometimes claimed between families, and the dispute is then channeled off in this direction, it being left to those families to effect some kind of settlement. This may result in the family belonging to the offending band staying behind and visiting with the others, temporarily swelling their hunting strength. Once again, however, the band has no control over the family, and a family seeing itself being maneuvered into an awkward situation may suddenly leave altogether and go somewhere else. Neither lineal seniority nor political authority (chieftainship) are ever even mentioned in any attempt to influence a family's movement. When Manyalibo and Masisi, who shared the same grandfather (Manyalibo being the lineal elder), fell out and moved into separate camps, it was Masisi who took the initiative, and although Manyalibo claimed that Masisi ought to respect him because of age, he never suggested that Masisi was subject to his authority. He even stated openly that Masisi had the right to move wherever he wanted, but that it was not good for "brothers" to separate.

Thus interfamily exchange can only be regarded as a direct relationship between two families which, if they happen to be in separate bands, creates a relationship between their respective bands allowing for further such interchanges. Such bands respond to each other's needs with regard to optimum economic size, occasionally cooperate, and possess an additional mechanism for the settlement of interband disputes concerning trespass or marriage exchange.

BAND TO VILLAGE

In examining relationships between the band and the village we find the same distinction, only more clearly made, between formal and informal relationships that are the most effective.

But whereas even latent antagonism between bands is minimal, there is considerable latent antagonism between band and village, manifest not only in opposed systems of economic exploitation but also in opposed systems of values. Open conflict would bring advantage to neither group, and we have to think, in view of the lack of necessary economic interdependence, of the exchange in connection with this antagonism. It does indeed offer each group ample opportunity for insulting the other, though individual exchange relationships sometimes remain amicable, and even intimate, for considerable lengths of time.

The outward objective, at least, of the general Mbuti/Villager relationship is one of economic exchange, for mutual convenience. There are a number of formal levels at which such exchange, and the necessary associated negotiations, may be conducted, using a corresponding number of media:

1. Band/Village: *capita*/Chief
2. Lineage/Lineage: Lineage elder/*Kpara*
3. Individual/Individual: *Karé*/*Karé*

We shall deal with each in turn to determine the formal nature of the relationship, and the degree to which it is effective.

Capita/Chief

The relationship of the band as a whole to the village as a whole would be a simple and effective one if the band were, as the villagers claim it should be, a unilineal entity based on the principle of patrilineal descent. However, as we have seen, the band is generally composite, and in any case its composition is constantly changing. Sheer territorial propinquity, however, encourages a relationship of economic exchange between these two units, regardless of the composition of either. Generally speaking there is no need for the village to relate to the band as a whole, food exchange being more easily effected at an interfamilial or interpersonal level. However, under the foreign economic pressures mentioned earlier, at certain times villages found it necessary to have the massed help of all the Mbuti they could muster. In such a case the village Chief summoned the Mbuti *capita* and made his wishes known. The *capita* relayed these wishes to the band, which then did whatever it thought expedient, after general discussion.

The *capita* seems to assume more importance as an institution in the villages of the archer area, to the east of the Epulu. However, even there the villagers themselves admit that the institution is foreign to the Mbuti. I have not once heard it claimed otherwise, by Mbuti or villagers. Among the archers, as among the net-hunters, old men and women are accorded respect, but they have no authority and their area of influence is limited in accordance with their age, and does not include the village. Such elders, then, have no more say than any other Mbuti concerning village matters pertaining to the band as a whole. But village affairs do not fall within the province of any age group, and the *capita* finds himself having to deal separately with each family, if indeed he takes that much trouble at all. Sometimes he may do so if a villager accompanies him to the camp in the hopes of adding strength to the village argument. I have seen this happen among the archers as among the net-hunters, in each case with a direct plea for all Mbuti to go to the village to help with the cotton harvest.

Usually the *capita* first made a plea from midcamp, and was listened to silently, but without respect and without reply. He then went from family to family, and from each family, despite the presence of the villager, received an emphatic and final negative answer. If the villager is not present on such an occasion, either the *capita* will act the clown as he delivers his message, or both he and his message will be ridiculed by others; there is, if anything, a greater chance of his achieving something for the village under such circumstances.

Respect for age is not conveyed upon the *capita* when acting in that capacity. Not only is he ridiculed, but if he persists in his efforts on behalf of the village, even his juniors, family members or otherwise, will combine to "shut his teeth." In areas where the occasional wealthy tourist passes by, the Mbuti regard him as they regard villagers, as animals to be eaten, and the *capita* fills the same role, but generally with more success for the rewards are usually more immediate and satisfying to all concerned. In other respects the situation is parallel to that of the village.

The difficulty is no less, even if the Mbuti are already in the village. If the villagers try to exert pressure on them as a band through the *capita*/Chief relationship, this precipitates an immediate return to the forest because the men will not even discuss the matter in the village. Their return may just be for purposes of discussion, but it may also lead to the return of the entire band. The men seem to regard it primarily as their province, the village, in a sense, being a hunting area calling for skill and courage, rather than a gathering area, and they explain their action in these terms, allowing that their wives could come if they really had something to say.

The band/village relationship, then, is not to be considered as highly effective, though there are times when the Mbuti find it expedient to act in concert in this way.

Lineage Elders/Kpara

The relationship of an Mbuti lineage to a village lineage is a little more effective, for while a band cannot be recognized as a unilineal entity, there are within it divers lineal units. One or more of these may well occupy a hereditary relationship with a village lineage, the head of which would be the *kpara*. They have no name for the head of their lineage except "old man," the term by which the villagers also refer to him.

As stated earlier, this relationship may be exceptionally cordial, and will then be maintained even if the Mbuti lineage is removed by a considerable distance from the village of its *kpara*. On the other hand the relationship may be extremely hostile, for if the Mbuti are not dealing with their *kpara*, they are certainly dealing with someone else and this causes a three-way antagonism. The *kpara*, having no political control over the Mbuti and being unable to apply any effective economic sanctions, take refuge in their belief in supernatural sanctions or else employ the local doctor to effect a curse. Their only hope of practical recompense lies in making a case against the villager with whom their Mbuti are dealing.

Insofar as the villages themselves have been tending to become somewhat divided, certain members being sent or simply going elsewhere to work, the situation is aggravated and it is difficult to assess the reasons, precisely, for the noneffectiveness of the interlineage relationship. Again the major immediate cause, though not necessarily the reason, is the fluid and composite nature of the Mbuti band, the periodic division of which may cut right across lineage divisions.

Karé/Karé

Male Mbuti individuals are related formally to male village individuals through the institutional *karé* brotherhood. The *nkumbi* initiations which take place periodically (every three years for the past twenty years or so, in the central Ituri) are not confined to individual villages, but draw candidates from a number of villages within the same major segment of the tribe. Frequently the *kpara* will try to see that members of their own immediate family are made *karé* to their Mbuti, but this is not always possible, and the *karé* relationship is liable to cut across the lineage relationship.

It is essentially a brotherhood pact avowing reciprocal obligations including and centering around economic exchange. But it is a more intimate relationship than can exist between the Mbuti and their *kpara*, particularly as they are related not only in terms of the knife but also in terms of age. During the period of seclusion in the initiation camp, *karé* are always expected to be close to each other, although any attempt of the one to comfort the other will be ridiculed. They are, however, frequently set tasks to perform jointly, or made to perform services for each other. A bond is begun with the knife, and may grow, under these circumstances, into a lasting friendship. It is because of this friendship, and not because of the knife, that an Mbuti may well maintain an exchange relationship with his *karé* throughout his life. It is also a question of friendship with the villager, but for him the relationship is further compelled by his belief in his own tribal lore, a compulsion not felt by the Mbuti. The Mbuti sometimes exploit this relationship with a *karé* as they may also do with their *kpara* for whom they feel no friendship, knowing that the strength of tribal lore, and the fear of supernatural sanctions upon themselves, will bring at least a grudging response.

Although essentially an individual relationship rather than a band relationship, failure on the part of an Mbuti to respond to his *karé* is considered by the villagers as a violation of village law, and can be made into a lineage/lineage or a band/village issue, but with predictable lack of success because of the absence of any effective agency of control. However, the attempt is sometimes made, and the band may at least be held responsible, in violation of *karé* brotherhood, for the actions of one of its members.

None of these formal relationships, then, brings about much effective economic exchange, and the political relationship is correspondingly ineffective. The mechanisms for political relationship are there, but their use is made impossible by the whole process of flux in Mbuti society. At the best those mechanisms are taken up and used momentarily when it is found to be mutually advantageous.

Individual Economic Relationships

There is, however, the last level, that of the nuclear family to the nuclear family, by which the band relates to a village. This is the effective level at which the bulk of economic exchange takes place among the Epulu Mbuti, and among most other net-hunting bands I have seen. In view of the flux that characterizes Mbuti society, it is indeed the only level that could provide any realistic basis of relationship.

It may not even necessarily be a family-to-family relationship. Individual members of the Mbuti family may go their own way and relate as such to village individuals. But once formed, these relationships are likely to remain fairly constant, for as long as the Mbuti family is hunting within that territory, or within reasonable reach. Several such attachments might be formed by the Mbuti, though generally not more than one in any one village. This leads to effective economic exchange but it provides no basis whatsoever for relating the band to the village, and it offers the villagers no more opportunity for control than they already have; namely, the fondness of the Mbuti for village luxuries. Bribery, indeed, may be said to be the only effective control the villagers have over the Mbuti. But it is short-lived and costly, and is on an individual or familial basis at the most. As far as internal relations are concerned, the band clearly exists as a territorial unit composed of a number of nuclear families cooperating in economic food quest. The Epulu band, and nearly all others studied, are characterized by a composite nature, negating the possibility of lineal authority. Any form of central authority is further negated by the constant changing of band composition. Leadership exists in respect to different fields at different age levels, and is nowhere centered in a single individual. Any attempt at the assumption of individual authority, or even of excessive influence, is sharply countered by ridicule or ostracism.

There is consequently no central leadership, in the form of an individual or even of a council, with which the centralized village leadership can deal in political terms. Nor is there any lineal leadership, let alone any stable lineal unit, with which village lineal units can relate, except in theory. The institution of *karé* brotherhood is primarily an individual relationship, and although its abuse can enlarge the relationship to a band/village level, there is again no mechanism of effective relationship at that level. Therefore the *karé* relationship, insofar as it is effective, only relates individuals.

Effective economic relationship of a stable nature can be seen to exist only between individuals or between families, determined by territorial considerations and by mutual satisfaction. The only control arises from these considerations, heightened by the Mbuti addiction to certain village foods. However, this fragments the band to such an extent that we can say the band simply ceases to exist, as such, in relationship to any village community. Neither the Chief nor the *capita* has the slightest authority or control over the band; flux renders a lineal interrelationship impossible, and we are left with no more than an agglomeration of person-to-person exchange relationships that may be economically effective but convey no political control to either side, the nuclear family being the largest effective unit, and frequently not even being that.

21. A young Mbuti mother, sitting on a log, prepares mushrooms, using a village knife. Another such knife lies across her left foot. It is probably the most widely used utensil for which the Mbuti are dependent upon the villagers, though still not indispensable.

22. A young hunter prepares meat on a smoking rack for bringing to the village.

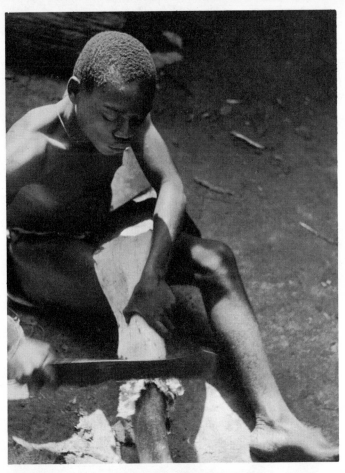

23. A youth, Kenge, strips a piece of bark before it is soaked, prior to hammering it into cloth.

24. Strips of bark, softened by water or smoke, are hammered into cloth up to eighteen inches wide. There are many individual preferences for different types of bark.

25. Akidinimba celebrates her puberty and her forthcoming marriage during an *elima* dance.

26. A young Mbuti mother, Epini, with her infant wrapped in a specially chosen piece of bark cloth. She will freely allow other women to fondle and even nurse her child, and will pass it around for the men to hold and admire.

CHAPTER 13

Magic, Witchcraft and Sorcery

MAGIC

To separate the world of magic from the world of religion is perhaps a dangerous pursuit, and not always profitable. In this instance it is done because we can thereby achieve a significant contrast between the world of the village and the world of the forest. By and large the village world is full of magic, witchcraft and sorcery, leaving little room for what might be considered the more spiritual, or religious, aspects of belief, faith or even hope, and certainly none for worship in the sense of devotion.

The forest world, on the other hand, is remarkably lacking in the former elements, and filled with the latter. But there is an overlapping and, necessarily, a meeting ground where any further overlapping is rejected and which becomes an area of conflict. The Mbuti have their own very simple forms of magic, but no witchcraft or sorcery, which they utterly reject. However, when faced with it in a village context, they are forced to come to terms with it and they have learned to turn these village institutions to their own advantage, in much the same way that they accept other village institutions such as the *nkumbi* initiation.

Increasingly one is aware of a curious ambivalence in the Mbuti attitude toward the village. This is not surprising in itself, when two opposed societies are in such close juxtaposition. But the vehemence of the Mbuti denial of witchcraft and sorcery seems at odds with the meekness of their acceptance, however nominal, of village domination in the village context. The answer lies mainly in the Mbuti attitude to the unknown, an attitude that is optimistic but open. In the realm of the known they can afford to be vehement, and they are perfectly aware of the social values of an institution such as witchcraft, and make use of it without accepting the belief. Similarly with the *nkumbi,* the Mbuti see submission as a means of acquiring status, which is necessary to them if they are to have any part at all in village society. They also see in it, and in witchcraft, a means of defeating the villagers on their own grounds, by proving their superiority. They can do this in the *nkumbi* by being excessively brave, either physically or by flaunting the taboos and thus exposing themselves to supernatural sanctions. They can achieve the same end similarly by pretending to be better witches than the villagers, and indeed the villagers often believe this to be the case.[1]

Nonetheless, the adoption of an institution, for whatever motive, brings a number of results, some of which will inevitably correspond to those expected and desired in the original context. This is a reality, a practical experience, and as such cannot help but somewhat alter the attitude of the Mbuti. In this way they may begin to partially believe in village magic or witchcraft or supernatural sanctions, at least insofar as such belief is not contradicted by the rest of their experience. This ambivalence is particularly marked when they are in the village, which is full of the unknown for the Mbuti, and is correspondingly much less pronounced in the forest. It is with this in mind that we should examine the magico-religious practices of the Mbuti, where there seems to be so much borrowing.

Magic is best defined, for all the tribes in the Ituri region, as the manipulation of material objects which in itself is believed to be the direct cause of certain results, with no invocation or spiritual intervention. It is essentially a natural and, from the local point of view, scientific procedure, having nothing to do with the supernatural.

The villagers have recourse to magical acts, so defined, for almost any circumstance over which they have no other form of control, yet which does not call for the invocation of supernatural intervention. Fertility of men, women and land may be secured by such processes, as may protection against thieves and adulterers; the weather may be influenced, illness may be cured. If the magic takes the form of an amulet to be worn, it may be secured from the local doctor; if it is something requiring more elaborate manipulation, such manipulation is generally considered a professional secret, and certain individ-

[1] The situation is somewhat analogous to that described by Lévi-Strauss (1955) for the Nambikwara chief who understood the principle of writing as a means of communication, and imitated it in order to heighten his status among his band and to intensify his measure of control. In each case the adoption of the institution was not for its original value, but to strengthen a somewhat precarious position. It is probable that the Nambikwara chief was thinking not only of his relationship with his own band but also of that with the European "band."

uals acquire the reputation of possessing the necessary skills. The doctors in particular possess such skills as part of their profession as diviners and curers, but even they recognize manipulative power in others, and do not try to effect a monopoly.

If the magic fails, it is considered that the manipulation was faulty and will be tried again. Several successive failures will be attributed to the intervention of supernatural forces, and will then involve witchcraft or sorcery.

As shown earlier (p. 54 *seq.*), village magic, even regarded as it should be, in context—as scientifically valid—has little to offer the Mbuti. It may nominally impinge upon their world, for there are, for instance, divers forms of magic to protect plantations against Mbuti raiders. But the Mbuti attitude to magic is different, for they recognize village magic as a mere attempt to control a situation, and not as a scientifically valid process. Brought face to face with such magic they may be wary, but primarily they are skeptical.

In their own world the unknowns are far fewer, and the need for control over events scientifically beyond their control is far less keenly felt. Such actions as may be described as magical, pertaining to health, weather or the hunt, involve an identification with the forest, being forms of sympathetic magic. In this respect, then, they are in a sense religious acts, for the forest is regarded as their protector. It would be difficult to determine whether the hunting fire is meant to placate or propitiate the forest, thus being a religious act involving a belief in a spiritual force, or whether it is thought to actively and directly affect the forest game, luring it into the nets. Mbuti attitudes, both expressed and observable, are mixed; the elements of religious belief, however, are never entirely absent.

The protective "magic" used to secure good health for a newborn baby, a vine bracelet and wooden charm, equally involves in a very real sense a religious belief in the power and strength and protectiveness of the forest, as well as making a more truly "magical" connection between the physical strength of the forest vine and trees and the weakness of the newborn baby, using the charms as a medium through which this strength can flow.

All this makes honey magic all the more outstanding, for it accords honey gathering far more ritual attention than is accorded to the economically incomparably more important activities of hunting and gathering. Some of the magic is slight and individual—a piece of bark cloth belonging to a girl or a woman is put in a cleft stick with a piece of honeycomb pressed down above it. Two sticks are prepared in this way by a hunter, and when the cloth is set on fire the hunter waves them both in the air. He then hands each of them to a youth, and the two youths run through the camp and out into the forest around the camp. The womenfolk clap loudly until the youths return and rather unceremoniously put the sticks down near the central fire.

The honey dance also separates the sexes, the women pretending to be bees, men the honey gatherers. Yet another separation, symbolizing the power of the women, is the medicine that is said to attune one's hearing so that one can hear the larvae wriggling in the honeycombs, high up in the trees. A woman prepares a stick which, when blown through, produces a misty spray. She blows into the ears of all the men. The men say that the bubbling noise they hear is the sound of larvae and grubs eating honey, and that it will guide them to the hives.

There is seldom any doubt as to where honey lies, and it is plainly the social rather than the economic importance of the honey season that is being celebrated. This is most clear in the great *angbe* medicine, in which the age groups are further differentiated and which includes attention to orientation that is quite unique in my experience (this, together with several other features, is so singular that it cannot be adequately explained at the moment, but is nonetheless described for its intrinsic interest).

At the *kuma'ngbe* (hearth of honey), a number of youths chop a special *tembu* wood into kindling (the only time I have ever seen kindling prepared). Four hunters supervise. The four hunters then put their honey axes down in the hearth, blades to the center. One of the hunters lines the axes up so they align with the cardinal points of the compass. This done, each hunter takes his ax and draws it toward him, cutting a trench along that line. In this way four trenches, two feet long and three inches wide and deep, are cut. In the center a square is cut so that the four corners indicate the intermediate compass points. The position of the sun is consulted to insure correct alignment.

A senior hunter has meanwhile cut four lengths of *teka* vine, carefully bound so that its juices do not escape. He removes the binding and allows the juice to fill the center square, after which water is added to fill the trenches. The combination of juice and water is said to be *mota*, or powerful. Each vine is laid in a trench, projecting at the extremities. Two youths then take out the vines and shake them in all directions, liberally sprinkling anyone who happens to be standing by. Other youths are by now standing about, whistling on their honey whistles, a form of *madi* called *singbe*. The kindling is then stuck upright in the trenches, beside the *teka* vines, which have been replaced. Children help with this.

A hunter then places a single ember, apparently drawn from any fire, in a *mongongo* leaf and, having filled the center square with *mongongo* leaf stems, he places the coal on top. More kindling is added, crisscrossed much like a house of cards, each piece carefully placed by youths and hunters together. Without fanning, the kindling catches and a dense cloud of smoke is given off. An elder then brings over a bundle of old leaves that have been used for collecting honey, and places them near the fire. He waits until the smoke begins to dwindle, then directs the operation of placing the honey axes in the hearth, waiting for the blades to get warm and then using them to split some *toangbe* wood. The *toangbe* tree and the *tembu* tree are both good honey trees, but the *tembu* tree has to grow "old and fat" before it is favored by the bees.

Elders then carefully arrange the old leaves, adding more as necessary, in a large circle around the fire. Four *singbe* whistles are stuck in the ashes of the fire, pointing to the cardinals. While elders stand and shout, women gather and loudly clap their hands, and both hunters and youths kneel on the circle of leaves, facing in to the hearth, and begin pounding their fists rhythmically on the ground. The tempo increases to a maximum and is broken off with a sudden shout. This is repeated twice more, after which the hearth is abandoned and camp life resumes as though nothing had happened.

The Mbuti themselves are unable to give any satisfactory explanation of the performance, and it seems to combine elements of genuine magic (for they talk of the smoke attracting the bees and bringing honey to them) and of invocation of supernatural intervention (the *keti* are said to hear the pounding on the ground and will know that the Mbuti want honey). Whatever it may be thought to achieve, however, *angbe* (also *angbelu*) undoubtedly reiterates the division of the band into age groups, a division that is evident throughout the net-hunting season but is not so necessarily a part of activity during the honey season.

However regarded, Mbuti magic implies belief and is to that extent religious, no matter how much it may also be thought to have direct causal attributes, and the belief always supposes the benevolence of the power believed in. There is not a solitary instance to show the belief in a malevolent power against which protection must be sought. This is plainly different from village magic, which is essentially pragmatic and not in any way related to a central value system. We showed earlier (pp. 53–62) how magic does not provide a means by which the villagers can control the Mbuti. By a comparison of the two systems of magic we can see in effect how clearly they indicate major value differences despite initial outward similarities. In particular, the Mbuti attitude to the forest as a benevolent central value in their lives can be seen, and while in village magic we see only the lack of such a central value, when we examine witchcraft and sorcery we see its exact polar opposite.

And it will be remembered how (pp. 57–59) the Mbuti recognize the difference in attitudes toward magic, and put it to good use. The villagers regard Mbuti culture as impoverished in all respects, and the lack of the magic so abundant in village life is part of their argument. In making this lack of magic an excuse for the allegedly poor hunting that has deprived their *kpara* of meat, the Mbuti turn the situation nicely to their advantage, and turn the argument of the villagers against them. Thus although village magic and forest magic are different and distinct, the areas overlap in such a way as to deepen the opposition between the two worlds.

WITCHCRAFT

With witchcraft the situation is different, for this is something peculiar to the village world. Earlier (pp. 59–60) we showed some of the ways in which village witchcraft (often confused by the Mbuti with sorcery) impinges on forest life. Again, the villagers regard the lack of witchcraft in Mbuti culture as a sign of cultural poverty, and in their own belief in the power of witchcraft they seek to use it in their constant struggle to impose some kind of control over the hunters. However, the Mbuti again make use of the village belief in witchcraft for their own ends, using it as a means of escape from situations in which they would otherwise be culpable and stand to lose a good exchange relationship.

In their own forest world, however, witchcraft plays no part, except insofar as it is recognized as a useful device for deflecting blame, and is thus occasionally used, tongue in cheek, to resolve a dispute. As indicated in the foregoing chapter, the prime objective in the settlement of a dispute is to avoid attaching blame to one individual or another, for this would result in a rift in the band. The blame has to be either deflected or dissipated, and the village notion of witchcraft is sometimes used to this end.

In the prolonged dispute over Ekianga and his three wives, the situation was aggravated by having, in the same band, Ekianga's brother-in-law, Amabosu, with whom he had exchanged sisters, and Amabosu's mother, old Sau. Sau made an ideal scapegoat, conforming to the village notions of what a witch should look like, and her role at times became rather like that of the camp clown. She would be accused of dancing outside people's huts in the middle of the night, and on one occasion she was distinctly heard to mutter in an exasperated voice, "Do they expect me to urinate inside my hut?"—for she had indeed emerged in the middle of the night to answer a call of nature. Nonetheless, on that occasion she rose to the needs of the moment and agreed that she had been dancing because she had been made to dance, and she was not responsible, and she was sorry for any harm she had done.

However, she was a major and active peacemaker in the family squabble, actively intervening to prevent Ekianga and Amabosu from fighting, and equally actively looking after the children of all the wives involved, passing them from one to the other and in this way helping to preserve reasonable relationships at least between her daughter and her son's wife.

All the more in the village was Sau used as a scapegoat. But whereas in the forest the scapegoat, even if the clown, feels the full weight of the blame he takes upon himself and may suffer some unpopularity, though temporary, in the village there is no such disadvantage, and old Sau played her role with zest. At a time when there were an unusual number of deaths through stomach disorders contracted in the village, the Mbuti were sharply criticized by the villagers for allowing this to happen and not taking the proper protective measures. It was plainly witchcraft, if not sorcery, and it was their duty to find the witch and have the necessary purification. An elaborate witch-hunt was held in the village, and of course Sau was finally "divined" and dragged out of her hut—where, at the time, she was dozing—complaining about all the noise.

Emerging into the center of the village she made all the usual protests, and performed the usual trick of stabbing herself with a knife, but holding it carefully so that it just nicked the skin sufficiently to draw impressive-looking streaks of blood. She was promptly stopped from "killing" herself, having it explained to her that she was only a witch and could not really help what she had done, and only had to purify herself.

However, the deaths continued and nobody else was willing to take Sau's role, and in the end there was no alternative but to accuse her of sorcery. In village belief, witchcraft substance is normally dormant but may become activated through a number of causes. A witch is a person who possesses this substance but has no control over it. Once discovered, the witch is under an obligation to keep the substance "cool." Sau obviously was not keeping hers cool, and it is said that if very bad people know they are possessed of witchcraft substance they may learn how to control it deliberately, and they then become sorcerers. Sau, then, was accused of deliberate and malevolent use of her witchcraft substance. She was formally condemned to be beaten to death. The Mbuti made a show of beating her but then stopped, telling the villagers that they did not want to kill her as then they would only have her spirit to deal with (using another purely village concept), which would be much more difficult to control. Exile was suggested instead, and Sau was duly exiled, and departed for her own village in great spirits, laden down with foodstuffs.

The deaths had caused the band, which originally had been gathered in the village for a wedding, to depart abruptly for the forest as soon as the Sau incident was over. It took a number of days to prepare themselves, taking fond farewells of their exchange partners, and Ekianga went ahead with three other hunters and their families to select the site. When the rest arrived they found Ekianga comfortably installed, with the sorceress, Sau, happily in an adjoining hut looking after his children. Her position in the forest was in no way changed. She remained a scapegoat, but her right to stay with the band was never seriously challenged, nor were the respect and affection with which she was regarded ever diminished.

The same use of witchcraft was found in other bands, and the same professional scapegoats. The other "witches," like Sau, occasionally made fun of the whole thing by miming all their alleged achievements as witches, including the legendary witch's dance and the casting of the "evil eye." In every case the "witch" occupied an otherwise perfectly normal role in camp life, having no more and no less respect than any other by virtue of being a scapegoat.

In forest life there is no need for witchcraft as a social institution, for there are other mechanisms to deal with the situations with which witchcraft, in village life, deals. As indicated, it may play a minor and supplementary role in the dispersal of blame in a dispute, but completely without involving any belief in the actual presence of witchcraft substance. It is highly significant that the concept of supernatural power in this form is utterly foreign to the Mbuti, and this places them in a somewhat disadvantageous position when brought face to face with the village notion of sorcery, and the practice of cursing.

SORCERY

While the Mbuti make limited use of village concepts of magic and witchcraft for their own practical ends, they make no such use of sorcery, having for it a complete abhorrence. The villagers themselves never admit to being sorcerers, for sorcery is by definition antisocial and evil, but they may use the threat of sorcery (pp. 60–62) and claim to have employed a sorcerer against the Mbuti. More likely still, they may seek the aid of the local doctor to effect a curse against the Mbuti for nonfulfillment of their side of a bargain.

From the village point of view there is a world of difference between a sorcerer's curse and a doctor's curse, but from the Mbuti point of view they are one and the same thing. The theoretical and institutional aspects of magic and witchcraft the Mbuti can appreciate and turn to their advantage. Confronted with sorcery they have no recourse but flight. Flight in itself is significant, for it is flight away from the village into the forest or, if already in the forest, then it is flight further into the forest. On the whole it is a firm belief that sorcery is ineffective outside the village, but sometimes circumstances (such as poison) combine to indicate otherwise, and then it becomes a question of proximity to the village. Once again, however, as with magic, we find the Mbuti regarding the forest as a place of refuge, a place where they are sure of protection.

Against witchcraft, all the Mbuti have to do is to acknowledge being witches and go through the necessary purifications; the belief never touches them. Against sorcery, apart from flight, they have no means of defense for there is no counterpart in their experience. Sorcery implies the use of supernatural powers to effect harm on someone. Two concepts are involved that are foreign to the Mbuti: one is that a supernatural power can be used for anything but the social good, and the second is that anyone could wish, anonymously as it were, harm upon another. Masisi put it as well as it could be put when discussing Aberi's death (pp. 61–62), allegedly due to an Ngwana's use of sorcery. The circumstances were such—the three healthy "accused" all dying within such a short space of time following the curse —that there was a general discussion of village sorcery. There was disagreement of opinion as to whether or not it involved supernatural power, as claimed by the villagers. Most Mbuti stated bluntly that this was impossible, for such power was necessarily good. They held that the deaths had all been caused by poison. Others were not so sure. But the crux of the discussion was that whether caused by supernatural power or by poison, the action was not that of a man. Masisi said, "If you have a quarrel with a man you hit him with a wooden club, and he sees who hit him. You do not go and hide yourself and kill him with your thoughts."

While the Mbuti seek to remove themselves as far as possible from sorcery, feeling as though they were contaminated by it, their attitude to other associated supernatural beliefs of the villagers is quite different, being determined by different experience. A villager who has cursed one man may claim that the sickness of that man's distant cousin is a result of his curse, or that the falling of a tree that nearly killed the man's child was equally a result of the curse. These are not allegations that can be proved or disproved, and the Mbuti consequently have a somewhat ambivalent attitude toward sorcery; their disbelief is tinged, at least, by a reluctant suspicion.

However, the villagers also believe that there exist various malevolent spirits, sometimes spirits of sorcerers, and that these spirits have to be avoided, for there is no sure way of placating or propitiating them. Their abode is the forest, which to the villagers is the abode of all evil. Their powers are phenomenal and almost insuperable, avoidance being the only sure safeguard, ritual propitiation being enough to prevent the spirits from entering the village. Thus the forest is a place to be avoided on account of the spirits.

The Mbuti see two things very clearly. One is that such spirits simply do not exist in their forest, and the other is that this particular village belief deserves to be maintained for as long as it is effective in keeping villagers out of the forest. Consequently the Mbuti, who are great storytellers at all times, delight in stories—among themselves and in front of villagers—that enumerate the powers and horrors of such evil forest spirits. Sometimes the stories are of village origin, embellished by Mbuti imagination; sometimes they are pure

Mbuti creations. But however much they enlarge upon the power and horror of the evil spirits, they always show that the Mbuti are not without power themselves, and the spirits are every now and again defeated and killed by Mbuti trickery. This confirms the village belief that the Mbuti are in fact in league with the spirits; just the fact that they coexist in the same forest is cited by many villagers as evidence of their affinity.

I cite two legends here (the KiBira versions of the same legends told by the same Mbuti are given in Appendix I), both of which show Mbuti ambivalence at its height. The first describes an Mbuti band in a village context (in a plantation) and pointedly refers to a myth that the Mbuti had bananas before the villagers. This is not generally believed to be true, but it is a way of expressing the undoubted prior occupation and ownership of the forest by the Mbuti. In this legend the Mbuti are threatened by a quasi-real enemy, the elephant. Elephants are indeed destructive to plantations and sometimes to Mbuti camps, but here, as seen at the end, the elephant is also a symbol for the villager (who is also destructive in his act of cutting down the forest). To rid themselves of the elephantine menace the Mbuti invent a story about evil spirits, making use of the knowledge that the elephant is basically stupid. When describing the elephant's fear of the spirits, the narrator comments, "Their fear was empty" ("*bachei ba bo*"), "for elephants are like villagers" ("*bambongu bua sopilabatu*"). The legend significantly ends with the promise that the narrator and his family will live happily forever after, but for "happily" the word *kobia* (more often, *ekimi*) is used. It means "quietly."

LEGEND OF THE MBUTI PLANTATION

In olden times we Mbuti had bananas before the people of the village. The people of the village stole bananas from us. We shared together, we Mbuti taking the leaves and the villagers taking the roots. They tricked us this way.

Our plantations of old were good, but the elephants used to bother us a lot. They killed many plantations. The Mbuti said, "What shall we do? The elephants are bothering us so much and are killing our plantations."

An old man, very old indeed, said, "When the elephants come again, we shall talk with them." The youths said, "What will you say?" The old man replied, "You shall see, children."

The elephants came. They began to kill all the bananas. They began to completely kill the plantation. The youths ran to the old man and said, "Oh, Father, the elephants have come again and are killing our plantation." [The old man said], "Good, I shall go and chat with them. All of you stay here, completely quiet."

The old man went to the plantation. He cried and cried. He threw himself on the ground. The elephants looked at him and said, "What thing is this? The youths have not come to chase us away, only an old Mbuti and he just cries. It is good, we shall eat quietly."

They ate many bananas, and the youths remained completely quiet in the camp. The old man cried greatly, "Oh, my children, all are dead. Oh, my children, where are they?"

The elephants heard, and said to the old man, "Why are you crying like that? And where are the youths? We shall eat up all the plantation." The old man replied, "Eat, eat it all. My children are all dead." And he continued crying.

The elephants said, "But you have many children. How did they die?" The old man said, "It was an evil spirit, very evil indeed. He walked with two spears.[2] He was very fat, like you. Every day I sent someone to cut bananas and the evil spirit ate him. Now he has eaten all my children. He said it was his plantation and that he would kill everyone who came here. Oh, my children have all died emptily. Why did the evil spirit not bother some other plantation, why did he curse mine?" He cried greatly and he left.

The elephants said, "Ha! If a spirit that bad has cursed this plantation, we should go somewhere else. Let us go quickly, before he kills us!"

Because elephants are like people of the village, and they are afraid of evil spirits. But they are afraid emptily. They went far. The old man called all his children and said, "Now the elephants will not come back. They think this is a place full of bad spirits. Thus we shall remain quiet. It is our plantation. Nobody else will bother us."

Although the scene is the plantation, thus asserting their claim to the plantations of the villagers, the Mbuti plainly are really referring

[2] Evidently a feature that to the Mbuti conveys a real fear of or respect for the supernatural, for in the morning rampages of the *molimo*, in its role as judge and when seeking Mbuti who are committing the crime of sleeping during the singing, the hunter acting the part carries a spear under each arm. See also in the second legend cited, where a spirit wanders through the night with two firebrands, which is the way in which the entrance of the *molimo* trumpet into the camp is often marked.

to their forest sanctuary, and describing their tactics for keeping it free of bothersome, elephant-like villagers. Hunting is not mentioned; the two spears (and in the next legend the two firebrands) are uniquely related to the *molimo*, which, as is seen in the next chapter, offers major roles to the elders and the youths; precise age levels are specified in this legend. Thus the defense of the forest is considered as part of the role of the *molimo*. There is significantly no talk of a resort to magic or witchcraft or sorcery, and the mention of the evil spirits is accompanied by no belief in them.

In the second legend, however, the first part is a very straight description of exactly how an Mbuti might cheat a villager simply by concealing a portion of his honey, whereas the second part describes how the Mbuti is himself cheated. The second part alone could be taken as another way in which Mbuti explain to villagers why they have no meat or honey for them (see a third legend at the end of this chapter for such an example), but in this juxtaposition seems to indicate a certain belief that the Mbuti themselves might be cheated in this way.

LEGEND OF DOUBLE TRICKERY

I went to the forest to collect honey. I went, I went, I went. I went very far, beyond the big river [an indication of trespass, perhaps, making it a situation displeasing to the forest; hence the ultimate defeat of the Mbuti?]. I heard the sound of bees. Way up high I saw the place of the honey. I said, "Ha! Nobody has enclosed this tree with a vine; it is my tree, it is my honey."

I sharpened my ax, very sharp indeed. I cut a vine, I fanned up my fire and put the fire [smoking embers] in my basket. I began to climb. I climbed, I climbed, I climbed. The honey was very high up, it was real honey, not *apuma* [a special fermented honey]. I reached it. I fastened the vine and I sat. I put the fire [in a leaf cone] into the hole and I blew. Much smoke came and the bees ran away. I chopped, I chopped, I chopped. While I was cutting I heard someone walking below. "Ah! Who is walking below me? It is my master [*kpara*]. He heard me cutting [the adverse aspect of noise] and followed me."

I began to sing. I sang loudly. He called to me, but I pretended that I did not hear him. I sang and I chopped. I sang, "Ah! I am chopping out honey to give to my *kpara!*" And slowly I chopped out the honey. I got a lot of it. But I only put part of it in my basket. The rest I put in a place where the tree had two arms [i.e., in a fork]. I sang, "Ah! There is only a little honey, but I shall give it all to my *kpara.*" I came down.

"Ah! My Mbuti, what are you doing here?" My *kpara* looks at the basket.

"Ah! My master. I came to search for my honey, but there is only a little of it. It is a bad year. It is heavy work. You must go back with my honey; if I get any more I shall come with it."

The *kpara* took my honey with him and returned to the village to say that he had eaten all my honey. His stupidity! [*Ndamdama nda'e!* or *Mbafu yaké!*] When he had gone I quickly climbed up above and I collected all the honey from the place I had put it, and I came down to return to the camp and share it with all my relatives. I walked, I walked, I walked. I arrived at the big river. Darkness began to come. I said, "Ha! Is night catching me in the middle of the forest like this? What shall I do?" I climbed up a big tree and lay there.

Halfway through the night I heard a sound and woke up. A little way off I saw two firebrands. "Ah! Who is walking in the middle of the night like that, with two firebrands? It is an evil spirit." I remained completely quiet. I heard a woman's voice. "Ah! My child, where is my child?" It was the voice of my grandmother, a very, very old woman. I was surprised. "Ha! Grandmother is looking for me in the middle of the night like this? Is it really my grandmother?"

"Ah! Where is my child? Either a leopard has caught him or he has lost the trail."

I remained quiet, but the two firebrands came right up underneath the tree. It was truly an evil spirit, but he had changed into my grandmother. I sneezed. "Ah! My child is up in the tree?"

"Yes, Grandmother. I am here. I was searching for honey, but darkness caught me on the trail."

"Oh, child, you have done badly, for when you did not return I thought you were dead and I left camp to search for you, and I have found you well. You have done very badly toward me. Give me my honey."

"Ah! Grandmother, it is very heavy. I shall carry it for you, I, myself. We shall return together."

"Nonsense! You are afraid of the night. You stay here. I shall return with my honey. Give it." I was afraid, because I knew it was an evil spirit. I threw some honey down. "Give me more, give me more." I threw down more. "Give me more."

"There is no more, Grandmother." "Yes there is, give it, my bad child." I was very afraid. I threw it all down and said, "That is all, Grandmother, take it and go. There is no more. Take it and return to your place. I shall stay here."

"Thank you, my child, I shall return. Stay well."

"Go well, Grandmother."

I sat with eyes [i.e., watchfully] and waited for daylight. When daylight came I climbed down. I looked for the footprints of my grandmother. There were no footprints. "Ah!" I said. "It was truly an evil spirit. I did well to throw down all my honey, or it would have killed me completely."

That is why I returned empty-handed.

If in telling the stories the Mbuti do so to such good effect that they half convince themselves, they more than convince the villagers. The advantages of the situation to the Mbuti are as obvious as they are considerable. But at the same time it has to be pointed out that the forest itself *is* hostile to the villagers, and they have very real reason to dislike and fear it. It not only makes their life as cultivators hard and uncertain but it makes communication through the forest highly dangerous, to the extent that, until the road along which the villages are now eagerly clustered was built across the middle of the forest, the villages were very self-contained units with little intercommunication. Even now villagers will walk twice as far or more by road to reach another village, rather than take a simple shortcut across the forest. Unversed as they are in forest lore, its dangers are real to the villagers and there are frequent instances of villagers disappearing without trace even while on a relatively short trip. They are promptly added to the legion of forest spirits by their relatives, who have an even greater fear of the forest from then on.

The Mbuti, however, know the forest and its ways, and the dangers it has to offer are exceptionally few and far between. There is certainly nothing in the course of natural events in the forest to suggest to hunters and gatherers any trace of hostility. There is a great abundance of material goods, and of health and security, all of which suggest benevolence. This is taken up in the final section on the forest world, dealing with the religious life of the Mbuti.

One of the best examples of the kind of use to which the Mbuti put village beliefs that do not tally with their own is seen in the following legend (quoted in *The Forest People*, Chapter 7). It makes use of the village fear and respect for forest spirits, but it also makes use of the village love for asserting their superiority and their paternalism. It even makes use of the village concept of kinship obligations, and the respect and obedience owed to a grandmother.

The occasion on which the legend was told was the return of Cephu to the camp, after a short absence in the village, laden down with village foods. It was known that he had gone empty-handed, and it was equally known that he was not on good enough terms with any of the villagers to get such a handout for nothing, that he was too lazy to have worked for reward and too wary of pursuit to steal. However, theft seemed the only answer, so he was asked from whom he had stolen the food. Always a great dramatist, Cephu told the following story in answer, and it quickly became a favorite.

"I am only a poor Mbuti; the forest is my father and my mother. But my village master asked me for meat, so I hunted and I hunted and I hunted. I caught *sondu* and *lendu* and *mboloko* and *sindula*, and I cut them all up and dried them carefully. When they were nice and dry I wrapped the meat in fresh *mongongo* leaves and put it all in my basket and set off for the village."

This much everyone knew to be completely false, but the implied ridicule of the villagers who would believe it was not lost.

"But on the way I saw a bad spirit coming toward me. I tried to escape but he caught up with me and demanded the meat. I said, 'No, this is for my master. I cannot give it to you. You may take all my own food, but not this meat—that is for my beloved master.' But the spirit was not to be put off, and I had to fight with him. Finally I managed to escape because I am strong, and a great hunter, and I ran on toward the village as fast as I could. Spirits are very bad things to fight. They would kill any villager; only we Mbuti can deal with them. But then I saw the spirit again, and this time he was more clever than I, and he changed into my grandmother.

"'A'i, Cephu, where are you going with all that meat?' she asked me.

"Now, my grandmother died many years ago and I had to be polite to her. So I told her I was taking it to my beloved master. But she got angry and demanded it, asking if I would refuse it to her, an Mbuti, my own grandmother, and bring it to a villager. I pleaded with her and begged her, telling her how good my master always was to me and how hungry he was for meat. But she snatched the basket from me, and because she was my grandmother I could not strike her or stop her, and she ran off down the trail.

"As she was running she changed into a spirit again so that she could run faster, and as soon as my grandmother was a spirit once more I could fight, so I fought and fought, and the spirit nearly killed me, and he went off in the manner of spirits and left me with nothing, not even my basket.

"When I came to the village I was crying because I had nothing to offer my master, and when my master asked me what was wrong I told him this story. He was terribly sorry because he knew what dreadful lives we Mbuti lead, surrounded by all these bad spirits. He said if it was not for the spirits he would come into the forest and hunt himself, but everyone knows how dangerous the spirits are to villagers. Then I asked him if I could have some rice, as I had lost all my own food as well as his. He said, 'Of course, my poor Mbuti. You have tried to help your master, and you can't help it if you are just an Mbuti and have to live among all those dreadful spirits.'

"So he gave me the rice and plantains and I came away happy. How kind the villagers are to their 'poor Mbuti'!"

Such stories are legion, being told by the Mbuti almost every time they are questioned by the villagers as to why they have brought no meat. They are equally, if not even more frequently, told, however, in the forest hunting camps, and are part of the constant effort of the Mbuti to affirm at all times the distinction between the two worlds, the forest and the village. Magic, witchcraft, sorcery and the belief in forest spirits are all turned to the same effect, among others, and combine to keep the worlds apart not only in theory but also in practice.

CHAPTER 14

Religion

SUPERNATURAL BELIEFS

In dealing with religion, Schebesta on occasion clearly states whether he is referring to the Sua, who are primarily net-hunters, or to the Efe, who are archers, so we are able to make some use of his data. However, religious belief among the Epulu net-hunting Mbuti does not coincide in detail with his account of Sua religion. Even among the very archer Mbuti where Schebesta worked I found the widest possible divergence of opinion, to the point of complete contradiction by one band of the stated beliefs of the other. The only systematic unity into which these allegedly Mbuti concepts fitted was that of the Lesé magico-religious system. However, Schebesta plainly saw throughout that though there were significant differences of opinion, there was also a subtle and powerful unity in trying to discover this unity. He was unfortunately hampered by his overwhelming desire to present a picture of a system applicable to all Mbuti.

Among the net-hunters, as among the archers, the dual use of magico-religious terms by the Mbuti, to refer both to village and to Mbuti practice and belief sometimes leads to an appearance of an Mbuti system somewhat akin to that of the villagers. However, ignoring the actual terminology—which is further confused by the proliferation of tribal languages in the Epulu region, in discussing concepts concerning life and death, the nature of the afterworld and so forth—there is not only difference of opinion from one net-hunting band to the next but even within any one band or any one family.

This should be no particular cause for surprise for, being a practical people whose physical existence is determined, in detail, by day-to-day context, they are far more concerned with the present than they are with the past or the future. With regard to the future, be it in this life or the next, they eschew speculation on the grounds that not having been there they do not know what it is like, and not knowing what it is like they cannot predict what their behavior will be. They say that to try and go into the future is to "walk blindly," and their response to villagers, missionaries or any who claim a knowledge of afterlife is to say, "How do you know. Have you died and been there?" They liken such discussion to the talk of a hunter who suggests hunting in a certain place without ever having been there, or a woman who goes off in a set direction to gather a certain kind of mushroom without having seen them growing in any particular place there. These are people who act "emptily," or whose heads are loose and not properly attached to the body.

However, this disclaimer to absolute knowledge of the nature of the future or of afterlife is in itself a characteristic that I found to be universal among the Mbuti, at least within my own experience. This did not prevent individuals from having ideas about the unknown, but as already indicated, such speculation was considered as fruitless, and took the form of legend and was listened to with interest, and often with amusement. Such speculations, whether spontaneous or in the form of established legends, do not reveal any consistency in detail, which appears to be a matter of individual imagination, but there are broad areas of belief that seem widespread among both archers and net-hunters.

There is a belief in a power greater than the Mbuti themselves and not of the natural order of the world they see and know around them. Insofar as this is stated to be a belief, and not knowledge, it may be considered a spiritual power, the spirit being a level of existence that the Mbuti do not claim to understand but which they see as necessarily existing in order to explain the nature of the world's unknowns. Again the terminology is hopelessly confused, the Epulu Mbuti using, in one instance, no less than five terms interchangeably—*pepo, keti, boru, roho, satani.* These terms are drawn from Lesé, Bira, Ndaka and Ngwana, among which tribes of villagers they are also to some extent interchanged, each change bringing a different shade of meaning. For the Mbuti they do not indicate clearly differentiated elements that make up the physical and spiritual being of man, but rather indicate this basic belief that man himself is in part spiritual and that his life derives not from the flesh but from some other source. All five terms are used equally to denote this personal force. But each one is also used to denote different aspects of that force, and the Mbuti usage again in no way coincides with that of the villagers, nor does the usage of one band necessarily coincide with the usage of another band.

The divers aspects of spiritual power that are generally recognized are as follows:

Each man and each animal (and according to most Mbuti, even the inanimate and vegetable worlds) is endowed to a greater or lesser extent with such power.

This power derives from a single source whose physical manifestation is the forest itself. Opinion differs as to whether this means the vegetable forest, or the forest totality, including the Mbuti themselves. Again there is a multiplicity of names to represent this single power source, and it is most easily translated simply as "the forest" (*ndura*), for this is ultimately how the Mbuti themselves describe it.

Also deriving from the prime source of spiritual power are certain disembodied spirits which, like the Mbuti, inhabit the forest. Their existence, for all practical purposes, does not impinge upon that of the Mbuti; they have no power to harm or help, though there is a vague belief that there might be a conflict of interests at times, and any unexplained mishap may be explained in this way. The disembodied spirits are generally thought of as living much the same kind of existence as the Mbuti, for as they themselves say, what other kind of existence can there be in the forest? Thus, someone who trips while chasing an animal may say he collided with a *keti* (the term used by the Epulu Mbuti for this disembodied spirit as well as for the more generalized spiritual power) who was chasing the same animal. The mysterious absence of game in an unhunted area is explained by saying that the *keti* must have hunted it out. But there is no sense of competition or rivalry, and the *keti* are thought about only when such explanations are needed.

The Mbuti also believe in individual personality, which is essentially of the body rather than of the spirit, but which is enhanced and activated by the spirit. This enables individuals to speak with conviction and to justify their actions or thoughts by saying that their "heart" is pleased, for the heart is generally considered the location of this personality, which when displeased jumps and leaps about inside the chest.

The same five terms, all of which may be used to denote the general concept of personal force, do, however, also have individual and particular meanings by which we can perceive something more of the system of belief of the Epulu Mbuti.

PEPO

The life force that animates all moving, living things, without which they would be mere vegetable growths, unable to move or think. The word *pepo* also has connotations of air and wind, and breathing is thought of as a manifestation of *pepo*. A gale of wind, then, is interpreted by some Mbuti as the breath of the forest itself (*pepo nde ndura*), as the breath of the disembodied spirits, or *keti* (*pepo nde baketi*).

KETI

Disembodied spirits, human and animal, who are not necessarily the spirits of the dead but may be independent manifestations of the forest, and who are disembodied only in that they are invisible to the Mbuti. They have an existence otherwise comparable to that of the Mbuti, and are likewise animated by *pepo*. There is no conflict of interests between them and the Mbuti, though occasionally the two worlds inadvertently become confused. An Mbuti may be in hot pursuit of an animal that suddenly disappears; he is likely to say that it must have been *keti*. An animal mysteriously drops dead; it was killed by a *keti* hunter (*keti a mu'e*) who thought he was in pursuit of a *keti* animal. Hallucinations and dreams are primarily the result of accidentally slipping from the one world into the other. All such meetings of *keti* and Mbuti are regarded as abnormal, and are never deliberately sought. They do not exactly induce fear, but there is undeniably the belief that one might cross over so effectively that one would never come back. The Mbuti say that if this happened you might not even know you had crossed over, which indicates that they conceive of the *keti* world as a mirror of their own.[1] Dreams, then, do not convey authority as being divine portents but, being real experience of a mirror world, they are, like all experiences, to be learned from. Thus Ambosu dreamed constantly that he was singing into the *molimo* trumpet. This did not give him the right to take up this role,

---

[1] On two occasions I heard *ekokomea* described laughingly as a dance of the *keti*. The dance, involving a reversal of the sexes, is primarily associated with the *molimo*, hence with the spirit and supernatural world. There is a hunting dance in which there is a rapid succession of changes in direction, the hunters becoming the hunted and vice versa. Yet another instance of Mbuti recognition of reversal is seen in the legend of the Mbuti plantation (see Chapter 12), in which the Mbuti are the cultivators threatened by the animals of the forest (elephants), who undoubtedly represent the villagers.

but everyone agreed that it was a clear indication that he should try. He became the leading trumpet singer, then, not through divine choice but simply through his experience in the *keti* world. He was not regarded as more spiritual, merely as more experienced. However, insofar as both Mbuti and *keti* derive their *pepo* from the forest, if the forest wills them to hunt together in the same time and place then the mirror images coincide exactly and it is, indeed, a "strong" hunt. Such coincidence is exhausting, however, and it is not something actively wished for except, possibly, in times of particularly poor hunting. Ideally the Mbuti and the *keti* should follow each other closely, but always remain just slightly apart.

BORU

A rather difficult concept of the "house" (*endu*—the same word as for a hut) inhabited by *pepo*. The human and animal body of flesh and blood is, in a sense, *boru*, and so is the invisibility of the *keti*. It is a term seldom used, but the concept affords a firm basis for a code of respect for the body, abuse or mutilation of which may drive away the *pepo*, causing "death" (which for the Mbuti is simply the departure of *pepo* and its return to the forest or the world of *keti*). Thus physical violence as a means of settling a dispute is abhorred as a sacrilege. A sound thrashing is perfectly in order, but any violence that produces blood causes an opening through which *pepo* may escape. For although associated with air and wind and thus with breath, it is not thought of as *being* any of these things, and its exact means of escape is unknown. The bodily apertures are all regarded as requiring attention, however, as possible avenues. It might be pointed out here that insofar as *pepo* is associated with life and may escape through these apertures, this is perfectly consistent with the Mbuti recognition of the sexual act as a means of conveying life, though they do not explicitly refer to semen as *pepo*. It is also consistent with the variations on the sexual act found in the *ekokomea* dance, where not only are the sexes reversed but attention is drawn to the less usual apertures, to be somewhat delicate. The role of *ekokomea* as a major feature of the death festival becomes immediately more understandable, its burlesque form allowing for the stated antipathy of the Mbuti to the unproductive forms of sexual perversion *ekokomea* so graphically depicts.

ROHO

The personality of the individual dies with the body and is the combination of a particular *boru* and *pepo*. It is associated with the heart and is spoken of as being hot or cold, sometimes as noisy or quiet. Hot and noisy are generally bad qualities, cool and quiet are good. But properly controlled heat and noise can be useful, though dangerous, for both are sometimes thought of as being "strong." The state of an individual's *roho* may be cited as justification for his actions, and nobody can gainsay him, for it is bad to go against one's *roho*. However, a man or woman who is constantly calling on his or her *roho* to justify antisocial acts such as laziness or quarrelsomeness may be said to have a bad *roho*, and will be shunned.

SATANI (also *Shaitani*)

This is a concept derived from the villagers, and is for the Mbuti more in the realm of folklore than belief, for *satani* are, to the villagers, malevolent and dangerous forest spirits. The Mbuti use the term in this sense only when recounting a village tale or a tale concerning villagers, for they essentially disbelieve in such evil spirits. However, they sometimes use the term, particularly if talking in Ngwana (to which language it belongs), as synonymous with *keti*. An additional complication: When talking in Bira, they may use *keti* (a Bira word) in the sense of the village Bira, which is the same as the Ngwana *satani*, or evil spirits. However, in the forest context there is no concept of *keti* or *satani* as conceived by the villager, the only spirits being the *keti* as described above, invisible mirror images of the Mbuti themselves, no better and no worse. (Conversely, in the village world all the spirits of the forest are malevolent and dangerous; there is no concept parallel to that of the Mbuti concept of forest spirit.)

THE GODHEAD

As the Mbuti themselves strenuously refuse to admit there is any sense in trying to describe what we here call "the godhead" unless you have seen it, there is not much sense in our trying to do so. Rather, by looking at various aspects of Mbuti life we can discern the existence of a belief in such a spiritual being, and its nature as being generally that of "the forest." From the foregoing description of the two levels of existence, human and *keti*, and of the generally accepted principle of spiritual animation, it is plain that there should be a source of such spiritual force. The mobility of the Mbuti, the composite nature of the bands and the frequency of interchange between bands all lead to a confused scattering of the various terms that appear in the village religious systems. I have been utterly unable to discern any pattern in which the godhead is divided into entities concerned with different aspects of Mbuti life, each with a distinct name; e.g., a god of the hunt known by one name, a god of the bush known by another, and so forth. Even within any one band it seemed singularly clear that there is only one godhead, though different individuals in that band may well use different names.[2] The forest *is* that godhead (*ndura nde kalisia*, or *ndura nde mungu*), rather than being thought of merely as its abode; hence the sanctity of the forest, and the profanity of anything that is not of the forest. That this is so is seen in the almost universal answer given when faced, either among themselves in the course of discussion or directly, by the question of where *pepo* derives from. The answer is that it derives from the forest itself (*pepo a kidi suba ndura*). Not just the trees or streams, or the sky or the soil, but from the totality, down to the last grain of sand.

We have shown earlier how the Mbuti frequently sing and shout to the forest, addressing it as "father" or "mother." They also sometimes address it as "friend," or even "lover." They are perfectly well able to explain this, for they say that "the forest is everything"

[2] Schebesta (1952, 303) says that the Basua (net-hunters) refer to the divinity as *mungu*, *keti*, *kalisia*, and *songé*. I have found all these terms used, but without any different significance in the forest context, while they each have a special and separate significance among the villagers. The important point is that Schebesta recognizes that the divinity "loves" the Mbuti, who owe everything to him, while the villagers are afraid of him. Here I believe Schebesta to have come across the forest as it is considered by the Mbuti in the evening *molimo*, the source of all good. In discussing the archer concept of the divinity, Schebesta (1952, 305–6) refers to the different visualizations they have of *toré*, frequently ugly, noisy and menacing. I found these same interpretations of *toré* among the archers, but always in reference to the other aspect of the forest, not as the mother provider but as the father lawgiver. Among the net-hunters, when the morning *molimo* comes into camp to wreak havoc, it is greeted with cries of *e téré, e téré*, it being openly agreed that this was a form of the archer word *toré* and referred only to this aspect of the *molimo*. But my informants would add, "It is all the same thing, it is all the forest." Schebesta's description of *toré* not only corresponds to a different aspect of the Mbuti *molimo*, but it also corresponds closely to the description given by Vergiat (1936, 53–7) of the "génie de la brousse" among the Ubangi villagers, to the northwest. Here, as by the Lesé/Efe, that divinity is described as a grotesque caricature of an Mbuti, fearful to all villagers but strangely friendly to the Mbuti hunters.

(*ndura nde bokbu*), and if pressed begin to enumerate the totality of their experience. Primarily, however, they refer to the forest as mother or father, according to context. On the hunt the men address it as father, the women as mother. A man receiving a sudden unexpected favor, as he sees it (coming across a cache of highly prized mushrooms), is apt to address the forest as mother. A woman who is having a hard time finding the leaves or saplings she wants will, getting into a tangle of undergrowth, almost certainly start addressing the forest as father and accuse it of being far too severe and strict. The terms are so widely and frequently used that I have no means of saying which is the more prevalent. If anything, I would hazard a guess that "mother" is used more often than "father." The Mbuti themselves say that which term they use and when is a matter for their *roho*.

The extent to which the Mbuti personify the forest is seen when in explanation they say that the forest gives them not only food and shelter, warmth and clothing, but also affection (*ndura pisasu bendu, pisasu isa, pisasu ngombe; ndura ekondisu*). The intimacy of the relationship between the individual Mbuti and his forest godhead is most plainly seen in the incident described more fully in *The Forest People* (Chapter 15), where a youth was found dancing all by himself in the moonlight, singing a wordless song as he danced. When questioned as to why he was dancing alone, he answered, "I am not dancing alone, I am dancing with the forest, dancing with the moon."[3]

[3]   *Kanga me bi akilé: me bi na ndura, me bi na songé.*

Schebesta (1952, 303) refers to *songé* (moon) as being one of the net-hunting names for God, regarded as the creator of all things (1952, 305), particularly of man, which *songé* creates by means of menstrual blood. He does not, unfortunately, give more information or documentation on this interpretation, but there is no doubt that the moon is, to the Mbuti, an object of interest and (as seen above) affection, and at the same time in common discussion they do connect the moon with menstruation, and menstruation with fertility. I have myself not come across any instance of the moon being worshipped as such, unless this moonlight dance be regarded as worship, except in one song of the *molimo*, the words of which were:

> *Ema songé,   ema,   ema;   okisu ema;   pika'i.*
> Mother moon, mother, mother, hear us mother; come.

This is remarkably similar to a translation given by Bowra (1962, 70) of a song of the Gabon pygmies cited by Trilles (1945, 157).

> Moon, O mother moon, O mother moon,
> mother of living things,
> Hear our voice, O mother moon!
> O, mother moon, O mother moon,
> Keep away the spirits of the dead,
> Hear our voice, O mother moon,
> O mother moon, O mother moon.

This was not an isolated instance, though such dancing and singing are generally confined to youths and younger married people. The
erotic aspect of the relationship between forest and Mbuti is also seen
in the very clear individual preferences for certain types of place in
which it is found good to the *roho* to have sexual intercourse, such as
by a stream, or in dark shade, or in a patch of sunlight or moonlight,
or during the hunt, but in the forest rather than in the hut.

The perennial certainty of economic sufficiency, the general lack
of crisis in their lives, all lead the Mbuti to the conviction that the
forest, regarded as the source of *pepo* and of their whole existence,
is benevolent, and that the natural course of life is good. The absence
of magic is not necessarily an indication of technological mastery; in
this instance it is simply an indication of the normal absence of
crisis. We indicated that such magic as existed was not without its
spiritual aspects, and might possibly be better classified as religion.
For instance the use of vine and wooden charms on an infant to convey the strength of the forest to the child is not thought to achieve
its end directly, by physical transference alone. Physical contact with
these materials is considered strengthening, and certainly the juice
of the vine in which infants are bathed is thought to have strengthening properties, but these things are also considered "pleasing to the
forest" (*babongisa ndura*). This phrase constantly recurs, and shows
the belief in the awareness by the forest of its "children" and their
needs. Such acts and many others, by physically relating the individual
to the forest, are believed to create an added awareness of the Mbuti
by the forest. It is not only the strength of the forest that is wanted,
but its affection.

THE POWER OF SOUND

Birth is attended with an undemonstrative concern to establish
this relationship between the forest and the individual, and it is re-
inforced at puberty by what might also be considered in some respects
as magic, but which is more essentially religious, and that is song.
The mere attachment of a vine to the wrist or around the waist
requires that amount of effort and no more. Song requires continued
effort, is more direct and personal, and consequently more powerful—
its goal is identical. Song above all else is believed to attract the attention of the forest, and to please it. "Sound is very strong indeed;
noise is bad, but song is good" (*S'uti mota ningo'e, akami sinand'e;*

imba nde bonga'i). The positive emphasis on *ekimi*,[4] or quiet, is in
no way thought of as being in conflict with song, for *ekimi* is cool,
and so is song, and both are pleasing to the forest. Song is in no way
associated with noise, though both are recognized to be sound.

There is no such thing as secular song among the Mbuti. Songs
sung by the Mbuti in the village, apart from being quite different in
musical form from those sung in the forest, are spoken of as "empty
sound" (*s'uti bobo*) or even as "noise." There are distinct musical
forms for distinct occasions of importance in forest life such as hunting, honey gathering, puberty and death. The absence of any specific
Mbuti form for village events, including *nkumbi* initiation or village-
arranged marriages, is an indication of the lack of importance of these
events in the forest life of the Mbuti.

There are, apart from the four major types of song listed above,
two other types that are less formalized, but which are considered
more in the nature of "sound" than "song." One is the lullaby, which
is an individual creation (unlike any other forms of song, all of which
require group participation), and the other is the play song, accompanying hoop-jumping, skipping or divers other rhythmic games.

Of the four major types, two concern economic activities and are
sung on the appropriate occasion, each involving men and women.
The other two are more directly religious in nature, being concerned
with puberty and death, though the field of each is somewhat wider
than these precise moments in the life cycle. The puberty songs
(which have nothing to do with the *nkumbi*, not being sung on that
occasion and in no way resembling the village songs that *are* sung at
that time) concern primarily the women and youths (male and female), and are first learned and sung at puberty but may be sung at
other times similarly critical to growth, birth and marriage. (Normally
elima songs, or puberty songs, are sung at birth only if there is some
special concern over the child's welfare, and at marriage only if it is
desired to consecrate an otherwise "empty" marriage taking place in
the village. Then not only is an *elima* song sung but leaves are brought
in from the forest, and the bridal couple are completely surrounded
by them to indicate that they are, in fact, joining together in the
forest.)

Death songs are normally sung at the death of an adult, male or

---

[4] *Ekimi* is the word most frequently used in this band for quiet. Like many other
words it is a dialectal form, in this case of the Ngwana word *kimia*. In KiBira the equivalent would be *kobia*.

female, during the ensuing festival (*molimo*), but some of them may
be sung at other times of crisis that threaten life, notably sickness
or poor hunting. Certain songs seem to be reserved for actual death,
but my impression is that this is a matter of personal attitude, for
there are other ways in which a distinction is more clearly made between what are called the lesser and the greater *molimo*, the latter
being the festival concerned solely with death.

To the same extent that the *elima* songs are of rather more importance to women than men, so are *molimo* songs considered more the
concern of men. There is, however, no absolute exclusion. On the
contrary, the male youths are an integral part of the *elima* festival,
which celebrates their puberty just as much as it celebrates that of
the girls, and although the actual festival is occasioned by the physical
maturation of the girls, who are then taught the *elima* songs, the
male youths are needed to sing the chorus to certain of those songs.
In the *molimo*, at one point, the roles of the sexes are reversed (as in
ekokomea), with the women taking over the men's songs, the men
sitting back and listening, like women.

An examination of Mbuti song form not only reveals areas of concern to the Mbuti, such as their food-getting activities, life and death,
but it also reveals the concern of the Mbuti for cooperative activity.
Each type of song requires a group of people to sing it, and if there
is a solo it is sung over a chorus, and the solo is passed around from
one individual to another. This is similar to the Mbuti rejection of
individual authority and their concern for dispersing leadership as
widely as possible. There are certain parts of certain songs that are
sung by youths, hunters or elders, strictly according to age, and song
form thus also reinforces Mbuti concern for the age differential as
an important element of their social structure. The songs are most
frequently in round, or canon, form, and the hunting songs, in order
to heighten the need for the closest possible cooperation (the same
need that is demanded by the hunt itself), are sometimes sung in
hoquet.[5]

There are certain similarities between the hunting songs and the
molimo songs, but this is an area that requires a great deal more care-

[5] This is a technique in which each note of the melodic line is taken by a single individual who sings that note alone, at the correct moment. The melodic line is thus
literally divided among the participants (sometimes singing in groups of two or three),
and the melody can only be reconstituted and heard by the cooperation of all. The
complications are heightened by the use of canon, and by the use of a harmonic pattern
which is also sung in *hoquet*, and proceeds clockwise as the melodic line proceeds, as
always, counterclockwise.

ful analysis by competent musicologists.[6] As described, the above divisions represent divisions recognized by the Mbuti, and visible in differences of musical form. There is sometimes an additional category stated, that of the elephant-hunting song, which seems to overlap both the ordinary hunting song (specifically referred to by the Epulu Mbuti as a net-hunting song) and the *molimo* song. In view of the possible elephant symbolism in the *molimo* festival, this could be of importance, though not enough is known at the moment of the elephant-hunting song to properly assess its position in the system. In this respect it should also be remembered that the Ngwana term *esumba*, or *lusumba*, frequently used by the Mbuti in the forest context as synonymous with their *molimo*, was originally for the Ngwana in the nature of elephant-hunting magic.

All songs share the same essential nature, sharing the same power of sound. The sound "awakens" the forest, in Mbuti terminology, and the nature of the song indicates the particular area of interest of the Mbuti at that moment, thus attracting the forest's attention to the immediate needs of its children. It is also of the essential nature of all songs that they should be "pleasing to the forest."[7]

Rather more magical in nature, perhaps, is the way the Mbuti use other forms of sound than song. A sudden noise of any kind is considered "strong," and generally bad; an isolated hand or arm clap, or a single loud shout, will bring complete silence to a camp or to a hunt. Whistling is considered very "strong" indeed, but here the word

[6] It is interesting to note here the elephant-hunting significance of the Ngwana *esumba* ritual, and the linguistic confusion between *esumba* and *molimo*. Frequently, I have seen in the forest the remains of what seems like the model of a spear-fall, and have always been told that a *molimo* had been held there. Most often such sites were in old, deserted camps, once or twice (particularly in archer territory) on the trail.

[7] Pahlen (1949) gives an excellent general background to the primitive concept and use of music, though his acceptance of the sounds of nature as symbols of supernatural powers is not demonstrated. He points out (p. 18) how in ancient cultures music went hand in hand with religion, "the synthesis of wisdom, beauty, kindness and solace." He is referring primarily to countries with "highly developed cultures," but much of what he says is applicable to primitive society. It is certain that an acute analysis of Mbuti music would reveal much that parallels the structure of Mbuti society. The extraordinary level of polyphonic achievement is surely related to a highly developed individualism that would hardly tolerate the confines of unison. The Mbuti musical categories of *berai* and *imiai*, chorus and solo song, indicate a system of recognized relationships between the group and the individual, and the technique of *hoquet*, already mentioned, further mirrors social relationships. Such considerations, however, should not obscure Pahlen's major point that music also mirrors social values. It is an analytical tool, requiring little musical training, that has been much neglected by anthropologists, and it is hoped that a systematic analysis of Mbuti music now being undertaken at Columbia University will provide data from which not only may further light be shed on Mbuti society, but from which may emerge the beginnings of an ethno-musicological methodology.

"strong" has the same double meaning that it has when used to describe song. In using either the Ngwana term (*nguvu*) or the Bira term (*mota*), the Mbuti may imply difficulty as well as sheer physical strength. A sudden noise that is *mota* has an inherent power of its own. A song or whistle has power only if it is properly performed. The proper performance is not so much the following of a prescribed pattern, though there may be and usually is such a pattern, if general, but rather the transference of *pepo* so that by contact with *pepo* the song or the whistle becomes *mota*. Singing or whistling not so touched with *pepo* is "empty noise," and doubly bad. Whistling is widely used to arrest action of any kind. In everyday life, whistling brings the movement of all hunters and beaters to an immediate stillness and stops all sound among them. The sign for them to continue is an imitated animal cry. In the camp, if someone thinks he hears a foreign sound—of approaching people or game, of a "crying" tree (a tree starts creaking some days before it falls, and this is referred to as "crying")—he whistles to call for silence so that all may listen and hear. During the *molimo* songs, particularly, but during any song, also, whistling softly brings the song to an end. A sudden storm is likely to bring shrill whistles, though nobody claims to even hope for them to stop the storm, though they all say it is worth trying. They explain that whistling is effective in other realms because it is the affair of the Mbuti, but it will not stop a storm because that is the affair of the forest.[8]

All such whistling is done with the lips. Whistles are also made of seeds and carved from wood, however, and though the seed-whistles are purely for children to play with, the wooden whistles (*piki, segbe*) have special usages. Rarely, a small whistle may be attached to a net, and although functional it is never blown. Similar whistles are used by those net-hunters who build a hunting fire in the camp, and are placed within the vine circle surrounding the fire, again not blown. Larger whistles made of two semicylindrical sections of wood and bound together by vine or *nkusa* twine, tapering to a point at one end (left open so it can be stopped with a finger) and notched for blowing at the other end, are sometimes attached to a fur cap worn by hunters, and may be blown before the hunt, possibly during a hunting dance. Similar whistles made of *angbe* wood, from the *angbe* tree that provides most of the honey, are used during the honey season

[8] Cooper (1941, 24 seq.), in drawing comparisons between the Semang, Andamanese, and Eta, finds much similar interest in noise.

"to call the bees" (in the sense of attracting their attention, not of summoning them). The belief is that these whistles will halt the game or the bees, so that they may be found more easily.

All such whistling, whether by lip or by *piki*, is done by men. Women rarely whistle, though they may do so to the same end as the men. If they do, it is considered all the more *mota*.

It could easily be explained by the Mbuti that the sound itself paralyzes the animals or the bees, and has this direct effect (and could so be more properly called magical), but they deny this strongly and say that the forest hears the *piki* and leads them to the bees or the game (or alternatively that the forest holds the bees and the game still for its children to find them).

In ordinary conversation, sounds are widely used to convey different ideas, a snap of the fingers indicating that the action being described was done suddenly, a high-pitched, drawn-out exhalation indicating it was done slowly. Wherever possible, the narrative is illustrated by imitations of the sound of the action described. Vowel sounds, unformed into words, are used in conversation similarly to heighten ideas, convey added emotion, to supply an element that would otherwise be missing and which is plainly of great importance to the Mbuti. For the forest is nearly always full of sound, and the Mbuti refer to this constant background by saying "the forest is talking" (*ndura a lufu*). The Mbuti listen, and interpret, and make use of what they hear. If the forest stops "talking," then it is a sign that something is very wrong and alerts the Mbuti to imminent danger.

It is not surprising, then, that sound so carefully controlled as song should be considered as *mota nengo*, *mota ngbekbekbei*, the "strongest" possible kind of sound, activated by the breath that is so mysteriously connected with *pepo*. Song is used to communicate with the forest, and it is significant that the emphasis is on the actual sound, not on the words. Frequently the mere vowel sounds are used, sometimes imitative of animals, birds or bees but more often simply to suit the melodic line of the song. When words are used they are most often trivial, and may be spontaneous and highly sketchy references to one or another event of the day. That the song is directed at the forest, and intended to awaken the forest, is most clearly seen in the *molimo* festivals, which are the Mbuti reaction to crisis. The *molimo* is named for the festival, for the society that performs the festival, and for the central and solitary piece of paraphernalia, the trumpet that echoes the song of the Mbuti on into the depths of the forest.

THE LESSER *MOLIMO* (*molimo madé*)

Apart from death there are two major crisis areas over which the Mbuti may have little or no effective control, poor hunting and sickness. But they do have a certain amount of control, and it is frequently effective. Poor hunting is more often than not remedied simply by hunting elsewhere, and it is rare that a band goes hungry for any reason except laziness. Against sickness the Mbuti have many remedies that are plainly effective. In particular they know how to clean open wounds and prevent infection, they know how to set and mend broken limbs, they know how to reduce fevers, and they know how to alleviate minor ailments such as headache, toothache and mild stomach disorders. They also have effective remedies against snakebite. So in case of sickness they either cure the patient, or else the patient becomes well of his own accord, or else he dies, the latter event leading to the greater *molimo*.

In such crises, then, time alone usually provides a solution, and the Mbuti are accustomed to waiting for these situations to improve. If bad hunting persists, however, or sickness shows no sign of alleviation, then it becomes a matter "of the forest." There is no rite or ceremony, but in the evenings the men gather around a central fire and sing *molimo* songs, thereby attracting the attention of the forest to their plight. The songs do not convey any specific request from the Mbuti for the betterment of their condition, it being considered necessary only to awaken the forest, for then it is for the forest to act as it will. Being benevolent, like a parent, whatever it does is accepted as being good, though it may not be understood.

Normally a lesser *molimo* lasts for only a few days, for during that time there is likely to be a change in the situation that is taken as an indication that the forest has awakened. The evening songs are not accompanied by any of the preliminaries that mark the greater *molimo*, nor are the women and children quite so rigorously excluded, and there is not the same order of dancing, which in the greater *molimo* is of the utmost importance. In the lesser *molimo* the dancing will be done by youths only, and be casual and mildly erotic. Above all there will be no use made of the *molimo* trumpet.

All adults youths and men are expected to take part, and although there will be criticism if someone does not attend, there will not be the same violent reaction that there is against such offenders in the greater *molimo*. In the case of a hunting *molimo*, the initiative is taken by the younger hunters, who sit together around a fire and simply begin singing. In the case of sickness, the initiative is taken by the adult men of the family concerned if the sick person is a child, and if the sick person is an adult the *molimo* will be initiated by his or her male age mates.

The hunting inevitably gets better sooner or later, and the lesser *molimo,* once begun, will continue until it does. But sickness may develop into death, in which case there will be an immediate change of camp, following an uncomplicated and informal burial, and the commencement of the greater *molimo*.

THE GREATER MOLIMO (*molimo mangbo*)

In a previous account (Turnbull, 1960, pp. 307–340), the general procedure of the greater *molimo* was outlined, and it was indicated that there is no set rule as to when a greater *molimo* should be held. Certainly it is not held for every death within the band, not even for every adult death. It may, on the other hand, be held for a child. It is largely a question of *roho*, and this is determined by a number of considerations such as the nature of the death, the importance of the deceased to the band, and the general tenor of life in the band at that moment, particularly the condition of hunting. A combination of poor hunting and ill humor and general sickness, associated with the death of a child, even of a stranger child temporarily within the band, may well occasion a *molimo*, for the total combination indicates that the forest is "sleeping" (*é langé toro*). On the other hand, the death of a great hunter, through his own fault or through sickness but at a time of good hunting and general contentment, may pass unmarked except by the usual summary burial and change of camp, all expression of grief being confined to the immediate family concerned.

One other consideration not without importance is the fact that whoever initiates a *molimo* festival undertakes a responsibility that may become a burden. He has to see that everyone cooperates in providing food, and when, as sometimes happens, the response is meager, he has somehow to provide enough himself for the society's evening repast. As a greater *molimo* is not likely to last under a month, except possibly for a child under circumstances which otherwise become quickly improved, the economic burden is one to cause careful consideration.

An occasion such as that described (Turnbull, *ibid.*) for old Balekimito would lead to a greater *molimo* without any hesitation, however, for the death of this much loved old lady affected everyone's *roho*. On the other hand, the *molimo* held for Cephu's daughter Teresa was initiated by Njobo, Cephu claiming he did not have a trumpet. It was held not so much out of respect for the girl but because conditions were bad at the time, there being much sickness and discontent. However, Cephu did not seem to be pulling his own weight, economically, and so the festival came to an abrupt end after only a week. If people found their *roho* upset at all, that was more because of Cephu's cupidity than because of the death of his daughter.

To recapitulate the essential elements of the greater *molimo*, as held for Balekimito:

Death is accepted as a natural event and does not lead to any accusations of witchcraft or sorcery, except in the village context. Such grief as is expressed is genuine, and not formal, again except in the village context. It is accepted with regret, and although regarded as natural and inevitable, there is nonetheless a feeling that this is the one really imperfect thing in Mbuti life. The expressed belief that death comes when the forest is sleeping does not quite tally with the factual acceptance of death by the Mbuti, but there is absolutely no feeling of resentment or blame attached to the forest because of death. The felt need to "awaken" the forest and to "rejoice" the forest is occasioned more by the fact that all the living have been brought closer to death and have, to some extent, been touched by it. They consequently need reassurance, not only for the continuation of their own lives but for the continuity of the Mbuti.

The factual attitude to death is seen in the practice of burial, which in the forest is performed as simply and quickly as possible. It is prolonged and attended by ritual only in the village context (see p. 74 *seq.*, 143). Burial is primarily the concern of the immediate nuclear family, who may be assisted by friends or relatives. Too much display of grief is considered very bad, and one of the major concerns of the ensuing *molimo* is to reaffirm life. In a sense, then, the *molimo* is more properly associated with life, occasioned though it may be by death.

The burial over, the camp is abandoned and the mourners are at once under an even stricter obligation to minimize their demonstrations of grief. The opening of the *molimo* festival is informal and casual, and depends on how long it takes for the new camp to get settled, how good the weather is, and whether or not visiting relatives or friends are expected. Within a few days, however, the festival will begin, and from the moment of its inception its stated concern is to awaken and, even more important, to rejoice the forest. The lesser *molimo* is more often spoken of as "awakening" the forest (*su kongi ndura*), though that too has to be done in a way that will rejoice it. The greater *molimo* should ideally be a festival of sheer joy. The course of the festival becomes more and more a symbolic triumph of life over death, the death of the individual being recognized in the final dramatic stamping out of the *molimo* fire, the fire of life. This is not done, however, until time and time again the fire has been attacked in an effort to destroy it, but has been regenerated by the dances of the men, who in a dance that imitates the act of copulation, with the fire as their partner, fan the scattered fire back into a blaze of life.

It is normally the old woman, who is an integral part of every greater *molimo*, who either by herself or with a girl attacks the fire, dancing through it and scattering it all around. Thus the woman who gives birth to life also seeks to destroy it. She is referred to by no title other than "mother," the same term of address used for the forest in its capacity as giver of life and death. It is primarily the young men who hastily rebuild the fire and fan it back into a blaze with their dance of life. It is frequently said that the women used to possess the *molimo*, but it was stolen from them by the men, and this dance, together with the tying up of the men by the old lady (Turnbull, *ibid.*, p. 323), may well represent in part this early conflict, and the attempt of the women to regain possession of the *molimo*. Whatever the symbolism, it is nowhere clearly stated by the Mbuti, each individual claiming to see something different in the performance. It is generally agreed, however, that it shows how strong the women are, and that they have to be respected by men.

Whether or not there is thought to be any correlation with *pepo* (breath), the power of breath to fan sparks into fire is demonstrated when coals are placed in the end of the *molimo* trumpet. The singer blows as he sings, and the sparks that fly out of the end of the trumpet are greeted by murmurs or even shouts of acclaim.

The trumpet is sometimes referred to as an "animal" of the forest, though this is generally in connection with its morning appearance. Nonetheless it is referred to as needing food and water, and these it symbolically receives. It is also passed through the *molimo* fire and

given fire to eat, just as water is passed through it to "cool" it. It is
rubbed with ashes and earth. It is brought into direct contact with
every individual by being passed over their heads as they sit around the
fire singing, and each individual will at some time or another, at his
own whim, scoop up ashes and rub the trumpet with them. And in
the evening appearances of the trumpet at the *molimo* hearth, while
the singer holds one end to his mouth and sings, the youth holding
the far end pumps it up and down as he dances in imitation of the sexual act, sometimes holding the mouth of the trumpet close to his
genitals, imitating the part of either man or woman. Little doubt is
left about the symbolic connection between fire and life.[9]

There is an important distinction between the evening and the
morning appearances of the *molimo* trumpet, and between the roles
played by different age groups. In the evening the singing is primarily
in control of the *mangesé*, or elders. Frequently, they have their own
fire, the hunters have theirs, and the *kiyana*, or male youths, have
theirs. Everyone joins in the singing, the elders maintaining over-all
control and the hunters being the most prominent singers, except for
the *molimo*-trumpet singer, who may be a youth or a young hunter,
being chosen because of his ability as a singer rather than for any
other reason. It is the youths that do most of the dancing at their fire
or at the central *molimo* fire (from which theirs is made by taking
burning embers and setting them separately). The whole intent of
the evening is to rejoice the forest, and this is done by singing throughout the night, and by eating a feast specially prepared from food contributed to the *molimo* hearth. (Just as with food, so with firewood
and with fire itself—every single household in the camp is expected to
contribute.) In the early days of the festival the old lady does not appear, and there is no attempt to stamp out the fire, though erotic
dances are constantly being danced around and over it. It is only toward the end of the festival that the nightlong songfest is drama-
tized by the appearance of the old lady, her dancing through the fire
in an attempt to destroy it, and her tying up of the men (referred to
as both tying up the hunt and tying up the *molimo*). The evening
meetings of the *molimo*, though full of the joy the Mbuti wish to
convey to the forest, are nonetheless solemn in that the purpose is

---

[9] Fire is primarily connected with women; the hearth is often referred to as the vagina;
the association of blood and fire is considered particularly dangerous. Thus the association of the male *molimo* trumpet with the fire and the ashes gives the trumpet phallic
significance in this context. Elsewhere, this precise symbolism seems unimportant, the
important factor being simply the trumpet's masculinity.

never lost sight of. The trumpet itself, while avowedly an "animal" whose animal noises (mainly in imitation of elephant and leopard) are designed to scare women and children and keep them in their huts, is the only sign of the presence of a supernatural power. The main function of the trumpet is to sing, and to pass on the song of the Mbuti into the forest. It is taken off to a distance from where it picks up the song from the men around the *molimo* hearth and echoes it on into the night. This way, the Mbuti say, the forest is sure to hear it and be pleased.

Normally a trumpet is kept high up, concealed in a tree. During a festival, however, it is kept in water except when in use, for it is considered to represent the power of the forest for chastisement. Keeping it in water keeps it "cool." It acts, it seems, as an intermediary, passing on the song of the Mbuti to the forest, but returning in the morning with power, and sometimes with anger. When it appears in the morning, just before dawn, the men have had at the most an hour's sleep, and this is a signal for them to begin singing again. An adult male who fails to sing during a greater *molimo* festival is allegedly killed, and when the trumpet appears in the morning its first act is to search for sleeping men. It is held by a number of youths, who run up and down the camp in search (this may also happen during the evening). But then, to show its power, the trumpet is carried from hut to hut, the youths beating on each with branches and tearing leaves off the roofs. The huts of any troublemakers are particularly singled out, though with due regard for the process described under "Government," by which individual blame is avoided. The older men and even the women may yell at the *molimo* to go away, or to go back to the water, but on this occasion the youths are effectively in charge. There is generally a mock battle in which some of the youths will try to block the path of the trumpet, borne by other youths, or to deflect it in another direction. There may even be a tug-of-war, with some youths pulling it in one direction, some in another, though such contests are formal and enacted more as a dance than as an actual test of strength. All the time, those carrying the trumpet keep it concealed behind leafy branches, or simply by holding it between them. In the end it is carried out of the camp triumphantly as dawn breaks, and with a few defiant bellows returns to its secret hiding place in the water. A vine stretched across the stream warns women and children to keep away.

It is noteworthy, however, that the trumpet is not considered as sacred in itself, hidden though it may be. There was one instance when a trumpet was stolen by a member of a different family and a different band, simply because it had such a good "voice" and could sing so well. Whatever power it possesses it is believed to possess through the quality of its "voice." The fact that it can be stolen or lost (they sometimes get washed away in the floods that follow a particularly torrential downpour), without causing any ritual crisis, is in keeping with the lack of concern for inheritance of the trumpet. It is said by youths that anyone who wants to make one can have it, but that if they do not want to be bothered they need not, for "the *molimo* is a lot of work." Elders, however, say clearly that there used to be one for each family, and by family they plainly defined a minimal lineage, all male members descended from a single living grandfather or from the same father, living or dead.

The fact that they also say that the *molimo* used to be the concern of the band only, perhaps indicates an earlier but now less pronounced emphasis on the principle of patrilineal descent; be that as it may, a noted feature of *molimo* festivals today is their utterly nonlineal nature (Tables 9 and 10). With reference to the greater *molimo* held for Balekimito, there were at one time three *molimo* trumpets in action, only one of which belonged to a member of Balekimito's lineage, the second belonging to her son, the third to Kokoyo, whose wife's step-mother's brother was married to a woman of the same clan as Balekimito—a rather distant claim to lineage—but Kokoyo and Ekianga brought out their *molimo* trumpets because their *roho* wanted it. Thus, by this means they emphasized the importance not of lineage membership but of membership of the band, and the *molimo*, as of old, was at least a band festival, if not a lineage festival.

A more systematic analysis in the next chapter shows the importance of the *molimo* festival as an integrating factor in Mbuti life, and indeed the importance of their whole religious system, based as it is upon a belief in the benevolence of a forest spirit or power. It can, for the moment, be seen clearly enough that it expresses among other things the latent antagonisms that exist between the sexes, because of the same lack of clear, formal sex delineations that characterize the *molimo* itself. It also unites the band (regardless of kinship considerations) in a common expression of the dependence of the Mbuti upon the forest, not only as an economic entity but also as a spiritual entity, a spiritual power that looks after their needs but which is also able to inflict hardship and punishment. The *molimo* heightens the practical economic dependency of the Mbuti upon the forest, which is felt and acknowledged, by forcing an acknowledgment of the most basic dependency of all, that of life and death. The association with the festival of all the basic elements—fire, water, air and earth—and the central importance of food and sex, all combine to create a highly direct, personal and intimate relationship between the Mbuti and the forest, while at the same time binding them together as a band, the one individual dependent upon the next.

CHAPTER 15

Principles of Organization (1)

THE FOREST CONTEXT

While reaffirming our introductory belief that this single-band study is the first essential in the wider study of the Mbuti hunters and gatherers, and that such a study cannot warrant generalizations of wide or final value, some generalization is obviously called for and must now be made to provide a basis for future comparative studies. While we have, in the section on "The Forest World," outlined the nature of Mbuti activity in domestic, economic, political and religious life, insofar as it is lived by the Epulu band of net-hunters, we now have to draw this picture together in an organizational framework. Within this the principles discerned should be specific enough to explain the unity and integrity that plainly persist despite the remarkable degree of flux, and at the same time be general enough to have wider application beyond this specific situation.

In the absence of central government it is customary to look for principles of organization in the kinship system of a society, and although the society in question does not conform to the expectations of Steward (1955) or Service (1962), and although its departure from their norm of patrilineality[1] cannot be demonstrably shown to be due to "evolution" or even to changes wrought by the influx of village cultivators, there is still much to be gained from a study of Mbuti attitudes to kinship. Embedded in their terminology, simple as it is, are attitudes expressed in behavior in all realms of their life.

We have seen how little emphasis is placed on kinship, except at the level of the nuclear family, where there is a strong affective element between young children and parents. This is most clearly seen in the terminology of interpersonal address and reference, which is

[1] Service was more perceptive in shifting the emphasis from lineality to locality, but his generalizations still lack substantiation.

of the generational type, dividing Mbuti into age levels that cut horizontally across the vertical lines of lineage. This terminology recognizes four age levels, but is misunderstood if thought of as a means of relating one generation to the next. Although *miki* can be correctly translated as "child," *apua'i* as "sibling," *eba* and *ema* as "father" and "mother," and "*tata*" as grandparent, these terms are not obligatory in address, and are used only where convenient in reference, or where it is desired to emphasize the age differential (for instance, in discussing activities specific to one age level or another). To use any one of these terms to address or refer to a person of a different generation, far from stressing kinship bonds, stresses generational separation. Even *eba* or *ema*, outside the affective nuclear-family usage, is generally a way of expressing distance, and may sometimes imply attitudes such as hostility or at least reproof.

Having stated what the terminology is, one has obviously to go further and look more closely into its actual usage, rather than be content with simple translations. In practice, the terms refer not to degrees of kinship at all, but to conditions of life: childhood, youth, adulthood, and old age. Of all the terms, the only one that effectively creates interpersonal bonds that are recognizable in daily life is the term *apua'i*. As with all the other terms, it is classificatory in the widest possible sense, extending even beyond bilateral connections to include equally affines or unrelated friends. Effectively, then, rather than "sibling," it should be translated "age mate." However, the English familial term is more pertinent in that it conveys something of the affection involved in the Mbuti relationship, and the intimate degree of unity.

The term *apua'i*, obviously, is used at each of the four age levels between members of that level. It is used widely, constantly, and always affectively, never with reproof or hostility. To address or refer to someone as *apua'i* is to indicate that all is "quiet" between you. Quietness (*ekimi*) is always associated with *apua'i*, whereas noise (*akami*) is invariably associated by any one age level with any of the others—that is to say, any crossing of the levels is liable to produce *akami*. The ideal state is quiet, or *ekimi*, therefore the ideal relationship is that pertaining between *apua'i*. Interlevel relationships (particularly those between adjacent levels) are spoken of not only as producing *akami* but also as being *mota*—strong, powerful, difficult, inclined to be hot, and therefore dangerous though not necessarily bad.

If we forget the usual genealogical associations of kinship and think in a strictly classificatory manner, we do have here an institutionalization of a kinship relationship and the beginnings of a kinship system, for we have already seen the vital importance of age in determining one's realm of activity and responsibility among the Mbuti, and how each of the four levels of *apua'i* act together in distinction from the other levels. But there seems little point in persisting any further with the term "kinship system" in this instance unless we define kinship so as to contradict its very fundamental significance in the more highly structured societies. With the Mbuti we are dealing with kith rather than kin, and the terminological division of the society into four age levels is best thought of as completely divorced from kinship except, and it is a vital exception, insofar as the nuclear family, and the ideal relations that should pertain among its members, are taken as the model relationships for the band. With this in mind, let us examine other relationships implicit in the terminology.

It is noticeable that the terminology distinguishes age levels, and only distinguishes between the sexes at the parental level (*ema* and *eba*). Children, siblings and grandparents (in their widest classificatory sense) are considered without emphasizing any male/female polarity. Sex differentiation can be made, and where necessary this is done, but only in the same rather roundabout way in which any genealogical connection can be traced. In order to differentiate an *apua'i* who is merely a friend from one who is a uterine brother, one has to add the expression "from one stomach" to designate the latter. Similarly, one can add the terms designating male or female to any term of address or reference except that of mother or father, where it is not needed.[2]

This avoidance of sex differentiation is consistent with the interdependence between the sexes that is so characteristic of Mbuti economic life, and with the egalitarianism that exists between them in the realm of government. A woman is in no way the social inferior of a man, and there is little absolute division of labor along sex lines. Among the net-hunters in particular, and among the archers during the *begbe* beat-hunt, cooperation between the sexes during the hunt

---

[2] I have come across instances where a vowel or consonant change has been said to indicate the sex differential (as happens in some Sudanic Languages), such as *tata* and *taté* for male and female grandparent, *apua'i* and *amua'i* for male and female sibling, but there was no consistency in the practice. Wherever it was necessary to make the difference, there was need for stress, and this was in any case better achieved by the more dramatic addition of *moko* or *kali*. At the level where this most frequently is done, a male child would thus be distinguished from a female child: *miki a moko, miki a kali*.

is essential, and gathering, though done mostly by women, may also be done by men when opportunity affords. Perhaps the most significant activity that is generally performed by women is that of house-building. The only men I have seen build their own houses have been bachelors or widowers, and even then they will frequently get women to do this for them. The woman builds the house; she has the final say in selecting the site. She is in charge of the family hearth, where the cooking is done and around which the family eats and sleeps. Her husband may eat with other men at the central hearth, so the family fire may be said to be of major importance to her and her children. And it is precisely at the parental level that the personal terminology differentiates the sexes.

Looking for significant differences in attitudes and relationships between a child and its mother and father, it is plain that the mother is regarded as the source of food, despite the fact that the father is the prime force in the hunt. It might be worth mentioning again here that vegetable foods (entirely discounting village influence) form the bulk of any forest diet, and their nutritive value is probably equal at least to that of the game consumed. In any case, the father gives the game and any vegetables he may have gathered to his wife, who cooks the food and distributes it. A hungry child looks to any one of his classificatory mothers for food, not to his fathers. His most likely chance of finding it will be at the hearth of his nuclear family, but any mother is under as strong an obligation to feed him as the mother from whose stomach he came.

There is no doubting the difference in the emotional connotations of *ema* and *eba*, differences that are not found to exist in attitudes to the sexes at other age levels. *Ema* (mother) is associated with love (*ekondi*); *eba* (father) is associated with authority (*mota*). We have referred a number of times to the habit of the Mbuti addressing the forest as *ema* and *eba*, and although I can adduce no body of evidence to indicate on what occasions it is addressed by which term, it would seem to reflect the attitude of the individual at the moment of address, and the frequency with which the forest is addressed, as both indicate something of great importance in understanding the Mbuti value system, upon which social order so largely depends. The forest is not only the provider, it is also the ruler; it is to be regarded with affection and respect, and under all circumstances to be trusted.[3]

[3] Schebesta (1952, 340) asserts: "*Les noms attribués à Dieu relèvent de deux catè-gories. Ou bien on l'invoque simplement sous ceux d'afa, bapapa, odu . . . père, grand-*

Another important aspect of the terminology is that it does not differentiate between cognates and affines, and is used to include all, without any distinction of this kind. In an Mbuti hunting band, a hunter may well have a uterine brother hunting to one side of him and his uterine sister's husband to the other side. He depends on each equally for both success and for safety, and any preferential behavior, such as might be signified in another form of terminology, must be avoided. To distinguish between cognates and affines in the daily hunting and camp life of the Mbuti, as to distinguish between matrikin and patrikin, or even between kith and kin, on any grounds except age and locality, is not only needless, it is destructive of the sense of unity that is vital to the close cooperative nature of Mbuti economic and political life.

Mbuti personal terminology, as in the more conventional kinship systems, equally reflects interpersonal bonds, then, but they clearly cut across all strictly kinship considerations. This can to some extent be construed as a denial of kinship ties, and it certainly implies that such ties do not form the basis of social organization in the band. But it is better expressed as a lack of concern for kinship that, whatever its origins, is particularly well suited to one of the band's major objectives, the preservation of the greatest possible political distance between itself and the village. It will be readily seen that whereas lineage considerations would divide the Mbuti, the generational system, if considered vertically, effects the widest possible classificatory unity from which the villagers are absolutely excluded. But for the moment to keep to the forest context, the same unity is in perfect consonance with the nonlineal nature of the band, the unity of which any lineal system would destroy. Here we have to refer to one other usage of the same personal terminology; namely, when the Mbuti refer to themselves as *bamiki ba ndura,* the children of the forest. This, together with their habitual reference to the forest as mother and father, extends the nuclear-family model to incorporate the larger

---

père, père des pères; ou bien on se sert de termes qui remontent à certaines représentations mythiques, et dont le nombre est très èlevè." ("Names attributed to the Godhead fall into two categories. Either one simply invokes the name *afa, bapapa* or *odu* . . . father, grandfather, or father of fathers . . . or else one uses terms that derive from mythological beings, of which there are a very great number.")

This indicates the same filial attitude to the forest that I found among the net-hunters. Among the archers, I myself most frequently heard *afa,* used with the same degree of affection as *ema* or *eba.* However, among the archers I equally often heard the forest (God) addressed as *ema* (mother), rarely heard *bapapa,* and never *odu.* My participation in the religious life of archer bands, however, was limited.

group—be it the sub-band, the band, or even the total Mbuti population—as a politico-economic unity. The situation is somewhat analogous to the more common lineal patterns, where a people see their ultimate unity in descent from a common ancestor; the Mbuti find their unity in their common dependence upon the forest.

Taking care not to become involved in issues of causality, we can now see the structural implications of this lack of concern with actual kinship, for it alone makes possible not only the nonlineal nature of the band but the fluidity of its composition. But here we have to introduce another factor, the absence of which would lead to the rapid disintegration of the corporate nature of the band. In the absence of the continuity provided by any kinship system, particularly under the condition of flux we have described for this Mbuti band, continuity and corporateness are seen in terms of territory. We have pointed out that the band can be defined only in terms of territory, the individuals forming that band changing from month to month; perhaps even this is implied in the personal terminology which, as seen, differentiates the sexes only at the parental level in terms of the family hearth—the most basic territorial unit of all.

The system also indicates a lack of concern with problems of superordination and subordination. Even problems are resolved in the forest context by the use of relative age. Their resolution is only truly difficult in one vital context, once again the forest-village relationship. It is consistent with the essentially egalitarian nature of Mbuti social behavior, and it successfully avoids lending any support to the assumption of individual authority on grounds of lineal seniority, which authority would again destroy the essential cooperative unity of the band.

The non-lineal nature of the band itself calls for some explanation, and now we are in a better position to understand it, for we can see clear structural elements that are only obscured when seeking to find principles of band organization in terms of kinship. The terminological system reflects as neatly as could any diagram the essential principle of age. This is the one factor it emphasizes above all others, except the common Mbuti unity as *bamiki ba ndura* (children of the forest). We have seen throughout our description of Mbuti forest life how activity and responsibility are regulated according to age level, and the terminology clearly indicates where one's loyalties lie. Such loyalties are entirely incompatible in so small a cooperative society with the crosscutting vertical loyalties of a lineal kinship system. The territorial band is the only reasonable answer.

We use the term "territorial" rather than bilateral, for the latter term still overemphasizes considerations of vertical descent. This is to negate the whole functional value of the generational system as used by the Mbuti, who use it to establish firm bonds between age mates, and to assign different and essential tasks to different age levels, thus avoiding the remotest chance of centralization of power or authority. But we certainly do not use the term as does Steward (1955, 143), who uses it "to designate certain primitive societies which consist of many unrelated nuclear or biological families." Steward implies that relationship (he does not state what degree of relationship) not only is of no concern, but that it does not exist between member families of the band. It would be difficult to find a more composite Mbuti band than that of the Epulu, yet a glance at Table 4, giving the band membership at the close of 1957, shows that every single individual, representing some twenty-two different lineages, is "related" by clear consanguineal or affinal bonds to every other. No individual stands alone, though the relationship may sometimes be remote.

And most certainly while stating that age and territory are more effective principles of organization than kinship, we do not deny that kinship is recognized. We are merely stating that social interaction among the Mbuti is based on generation and territory. A system, to deserve the term, must be effective in action, and we have seen how seldom kinship relationships are called into account among the Mbuti, the major occasion being a proposal of marriage. There the concern with kinship is not so much in terms of the politico-economic implications of the marriage, as a clear-cut consideration of lineal distance. The stated prohibition is against marrying on the side of either the mother or father, but so long as the memory of the elders can trace no connection, there is no further concern.

Sister-exchange marriage preserves the unity of the apud'i, and indeed enhances it when, as can happen in the composite band, the two couples reside side by side. The lack of marriage and divorce ritual does not indicate any lack of concern for one's age level, for one always marries within that level and so is never lost to it, but it is another symptom of the general lack of concern with kinship, this time with affinity rather than lineality. A marriage is effected by living together; divorce is effected by one or other spouse simply going to live elsewhere. If this is taken to indicate a lack of concern not only for kinship but also for social stability, it can also be regarded, precisely because of the freedom it allows, as a further mechanism by which the constant flux so characteristic of the band is maintained. That this flux itself has a function will be seen in the final chapter, when we deal again with the Mbuti/Villager relationship.

The different functions of each age level have been described (pp. 110, 111, 112 *seq.*), and the organizational value of making the horizontal distinction in the composite band is self-evident. Each age level is cooperative in activity, certain activities (such as the hunt) calling for cooperation between two or three age levels still preserving the distinction by allocating different roles to each. Interpersonal relations are determined primarily by age level, and authority has also been seen to be diffused through the different levels.

The transition from childhood to youth is marked for boys and girls alike by participation in the *elima*. Adulthood is conveyed by the act of marriage, which carries with it the right to own a net. The rare bachelor who proves himself as a great hunter and still does not marry may, by combined virtue of his age and his skill, own a net, but the accepted qualification is that of marriage, emphasizing another major Mbuti concern, that of procreation.

Transition from adulthood to elderhood is less clear-cut and more filled with tension, for though an elder enjoys many privileges and has, set aside for him as such, certain vital roles in the social organization, he misses the excitement of the hunt, the pride and satisfaction of rearing a family, and he certainly recognizes that this is the final transition.

The nonlineal (or cognatic) band, then, divided horizontally into age levels rather than vertically into lineages, effects an absolute unity throughout each level, whereas it would otherwise be divided into as many sections as there were lineages. Its persistence and continuity are seen in terms of territory. There may well be a tendency for certain lineages to remain within the same territory for successive generations, but such association is incidental rather than structurally determined. The demography and internal organization, while allowing for marriage within the band, make it essential for much marriage exchange to take place between different and preferably not adjacent bands. Since the residence of the newlywed couple is determined by immediate economic considerations, such as the relative size and composition of the two bands, territory is obviously not an individual value (though an individual generally knows and therefore feels at home in one territory more than in others) so much as a group value. The stated concern of the Mbuti is not to perpetuate lineage but to perpetuate the band, and bands are not only defined but named by territory. Individual camps are given specific names according to their locality. *Apa toangbe* is the camp under the *toangbe* trees; *apa* Lelo is the camp by the Lelo River, and so forth. It is significant that when referring to another band it is generally referred to by its current camp name, or the last camp name known, rather than by the more general name by which its whole hunting territory is known. This implies a recognition of the changeability of the composition of the band, and an emphasis on what the band is at any given moment, defined by the particular part of its territory it is hunting at the moment.

Practical considerations of territory are that birth in a territory conveys the right to hunt with that band throughout life, and it generally conveys a sentimental attachment to the territory that may well act as a stabilizing factor. Cognatic or affinal relationships may be utilized to acquire the right to hunt in other territories, but one then becomes a member, if temporary, of the band in which one is hunting.[4] But it is when one widens the concept of territory, so that it implies more than a mere area defined by boundaries, that the notion acquires its most fundamental importance. As a definable area it is of economic and political significance in providing the framework within which hunting by different bands can take place without danger of shortage or need for conflict; it is also of social significance in providing a symbol of band unity, and the promise of continuity. But the term used by the Mbuti for territory is the same word used for forest, *ndura*. Regarded in this light, territory assumes vastly added significance.

When an Mbuti says "This is our forest" ("*Nde ndura ndasu*"), he may be defining the territory of the band in which he is a current member, or he may be defining the Mbuti as against the villagers. Alternatively, if in the honey season among the net-hunters, he may be defining the territory in which his particular subsection of the band

---

[4] This again is an example of different degrees of kin relationship being recognized but not made explicit, because explicit recognition would alter the distance between the individuals and so disturb the *apua'i* relationship. Once in the new camp, the visitor is assimilated into the age-level system of that band regardless of the nature of his kin relationships. In giving his reasons for making the visit, either to his own band or to the band he is visiting, an Mbuti will not spell out the relationship but will most likely use the personal name, coupled perhaps with the appropriate generational term. The term alone would plainly not indicate clearly enough whom he was going to visit.

27. A common way of showing displeasure is to sulk, talking to no one. A young girl here keeps her back to her husband, wherever he might be, and refuses to cook his food.

28. Moké, an elder and a peacemaker, with two of his adopted families. It is considered no shame for an Mbuti male to fondle and care for the needs of even the youngest children.

29. A hunting fire is lit to announce to the forest that the hunt is setting out. Hunters on their way will pass by, but no special ritual is performed.

30. The hunt sets off, well camouflaged against the leafy background. The men and youths generally go separately from the women

31. Cephu's wife, carrying an ember of the family hearth wrapped in fire-resistant leaves, and with her carrying basket on her back, sets off after the hunt. She will act as a beater with the other women and children, and will gather wild foods on the way.

32. Masisi stops on his way to the hunt to try for a monkey in the treetops. For net-hunters the bow and arrow is only an incidental means of food-getting. As seen here, poisoned arrows are preferred to those with metal tips provided by the villagers.

33. Two youths, armed with spears, carry their fathers' hunting nets. They will not have nets of their own until they are married but may, on occasion, take the place of their fathers on the hunt.

34. A youth, recently initiated, is still considered far from manhood in the forest. Here he helps an older brother set up the net.

35. When an animal falls into the net it is quickly caught by the hunters and carefully extracted before it damages the netting. A youth stands by for the kill.

36. When the kill is assured, a youth signals back to the camp and to other hunters, to let them know what kind of game has fallen into whose net. Relatively complex messages can be signaled in this way, variations in rhythm combining with variations in pitch achieved by flexing the elbow, which forms a sound box when clapped with the other hand.

37. Honey-gathering usually involves climbing to great heights, but honey is occasionally found near ground level. Only if found in fallen tree trunks can the honey be collected by women.

38. Honey is highly prized, but is nonetheless shared among all. Here Kelemoké's uncle, Masalito, shares with his favorite nephew.

39. The musical bow, apart from the wooden clappers used during the *molimo* and during the honey season, is the only musical instrument that seems to be original to the Mbuti. Even this is slightly used, the one here simply being a hunting bow tapped by an arrow, the mouth acting as the resonator. An extremely musical people, the Mbuti are, unlike the villagers, vocal rather than instrumental.

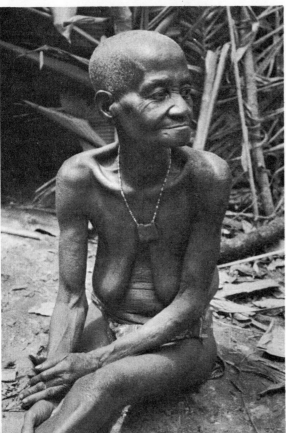

40. Balekimito, the old lady who "died well," and for whom the exceptionally long *molimo* festival was held. The charm around her neck, stolen from the villagers, would have been regarded by the Arabized Ngwana as powerful magic. For her it was a mere ornament.

41. A spot like this, in the Lelo River, was the resting place of the *molimo* trumpets used in honor of Balekimito. Vines are stretched across the stream to warn intruders to keep away. The precaution, however, is as much for fear of theft as for fear of desecration.

is resident. It is seldom that he refers merely to geographical boundaries, for trespass, as seen, is rare and of little consequence. Yet it is a
term he frequently uses, and as an organizational principle it is equal
in importance to age.

While agreeing with Steward that the environment may to some
extent be determinant as well as permissive of certain elements of
social organization, I find it impossible to see the validity of his wider
deterministic claims for cultural ecology.[5] But while Steward seems
to have overreached himself, or rather overreached his material, in
trying to draw up general principles of culture change, nonetheless
in regarding cultural ecological adaptations as "creative processes"
(1955, p. 34), his stress on cultural ecology as a particular factor is
highly relevant to the Mbuti and in itself an important contribution.
We have seen throughout the importance of the economic abundance offered by the forest, permitting economic independence to
each band. While the presence of the village tribes is sufficient indication of the permissibility of cultivation, at the technological level of
the Mbuti one might say that the environment determines hunting
and gathering. It is certainly relevant to say that the Mbuti, at least,
would agree with Steward, for they say it is the only way they can
live, that if they cultivate they will die. The truth of their assertion
is not relevant here; its importance lies in that it reveals the depth
of their felt dependence upon the forest.

Nothing is gained, however, by saying that the Mbuti exploitative

[5] Indeed, it would be impossible to do so since Steward uses the Mbuti as an example
of an ecologically determined patrilineal band, content to base his analysis on Putnam
(1948) as interviewed by Carleton Coon and represented in a brief and obviously general and sketchy article. Steward's only other Mbuti reference is to Schebesta's preliminary seventeen-page field report in *Anthropos* (1931). A minimum of inquiry would
have revealed numerous other sources, which while admittedly unsatisfactory would,
through their very divergence, at least have demonstrated the inadvisability of relying on
the two sources quoted (ref. Turnbull, 1965). Further evidence to support his theory,
for the Central African Negritos, was drawn by Steward from the reports of Schmidt
(1910) and Trilles (1932). Not one of the many articles in *Zaïre, Congo,* or *Kongo-
Overzee,* is cited, nor is Schebesta's major work, *Die Bambuti Pygmäen vom Ituri,* nor
the abridged and revised edition of that work which appeared in French in 1952, *Les
Pygmées du Congo Belge.* Unsupported assertions such as that "the exploitative patterns
produced the features typical of the patrilineal band" (Steward, 1955, p. 128) are bad
enough; the apparent ignorance of major texts (for Steward nowhere gives any reasons
for not using them) is worse; but still worse is the sheer misrepresentation of the facts
he does claim to have at his disposal. Thus he claims that the populations he has selected to illustrate patrilineal bands—the Bushman, Congo Negritos, Australians, Tas-
manians and Fuegians, "and others"—are similar "because the nature of the game and
therefore of their subsistence problems is the same in each case" (1955, p. 38). It is
difficult to see much similarity between subsistence problems of the Kalahari Desert
and the Equatorial Rain Forest, even if they are on the same continent.

patterns produce "features typical of the patrilineal band," for the patterns differ from group to group, and within each group from one time of the year to the next. At one time or another, each group, net-hunters or archers, will be able to present bands that resemble patrilineal units; at other times the same bands will be utterly nonlineal, even though the exploitative pattern may not have changed.

Nonetheless, the environment itself does play a vital structural role, and while not necessarily determining the exploitative activity, or the dependence of the Mbuti upon it, is determinant of their value system so long as that dependence is felt. For, feeling that way, regarding the forest as *ema* the provider, and as *eba* the ruler, believing that any deviation from the way of life ordained for them by the forest would be fatal, the Mbuti effect what control they can over their lives by a constant effort to "rejoice the forest."

Conceiving that the forest is intelligent, the Mbuti conceive that it is like them, and consequently the ideal that they hold for themselves is the ideal they attribute to the forest. While age and territory are effective in organizing the band, dividing it into significant units, binding it together as a whole, and determining the general nature of interpersonal relationships, the territory enlarged into the forest seen as mother and father acts as the ultimate sanction of all behavior. There are certain recognized forms of behavior that lead to a "good" band, and others that lead to a "bad" band. The appropriate positive and negative sanctions are formulated in such a way that all actions are either pleasing to the forest—leading to the ideal of *ekimi*, or quietness—or displeasing to the forest, leading to *akami*, or noise. (*Ekimi* and *akami* are, in practice, essential elements in determining the success or failure of the hunt.)

Thus it is recognized that cooperation is essential for the success of the hunt, so it is stated that laziness and aggressiveness and disputatiousness are all displeasing to the forest, leading to *akami* (as indeed they do). The *akami* is their own reward, for *akami* destroys the hunt and "kills" the Mbuti. On the contrary, to hunt well, to have a full stomach, to sing and dance, is to please the forest and lead to *ekimi*, or "quietness," and *ekimi* in turn brings good hunting, and is associated with singing and dancing and feasting.

Here is a very clear example of the closest possible association between religious belief and ethical behavior. The distinction made by Radcliffe-Brown (1952, p. 172) between law, morality and religion, upheld by legal sanctions, sanctions of public opinion, and religious sanctions, does not hold good for Mbuti society, where the three principles are inextricably fused. One might be able to talk of law, even if law implies sanction by force, for the Mbuti believe that the forest has such power and force and will use it. Indeed, in their experience it does, for transgression is met with the force of *akami*, which kills. This is thought of as a very direct and practical response on the part of the forest as the law. On the other hand, public opinion can hardly be said to exist, for there is no public spokesman, and every opinion on behavior is expressed in terms of pleasing or displeasing the forest. Such public action as may be taken—ridicule or ostracism —is taken in the name of the forest. Exile is literally being sent to the forest to meet it directly. Religious sanctions are not differentiated from any others; the threat is the same—noise and displeasure.

Ultimately, then, in our consideration of territory, despite the obvious practical values involved and a certain extent of ecological determination of behavior patterns, the territory as a principle of organization must be regarded as a religious principle. Indeed, life itself, for the Mbuti, can almost be regarded as a ritual designed to please the forest and secure *ekimi*. There is, as noted, an almost total absence of magic, and the only ritual that can be truly considered as such, and is not otherwise a necessary daily activity, is song. We have seen that song is designed specifically to rejoice the forest, and to draw its attention to its children, but beyond this and its reinforcement, through musical technique, of the values of age and cooperation, there is nothing particularly remarkable about it as a social institution.

It is only when we come to death that there is a marked departure from the normal tenor of life, and a ritual, the *molimo*, that might be regarded as a ritual in the Durkheimean sense of recreating society and reaffirming the social sentiment. While any interpretation of religious ritual of this kind is highly questionable, the attempt has to be made.

Leaving aside the "legal" aspect of the *molimo* when it appears in the early hours of the morning to wreak havoc in the camp, there are few rituals that could be more explicitly concerned with the "recreation of society" in the most literal sense. Death is the most final and inescapable of all crises, and for it there is no remedy. But it threatens more than the life of the individual; it threatens the continuity of the band, and so threatens the ritual of life by which the forest is pleased. Death itself is recognized as deriving from the forest, so is accepted with regret, but there is enormous concern to conceal the regret and avoid any excessive show of grief, for crying is *akami*. The uncomfortable fact of death has to be obliterated from the memory as quickly and effectively as possible, and the band, which has received a blow at its strength, must be rejuvenated in an exaggerated display of all the things pleasing to the forest—good hunting, singing, dancing, feasting and, above all, *ekimi*. More than this, the *molimo*, as we have seen, is a means of reaffirming the effective division of the band into age groups, and through both the participation of the old lady, who demonstrates the power of the women over the men, and through the *ekokomea* dance, the lack of sex differentiation is emphasized. *Ekokomea* may also be regarded in a similar light as the erotic dance over the fire, where the men symbolically copulate over the scattered embers, fanning them to life. Certainly the sexual act is represented in the *molimo* dances, if not in the symbolism of the *molimo* trumpet itself and the way in which it is handled, and there is very evidently expressed concern with the regeneration of life.

The *molimo* is also an occasion on which the band reaffirms all its interpersonal loyalties, and its unity as a band, regardless of kinship considerations. (This is not to deny that the band, and the *molimo*, may at one time have had a more definitely lineal structure.) It is significant that it insists on participation by all adult males, including not only affines but adult visitors living temporarily with the band under an obligation, default in which is punishable by death. Such death itself is said to be brought by the *molimo*; informants differed as to *how* death would actually take place—some said by two spears, some by beating—but in all cases it was held that the *molimo* would bring death to any who did not fulfill his obligations.

Thus the forest is intimately associated with the Mbuti at death, just as it is at birth. The same forest that gives life and strength through the juices of the vine, and through the vine and wooden charms tied around an infant's wrist, may bring death to that infant, if as an adult he fails to rejoice the forest during the *molimo* festival.

Fire, which is the gift of the forest, but whose ownership is disputed, is central in the life of the Mbuti, representing life itself. (One legend has it that fire was first owned by a chimpanzee; another by woman; another by the *keti*. In any case, man [Mbuti] ultimately stole it and now possesses it.) During the *molimo*, men pass their hands through the flames and then rub gently over their faces. The *molimo* trumpet is passed over the flames. Sometimes men put coals in their mouths, or hold them in their hands. Burning coals are put in the mouth of the trumpet. When the trumpet enters the camp at night it is preceded by a youth carrying burning embers which he waves in the air and touches to the ground to leave a trail of glowing cinders, the "footsteps" of the *molimo*. And of course the *molimo* fire is the object of attention of the old lady and her attendant. The final extinction of the fire is the signal for the return of the *molimo* to the forest, and the end of the festival.

The festival emphasizes and reaffirms everything of importance in the life of the Mbuti. And perhaps one of the most important things it emphasizes is accompanied by the least ritual—the closing of the path leading to the village. To the same end, but more dramatic, is the way in which a *molimo* festival will come to a complete halt if a villager comes to the camp. For the *molimo* not only reaffirms the unity of the band; it reaffirms the unity of the Mbuti in opposition to the village. It is essentially a "matter of the forest," and the entire system that it upholds operates only in relation to the forest.

In the same way that a solitary villager can transform a forest camp into a village camp, just by his presence, so is any contact between the two worlds, except one of opposition, impossible. The system that the *molimo* recreates in the forest, the very life of the Mbuti that in itself is a ritual of pleasing the forest, cannot persist in the village. The ritual closing of the path is clearly symbolic of the Mbuti concern to keep the village out of the forest, to keep the two worlds apart. When they, as individuals or as a band, leave the forest and visit the village, they do precisely that—they leave the forest. It is this opposition, which is so sharply defined in the *molimo*, that is the basis of the Mbuti relationship with the villagers.

CHAPTER 16

Principles of Organization (2)

THE VILLAGE CONTEXT

The principles of organization that have begun to emerge with reference to the forest world of the Mbuti only become fully comprehensible when we relate them to the village world. Gluckman (1960) gave some general but highly pertinent indications of a somewhat similar situation involving a dichotomy in the lives of Africans in North Rhodesia and Nyasaland. In that situation the conflict, or rather the opposition, was between the ancestral land and the town. The land represented subsistence to some extent, but primarily security; the town was a place to raid for money. While Gluckman did not see any "detribalization" involved, he pointed out that the African is tribalized, in towns and in rural areas, in two different ways, tribal attachments in urban areas having to work within a setting of urban associations: "Hence the African in rural areas and in town is two different men; for the social situation of tribal home and of urban employment determine his actions and associations, within the major politico-economic system covering both areas" (1960, p. 11).

Gluckman refers to the consequent social and mental conflict, and sees "considerable resolution of this conflict through the separation of the spheres of activities" (1960, p. 11). In assessing the Forest/ Village relationship we see a similar situation, with the village being regarded as a place to raid, creating numerous social and mental conflicts which again are largely resolved by separation in what I have called a system of indigenous apartheid. There is more to it than that, however. We cannot suppose, however complete the barrier, that the Mbuti live an utterly schizophrenic existence; even within the opposition there must be order. Nor can we suppose that the order comes from a mere dilution of forest values when the Mbuti come to the village; it is rather, as Gluckman says, that the same values have to work within a setting of urban (village) associations.

Indeed, certain elements of the forest system can only be explained in relationship to the village context, such as the excessively fluid composition of the band and the almost paranoid attitude to a single villager passing through a hunting camp, sufficient to suspend the vital and central, all-important *molimo* festival, even at its height, or transform it into a village-style parody. This quite singular feature has found no explanation in terms of either the village alone or the forest alone. Let us then briefly review the forest system, and look at it again in the village context. The following elements have emerged as having the greatest structural significance:

1. THE BAND is the basic unit, its membership being influenced by economic rather than kinship considerations. Constant association and cooperative compatibility outweigh kinship even within the band in regulating the process of fission and fusion. This latter process is related to the annual honey season, but it is not determined by it. The over-all size of the band, or of its subsections, is, however, determined by ecological factors resulting in a maximum of about thirty nuclear families for a band, and a minimum of three families for a subsection. Although the band is nonlineal, the network of consanguineal and affinal interpersonal relationships is recognized to link all members, so that the terminology, while referring to age levels regardless of actual or fictive kinship, still has the same affective qualities of kinship terminology, the term referring to age mates (*apua'i*) being the most widely used, and the most effective.

With the best will in the world, it is not possible to apply the kind of analysis suggested by Lévi-Strauss (1958) for following his argument (that the biological family makes a poor starting point); further we must also abandon the affinal family and the system of affective relationships that Lévi-Strauss saw to pertain there. For among the Mbuti affective relationships are determined more by age than by kinship, consanguineal or affinal. We simply cannot follow a set formula that takes no account of the age factor. Thus f/s is positive when s is a child.[1] It is negative when s is a youth, becomes less strained when s becomes a hunter, but only approaches positive again when f becomes an elder. In other words the relationship is positive as long as f/s are not in adjacent age levels. The greatest friction arises when s approaches adulthood and is about to become a hunter, a signal for the retirement of the father into elderhood. It

[1] f = father; s = son; m = mother; d = daughter; b = brother; z = sister.

would be difficult to notice much difference in this respect between
f/s and *mb/zs*.

b/z and *h/w* are both positive, though *b/z* swings to negative
briefly at the youth's age level, friction being an inevitable potential
of the sister-exchange practice, loose as it is. *m/s*, almost as uniformly
positive as *h/w* throughout all changes in age level, might be said to
reach a double-positive stage when *s* becomes a hunter, and is certainly pronounced during his youth—just at the time, in fact, when
his relations with his father are at their worst.

If we consider the age factor we get something like the following
(allowing for the fact that there is no very precise way of determining
attitudes, particularly among the somewhat volatile Mbuti):

	mb/zs	:	*b/z*	::	*f/s*	:	*h/w*
When *s* is a child:	+		+		+		+
youth:	−		−		−		+
hunter:	−		+		−		+

Or, if set out in a different form, considering only age, the thick
lines joining positive relationships, the thin lines joining those points
at which the relationships are negative, we see most clearly the correspondence of attitudes to age. Only when the sex difference is considered—i.e., allowing for negative *b/z* and positive *m/s*—is the
symmetry spoiled.[2]

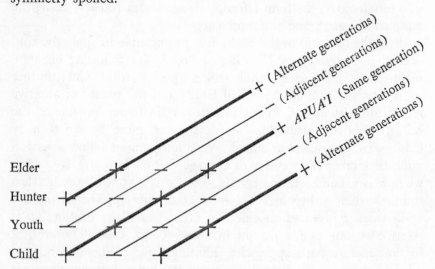

_____

[2] The system, and the results, might be considerably improved by replacing the in-
flexible positive and negative signs with a scale analysis.

Despite all of which, and the lack of structurally significant rules of inheritance of property or status (names sometimes being handed on down to alternate generations, but not necessarily so), and with no apparent concomitant inheritance of status, certainly not of property, there is a recognition of the patrilineage, and a tendency toward patrilocality.[3]

2. AGE is the prime factor in dividing the band into significant units, the significance being seen in terms of domestic, economic, legal and governmental responsibilities. Each age level has a distinct role that contributes to the total social order, and in all these aspects of life it is consistently of greater import than kinship. The consistency still remains as firm in religious life, and following the ultimate crisis of death. The dead belong, as it were, to yet another age level, and one that is almost dissociated from the four levels of the living. Thus after death there is no familial concern for the dead, as seen in the complete lack of concern with ancestral ghosts. Far from disclaiming the dead relatives through fear[4], the Mbuti continue to regard them with affection insofar as they regard them at all. Their preference for forgetting the dead reflects an attitude toward death, not to the individual dead.

Each age level has its own way of earning the respect of the band as a whole, by fulfilling what is referred to as its "duty." Thus the duty of children is to grow up in good health. The duty of youths is to sing, flirt and play—and help the parental level. The duty of the hunters is to hunt and, oddly enough, to create *akami*, or noise, and the duty of

[3] We have to assert that there is, for the moment, no evidence that the territorial band is a product of special considerations, as suggested by Steward and Service (in whose terminology the band is "composite"). In particular we must reject, for the Mbuti, the assertion of Service (1962, p. 49) so convenient to his argument for virilocality, that all such societies were, before they were "so thoroughly subjugated," characterized by fighting between "unrelated groups," resulting in "fears, dangers and enmities." Also it is necessary to deny his assertion that such societies are "enclaved among more powerful neighbours—and cannot but lose or be heavily punished for any breach of the peace." If anything, in the Ituri, it is the villages that are enclaved. Further gross misrepresentation, perhaps owing to paucity of reliable material, is offered by Service (1962, p. 108) in the bald statement: "The composite band, on the other hand, is obviously a product of the near-destruction of aboriginal bands after contact with civilization. In all cases there is conclusive evidence of rapid depopulation by disease which, when combined with ending of hostilities among the aborigines themselves under the dominance of the common enemy, resulted in the merging of previously unrelated peoples." The evidence now available, while not denying the possible validity of such historical reconstruction, in no way supports it. Indeed, there is evidence to the contrary.

[4] For an example of precisely the opposite situation, see Beattie (1960, p. 76), where concern for kinship obligations during life is continued after death, resulting in a desire to disavow relationships.

the elders is to restore *ekimi,* or quietness, and also, following their alternate generation, to play and sing, if in a somewhat different manner. The elders may also flirt.

Above all, each age level has its own responsibility in the total band economy.

3. TERRITORY is the principle by which the band, divided horizontally by age, sees its unity vertically, through all four generational levels. Territory, represented by the hearth, recognizes the divisions of the band from the nuclear family, represented by the family hearth, to the four age levels, represented by the different hearths at the *kumamolimo,* for youths, hunters and elders (children remaining by the family hearths). Territory, represented by an area enclosed by recognizable boundaries, defines and is the symbol of unity of the band. In its widest extension, the forest itself, territory forms the basis for the unity of all Mbuti in their common opposition to the village world. The village world is frequently referred to as *indenji aku,* or in the lingua franca, KiNgwana, as *inchi ingina*—directly translated as "another territory." Each band has its own *indenji,* and intermarriage between noncontiguous bands is preferred because of the rights it conveys, each to the other's territory. The Mbuti themselves say it is good to have relatives (friends) in many camps, for then one never "walks emptily" (*tamba bulé*). One of the great *molimo* songs is *"me tamba bulé"*—"I am walking emptily." The importance lies not in the initial or future residence of the married couple, but in the exchange relationship established by their marriage, enabling individuals or families of each band to exchange visits with members of the other, never having to "walk emptily."

For the Mbuti territory in its widest aspect, as the forest, also represents the spiritual source of their entire being, and effectively operates as the ultimate sanction of social behavior.

4. NOISE, or *akami,* is another element of structural significance, and must be considered in relation to its counterpart, *ekimi*—quiet. Noise is recognized as having considerable practical significance, such as its effect in scaring away animals. This can be desirable or undesirable, depending on the situation, and so can noise be desirable or otherwise. Ultimately, however, noise kills, and so generally is to be avoided. It may be used in times of danger or crisis for protective purposes, and apart from shouting to frighten away wild animals while on the trail, the Mbuti also whistle to stop all human sound, in

the camp or on the hunt, and they also sometimes shout at a storm or at rain to drive away bad weather.

But more important than Mbuti recognition of the practical power of noise is their recognition of its social value. When they say it is the duty of the hunter age level to make noise, they mean just that, even though it is precisely noise that will negate the hunter's other duty, to hunt. The Mbuti do not connect the two duties—the one refers to the hunt, the other to camp life. It is in the camp that the hunter is expected to make noise; that is, to be disputatious. For the countervalue, *ekimi*, is only "quiet" and does not refer to silence (*kobinengo*), which is considered as an indication of great and imminent danger. A silent camp is considered a bad camp and the badness is destroyed by destroying the silence, which can be done in two ways. One is by singing, which is recognized as sound but only described as noise when it takes place in the village. Singing, as we have seen, is essentially a form of communication, even of communion, with the benevolent forest divinity. It destroys silence and "rejoices the forest" at the same time. But this is recognized as having only temporary efficacy. To strike at the roots of silence, one employs "noise" in the sense of argument, which is certainly its most common connotation.

Silence in a camp betokens unusual ill humor, which is common among the Mbuti when in their village camp, but not in the forest (except when the hunt is spoiled by rain). Disputes seldom remain hidden for long because of the intimate nature of camp life, but any length of time is too long, and when a camp is silent it is invariably the hunters who find some cause for "making noise." It matters little what they pick on, but it is preferably not the underlying dispute causing the silence. It may be directed at the cause if personal feelings run high, but then the hunters are criticized for making too much noise, *akami ndasi*. Youths and elders will alike shout at the hunters and tell them this, but the noise will not die down until the disputants have either come into the open with their dispute, putting it before the band, or have been forced to join together in some common but unrelated cause.

Thus there was an occasion on which Amabosu, for no evident reason, took to beating his wife, Amaloku, with unwonted vigor and regularity. A certain amount of wife-beating is considered good, and the wife is expected to fight back. But Amaloku was aware of the real reason for her husband's behavior, which was her own brother's persistence in sleeping with Amabosu's sister despite her having just given birth to a child. She evidently felt shame for her brother, but whatever the reason she did not fight back. This only enraged Amabosu further so that his beatings grew to the point where Amaloku was bruised and lame and perpetually in tears. After a week of this the band was well aware of the underlying cause, but it was nonetheless concerned for the restoration of good relations between Amabosu and his wife. Being outwardly a domestic squabble, nobody interfered, and the camp was silent. The silence was very real, as it can be when the Mbuti get moody, and it settled on the whole camp the moment each beating began. Masisi tried to create minor disputes about hunting, in the hope that Amabosu and his wife would join in, but they were not to be drawn so easily. Even when one very real dispute raged beside them (Pepei having stolen some meat from Sau, Amabosu's mother) they maintained a sullen silence that overcame the band as soon as Pepei had been dealt with by a sound beating.

It was not until Amaloku, in an effort to run away from Amabosu, tripped and fell by Tungana's hearth that the camp had its chance. As she tripped, Amaloku scattered several logs from the fire, upsetting a piece of meat that had been roasting over the coals, casting it into the ashes. Old Tungana let out a yell and his wife slapped Amaloku hard. Amaloku wailed as she had never wailed before, whereupon Masisi and Manyalibo, both great hunters, went to the middle of the camp and jointly denounced Amaloku as a troublesome girl who should be sent back to her people. She had been badly taught, because no Mbuti ever treats fire like that, or throws food into fire. She was no good as a daughter, no good in camp, and evidently no good in bed because she was still without child.

This utterly unjustified and personal attack brought out not only Amabosu but also Ekianga (Amaloku's brother, the basic cause of all the trouble) in common defense of the weeping girl. Masisi and Manyalibo put up a good argument, for it was indeed considered bad to accidentally step into a fire, and the camp was soon in an uproar with the sister-exchange section uniting in defense, supported largely by the youths. The hunters, with the exception of Ekianga and Amabosu themselves, allied with Masisi and Manyalibo. Finally old Tungana stopped everything by whistling and then making one of his rare speeches. It was to the effect that everyone was behaving like villagers, so he might as well go to the village and stay there. He called to his wife to pack her things, and grumbling loudly he grabbed his bow and arrows and started to walk out of the camp. His son Maku-basi, one of the hunters, called after him that he was going "emptily" (*ue ke bulé*)—using the KiNgwana word for "emptily," with its con-notations of war—(See footnote to p. 295) and without reason. Makubasi pointed out that all the noise had ceased and that now there was *ekimi*, or quiet. Tungana stopped, listened, said that he did not want to kill the camp so he would come back, but from now on there must be nothing but *ekimi* and no more jumping in and out of his hearth, spoiling his food, destroying his fire.

Ekianga continued to sleep with Amabosu's sister, but Amabosu no longer beat Ekianga's sister in retaliation. On the contrary, even before Tungana's grumbling protests had died down, he was off get-ting some herbs to soothe his wife's wounds. And if the camp had been upset by noise rather than silence, the hunters would have killed it with more noise. The ultimate solution generally lies in the hands of the elders, but the process of restoring equilibrium is initiated by the hunters' fulfilling their duty of making noise. Thus though noise cannot be said to be good, its use (properly controlled) is recognized as having beneficial potentialities.

5. QUIET (*ekimi*) is not merely the opposite of noise; it is some-thing else and it is the ultimate goal toward which life is directed. As with noise, its practical advantages are plain, particularly on the hunt. It is also recognized as an indication that all is well; a quiet camp is a camp untroubled by dissension, a quiet child is a well-fed child, and so forth. In the same way that noise is associated with heat, so is quiet associated with coolness, and this is generally a de-sirable quality, whereas heat is undesirable.[5] The plaintive cry of the elders when trying to stop an argument or settle a dispute is often "*Me oki akami, me toni akami; me kondi ekimi, ndura ekondi ekimi*" —"I hear noise, I refuse noise; I love quiet, the forest loves quiet."

The ideal is quiet, and quietness is associated with the forest. The concept is inseparable from the concept of joy, which is *ekimi mota*, or "powerful quietness." Joy is an intensification of quietness and is brought about by the occurrence of the norm: good hunting, good weather, good health, harmonious relations, plenty of children. These conditions do not always prevail, in which case active steps have to be taken to improve the hunt, to be less disputatious, to keep better health, to have more children, and to drive bad weather away. En-

[5] The village is in fact, as in thought, hot and noisy, whereas the forest is cool and quiet.

deavor of this kind, however, is recognized as being fraught with difficulty, and there is another way that is both easier and more sure, for *ekimi mota* is produced by song. The process of "rejoicing the forest" is a process of creating *ekimi mota* where it does not exist, of intensifying mere *ekimi* through song.

The term for "rejoicing the forest" in the Epulu area is *bongisa ndura*. In KiNgwana the verb is either *furahisa* or *ponisa*, there being no precise equivalent to *bongisa*. *Furahisa* is closer to the English concept of joy, involving festivity; *ponisa*, however, means to cure. The KiNgwana words are both used by the Mbuti in this context, interchangeably, and the meaning of *bongisa* lies between them, derived as it is from *bonga*, meaning good, in an all-inclusive sense.

Perhaps the exact connotation of "rejoicing the forest" is best described by the process itself, which brings joy through joy. Singing gives the Mbuti intense satisfaction. They say it makes them feel good, in the sense of feeling joyful. The mood of song is joyful, even when it is a *molimo* song on the occasion of death. By creating a mood of joy within themselves the Mbuti convey that joy to the forest, which returns it, restoring *ekimi* or even *ekimi mota* to the camp. To describe song as mere "curing" would not quite cover the essential sharing process implied by the term *bongisa ndura*. Song is known, to the Mbuti, to have the infallible power of filling the forest with *ekimi mota*. It is sometimes described as being like the act of copulation in the moonlight, or wherever the individual talking feels that act to be the most intense and beautiful. The Mbuti say *"su bongisa ndura, ndura pisu ekimi"*—"we rejoice the forest, the forest gives us quiet." The distinction is simple, for joy is *ekimi mota*, an intensification of *ekimi*, and as such is not the norm and can only be temporary. Far more important to the Mbuti is that they should have, on a less temporary if less exalted level, the norm of *ekimi*.

While the forest cannot fail to be rejoiced by song, it may well, for one reason or another, be displeased, as a father may be displeased with his children (a perfectly common Mbuti metaphor), and withhold *ekimi* for a long time. The fact that singing brings joy to the Mbuti, filling them with *ekimi mota*, does not mean that it is not also hard work. For the forest is not content with one song. If singing is undertaken at all, and particularly if it is undertaken for purposes of restoring lost *ekimi* (i.e., if it is to be a *molimo* festival), it must be long and continuous. After a fest of singing every night, from shortly after dusk to an hour before sunrise, the Mbuti set off to hunt with excessive vigor. It would be an insult as well as *mbafu* (stupidity) to take all the trouble to rejoice the forest by song and then displease it by not having a particularly vigorous hunt. A month of this leaves the stoutest Mbuti more than a little tired, so although the remedy for *akami* lies in their hands, through song, at all times, it can be arduous and, since it is *mota*, it can be dangerous. Thus the supernatural sanction on social behavior is in no way lessened: the Mbuti all state that the forest, in its manifestation through the morning *molimo*, may punish and kill.

The system as described can be seen easily enough to maintain internal order, and it can also be seen well enough how it operates, as an essentially forest-centered system based on age and forest values, to maintain separation from a village system based on kinship and anti-forest values—for one of the cardinal village beliefs is not simply that the village is better than the forest, but that the forest is the source of all evil. But now we have to see how these same elements that make for social order in the forest (the nonlineal band, age, territory, noise and song) operate within the village framework.

Winter (1956) describes the relationship between the eastern extension of the Mbuti, the few who live among the Amba on the Uganda/Congo border, and the Amba themselves. Each group denigrates the other's mode of existence, yet they evidently live in the closest association with each other, in what Winter calls symbiosis. More important, he describes how two Mbuti groups are fitted into the Amba lineage structure, but only partially so. They are both attached to Bulibuli lineages, each to a maximal lineage as a whole; yet they do not share full and equivalent relationships as Bulibuli with the other lineages of the same clan. Winter mentions that they stand in a joking relationship with only one of the maximal lineages.

Joking relationships are generally thought of as pertaining between individuals who stand in a specific relationship to each other, involving both proximity and distance. The proximity is thought of in terms of kinship, the distance is due to a difference, if not a conflict, of interests. The relationship can involve considerable amity and mutual cooperation, but nonetheless contain elements of hostility, particularly in its outer expression (Radcliffe-Brown, 1952, p. 91). The exact formularization varies from situation to situation, tolerating or compelling joking behavior, on a symmetrical or asymmetrical basis.

The essential elements of this form of relationship are all present

in the Mbuti/Villager situation. The basis of the proximity and distance elements does not rest on kinship, and the relationship is as
much between the two groups as it is between individuals, otherwise
the situation conforms to Radcliffe-Brown's model quite clearly—viz.
(1952, p. 95): "The show of hostility, the perpetual disrespect, is a
continual expression of that social disjunction which is an essential
part of the whole structural situation, but over which, without destroying or even weakening it, there is provided the social conjunction
of friendliness and mutual aid."

In the Mbuti/Villager situation the relationship appears to be symmetrical and permissive, though both sides do occasionally take offense, the village side even sometimes taking counteraction. The
ineffectiveness of taking offense or action, however, only serves to
heighten the characteristic "social disjunction," and there is no doubt
that beneath the display of hostility and disrespect there is cooperation, and even considerable amity. Considering the completely opposed value systems of the two worlds, this is, indeed, the only way
in which the two peoples could meet and still retain a separate
identity. The reasons for the meeting taking place at all, as we have
already seen, are circumstantial—the historical invasion of the forest
by the villagers, and their use of the Mbuti as guides; the continued
parasitism of the Mbuti upon the villagers long after the original
need for cooperation had gone; the contemporary mutual convenience
of economic exchange; sheer territorial propinquity. These reasons do
not lead automatically or easily to a structured relationship, particularly when the values of the two peoples are so divergent, so while a
form of joking relationship helps to stabilize the alliance, maintaining
the combination of Radcliffe-Brown's "conjunctive and disjunctive
components," it is not by itself enough.

We have seen the methods by which the villagers have sought to
further stabilize the situation, through a formal economic-exchange
system, a fictive parallel-kinship system, and through introduction to
village supernatural sanctions by establishment of magico-religious
bonds through karé blood brotherhood and nkumbi initiation. Any
one of these, had it worked, would have reduced the Mbuti to subordination, yet this plainly has not been done. The defense of the
Mbuti has lain in their own indigenous forest system, which works
not only to maintain internal cohesion but also to maintain the utmost possible structural distance from the village world while allowing a minimal amount of "mutually convenient" economic exchange.

Let us look, then, at these same structural elements, having just considered them in their forest context, and place them in a village context.

1. THE TERRITORIAL BAND, while in no way lessening the efficiency of the hunting band, and while still preserving band unity through the concept of territory and the use of an age-level system, presents to the village system only disunity and flux. The flux that is a natural part, it seems, of the seasonal fission and fusion of all Mbuti bands renders it next to impossible for any form of village authority to be exerted over the Mbuti, either as bands or as individuals. The preference of the Mbuti for marrying into distant bands, and of thenceforth maintaining an exchange of visits and even of membership with these bands, directly counters the authority of the villagers, which is based on localized lineages and is therefore itself localized. The Mbuti are as likely as not to exchange visits with each other over distances that exceed not only the territorial limits of the clans of the village tribes but even of the tribes themselves, between which there are no political relationships except hostility. In view of the lengths to which the Mbuti carry the joking relationship, if it can be called that,[6] it is not surprising that they find it convenient to maintain their bands in such constant and otherwise unnecessary flux. The Mbuti constantly raid village plantations, openly ridicule the villagers, and steal from under their noses, unless the villagers are particularly generous. I have not met a single villager, even among those most popular with the Mbuti, who has not complained of being "eaten," and complained at the same time of the impossibility of applying legal sanctions over tribal boundaries.

2. AGE divides the hunting band into significant horizontal sections crosscutting all lineal considerations.[7] The emphasis on age is con-

---

[6] The Mbuti in their own parlance regard the village as a place to hunt and eat. They say "in the forest we hunt, in the village we hunt" (*subandura su wendi, subananji su wendi*), also, equally frequently, "We eat animals, we eat villagers" (*Sule banyama, sule Batubanji*). Hunting calls for trickiness, cunning, using tactics appropriate to the game, often imitating it and assimilating, temporarily, its personality. Such tactics in the village include bringing in a certain amount of meat as bait, performing some service, and occupying a generally subservient position. When asked why he forced his son to take part in the *nkumbi* initiation at the hands of the villagers, one father said, simply, "When we hunt elephant we cover ourselves with elephant dung" (*Su wendi bambongu su pati mavi nda'bo*).

[7] Turner (1957), following Gluckman (1954), finds among the Ndembu, a society that is mobile and fissionable, also lacking the more formal political institutions, an essential crosscutting of opposed groups. He also found, as we have found, that (Turner 1957, p. 289) ". . . links of kinship and of political and economic co-operation *per se*

sistent as a major principle of organization in all realms of Mbuti life, with a consequent lack of interest in lineage. This adds both to the compositeness of the band and to its fluid structure. The division of authority renders the band, at any stage of its existence, without the slightest trace of individual leadership other than fictive to which the village headmen or chiefs could relate. Even more important, it means that the band has no constant kin grouping by which it can be related to the village unilineal descent group claiming hereditary ownership over a comparable Mbuti group. The comparable Mbuti group only exists in the minds of the villagers, and functions among them as an institutionalized means of regulating intervillage disputes over Mbuti "ownership." The effect of placing a horizontally divided hunting band in a vertically divided village is fragmentation. The only effective relationships, even when the Mbuti happen to be in a village where their *kpara* resides, are interpersonal. The loyalties that the Mbuti feels toward an age group are negated by the lineal loyalties of the villager, and conversely.

Again the Mbuti employ the joking relationship to their advantage. They invoke claims upon *kpara, karé,* and "kin" without the slightest compunction, but when the same claims are reversed, they either deny or ridicule them.

3. TERRITORY, which acts in one respect as a focus of band unity, is the only principle that also, in this limited respect, offers any measure of consistency in intergroup contact. Thus while the villagers in any given village may never be sure of just which Mbuti they will be dealing with in the adjacent hunting territory, they are always able to look to that territory for *some* Mbuti. There is, in fact, a reasonable continuity within the band, achieved by territorial considerations, and this helps stabilize relationships with the neighboring village to some extent. But in its wider extension, as the forest, territory only serves to unite the Mbuti in common opposition to all villagers.

4. NOISE is associated with the village, and noise is associated with death. The term *akami* is used together with the terms *bulé* or *tupé*

---

are insufficiently strong to hold together village and nation." The "consciousness of national unity" (*ibid.*) that exists among the Ndembu nonetheless is, according to Turner, because that unity is moral rather than political, its source lying in the value system.

In considering Mbuti society we have to think of opposition within the forest society, such as that created by the age-level system, and within the total society, such as that created by the "kinship" system. At each level there are indeed opposed groups, with crosscutting membership. The absence of a common value system between forest and village, further, is accompanied by a corresponding absence of a wider unity.

(empty), *mbafu* (stupid) and *mota* (in the sense of dangerous) as assessments of all village institutions and beliefs. A certain amount of this ridicule is again a part of the joking relationship, but it is significant that the Mbuti do not frequently accuse the villagers of being *sinana*, "bad," however much they might refer to the village itself as a "bad place." From the forest standpoint, however, there is no question but that the village system is singularly inapplicable, and therefore at least *bulé* (empty) and possibly *mbafu* (stupid), if not actually *mota*, or dangerous. The village does become *mota*, and very much so, the moment it impinges upon the forest, and any villager in this situation becomes truly *sinana*, or bad. But as seen, in forest life even *akami* can be turned to good use, and the noise of village life, while in itself definitely not good, can be turned to advantage. In the same way that *akami* is the duty of hunters in the forest, as a means of resolving disputes, or at least bringing them into the open, so may *akami* in the village be used as an institutionalized means of resolving a dispute without settling the blame on any single Mbuti. Thus individual villagers, village demands, or village allegations of witchcraft or sorcery can all be invoked to explain what could otherwise only be explained by Mbuti delinquency. Individuals or families who are under criticism, openly or covertly, may decide to go to the village to fulfill some obligations to village *karé* or *kpara*. The village generally is a place for relief from the tensions of forest life, and by bringing their *akami* to this center of *akami* the Mbuti often hope to shed their own internal dissensions. The village is associated with "war" (*vita*).[8]

In the sense of constant interpersonal conflicts, there is no doubt that for whatever reason an Mbuti band reassembles after a stay in a village, it is likely to reunite in the forest with considerably more *ekimi* than it possessed on leaving. In the same way that individuals leave a forest camp for a visit to the village because of *akami* (probably of their own making), so whole bands move to the village when

[8] Vita is, strictly speaking, a KiNgwana word, but is invariably used by these Mbuti, as are some other words of the same language, even when speaking in KiBira. A future study of such usages might reveal significant connotations in Mbuti thought. Certainly the wars still uppermost in the minds of the Mbuti, as of others in this region, are those of the Arab slavers, whose pawns the Ngwana were. Similarly the KiNgwana word *bulé* (empty) is used far more than its KiBira counterpart (*bobo*) when the implication is particularly derogatory. Thus *kelele bulé*, which is all KiNgwana, means empty noise, a phrase that might be used to describe a dispute that has no just cause. If an Mbuti were to refer to a dispute as being *akami bobo*, it would have a similar connotation. However, if he said *akami bulé*, it would no longer describe a merely pointless dispute, but one that is both without just cause and with deliberate hostile intent. In fact the odium of *vita* clings to almost every KiNgwana word, as does that of *mayelé*, or trickery.

the camp is filled with *akami*—not in search of *ekimi*, but in the hopes of doing as the hunters do, killing noise with more noise.

5. SONG brings us to the crux of the opposition between Mbuti and villagers, for all song in villages is by definition "empty," even if sung by Mbuti, and even if, as is rarely the case, the song is strictly Mbuti in origin. That is, while in the village the Mbuti no longer have the ultimate safeguard of being able to "rejoice the forest" through song. Even if they tried, it would be *bulé*. Song being directly associated with *ekimi*, it follows, and the Mbuti affirm, that there can be no *ekimi*, or "quiet," in the village. *Ekimi*, as stated, is the ultimate goal of the Mbuti, and it is only *ekimi* that can please the forest. Visiting the village, then, would be a treacherous act beyond reconciliation under Mbuti values if it were not for the Mbuti attitude to such visits as being a form of hunt, for hunting is pleasing to the forest, and hunting is also associated with noise and danger, *akami* and *mota*. The rationalization may seem a feeble one, but to the Mbuti it is adequate and convenient.

Thus while the more formal institutions of the band, age levels and territorial affiliation, work internally to achieve stability and externally to directly counteract village attempts to subordinate the Mbuti, so do forest values directly counter village values, maintaining the complete separation of the two peoples. The economic exchange that takes place, while undeniably mutually convenient, may also be in part a mere recognition of territorial propinquity and of mutual opposition, a mechanism for avoiding open hostility, which would otherwise be the only possible relationship.

The strongly forest-oriented value system of the Mbuti, while operating toward the maintenance of internal order, completely counters the attempts of the villagers to assert their dominance by supernatural sanctions based on village values. But the answer to the question as to why the Mbuti go to the extreme of allowing themselves to be circumcised and initiated by the villagers may be more than that offered by the Mbuti hunting metaphor.

The metaphor recalls the technique of a hunter in taking on the appearance (and smell) of his quarry, of rubbing himself with a paste made of the heart and brains and eyes of the animal so that he can feel and think and see like his quarry. It is not a technique widely practiced, though it *is* practiced by elephant hunters, and by some archers, and by elders who are out hunting on their own. It is more widely practiced in the mimetic hunting dances, by which it may be supposed that the dancer is trying, magically, to influence the action and movement of the game. In this light the Mbuti acceptance of the *nkumbi* seems more plausible, as a "magical" means of gaining power over the villagers. It is not entirely unlike the situation described by Beattie (1960, p. 78) for Nyoro reactions to foreign powers such as Europeans, Polish expatriates, and airplanes. The Nyoro attempt was to gain some control over the situation by becoming possessed by the spirits of these foreign powers.

There may also be a certain amount of seepage of village beliefs into the Mbuti subconscious, despite the formidable structural opposition they have raised to all such influences. There is certainly cause to think that the village beliefs of witchcraft and sorcery, confused as they are by the Mbuti, nonetheless have for them a certain sinister ring of conviction.[9]

It is perhaps for that reason that the only plainly discernible symbolism evident in Mbuti ritual is concerned with life. Of all the oppositions between the forest and the village, such as abundance/hunger, unity/disunity, moral/immoral, equal/unequal, cool/hot, song/silence, quiet/noise, the most significant are undoubtedly the last two, for silence and noise are associated ultimately with death. If the Mbuti suspect there are, in the village, supernatural powers with which they should come to terms, it is for purposes of defense. And they see their major defense in the power of their own supernatural, the forest.

Their desire is to counteract the forces of hunger, disunity, immorality, inequality, heat, silence and noise, forces that amount to death for the Mbuti. Their focus of attention is on the preservation and continuation of life. The relatively simple ritual, if it can truly be called that, of the *molimo* festival is supercharged with an emotional concern, a burning desire, for life. As might be expected, it reinforces those aspects of Mbuti society that require constant attention: age divisions are clearly symbolized in the three fires for the three upper age groups; the value of sharing (on nonlineal grounds!) is emphasized in the technical division of the songs, again bringing in division along age lines and demanding close cooperation; the reluctance to share is symbolized at the same time as the friction between youths

[9] Again, a linguistic study might help greatly, not only through separating institutions and concepts that derive from different tribes, but in revealing the location of hidden areas of forest/village opposition. Unfortunately we still lack any published studies of KiNgwana, KiBira and KiLesé, let alone of the divers Mbuti groups.

and fathers when youths go around trying to snare food from each hut (the women ultimately letting them have it, often ostentatiously). The opposition of adjacent age levels, and particularly the hostility between sons and fathers, is plainly manifest in the morning rampages of the *molimo* trumpet. The forest itself is symbolized by the leaves that conceal the trumpet (itself the symbol of the life-giving organ), and *ekimi* is the avowed objective sought through song. *Akami*, its antithesis, is symbolized again in the morning rampage, frequently a physical battle between older and younger youths (dividing brothers) and between youths and hunters, and always a wordy battle, with the hunters winning if for no other reason than that there is a limit to the energy even of Mbuti youths.

Thus the *molimo* admirably reinforces social values and allows for the harmless expression of hostility in areas of conflict. The only symbolic representation of sexual conflict is *ekokomea*, and of course the fire dance. But here the symbolism runs deeper, and concerns the ultimate end, for just as *akami* is associated with death, so is *ekimi* associated with life. The fire is not as realistically symbolic as the trumpet, though it is undoubtedly as feminine as the trumpet is masculine. But it is impossible not to be reminded of other instances of the use of fire and sex symbolism.[10]

And perhaps we should see this concern with life not only in terms of the threat of death from the village. Death is a threat to all societies, and for the Mbuti it is probably the one imperfection in an otherwise perfect life; that is to say, it is the one thing for which they have no certain answer, and to a practical people such as the Mbuti uncertainty is imperfection.

Ultimately the efforts of the Mbuti, if not of their system, are directed to keeping the villagers physically out of the forest, an effort that is successful largely because the villagers are only too thankful not to have to go into the forest. But just the fact that one villager can set up a fishing camp in mid-forest and be visited by other villagers, or that a chief can send his representative to a hunting camp to demand (but not necessarily obtain) meat, means that even the forest

[10] For instance, Audrey Richards (1956) writes of the Bemba that access to the ancestral spirits is to be had through the correct handling of fire and sex, and stresses (*ibid.*, p. 30, *seq.*) the ritual association of sex, blood and fire as the *idée maîtresse* behind most of the ritual behavior of the Bemba. Hocart would certainly have seen the *molimo*, and the "baptism of fire" (when Moké passes his hands through the flames and rubs them over his face, then gently touches the hands of all those around), as a request "for the gift of undying life" (Hocart, 1952, p. 47).

cannot offer absolute sanctuary, for each one of these villagers brings with him *akami* and, even worse, the threat of witchcraft and sorcery. In the last resort, then, the only recourse of the Mbuti will be to learn to master these arts themselves, unless in time they learn to discern between the possibilities of the one as a legal mechanism and the practical ineffectiveness of the other as a physical threat.

In other areas of the forest, where the village tribes are less afraid of the forest, living and hunting in it themselves, as well as cultivating, the attempted exploitation of the Mbuti has been no less and its general pattern and degree of success have been similar, but there has not been the same attempt by villagers to assimilate the Mbuti. This seems to be true not only in the northern part of the Congo, but also further west and in the Gabon.[11] But while in those areas the hunters may not be assimilated into the village system to the extent of being admitted to initiation, they are also, it seems, more ready to accept village beliefs such as those in witchcraft and sorcery, and are evidently more dependent upon the villagers in other respects. However, these areas need considerably more investigation before any useful comparisons can be made. Here it is sufficient to stress that in a situation where the village cultivators are afraid of the forest and unwilling to move freely within it and exploit it, and perhaps correlated with that fact, the Mbuti maintain a form of social organization based on recognizable principles that plainly have a dual function— the maintenance of internal order and the maintenance of separation and distinction from the villagers. In such a situation, the Mbuti adopt only the outer form of the village social organization while in the village, in a form of jóking relationship between the two groups. The joking relationship and the dual function of the Mbuti principles of organization effectively counter all attempts of the villagers to effect an institutional subordination of the Mbuti. The value systems of the two people are in complete opposition, and this reflects the whole nature of the relationship between them. The ultimate attempt of the villagers to assert supernatural authority over the Mbuti, while derided by the Mbuti as *bulé*, or empty (but malevolent), might be a cause of Mbuti willingness to undergo the *nkumbi* initiation, as a means of acquiring power through assimilation of like power, to combat this authority.

On the other hand it might be argued that the villagers, in initiat-

---

11 Information on the relationship of the pygmies of the Gabon to the village cultivators was supplied by Mr. Leon Siroto, from unpublished field notes.

ing the Mbuti, are not only trying to subject the Mbuti to the authority of village supernatural sanctions but are also trying to assimilate from the Mbuti some of the spiritual power they believe to reside in the forest.

The ultimate nature of the relationship between the two people cannot be determined until further studies have been made of similar situations from both the Mbuti point of view and, a major need at the moment, from the village point of view. For now, it seems sufficiently clear that the general nature of the relationship is one of opposition, and that Mbuti society, in response to the demands of the situation or by fortuitous chance, meets it with an organization based upon the very antithesis of village organization. Against political centralization it offers complete decentralization and diffusion of authority. Against a sedentary, patrilineal, patrilocal village it matches the nomadic, nonlineal, territorial band. The vertical village kinship system is countered by a horizontal age-level system. Village values are directly opposed by forest values. And within itself Mbuti society uses these same principles, in a state of almost perpetual flux, to maintain a cohesion fully as powerful as that found among the villagers. Instead of looking to the more conventional structural principles for the source of unity of Mbuti society, we have had to look rather to values, and it is in terms of values that the over-all society, of Mbuti and villagers, has its ultimate being and significance.

The Legend of Double Trickery
and
The Legend of the Mbuti Plantation

THE LEGEND OF DOUBLE TRICKERY

me ke nandura ka ba boki.
I went to the forest to collect honey.

me ke a'i, me ke a'i, me ke a'i.
I went, I went, I went.

me ke akurahwa, ku pia libo mangbo.
I went very far, beyond the big river.

moki li suanjoki. me oni neko kuma boki.
I heard the sound of bees. I saw up high the place of honey.

me lufudo, "toka bo nangoli; nde mendamo; nde boki ndamo."
I said, "Nobody has enclosed the tree with vine, it is mine; it is my honey."

me poki loka phelea, phelea bekbekbe'i.
I sharpened my ax, very sharp indeed.

me teningoli. ke kongi isa, me pisi isa subaso.
I cut a vine. I fanned my fire, and put the fire in my basket.

me pedi oda phangoli; me daphi, me daphi.
I began to climb; I climbed, I climbed.

boki neko kurahwa. nde boki, boki sandenengo, kanga piso.
The honey was very far. It was honey, real honey, not *apuma*.

me kidi. me boingoli, me liki. me pisi isa suba eboso.
I reached it. I fastened the vine, I sat. I put fire into the hole.

me lophi. me ki abi bekbekbe'i, me che'i banzoki.
I blew. I got much smoke, I drove out many bees.

me ko iti, me ko iti, me ko iti.
I chopped, I chopped, I chopped.

me ko iti, me mua kito, a mua pika na dodo.
While I was chopping I heard someone walking below.

"nu andea a mua pika pecha me?" nde mukpara ndamo.
"Who is walking below me?" It is my master.

"a oki kueta mboki ndamo, a me beli." me wanzi nimbo.
"He heard me cutting my honey, he followed me." I began to sing.

me nimbi bekbekbei, akini melufu. kanga me oki.
I sang loudly, but he called me. I did not hear.

me nimbi, akini me kweti.
I sang, but I chopped.

me nimbi, "Ha! me kweti boki. me ko oka kapa'i akpara mamo."
I sang, "Ha! I am chopping honey to give to my *kpara.*"

me kweti bisa, me kweti boka. boki a bi lenga'i.
I chopped slowly, I chopped honey. There was much honey.

akini me pisa depha subaso.
But I only put part of it in my basket.

me pisi ndetina a su soro kokomea.
The rest I put where the tree had two arms.

me nimbi, "Ah! boki a bi depha, me ka bokbu akpara mamo." me ki a dodo.
I sang, "Ah! There is only a little honey, I shall give it all to my *kpara.*" I came down.

"Ah! mambuti mamo, me siye ema?" mubira a si pi so.
"Ah! My Mbuti, what are you doing here?" The MuBira looks at the basket.

"Ah! akpara mamo, me piki ka ba boki ndamo, akini me pati na che.
"Ah! My Master, I came to search for my honey, but I got only a little."

"me mua ka pa'i bokbu. me sia bo'u."
"I am going to give it all. I will stay empty."

"ue nde mambuti manza. me ka pa eboko mboye siki nanji."
"You are a good Mbuti. I shall give you bananas when you come to the village."

"Ah! akpara mamo, me lika nandura a ka ba boki, akini nde depha."
"Ah! My Master, I shall stay in the forest to search for honey, but there is little."

"nde mwaka sinana. nde kazi ndangbo."
"It is a bad year. It is hard work."

"ue sikia nanji na boki ndamo. me pati ndetina, me piki na'u."
"You go to the village with my honey. If I get more, I shall come with it."

akpara a bu boki ndamo, a siki nanji nda'e.
The *kpara* took my honey, he went to the village with it.

asibande a bi boki ndamo bokbu. ndandama nda'e!
He would say he had eaten all my honey. His stupidity!

ake me daphi umana'o, me bu boki ngbokbu, kumande me pisibi.
I quickly climbed up again, I took all the honey from the place where I had put it.

me simi ya dodo a sia n'apa a kapa banama bame.
I came down to return to the camp and shared it with everyone.

me tambi, me tambi, me tambi. me kidi apua libo mangbo.
I walked, I walked, I walked, I arrived at the big river.

tokwaba a wanzi pika. me lufu. "ha! tudu a me pedi a me mandula? me sao mabo?"
Darkness began to settle. I said, "Ha! Is night catching me in the middle of the forest like this? What shall I do?"

me daphi kua me mangbo, me langi neko.
I climbed up into a big tree, I lay there.

ame mangondo moki liso. me oni kurahwa isa ebaré.
Halfway through the night I heard a sound and woke. I saw far away two firebrands.

"mondea na tamba kifa, na isa ebara bende? nde ketiba!"
"Who is walking in the middle of the night, with two firebrands? It is an evil spirit!"

me kobi nengo. m'oki liso kali.
I remained completely quiet. I heard a woman's voice.

"a miki mamo, miki mamo; miki mamo mu ma?" liso a tata, mozee nengo.
"Ah! My child, my child; where is my child?" It was the voice of my grandmother, a very old person.

me moboki nengo. "Ah! tatamua kaba me amemangondo? nde tata mamo nengo?"
I was very afraid. "Ah! My grandmother is looking for me in the middle of the night like this? Is it really my grandmother?"

"ah miki mamo mu ma? au moli a pedi, au a bungi?"
"Ah! Where is my child? Either a leopard has caught him or he has lost his way?"

me kobi nengo, akini isa ebaré akidi tina me.
I kept quiet completely, but the two firebrands came right up underneath the tree.

nde keti nengo, akini akeoki tatamamo.
It was truly an evil spirit, but it had turned into my grandmother.

me teni kisio. "Ah! miki mamo amu neko?"
I sneezed. "Ah! My child is up in the tree?"

"e'i tata, me mu be'i. me ka bi boki tudaha a me pedi a phe."
"Yes, Grandmother, I am here. I was searching for honey but darkness caught me on the trail."

"Ah! miki, ue mesi sinana. ue a bia sisia abende neku, me toli akaba'o; me tondi mota'o. ue si sinana nengo. pisa boki ndamo."
"Ah! Child, you have done badly. When you did not return, I thought you were dead and I left to search for you; I found you strong. You have done very badly towards me. Give me my honey."

"ah! tata, nde tida'i; me kumbandi susia kumekadi."
"Ah! Grandmother, it is very heavy. I shall carry it for you, we shall return together."

"mbe, ueche todahwa; ue lika ma. me sia na boki ndamo. pikisa."
"Nonsense, you are afraid of the night. You stay here. I shall return with the honey. Give it."

me che'i nengo gunde me upi a bi keti.
I was very afraid, because I knew it was an evil spirit.

me maké boki na dodo. "pikasa ndetina, pikasa ndetina."
I threw some honey down. "Give me more, give me more."

me maké ndetina. "pikasa ndetina."
I threw down more. "Give me more."

"ndetina a munda, tata." "mbe, pikisa, miki masinana."
"There is no more, Grandmother." "Nonsense, give, my bad child."

me che'i nengo, me maké bokbui me lufu:
I was very afraid, I threw it all down; I said:

"e ngbokbu, tata, bo'a, ue ke, ndetina amunda. peda ue sia nda'o. me lika oma."
"That is all, Grandmother, take it, you go, there is no more. Take it and return to your place. I shall remain here."

"ebo. nde bonga'i, miki mamo. me siki d'o. ue likato."
"Good. It is good, my child. I shall return. You stay on."

"ue kato'e, tata."
"Go then, Grandmother."

me liki na siu, me bonji mané. mané a piki, me simia a dodo.
I sat with eyes, I waited for daylight. When daylight came I climbed down to the ground.

me ka bi anga batu; anga munda.
I looked for footprints of humans. There were no footprints.

"Ah!" me lufu, "nde keti mabobo. me si ndanza me ka boki bokbu. a bia mua me nengo."
"Ah!" I said, "It was an evil spirit, truly. I did well to throw down all my honey. It would have killed me completely."

akini, gunde me sibo.
But, empty-handed I return.

THE LEGEND OF THE MBUTI PLANTATION

mosa besu bambuti subua'ini eboko. mosa ma batu banji.
In olden times we Mbuti had bananas, before the people of the village.

batu banji baku biai eboko ndasu. su kangia'i.
The people of the village stole the bananas from us. We shared them.

besu bambuti sukonia ekasa, bakpara bua'i poko. Seyuma mayeli bendo.
We Mbuti took the leaves, the *kpara* took the roots. That was their trickery.

samba ndaso nde mosa bindanza. akini bambongu pikiai dongasu.
Our plantations of old were good. But the elephants came and troubled us.

basudongia'isu. ba bumia'i tiko su.
They troubled us. They killed our plantations.

bambuti balufa'i, "su samabo? bambongu basu dongibé, babuniasu tiko ndasu."
The Mbuti said, "What shall we do? The elephants trouble us so and are killing our plantations."

mangesé, mangesé mangbo, alufa'i, "bambongu bapiké su lufua nabé."
An elder, a very old man indeed, said, "When the elephants come again, we shall talk with them."

bachahwa balufa'i, "ue semabo?" mangesé a lufa'i, "ue sipa, bamiki."
The youths said, "What will you say?" The old man said, "You wait, children."

bambongu bakidi. bawanji a lea'eboko bokbu. ba wanjia'i buna tiko.
The elephants came. They began to eat the bananas. They began to destroy the plantation.

bachahwa bache'i aka mangesé, balufua'i, "ombo, epa, bambongu bkidi; ba bunia tiko ndasu."
The youths were afraid and ran to the old man, saying, "Oh! Father, the elephants have come; they are destroying our plantation."

"ndanza. me mua ka totiambino. beningbokbu mu likana; nekobi anenengo." mangesé a ke d'i na tiko.
"Good. I shall go to chat with them. All of you stay here, completely quiet." The old man went to the plantation.

a kamia'e nengo. engbue na dodo nengo. bambongu ba li sipi.
He cried greatly. He threw himself on the ground. The elephants looked at him.

balufu, "nde'i'i? bachahwa kabapiki dongasu, paka mangesé a piki ngamo nde ndanza sulea kobia nasu."
They said, "What is this? The youths have not come to trouble us. Only an old man has come. Good, we shall eat quietly."

balea ebokosu, bachahwa bakobia nengo apa.
They ate many bananas, the youths stayed very quiet in the camp.

mangesé a kami, "Ah! bamiki bamo bau. Ah! bamiki bamo buma?"
The old man cried, "Ah! my children, all are dead. Ah! my children, where are they?"

bambongu ba'oki, balufu'aka mangesé, "angbe ue ka mi? bachahwa buma? su lea tiko bokbu."
The elephants heard, they said to the old man, "Why are you crying like that? The youths are where? We shall eat the whole plantation."

mangesé a lufu, "lea, lea ngbokbu. bamiki bamo baku." a kami.
The old man said, "Eat, eat everything. My children are all dead." He continued crying.

bambongu balufu, "akini ue mua bamiki si angbe e'ebaku?"
The elephants said, "But you have many children, how did they die?"

mangesé a lufu, "nde keti, keti ma phele'a. a tambi na kongé ebaré nde bia nengo, sawa na ue.
The old man said, "It was an evil spirit, very evil indeed. It walked with two spears. It was very fat, like you.

"siku bokbu, me mengia na'u kapié eboko, keti a mua'e, a nia'e.
"Every day I sent someone to cut bananas, the evil spirit killed him, it ate him.

"makati i'o'elea', bamiki bamo bokbu. a siainbende nde tiko nda'e, batu bakidié, e muangbokbu.
"Now it has eaten all my children. It said it was its plantation and whoever came it would kill them all.

"ah! bamiki bamo baku bo'u. angbe'e keti kadongimbe tiko ndetina?
"Ah! My children have all died emptily. Why did the evil spirit not trouble some other plantation?

"angbe a loki tiko ndamo?" mangesé a kami, a ke.
"Why did it curse mine?" The old man cried, he went away.

bambongu balufu, "Ah! akini keti nde sinana, a loki tiko ndamané, su bua ka komanda; suke umana, kabe su mua."
The elephants said, "Ah! But if the spirit is that bad, and has cursed the plantation, we had better go elsewhere; let us go quickly, before it kills us."

gunde bambongu bua sopilabatu bananji, bache'i baketi bobo.
Because elephants are like people of the village, they are very afraid of spirits.

ba ke, ba ke, kurahwa. mangesé e oki bamiki bokbu.
They went, they went very far. The old man called all his children.

a lufu, "bambongu ka ba piké noma. ba bia sisia kuma keti masinana.
He said, "The elephants will not come back again. They think this is a place full of bad spirits.

"su likia kobia nasu tiko ndasu.
"We shall remain quietly in our plantation.

"batu betina bunda basudonga."
"Nobody else will bother us."

APPENDIX II

Medical Treatment

MEDICAL TREATMENT

The following list represents only a third of the total number of treatments noted; for the rest it was not possible to obtain exact identification of the plants used. Only the general identification is given below of the treatments cited here, the full details being lodged with Smith, Kline, & French, who generously supported the project.

HEADACHE: *amongolo pepé* (menispermaceae)
Leaves are pounded and rubbed into forehead.

doré (violaceae)
Seeds are pressed, and the juice is lightly rubbed on the forehead.

sungusungu (orchidaceae)
Leaves are roasted, then rubbed into light incisions in the skin of the forehead.

KNEE ACHE: *amakokosu* (uragoga pedunculari)
Stem, leaf and bloom are roasted, then rubbed into incisions on knee.

tapha (strychnos icaja)
Leaves are roasted and applied to incisions.

SORE THROAT: *kasa* (mapana bieleri)
Leaves are wrapped tightly around the throat.

EYE INFLAMMATION: *manoka* (manotes pruinosa)
Leaves are rubbed well between the hands, then put into a leaf cone. A little water is poured into the cone and allowed to drip into the eye.

STOMACHACHE: *amasobo* (violaceae)
The bark is stripped from young shoots, the core being pounded and roasted. The ashes are rubbed into incisions made over the afflicted area.

apisikalukba (araceae)
Leaves are pounded, water added, warmed, and drunk.

karama (dracaena maculata)
The leaves are pounded with salt, mixed with water, the concoction drunk. (The juice of the pounded leaf, without salt, is also put in the eyes of children "to make them see well.")

ebambu (annonaceae)
Bark is cut into small pieces, water is poured over it; when the water is red, a small quantity is drunk.

IMPOTENCE IN MALE: *tededasi* (rubiaceae)

Leaves are roasted, and the ashes rubbed into light incisions made above the penis.

teba (rubiaceae)

Leaves are roasted, and if the penis pains, the ashes are rubbed into incisions in the skin of the penis itself.

TOE ROT: *apatekaka* (hippocrateaceae)

Leaves are roasted and rubbed into incisions.

FOOT SORES: *ikengbe* (ochnaceae)

Stem of plant is warmed over a fire, then blown through, so that the juice enters the sores.

ikengbe (convolvulaceae)

Same as above.

HEART PAINS: *banga bamemé* (compositae)

Leaves are pounded, soaked with water, which is drunk when it becomes red.

HEMORRHOIDS: *amekulu* (beilschmieda spp.)

Stem is roasted, the ashes rubbed well into the buttocks around the affected area, and left on. Repeated after three days.

TOOTHACHE: *amabulubulubu* (tiliaceae)

Leaves are pulped to a juice, diluted with water for a child, funneled through a leaf into the nostrils. Said to afford instantaneous relief.

manganza (leeaceae)

Berries are roasted, crushed, and the ashes rubbed into incisions on the jaw.

OPEN WOUNDS: *ndindimia* (connaraceae)

The bark of a twig is carefully shaved, and the juice blown through the twig into the sore or wound. The bark is then packed into the wound to stop bleeding and to prevent dirt from entering. After three days the bark is removed and a fresh application is made, using less bark shavings to allow the wound to close gradually.

Maps, Tables and Plans

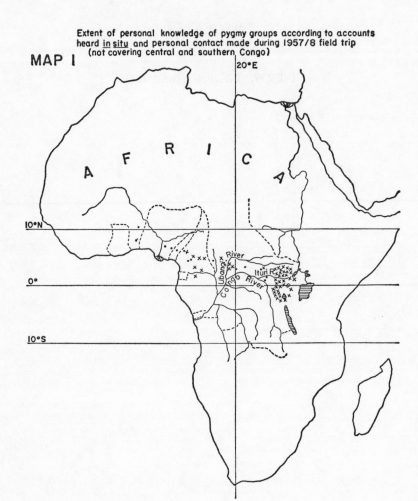

Extent of personal knowledge of pygmy groups according to accounts
heard in situ and personal contact made during 1957/8 field trip
(not covering central and southern Congo)

MAP I

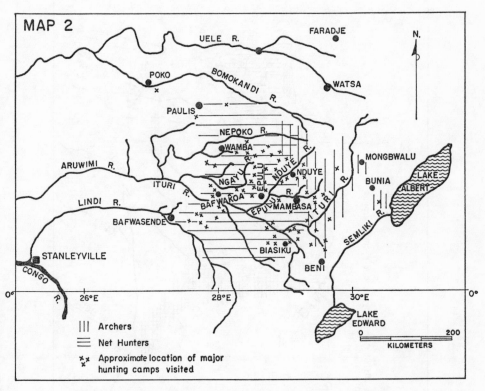

Approximate location of hunting bands visited in the Ituri.

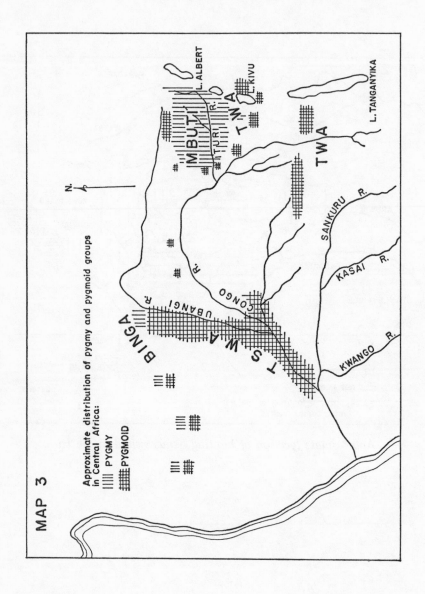

MAP 3

Approximate distribution of pygmy and pygmoid groups in Central Africa:

|||| PYGMY

PYGMOID

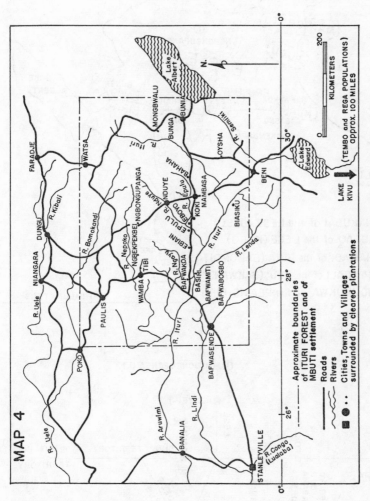

Boundaries of Ituri Forest and of Mbuti settlement.

MAP 5

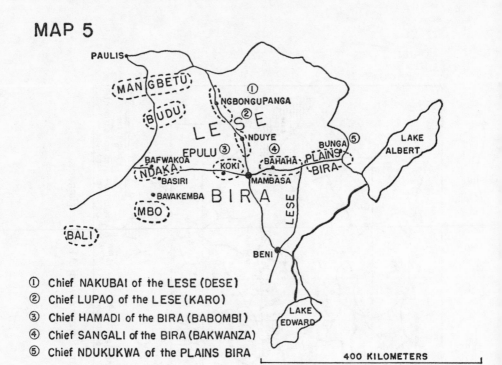

① Chief NAKUBAI of the LESE (DESE)
② Chief LUPAO of the LESE (KARO)
③ Chief HAMADI of the BIRA (BABOMBI)
④ Chief SANGALI of the BIRA (BAKWANZA)
⑤ Chief NDUKUKWA of the PLAINS BIRA

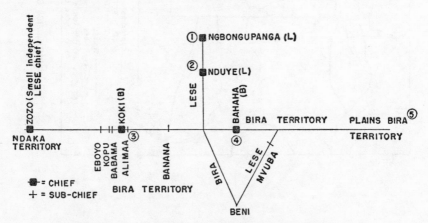

Village tribes and location of tribal Chiefs in the Ituri.

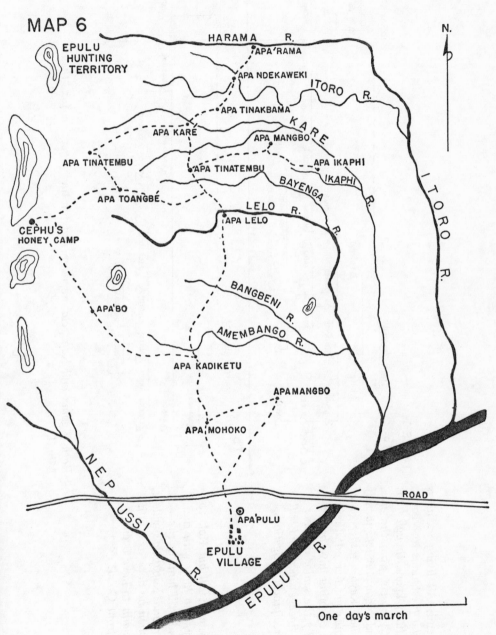

The Epulu hunting territory.

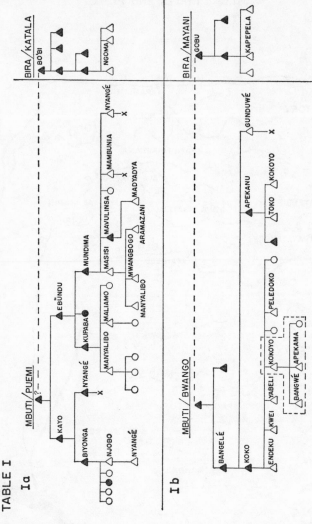

TABLE I

Ia

Ib

TABLE 1a
Mbuti/Puemi: All living members
make regular prestations to Ngoma,
their hereditary kpara, though he is
permanently absent from the area.
Njobo and Ngoma independently
declared that Kayo's father allied
with Ngoma's great-grandfather,
Bo'bi. His offspring have been
inherited by the senior member
of Bo'bi's lineage since, and still
recognize reciprocal obligations.

TABLE 1b
Mbuti/Bwango: All but Kokoyo
and family, who hunt with the
Epulu band, still hunt in the
territory around Kapapela's village,
moving, when he does, as a unit.
They all claim to have been
inherited from Gobu.

Both Ngoma and Kapepela are renowned for their affection for "their"
Mbuti.

TABLE 2

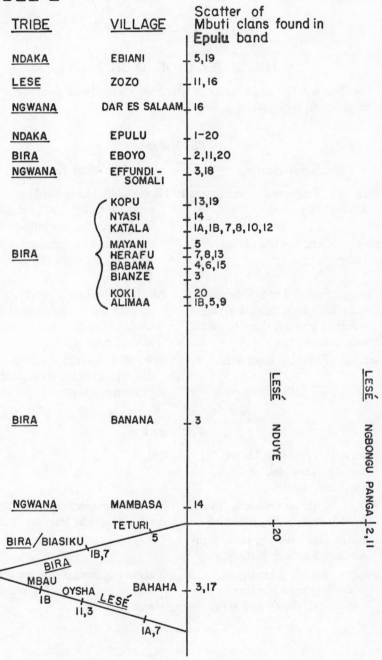

TRIBE	VILLAGE	Scatter of Mbuti clans found in Epulu band
NDAKA	EBIANI	5,19
LESE	ZOZO	11,16
NGWANA	DAR ES SALAAM	16
NDAKA	EPULU	1-20
BIRA	EBOYO	2,11,20
NGWANA	EFFUNDI - SOMALI	3,18
	KOPU	13,19
	NYASI	14
	KATALA	1A,1B,7,8,10,12
BIRA	MAYANI	5
	HERAFU	7,8,13
	BABAMA	4,6,15
	BIANZE	3
	KOKI	20
	ALIMAA	1B,5,9
BIRA	BANANA	3
NGWANA	MAMBASA	14

TETURI 5

BIRA/BIASIKU 1B,7

BIRA

MBAU 1B   OYSHA   LESÉ 11,3

BAHAHA 3,17

1A,7

LESÉ NDUYE 20

LESÉ NGBONGU PANGA 2,11

Distribution of Mbuti "clans" found in the Epulu band.

TABLE 3a

FOREST/VILLAGE EXCHANGE

To illustrate the major areas in which an exchange of goods or services does or could take place.

The Village

Forest Produce	Village Produce
SHELTER: Phrynium leaves, small saplings, firewood.	House poles; large saplings; leaves; mud for walls; wood for doors, furniture, etc.; clothing.
FOOD: Meat, rarely nuts and honey.	Bananas, manioc, peanuts, rice, corn, beans, palm oil, dried fish (trade).
LABOR: Partial hut-building, guarding plantations, carrying goods to market, drawing water, entertainment.	All major building, furniture-making, marketing, plantation work, clearing, canoe-building, fishing, road work.
SKILLS: Effective medicines.	Pottery, metalwork, toolmaking, divination, ritual specialization (circumcision).

The Forest

SHELTER: Phrynium leaves, saplings, firewood, clothing, furniture.	Nil
FOOD: Meat, mushrooms, fruits, nuts, berries, roots, honey.	Bananas, manioc, corn, beans, palm oil, rice (with relevant utensils).
LABOR: Hut-building, bark-cloth-making, hunting, gathering.	Nil
SKILLS: Effective medicine, manufacture of hunting equipment, dance and song.	Metalwork (metal tips for arrows and spears, blades for knives and axes).

TABLE 3b

ACTUAL EXCHANGE BETWEEN VILLAGE FAMILY AND MBUTI FAMILY DURING FIVE-DAY VISIT OF LATTER TO EPULU VILLAGE

Brought for villagers:

One *mboloko* antelope (enough for two adults for one meal)
Two loads of leaves (enough for ⅛ roof, or for one over-all temporary repair)

Work done for villagers:

Woman:
husks rice: four hours
watches over cooking: twelve hours
helps fetch water: two hours
carries one load of bananas to market: three hours
takes part in two dances: two evenings

Man:
fetches one load of firewood: four hours
helps re-leaf roof: three hours
takes part in two dances: two evenings

Two children: watch plantation for three mornings

Obtained during stay from the villagers:

Village food for four, or five, days
1½ packets of cigarettes
1 bottle of palm oil
1 musical instrument (*lukembi*)
2 arrow points

1 ax blade
1 bottle of beer
1 shirt
1 bar of soap

Taken back to forest after five days:

1 stem of bananas (enough for the family for fourteen meals)
manioc (enough for four meals)
beans (enough for two meals)
corn (enough for three meals)

peanuts (enough for one meal)
½ bottle palm oil
1 bar soap
1 handful of salt
1 handful loose tobacco

[*Table 4 is located inside back cover.*]

TABLE 5

LINEAGES CONTRIBUTING TO THE COMPOSITION OF
THE EPULU NET-HUNTING BAND DURING 1957–1958, NOT
INCLUDING VISITORS STAYING LESS THAN THE
DURATION OF ONE CAMP

		married		unmarried
Bambaka		14	13	15
Bandohwa		1	—	3
Bi		—	2	4
Bokele	(1)	2	3	4
	(2)	9	5	11
	(3)	—	1	—
Bolima		2	—	—
Bomasua		3	8	8
Bongwana		2	5	5
Buela		1	1	
Bwango		2	1	3
Meki		—	2	2
Molomba		—	2	1
Ngamo		5	—	7
Pasama		—	1	—
Pokama		1	—	4
Pokbaya		2	2	5
Poté		—	1	—
Poteba		3	2	5
Potola		1	2	—
Poya		2	—	5
Puemi	(1)	5	4	7
	(2)	6	3	12
Pukena		—	2	2
Puma		1	2	4
Pumasa		—	1	—
Pusa		—	2	5
Pusei		—	1	1
Tisi		—	—	1
Ungbausu		3	—	7
Totals:		65	66	121

Individual members mentioned in text by name are indicated on Table 4.

To get some idea of the extent of mobility from band to band, the figures in Table 5 (total) should be compared with figures that could be reasonably expected to apply to an average-sized camp of this band; i.e., of 17 huts, each containing a married couple and three or four unmarried children.

Any one such "average" camp would be composed of little more than a quarter of all those who, at one time or another during the year, would be band members.

TABLE 6

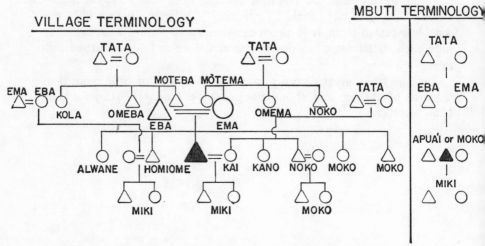

Mbuti terminology may also vary according to age, if one brother or sister is much older than another, thus:

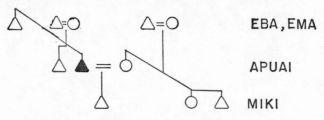

Village and Mbuti kinship terminology.

TABLE 7
EPULU 1958
7a

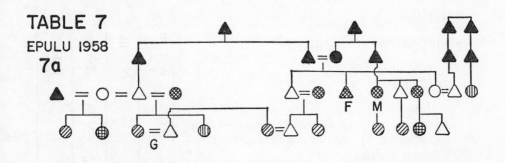

7b
EBOYO
1958

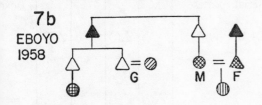

7c
EBIANI
1957

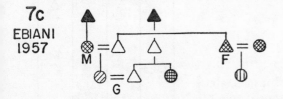

7d
KOKI
1958

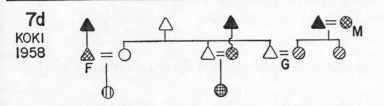

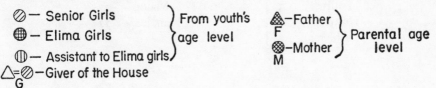

⊘ — Senior Girls   } From youth's
⊕ — Elima Girls   } age level
⏛ — Assistant to Elima girls
△=⊘ — Giver of the House
 G

▲ — Father
F
⦻ — Mother
M

} Parental age
  level

TABLE 7a–d *elima* participation

Table 8

FIELDS OF AUTHORITY

	Nuclear Family	Youths	Hunters	Elders
1. Economic				
Hunting ⎤			△	
Gathering ⎥ (Joint male/female authority among the net-hunters)			○	
Honey collecting			△	
Exchange with village	△○			
Industry (manufacture of material possessions)	△○			
Camp supervision (in absence of the hunt)		△○		△○
2. Ritual				
Birth	△○			
Puberty, betrothal and marriage: the *elima*		○		○
Death: the *molimo*		△		△
3. Legal				
Conjugal harmony	△○			
Individual disputes (personal insults, abuse, failure to share food or property, etc.)			△○	
Group disputes (any of the former that become enlarged beyond the realm of those directly concerned)				△○

Thus distribution of authority according to age and sex is almost equal as follows:

Family:	4 ⎤	
Youths:	3 ⎥	Male: 12
Hunters:	4 ⎥	Female: 11
Elders:	4 ⎦	

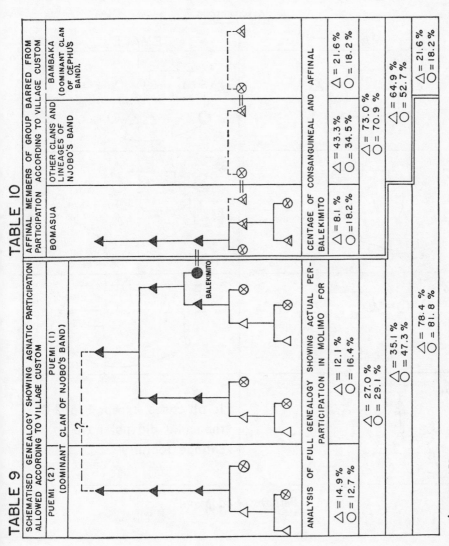

TABLE 9

TABLE 10

SCHEMATISED GENEALOGY SHOWING AGNATIC PARTICIPATION ALLOWED ACCORDING TO VILLAGE CUSTOM

AFFINAL MEMBERS OF GROUP BARRED FROM PARTICIPATION ACCORDING TO VILLAGE CUSTOM

PUEMI (2) (DOMINANT CLAN OF NJOBO'S BAND)

PUEMI (1) (DOMINANT CLAN OF NJOBO'S BAND)

BOMASUA

OTHER CLANS AND LINEAGES OF NJOBO'S BAND

BAMBAKA (DOMINANT CLAN OF CEPHU'S BAND).

BALEKIMITO

ANALYSIS OF FULL GENEALOGY SHOWING ACTUAL PARTICIPATION IN MOLIMO FOR

CENTAGE OF CONSANGUINEAL AND AFFINAL BALEKIMITO

△ = 14.9 %
○ = 12.7 %

△ = 12.1 %
○ = 16.4 %

△ = 8.1 %
○ = 18.2 %

△ = 43.3 %
○ = 34.5 %

△ = 21.6 %
○ = 18.2 %

△ = 27.0 %
○ = 29.1 %

△ = 73.0 %
○ = 70.9 %

△ = 35.1 %
○ = 47.3 %

△ = 78.4 %
○ = 81.8 %

△ = 64.9 %
○ = 52.7 %

△ = 21.6 %
○ = 18.2 %

▲ =DECEASED

△, ⊗ = NON-PARTICIPATING MEMBERS

TABLE II

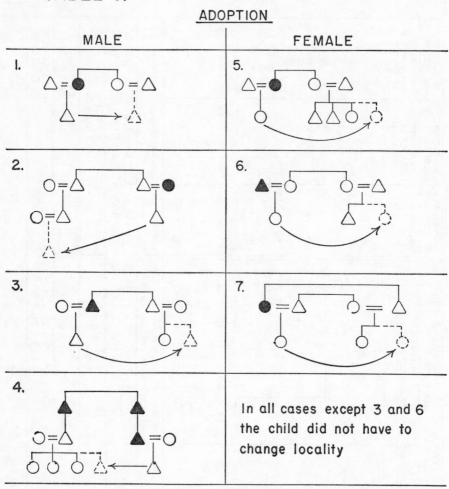

Patterns of adoption.

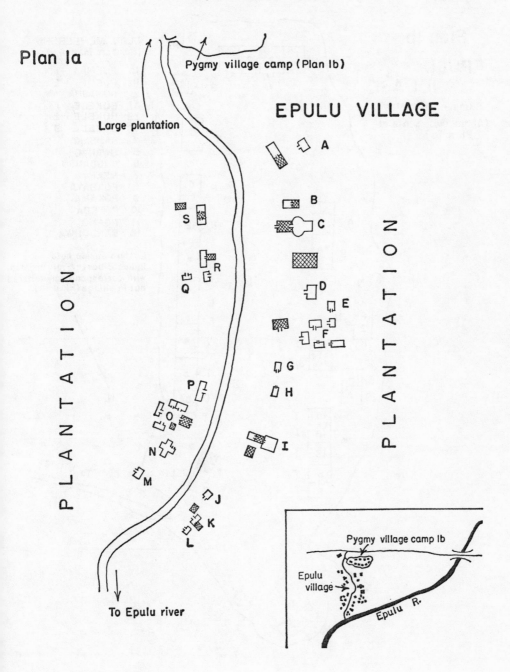

Plan Ia

Pygmy village camp (Plan Ib)

EPULU VILLAGE

Large plantation

PLANTATION

PLANTATION

A

B

C

S

R

Q

D

E

F

P

O

G

H

N

M

I

J

K

L

To Epulu river

Pygmy village camp Ib

Epulu village

Epulu R.

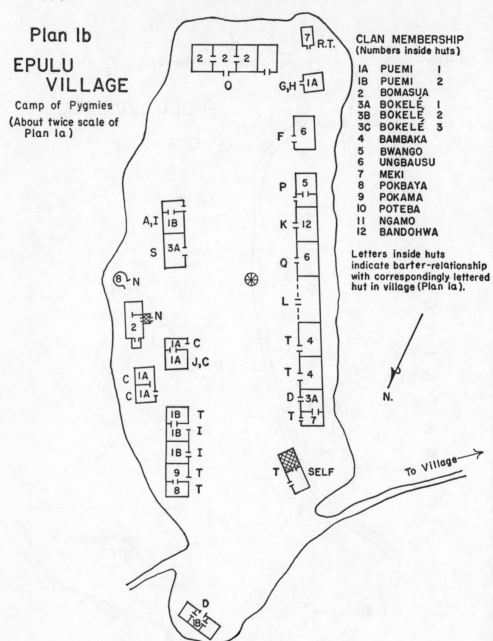

Plan Ib
EPULU VILLAGE

Camp of Pygmies

(About twice scale of Plan Ia)

CLAN MEMBERSHIP
(Numbers inside huts)

IA PUEMI   I
IB PUEMI   2
2   BOMASUA
3A BOKELÉ   I
3B BOKELÉ   2
3C BOKELÉ   3
4   BAMBAKA
5   BWANGO
6   UNGBAUSU
7   MEKI
8   POKBAYA
9   POKAMA
IO POTEBA
II NGAMO
I2 BANDOHWA

Letters inside huts
indicate barter-relationship
with correspondingly lettered
hut in village (Plan Ia).

N.

To Village

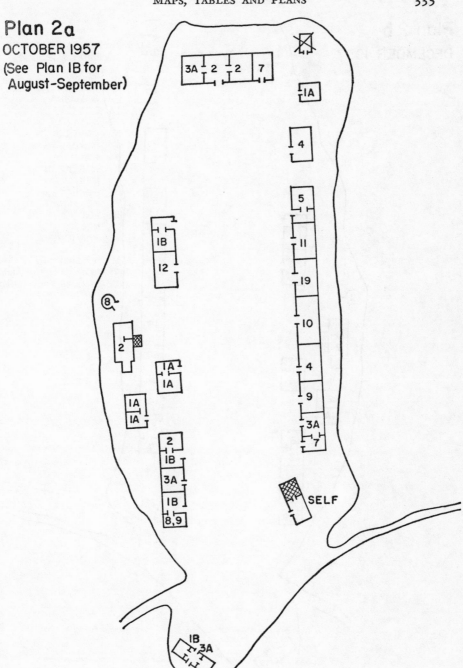

Plan 2a
OCTOBER 1957
(See Plan IB for
   August-September)

PLAN 2a–d *Village camp of Epulu Mbuti, October 1957–March 1958.*

Plan 2 b
DECEMBER 1957

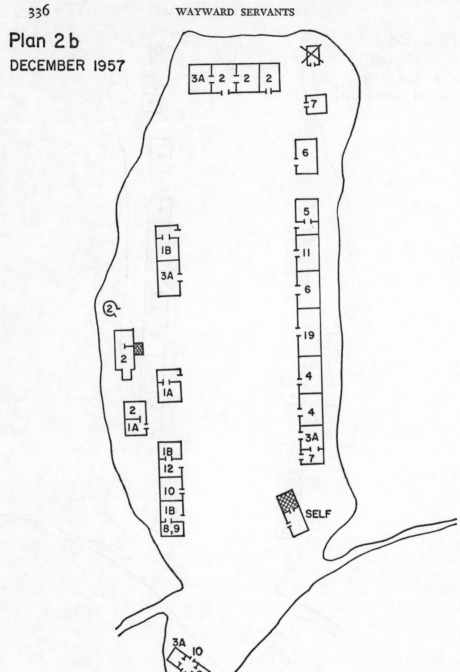

Plan 2c
FEBRUARY 1958

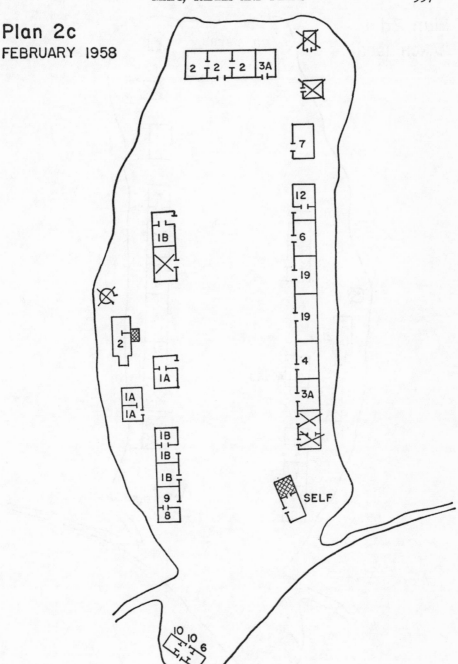

Plan 2d
MARCH 1958

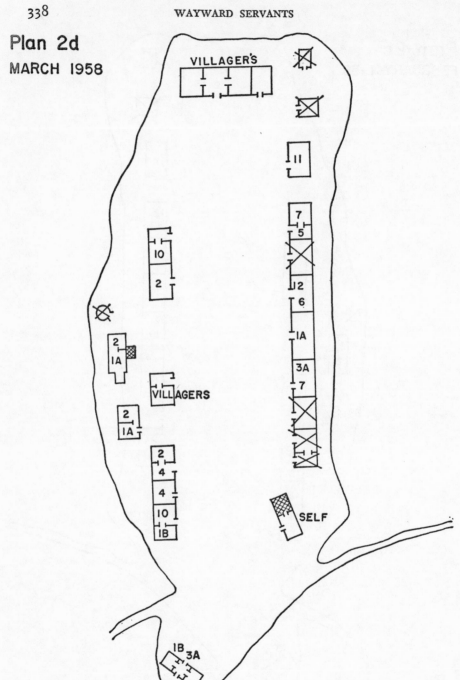

Plan 3a-g : KEY

▨ = Baraza (meeting veranda)

C, ⊐ = Hut

⬲ = Abandoned hut

⊗⧗ = Living but not in camp

⊕ = Hearth, used by more than one nuclear family

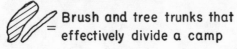 = Brush and tree trunks that effectively divide a camp

CLAN		TOTEM		CLAN	TOTEM
IA, IB	PUEMI	2	II	NGAMO	I
2	BOMASUA	I	12	BANDOHWA	2
3A,B,C	BOKELÉ	3,1,6	13	POYA	4
4	BAMBAKA	6	14	MOLOMBA	4
5	BWANGO	I	15	POTOLA	I
6	UNGBAUSU	2	16	PASAMA	5
7	MEKI	4	17	PONGWANA	2
8	POKBAYA	I	18	PUKENA	I
9	POKAMA	6	19	PUSA	7
10	POTEBA	I	20	PUMA	4

TOTEMS: 1 LEOPARD
     2 CHIMPANZEE
     3 BUFFALO
     4 SNAKE

5 ⎫
6 ⎬ Different kinds of rare antelope
7 ⎭

Plan 3a

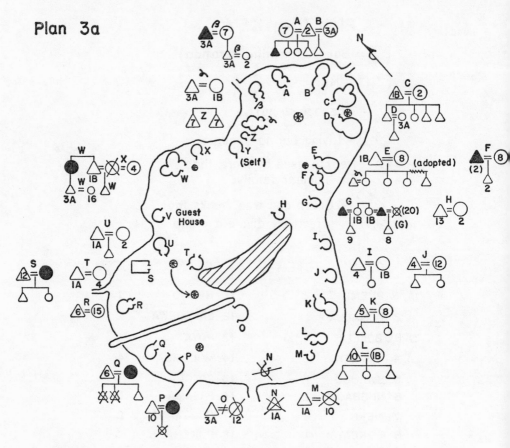

PLAN 3a–g *Composition of hunting camps cited p. 98 for large and small camps of Epulu band.*

Plan 3b

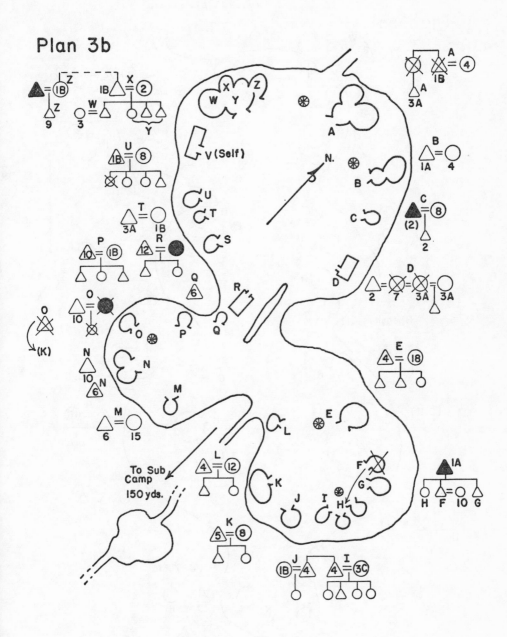

Plan 3c

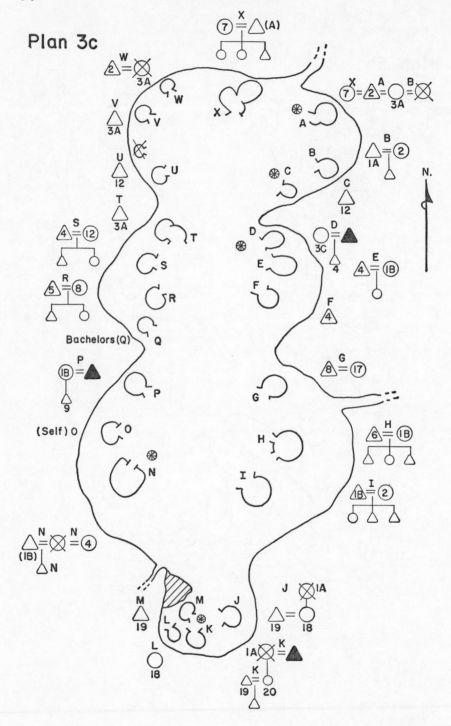

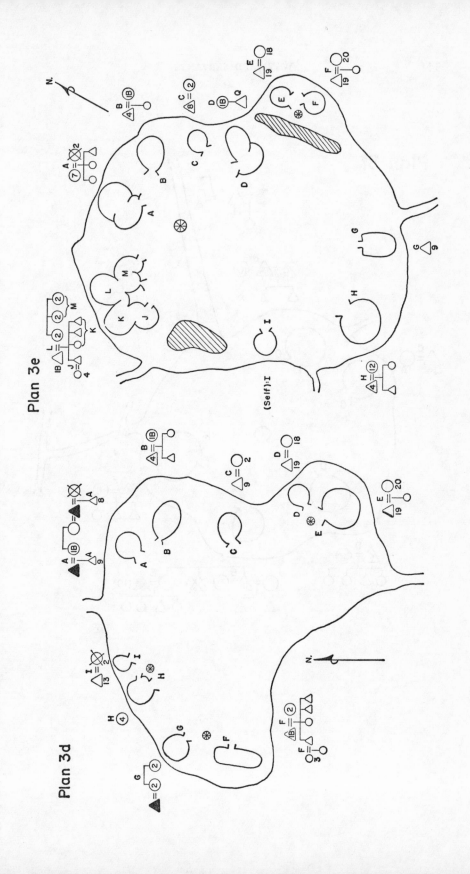

Plan 3e

Plan 3d

Plan 3f

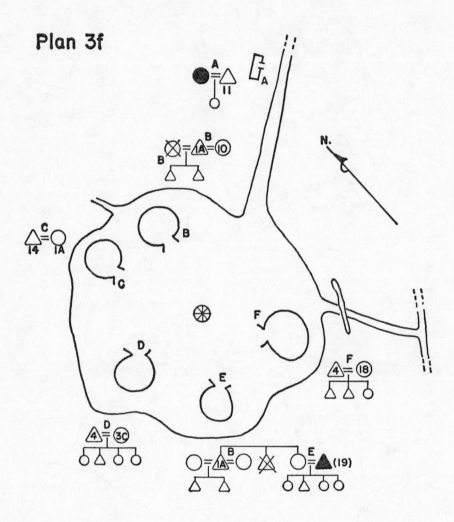

Plan 3g

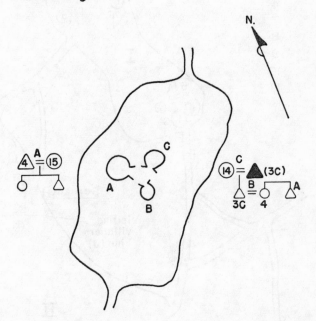

Plan 4a

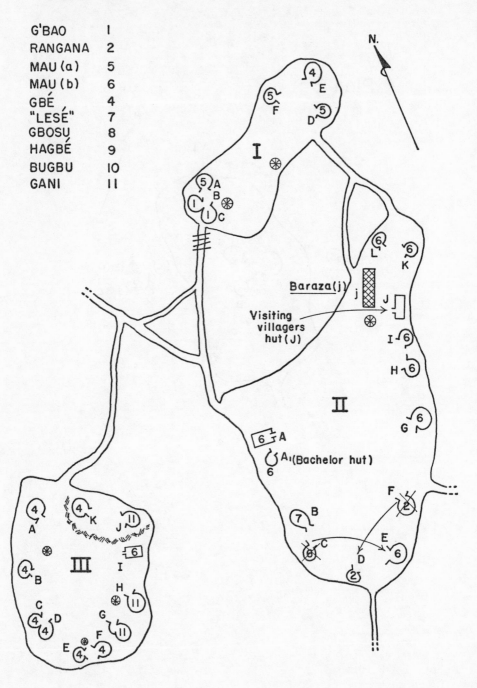

I

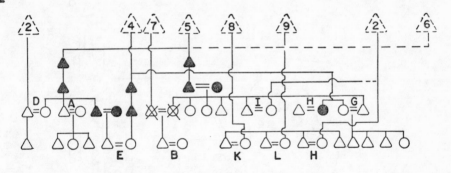

II

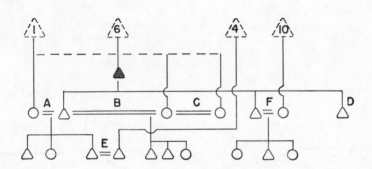

III

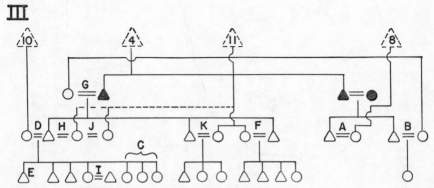

PLAN 4a–m *Hunting camps of net-hunters and archers other than at Epulu, showing composition.*

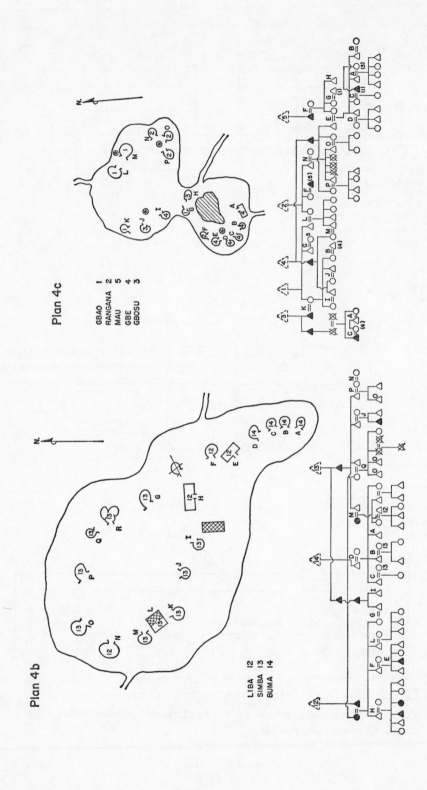

Plan 4b

LIBA 12
SIMBA 13
BUMA 14

Plan 4c

GBAO 1
RANGANA 2
MAU 5
GBE 4
GBOSU 3

Plan 4d

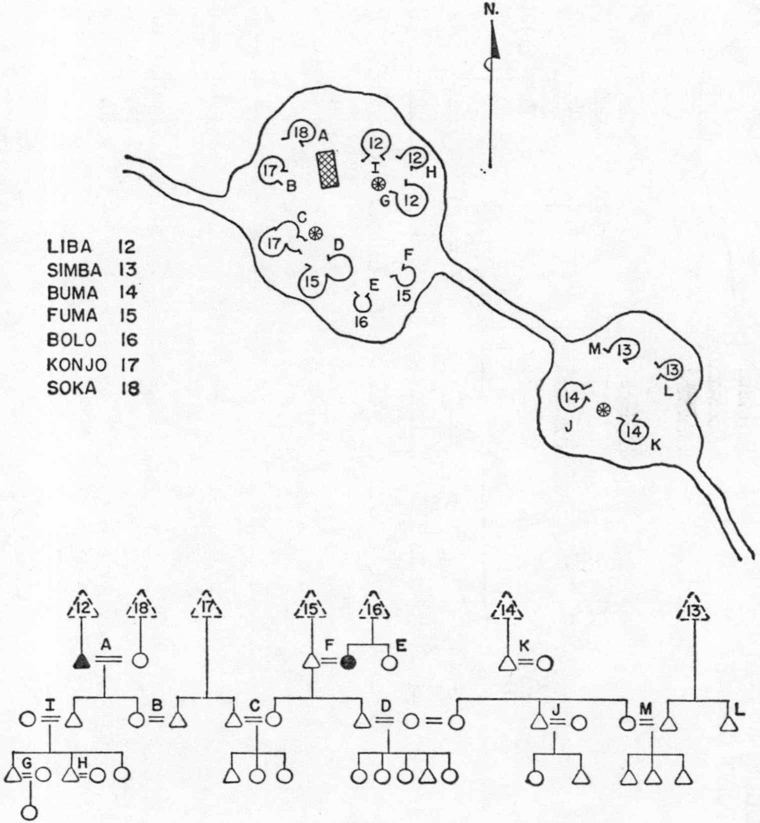

LIBA 12
SIMBA 13
BUMA 14
FUMA 15
BOLO 16
KONJO 17
SOKA 18

Plan 4e

LIBA 12
SIMBA 13
BUMA 14
BOLO 16
SOKA 18

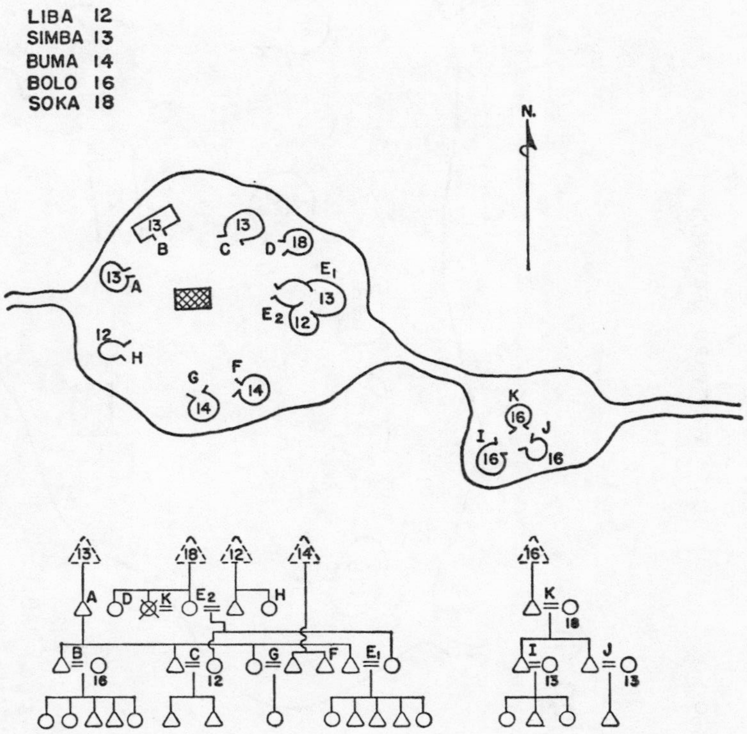

Plan 4f

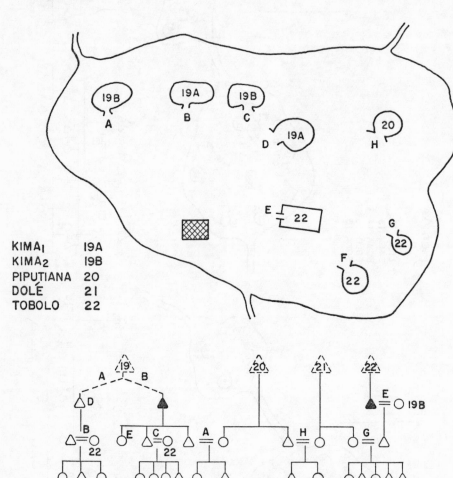

KIMA₁   19A
KIMA₂   19B
PIPUTIANA 20
DOLÉ   21
TOBOLO   22

Plan 4g

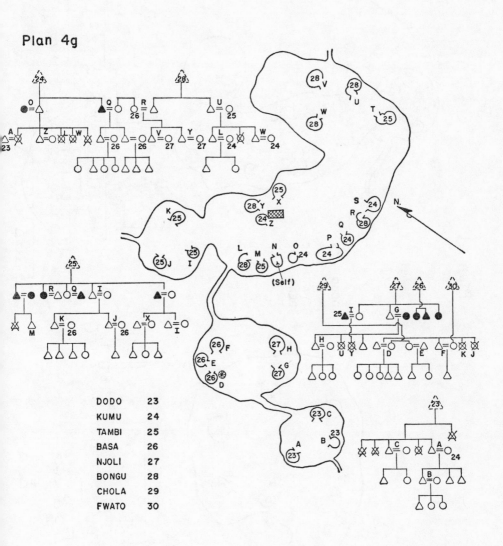

DODO   23
KUMU   24
TAMBI   25
BASA   26
NJOLI   27
BONGU   28
CHOLA   29
FWATO   30

Plan 4h

SEMBI 32
POKU 33
LINDA 34

Plan 4i

DODO 23
KUMU 24
FWATO 30
DENA 31

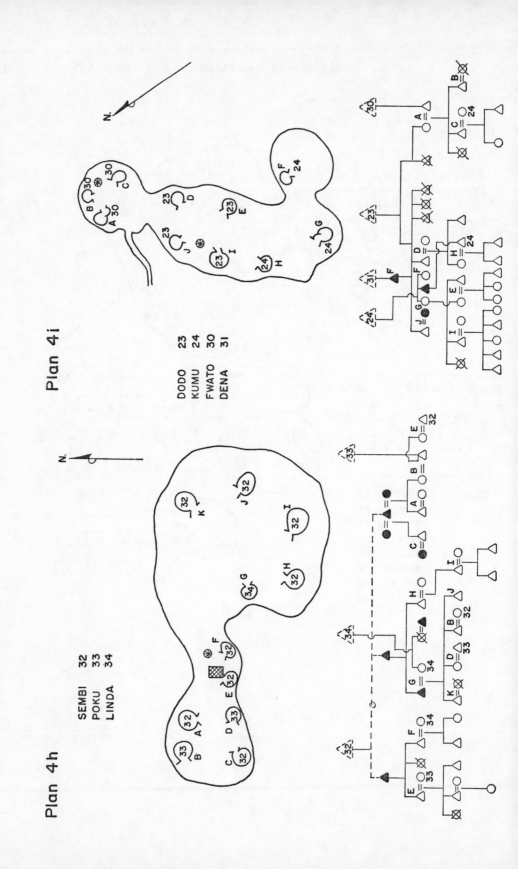

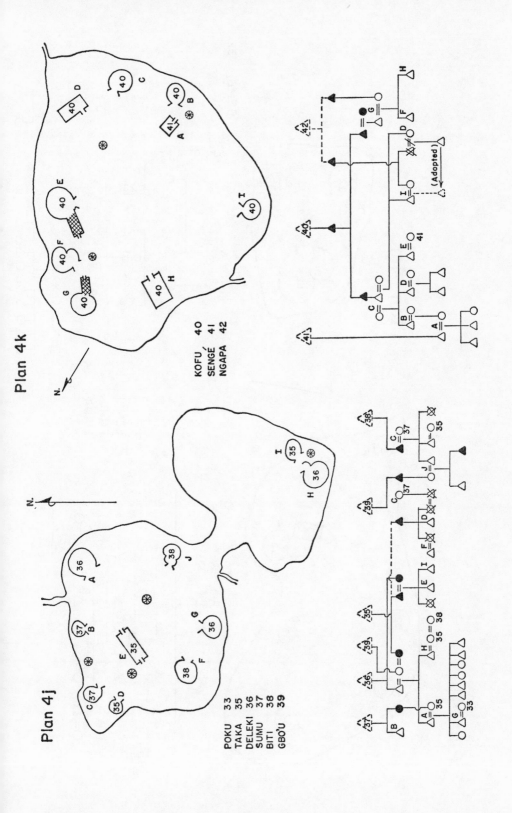

Plan 4k

KOFU 40
SENGÉ 41
NGAPA 42

Plan 4j

POKU 33
TAKA 35
DELEKI 36
SUMU 37
BITI 38
GBO'U 39

Plan 4L

Plan 4m

N.

SEMBI 32

SEMBI 32
POKU 33
LINDA 34

Plan 5
Apa Lelo
Male membership of patrilineages

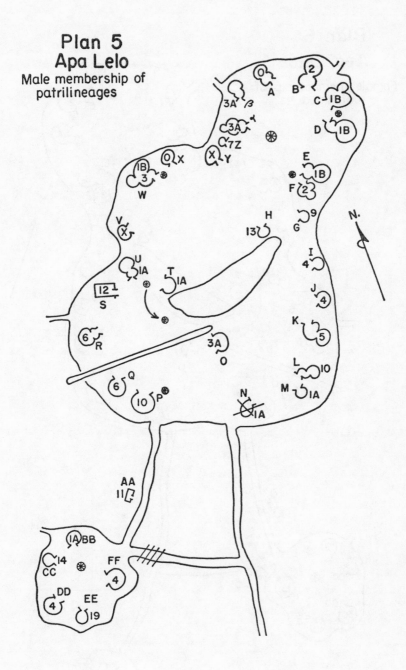

Plan 6
Apa Lelo

Female membership of patrilineages

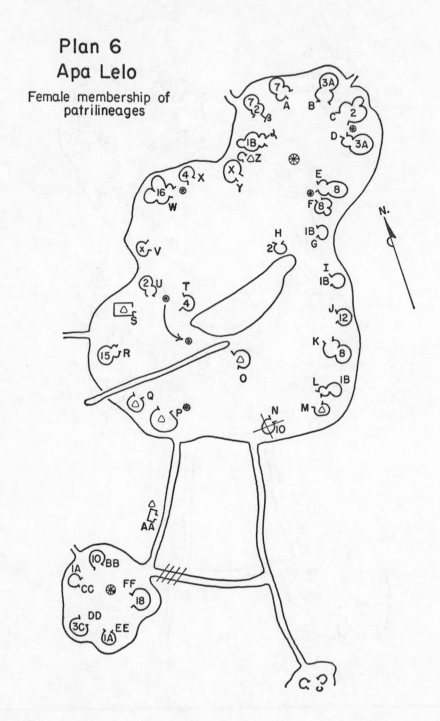

Plan 7
Apa Lelo
Changes in hut shapes
indicating personal friendships
and hostilities

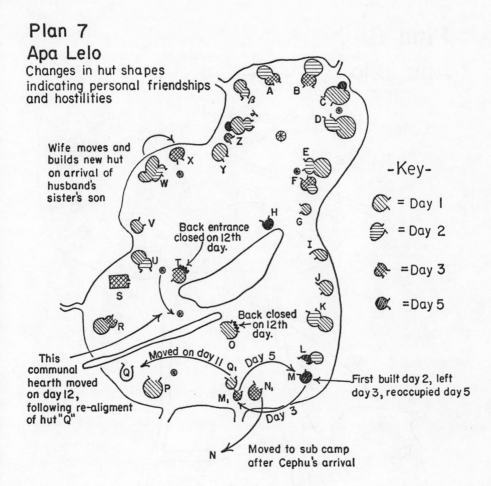

Wife moves and
builds new hut
on arrival of
husband's
sister's son

Back entrance
closed on 12th
day.

This
communal
hearth moved
on day 12,
following re-aligment
of hut "Q"

Moved on day 11

Back closed
on 12th
day.

Day 5

Day 3

-Key-

= Day 1

= Day 2

= Day 3

= Day 5

First built day 2, left
day 3, reoccupied day 5

Moved to sub camp
after Cephu's arrival

Plan 8
Apa Lelo

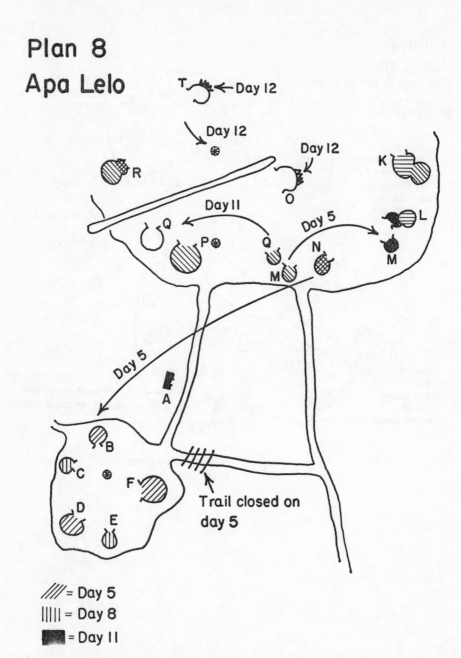

Apa Lelo: changes at southern end of camp due to Cephu's arrival.

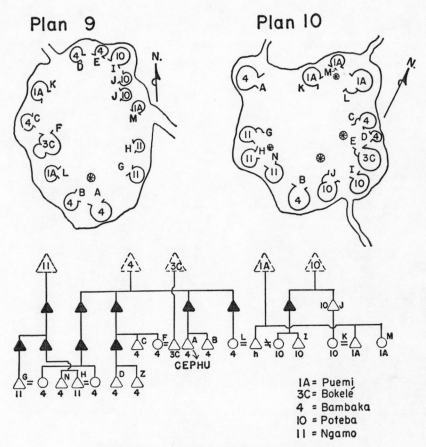

Cephu's camp before (Plan 9) and after
(Plan 10) his hunting offense.

[Plan 11 is located inside back cover.]

Glossary

This is a glossary of terms used by Epulu Mbuti, as cited in the text. Owing to the frequency with which the Mbuti mingle words originating from different local languages, while most of the words given here are of Bira origin, some derive from KiNgwana. Further, owing to the Mbuti habit of dropping or adding vowels or consonants for the sake of euphony, and to their ambivalent attitude toward prefixes, I give the words as used in speech without attempting to reduce them to roots, except where there is no doubt. Thus "*bo'o*" in Mbuti usage I give as the KiBira original, "*bobo*"; where in doubt I suggest a possible derivation such as "*ekimi*" from "*kimia*" (KG). Wherever the derivation is apparently from KiNgwana, I insert (KG).

akami: noise (from *kami*: to cry?).
angbe: a tree and the wood from the tree, important for honey.
angbelu: medicine for honey season (from *lu-* to talk, call?).
anjo: hunting medicine.
anza: good.
apua'i: friend, sibling.
bamiki ba ndura: children of the forest.
batu ba ndura: people of the forest.
batu banji: people of the village.
bekbekbe'i: very (much).
bera'i: melody (solo).
bo: good.
bobo: empty.
boki: honey.
bokbu: all.
bonga: good (in a fuller sense than *bo*).
bongisa: to make good, to rejoice.
bopi: children's playground.
boru: the "house" (*endu*) of the soul; i.e., the body.
bulé: (KG) empty, worthless, troublesome.
chahwa: youth(s).
chanja: (KG) to make light incisions in the skin, for tattoo or for insertion of medicines.
chawi: (KG) witch.
che'i: fear.
eboko: banana.
ekimi: (ref. *kimia* [KG]) quiet.
ekokomea: erotic dance for *molimo* and for honey season.

ekonga: spear.

ekondi: love.

elima: premarital festival in which girls and boys both take part, signaled by a girl's first menstruation.

ema: mother.

endu: house, hut, room.

epa: father.

esumba: (KG) ritual originally associated with elephant-hunting for Arab slavers, sometimes used interchangeably with the word *molimo.*

furahisa: (KG) to rejoice, make festive.

ganga: to mend, bind together, cure; hence *mganga* or *muganga,* doctor.

imia'i: chorus, refrain.

isa: fire.

ishumbwa: another form of *esumba* (KG), possibly of slightly different significance to the Ngwana, not to the Mbuti.

itaba: edible forest root.

kali: girl, woman.

kalisia: a name sometimes used for the godhead (forest).

kami: to cry, which is defined as making a noise (*akami* or *kelelé* [KG]).

karé: brotherhood in the *nkumbi* initiation.

kelelé: (KG) noise.

keti: a forest spirit, neither good nor bad to the Mbuti, but evil to the Bira.

kidi: come, arrive.

kimia: (KG) quiet (ref. *imia'i,* chorus, and association of song with the value of *ekimi*).

kiyana: (KG) youth(s).

kobi(a): fear, be wary or cautious, but more often used as:

kobi: to keep very quiet.

kobinengo: silence.

kondi: to love, have affection for.

kuma: hearth.

kuya: hunting net.

langé toro: sleep; lit., "to lie sleep."

le: eat.

leahwa: food.

lendu: an antelope.

lozi: (KG) sorcerer.

lufu: say, talk, call.

lukembi: (KG) musical instrument, an idiophone better known as *sanza* in Swahili.

madé: wooden whistle.

madé: lesser (as in *molimo madé*).

mangbo: great.

mangesé: elder.

mavi: (KG) excrement.

mbafu: (KG) stupidity.

mboko: buffalo.

mboloko: small antelope.

mbongu: elephant.

miki: child.

moko: brother.

molimo: men's religious association, a festival of crisis among both the Mbuti and the Bira, and also associated with a musical instrument among both, but otherwise quite distinct.

mongongo: phrynium leaves used for roofing (ref. *makongo* [KG]).

mota: hard, difficult, dangerous.

mukira: hunt, hunter (also in KG).

mungu: (KG) God.

nanji: village.

ndandama: stupidity.

ndasi: too much.

ndura: forest.

nengo: very.

ngbengbe: wooden clappers used in honey season.

nguvu: (KG) difficult, hard, heavy.

njelani: vine used for making baskets.

nkumbi: initiation of the Bira for boys.

nkusa: vine used in making twine and nets.

nyama: animal.

oki: hear.

oni: see.

pati: take to oneself, cover oneself, become.

pepo: vital essence, vital breath, life force of the forest.

pika: to come, bring.

piki: whistle of wood.

pisa: give, pass over, put.

ponisa: (KG) punish.

roho: individual self, personality (with different connotations when used by Bira or Ngwana).

satani: (KG, also *shaitani, saitani*) spirit, ghost, evil if used by villagers, or by Mbuti if referring to village "satani."

segbe: wooden whistle (as for *piki, madé*) for magical use.

shamba: (KG, also *samba*) plantation.

sinana: bad.

sindula: water chevrotain.

sondu: a large antelope.

songé: moon.
suba: within.
s'uti: sound.
tata: grandparent.
teré: the godhead, primarily in its judicial, authoritative aspect (ref. morning *molimo* cries of "*e teré*": "it is *teré*").
tiko: plantation.
toré: as for *teré.*
wendi: to hunt.

Bibliography

BATTEL, A.
1625. "On the regions and customs of the peoples of Angola, Congo and Loango." In, Purchas, Samuel: *Purchas, his pilgrimes*. London.

BEATTIE, J. H. M.
1960. *Bunyoro, an African Kingdom*. New York.

BLEHR, OTTO.
1963. "Action Groups in a society with bilateral kinship: a case study from the Faroe Islands." *Ethnology*, II: 3, pp. 269–275.

BOELAERT, E.
1936a. "De elima der Nkundo." *Congo*, 1: 1, pp. 42–52.
1936b. "Waar komen onze pygmoiden vandaan?" *Kongo-Overzee*, 3: pp. 22–25.

BOURITIUS, G., and J. JONK.
1954. Waarseggerij en Beheksing bij Bandaka en Arabisés." *Zaïre*, 8: 6, pp. 593–613.

BOWRA, C. M.
1962. *Primitive Song*. Cleveland.

BURROWS, G.
1898. *The Land of the Pigmies*. New York.

CAMBRON, L.
1923. "Circoncision dans la région de Beni et des environs." *Congo*, 1: 5, pp. 708–711.

CASATI, G.
1891. *Zehn Jahre in Aequatoria und die Rückkehr mit Emin Pascha*. Bamberg.

CHRISTY, C.
1924. *Big Game and Pygmies*. London.

CIPRIANI, L.
1933. "Osservazioni sui pigmei centro-africani." *Archivo per l'Anthrop. e Ethnol.*, 63: pp. 202–217.

COOPER, JOHN M.
1941. *Temporal Sequence and Marginal Cultures*. The Catholic University of America, Anthropological Series, no. 10, Washington.

COSTERMANS, B. J.
1937. "De Efe van Watsa-Gombari." *Congo*, 2: 5, pp. 526–532.
1938. "Toré, God en geesten bij de Mamvu en hun dwergen." *Congo*, 1: 5, pp. 532–547.
1947. "De gebouwen bij de Mamvu-Mangutu-Walese." *Zaïre*, 1: 3, pp. 281–295.

CUREAU, A. L.

1915. *Savage Man in Central Africa*. London.

CZEKENOWSKI, J.

1924. "Wissenschaftliche Ergebnisse der Deutschen Zentral-Afrika-Expedition 1907–1908." *Ethnog. und Anthrop.*, 6: 2, Leipzig.

DAVID, J.

1904a. "Ueber die Pygmäen am oberen Ituri (Bambuti)." *Globus*, 85: pp. 117–119.

1904b. "Notizen über die Pygmäen des Ituriwaldes." *Globus*, 86: pp. 193–198.

DAVIS, R. H.

1907. *The Congo and the Coasts of Africa*. New York.

DE CLEENE, N.

1933. "De oudheid der Pygmeeën van Centraal-Afrika." *Congo*, 1: 1, pp. 109–114.

DE HAENE, J.

1949. "Découvertes préhistoriques en Haute-Ituri." *Zaïre*, 3: 9, pp. 1003–1110.

DE LABROUGHE, O.

1933. *Chez les Pygmées*. Paris.

DENIS, P.

1952. "La tortue et le léopard dans les légendes Mangbetu." *Zaïre*, 6: 2, pp. 155–172.

DU CHAILLU, P. B.

1867. *A Journey to Ashango-Land*. London.

1890. *Adventures in the Great Forest of Equatorial Africa and the Country of the Dwarfs*. London.

1900. *The World of the Great Forest*. New York.

DURKHEIM, EMILE and MAUSS, MARCEL.

1963. *Primitive Classification* (tr. Rodney Needham). London.

EVANS-PRITCHARD, E. E.

1956. *Nuer Religion*. Oxford.

FIRTH, RAYMOND.

1959. "Problem and Assumption in an Anthropological Study of Religion." *J. R. A. I.*, 89: part II, pp. 129–148.

FORTUNE, R. F.

1935. *Manus Religion*. Philadelphia.

GEIL, E. W.

1905. *A Yankee in the Pygmy land*. London.

GLUCKMAN, M.

1954. "Political Institutions." In, *The Institutions of Primitive Society*. Oxford.

1960. "From Tribe to Town." *The Nation*, September, pp. 7–12.

GREGORIUS, P.

1952. "P. Schebesta's Expedities onder de Bambuti-Pygmeeën aan de Ituri-rivier." *Zaïre*, 6: 4, pp. 379–390.

GRIERSON, P. F. H.

1903. *The Silent Trade*. Edinburgh.

GUSINDE, M.

1942. "Die Kongo-Pygmäen in Geschichte und Gegenwart." *Nova Acta Leopoldina*, N. F. 11: 76, pp. 167–415. Halle (Saale).

1945. "Benennung der Afrikanischen Pygmäengruppen." *Mitt. Geogr. Gesell. Wien*, 88: pp. 47–53.

1948. Urwaldmenschen am Ituri: Anthropologisch-biologische Forschungsergebnisse bei Pygmäen und Negern im Östlichen Belgisch-Kongo a. d. J. 1934/35. Vienna.

1955. "Pygmies and Pygmoids: Twides of Tropical Africa." *Anthropological Quarterly*, N. S. 28: 3, pp. 3–61.

HOCART, A. M.

1952. *The Life-Giving Myth, and Other Essays*. London.

HUTEREAU, A.

1909. "Notes sur la vie familiale et juridique de quelques populations du Congo Belge." Ann. Mus. du Congo Belge, Brussels.

1924. "Les Négrilles de l'Uele et de l'Ubangi." *Congo*, 1: 4, pp. 495–514; 1: 5, pp. 693–711.

IMMENROTH, W.

1933. *Kultur und Umwelt der Kleinwüchsigen in Afrika*. Leipzig.

JADIN, J.

1936. "Groupes sanguins des Pygmées et des Nègres de l'Ituri (Congo Belge)." *Anthropos*, 31: pp. 177–186.

1938. "Aperçu sur l'état sanitaire des Pygmées de l'Ituri." *Anthropologie*, 16: pp. 69–83.

JASPERT, W.

1930. *Through Unknown Africa*. London.

JENSEN, A. E.

1933. "Beschneidung und Reifezeremonien bei Naturvölkern." *Studien zur Kulturkunde*, 1, Stuttgart.

JOHNSTON, H. H.

1884. *The River Congo*. London.

1902, 1904. *The Uganda Protectorate* (2 vols.). New York.

1903. "The Pygmies of the Great Congo forest." Smithsonian Inst., Ann. Rept. for 1902, pp. 479–491.

1905. "Pygmées et hommes Simièsques de la frontière de l'Ouganda." *Revue Scientifique*, 3: 15, pp. 449–454.

1908. *George Grenfell and the Congo*. London.

JOSET, P. E.

1947. "Notes ethnographiques sur les Babira-Babombi (Babira de la forêt)." *Bull. Assoc. Ancienne Ethnog.*, Univ. Colon, Belgique, 1: pp. 9–24.

1948. "Buda Efeba: contes et légendes Pygmées." *Zaïre*, 2: 1, pp. 25–56; 2: 2, pp. 137–157.

JULIEN, P.

1934. "Tusschen Nijl en Congo: Onwetenschappelijke ervaringen tijdens een Pygmeeënoverzoek in N. O. Congo." *Congo*, 2: 5, pp. 728–729.

1954. *Pygmeeën.* Amsterdam.

JUNKER, W.

1889–1891. *Reisen in Afrika* (3 vols.). Vienna.

LAMEN, K. E.

1928. "Languages used in the Congo basin." *Africa*, 1: pp. 372–380.

LANG, H.

1919. "Nomad dwarfs and civilization." *Natural History Magazine*, 19: 6, pp. 696–713.

LE ROY, A.

1897. *Les Pygmées: Négrilles d'Afrique et Négritos d'Asie.* Paris.

LÉVI-STRAUSS, CLAUDE.

1948. *La Vie Familiale et Sociale des Indiens Nambikwara.* Société des Américanistes, Paris.

1955. *Tristes Tropiques.* Paris.

1963. *Structural Anthropology* (tr. Claire Jacobson). New York.

LLOYD, A. B.

1899. *In Dwarf Land and Cannibal Country.* New York.

MAES, J.

1932. "Allume-feu des Pygmées de l'A.E.F." *Congo*, 2: 5, pp. 704–707.

1933. "L'Allume-feu des populations de Congo Belge." *Congo*, 2: 1, pp. 21–41.

1934. "Enquête sur la façon de compter et les mimiques des nombres employées par les Pygmées de la région de Gombari." *Congo*, 1: 4, pp. 564–571.

1935. *Volkerkunde van Belgisch-Kongo.* Antwerp.

MAUSS, MARCEL.

1923. "Essai sur le Don: Forme et Raison de l'échange dans les sociétés archaïques." *Année Sociologique*, N.S.I., 1923–4, pp. 30–186.

MEEUSSEN, A. E., and B. LECOSTE.

1955. "Systématiques des termes de parenté Ngwana." *Zaïre*, 9: 4, pp. 403–405.

MERRIAM, A. P.

1953. "African music re-examined in the light of new materials from the Belgian Congo and Rvanda-Urundi." *Zaïre*, 7: 3, pp. 245–253.

MOELLER, A.

1934. "Les grandes lignes des migrations des Bantous de la province Orientale du Congo Belge." *Bull. Inst. Royal Colonial Belge,* 5: pp. 63–111.

1936. *Les grandes lignes des migrations des Bantous de la Province Orientale du Congo Belge.* Brussels.

NEEDHAM, RODNEY.

1954a. "Reference to the dead among the Penan." *Man,* 54: 6.

1954b. "A note on the blood pact in Borneo." *Man,* 54: 129.

1962. *Structure and Sentiment.* Chicago.

NENNEN, O.

1927. "La circoncision chez les Samba (Baluba)." *Congo,* 2: 3, pp. 368–376.

NIPPOLD, W.

1936. *Rassen und Kulturgeschichte der Negritovölker Südost-Asiens.* Göttingen.

1937. "Umwelt und Rasse als Kulturfaktoren." Göttinger Gelehrte Anzeigen, pp. 544–564.

PAHLEN, KURT.

1949. *Music of the World: A History.* New York.

PARKE, TH.

1891. *My Personal Experience in Equatorial Africa.* London.

POSSOZ, E.

1954. Batoa, Batwa, Batswa. *Africa,* 24: pp. 257–260.

POUTRIN, M.

1910. "Contribution à l'étude des Pygmées d'Afrique." *Anthropologie,* 21: pp. 435–504.

1911. "Contribution à l'étude des Pygmées d'Afrique." *Anthropologie,* 22: pp. 421–549.

1912. "Contribution à l'étude des Pygmées d'Afrique." *Anthropologie,* 23: pp. 349–404.

POWELL-COTTON, P.

1907. "Notes on a journey through the great Ituri forest." *Jour. Royal Anthrop. Inst.,* 7: pp. 1–12.

PUTNAM, A. E.

1954. *Madami.* New York.

PUTNAM, PATRICK.

1948. The Pygmies of the Ituri Forest. *In,* Coon: A *Reader in General Anthropology,* pp. 322–342. New York.

QUATREFAGES, A. DE.

1887. *Les Pygmées.* Paris.

1895. *The Pygmies.* London.

RADCLIFFE-BROWN, A. R.

1952. *Structure and Function in Primitive Society.* London.

RICHARDS, AUDREY I.

1956. *Chisungu.* London.

SAUZY, M.

1926. "Les Pygmées au Congo Belge." *Géographie, 46:* pp. 24–32.

SCHEBESTA, P.

1929. "Chez les Pygmées de l'Ituri (entre la Lindi et l'Ituri)." *Congo,* 2: 3, pp. 415–421.

1931a. "Voyage d'exploration chez les Pygmées du Congo Belge." *Congo,* 1: 3, pp. 327–341.

1931b. "Les conceptions religieuses des Pygmées de l'Ituri." *Congo,* 1: 5, pp. 645–666; 2: 1, pp. 45–68.

1932. *Bambuti, die Zwerge vom Congo.* Salzburg.

1933. *Among Congo Pygmies.* London.

1934. *Vollblutneger und Halbzwerge.* Salzburg.

1936a. *My Pygmy and Negro Hosts.* London.

1936b. *Der Urwald ruft wieder.* Salzburg.

1936c. "Données essentielles sur la religion des Pygmées." *Congo,* 1: 13, pp. 321–331.

1937. *Revisiting My Pygmy Hosts.* London.

1938. *Die Bambuti-Pygmäen vom Ituri: 1* (of three volumes): *Geschichte, Geographie. Umwelt, Demographie und Anthropologie der Ituri-Bambuti.* Brussels (Mém. Inst. Royal Colonial Belge).

1941. *Die Bambuti-Pygmäen vom Ituri: 2, part 1: Die Wirtschaft der Ituri-Bambuti.* Brussels.

1947. "Tore, le Dieu Forestier des Bambuti." *Zäire, 1:* 2, pp. 181–195.

1948. *Die Bambuti-Pygmäen vom Ituri: 2, part 2: Das Gesellungsleben.* Brussels.

1949. "La Langue des Pygmées." *Zäire, 3:* 2, pp. 119–128.

1950. *Die Bambuti-Pygmäen vom Ituri: 2, part 3: Die Religion.* Brussels.

1952. *Les Pygmées du Congo Belge.* Brussels (Mém. Inst. Royal Colonial Belge).

1957. "Pygmy Music and Ceremonial." *Man, 57:* 78.

1958. "Bambuti-Initiation." *Kongo-Overzee, 24:* 3, pp. 136–161.

1963. "Colin M. Turnbull und die Erforschung der Bambuti-Pygmäen." *Anthropos, 58:* pp. 209–223.

SCHMIDT, W.

1910. *Die Stellung der Pygmäen-völker in der Entwicklungsgeschichte der Menschen.* Stuttgart.

1933. *Der Ursprung der Gottesidee: Die Religion der Urvölker Afrikas.* Münster.

SCHWEINFURTH, G.
1874. *The Heart of Africa*. New York.

SERVATIUS, P.
1932. "De besnijdenis bij de Bene-Nsamba." *Anthropos*, 27: pp. 525–542.

SERVICE, ELMAN R.
1962. *Primitive Social Organization*. New York.

SOORS, M.
1950a. "A propos des découvertes préhistoriques en Haut-Ituri." *Zaïre*, 4: 1, p. 59.
1950b. "Notes sur les Pygmées." *Zaïre*, 4: 3, pp. 299–301.

SPEKE, J. H.
1864. *Journal of the Discovery of the Source of the Nile*. New York.

STANLEY, H. M.
1879. *Through the Dark Continent*. New York.
1890. *In Darkest Africa*. New York.

STEWARD, JULIAN H.
1955. *Theory of Culture Change*. Urbana.

TORDAY, E.
1925a. *Causeries Congolaises*. Brussels.
1925b. *On the Trail of the Bushongo*. London.

TRILLES, H.
1932. *Les Pygmées de la forêt équatoriale*. Paris.
1945. *L'Âme du Pygmée d'Afrique*. Paris.

TURNBULL, COLIN M.
1955. "Pygmy Music and Ceremonial." *Man*, 55: 31.
1956. *The Bambuti of the Ituri Forest*. B. Litt. Thesis (Oxford, mss.), (to be published in 1965 by The American Museum of Natural History in the Anthropological Papers).
1957a. "Pygmy Music and Ceremonial." *Man*, 57: 157.
1957b. "Initiation among the BaMbuti Pygmies of the Central Ituri." *J.R.A.I.*, 87: 2, pp. 191–216.
1959. "Legends of the BaMbuti." *J.R.A.I.*, 89: 1, pp. 45–60.
1960a. "The *elima*: a premarital festival among the BaMbuti Pygmies." *Zaïre*, 14: 2–3, pp. 175–192.
1960b. "The *molimo*: a men's religious association among the Ituri BaMbuti." *Zaïre*, 14: 4, pp. 307–340.
1961. *The Forest People*. New York.

TURNER, V. W.
1957. *Schism and Continuity in an African Society*. Manchester.
1961. "Ndembu Divination: Its Symbolism & Techniques." *The Rhodes-Livingstone Papers*, 31. Manchester.

1962. "Chihamba: The White Spirit." *The Rhodes-Livingstone Papers*, 33. Manchester.

TYSON, E.

1699. *The Anatomy of a Pygmie Compared to that of a Monkey, an Ape, and a Man*. London.

VAN BULCK, G.

1948. Les recherches linguistiques au Congo Belge. Mém. Inst. Royal Colonial Belge, 16.

1953. "Les Pygmées Asiatiques et les Pygmées Africains, Constituent-ils une Race Unique?" *Zaïre*, 7: 8, pp. 845–850.

VAN BULCK, V.

1948. "Où en est le Problème des Pygmées de l'Ituri?" *Zaïre*, 2: 4, pp. 423–436.

1952. "Existe-t-il une langue des Pygmées en Afrique Centrale?" Wiener Beiträge zur Kulturgeschichte und Linguistik, 9, pp. 365–396.

VAN DEN BERGH, L. J.

1921. *On the Trail of the Pigmies*. New York.

VAN DER KERKEN, G.

1944. L'Ethnie Mongo. Mém. Inst. Royal Colonial Belge, 13.

VAN GELUWE, H.

1956. Les Bira et les peuplades limitrophes. Ann. Mus. Royal Congo Belge, 2.

1957. Mamvu-Mangutu et Balese-Mvuba. Ann. Mus. Roy. Congo Belge, 3.

VANSINA, J.

1956. "Migrations de la Province du Kasai: une hypothèse." *Zaïre*, 10: 1, pp. 69–84.

VERBEKEN, A.

1947. "La signification mystique des couleurs chez les Bantous." *Zaïre*, 1: 10, pp. 1139–1144.

VERGIAT, A. M.

1936. *Les Rites Secrets des Primitifs de l'Oubangui*. Paris.

VERNER, S. P.

1902. "The African Pygmies." *Atlantic Monthly*, August, pp. 184–195.

VON EICKSTEDT, E.

1934. *Rassenkunde und Rassengeschichte der Menschheit*. Stuttgart.

VON HOFFMAN, C.

1929. *Jungle Gods*. New York.

WARD, H.

1910. *A Voice from the Congo*. London.

WAUTERS, G.

1940. De Bilima van de Batswa der Evanaarsprovincie. *Kongo-Overzee*, 6: pp. 95–103.

WINDLE, B. C. A.
1894. *A Philological Essay Concerning the Pygmies of the Ancients.* London.

WINTER, EDWARD H.
1956. *Bwamba: A Structural-Functional Analysis of a Patrilineal Society.* Cambridge.

WISSMAN, H.
1890. *Unter deutscher Flagge (quer durch Afrika von West nach Ost).* Berlin.

Index

COLIN M. TURNBULL was born in London and now lives in New York City, where he is Associate Curator of African Ethnology at The American Museum of Natural History. He was educated at the Westminster School and at Magdalen College, Oxford, where he studied philosophy and politics. After serving in the Royal Naval Volunteer Reserve during the war, he held a research grant for two years in the Department of Indian Religion and Philosophy at Banaras Hindu University, in India, and then returned to Oxford, where he studied anthropology, specializing in the African field.

He has made three extended field trips to Africa, from which he drew the material for this volume, as well as his two previous books, *The Forest People*, a more informal study of the Congo Pygmies, and *The Lonely African*, a study of tribalism and cultural change in modern Africa. He is a Fellow of the Royal Anthropological Institute, and a Corresponding Member of Le Musée Royal d'Afrique Centrale.